SAMSON OCCOM

Religion, Culture, and Public Life

RELIGION, CULTURE, AND PUBLIC LIFE
Series Editor: Matthew Engelke

The Religion, Culture, and Public Life series is devoted to the study of religion in relation to social, cultural, and political dynamics, both contemporary and historical. It features work by scholars from a variety of disciplinary and methodological perspectives, including religious studies, anthropology, history, philosophy, political science, and sociology. The series is committed to deepening our critical understandings of the empirical and conceptual dimensions of religious thought and practice, as well as such related topics as secularism, pluralism, and political theology. The Religion, Culture, and Public Life series is sponsored by Columbia University's Institute for Religion, Culture, and Public Life.

For a complete list of books in the series, please see the
Columbia University Press website.

Moral Atmospheres: Islam and Media in a Pakistani Marketplace, Timothy P. A. Cooper
Karma and Grace: Religious Difference in Millennial Sri Lanka, Neena Mahadev
Perilous Intimacies: Debating Hindu-Muslim Friendship After Empire, SherAli Tareen
Baptizing Burma: Religious Change in the Last Buddhist Kingdom, Alexandra Kaloyanides
At Home and Abroad: The Politics of American Religion, edited by Elizabeth Shakman Hurd and Winnifred Fallers Sullivan
The Arab and Jewish Questions: Geographies of Engagement in Palestine and Beyond, edited by Bashir Bashir and Leila Farskah
Modern Sufis and the State: The Politics of Islam in South Asia and Beyond, edited by Katherine Pratt Ewing and Rosemary R. Corbett
German, Jew, Muslim, Gay: The Life and Times of Hugo Marcus, Marc David Baer
The Limits of Tolerance: Enlightenment Values and Religious Fanaticism, Denis Lacorne
The Holocaust and the Nakba, edited by Bashir Bashir and Amos Goldberg
Democratic Transition in the Muslim World: A Global Perspective, edited by Alfred Stepan
The Politics of Secularism: Religion, Diversity, and Institutional Change in France and Turkey, Murat Akan
Holy Wars and Holy Alliance: The Return of Religion to the Global Political Stage, Manlio Graziano
Faithful to Secularism: The Religious Politics of Democracy in Ireland, Senegal, and the Philippines, David T. Buckley
Pakistan at the Crossroads: Domestic Dynamics and External Pressures, edited by Christophe Jaffrelot

Samson Occom

RADICAL HOSPITALITY IN THE NATIVE NORTHEAST

Ryan Carr

Foreword by
Megan Fulopp and Amy Besaw Medford

Columbia University Press
New York

Publication of this book was made possible in part by funding from the Institute for Religion, Culture, and Public Life at Columbia University.

Columbia University Press
Publishers Since 1893
New York Chichester, West Sussex
cup.columbia.edu
Copyright © 2023 Columbia University Press
All rights reserved

Library of Congress Cataloging-in-Publication Data
Names: Carr, Ryan, author. | Medford, Amy, writer of foreword. | Fulopp, Megan, writer of foreword.
Title: Samson Occum : radical hospitality in the native Northeast / Ryan Carr ; foreword by Megan Fulopp and Amy Besaw Medford.
Description: New York : Columbia University Press, [2023] | Series: Religion, culture, and public life | Includes bibliographical references and index.
Identifiers: LCCN 2023020307 (print) | LCCN 2023020308 (ebook) | ISBN 9780231210324 (hardback) | ISBN 9780231210331 (trade paperback) | ISBN 9780231558365 (ebook)
Subjects: LCSH: Occom, Samson, 1723–1792. | Occom, Samson, 1723–1792—Criticism and interpretation. | Presbyterian Church—Clergy—Biography. | Mohegan Indians—Biography. | Religious literature, American—History and criticism. | American literature—Indian authors—History and criticism. | Brotherton Indians—History.
Classification: LCC BX9225.O323 C37 2023 (print) | LCC BX9225.O323(ebook) | DDC 285/.1092 [B]—dc23/eng/20230615
LC record available at https://lccn.loc.gov/2023020307
LC ebook record available at https://lccn.loc.gov/2023020308

Cover design: Milenda Nan Ok Lee
Cover image: Samson Occom, as captured in a lithograph published by Williams & Smith, Stationers (London, 1808), after a lost oil painting (1766–1768) by Mason Chamberlain

Contents

Foreword by Megan Fulopp and Amy Besaw Medford vii
Acknowledgments xiii

Introduction, On the Occasion of Samson Occom's
Three Hundredth Birthday 1

PART I

I   "Asylum for Strangers": An Approach to
Occom's Traditionalism 21

II Occom Obviously: Literary Studies and the Problem
of Indigenous Knowledge 50

PART II

III A Theology of Land and Peoplehood 85

IV   Piety and Placemaking: Styles of Strangerhood
Among Occom and His Kin 135

PART III

v   Seft at Last: Occom's 1768 Autobiography in Native Space   169

vi   "Time to Awake": Occom on Perception, Alienation, and "Pure Religion"   200

Conclusion: "Good Enthusiasm"   230

Appendix: Two Letters from Susanna Wheatley to John Thornton Concerning Samson Occom   239

Notes   245

Bibliography   293

Index   315

Foreword

Three hundred years after his birth, Reverend Samson Occom (Mohegan/Brothertown) continues to encourage "stranger-love," self-reflection, and communal dialogue. His words are also helping to foster lasting friendships across communities and between Native and non-Native people. At least, as two Brothertown women, this has been our experience with a book club that began in 2020. To illustrate, let us share a brief history of the Brothertown Indian Nation and then describe how "stranger-love," a term Ryan Carr introduced us to, has allowed this unique community to grow into a positive support for Brothertown Indians and our allies.

The movement that became the Brothertown Indian Nation started with seven Algonquin communities—Tunxis, Mohegan, Narragansett, Niantic, Montauk, and Eastern and Western Pequot. Responding to the colonial stranglehold that had left our ancestors in dire poverty and at the bottom rung of society, Joseph Johnson (Mohegan/Brothertown), the self-professed "very first mover of this design," envisioned a land his brethren could settle and spread out on; where they would once again be free to hunt game, chop firewood, provide for their children, and govern themselves without the negative influence of colonists. On March 13, 1773, individuals and families from the seven Christian villages gathered in Mohegan to discuss emigration.

We asked our Elder Brother, the Oneida, and they welcomed us into their territory in what is now upstate New York. By 1774, the land with rolling hills and lush forests around Oriskany Creek was chosen by, and gifted to, the people of these seven communities. Despite the extreme dangers surrounding the buildup of the Revolutionary War, the first groups arrived in March and April 1775. Building homes and planting corn were initial priorities, but by 1777 the Revolutionary War forced our people to flee for their lives. They returned to rebuild after the conflict ended. Occom memorialized our formation into a "body politick" in his journal entry dated November 7, 1785: "we Named our Town—by the Name of Brotherton, in Indian Eeyawquittoowauconnuck."

For nearly fifty years, the Brothertown Indians lived, worked, and governed their town in New York. Yet ever-increasing pressure from settlers, eager for more land, caused us to look farther west. Many years and several negotiated and renegotiated treaties later, the tribe began settling on the eastern shores of Lake Winnebago. Similar to our move to Oneida Territory, individuals and families moved in waves with the first of these arriving in the early 1830s. This area would eventually become the state of Wisconsin.

Almost immediately, the United States threatened to push Brothertown even farther west. Seeking a way to halt this removal and protect their new home and people, Brothertown leaders asked Congress to transfer the land into individual fee simple allotments. There was no response. The tribe followed up, adding a request for U.S. citizenship. In 1839, Congress passed an act granting both. Unfortunately, the move to individual allotments was not the panacea our ancestors hoped it would be. Bit by bit, the tax man reclaimed the land, many of our people moved away in search of better economic opportunities, and our elders "fell asleep."

Despite these tough times, Brothertown continues as a tribal nation. Our sovereignty, our spirit, our people persevere and thrive. We are doctors, lawyers, teachers, small business owners, office workers, elected officials, property owners, servicemen and women, and the list goes on. Today, our tribal headquarters is located in Fond du Lac, Wisconsin, on the southern end of Lake Winnebago, and our people live all across North America and around the world.

For us, our journey into Occom's writings began when a shared passion for our nation brought us together with two more Brothertown Indians: Mark Baldwin—who had been involved with the tribe for more than thirty-five years and had held a number of positions, including vice chairman of the Tribal Council, grant writer, and founding editor of the tribal newsletter; and Paul Werth—a federal law enforcement officer, retired Coast Guardsman, tribal volunteer, and descendant whose family still retains their original 1839 Brothertown Reservation allotment in Wisconsin (Lot 199). We met every Sunday to discuss the responsibilities of a Brothertown citizen. We also shared information about our families and history within the tribe. Soon we began hosting community events with authors, scholars, and Brothertown leaders. Our endeavors allowed us to build strong bonds and share our hopes and dreams for our tribe. Several times, we were also approached with unexpected opportunities and new allies. Eventually recognizing the communal benefits of doing things on a larger scale, we decided to create a nonprofit entity.

Calumet and Cross Heritage Society was established in 2017 under Mark's leadership and direction. Its purpose is to build community, encourage relationships, and share Brothertown history. In the spring of 2020, amid other projects, Calumet and Cross began a book club open to anyone interested. As word spread, more people joined. Now, neighbors, scholars, other Native people, and Brothertown Indians meet week after week to read and discuss Brothertown-relevant materials together. Each person brings something unique and meaningful to our group.

Beyond their individual life experiences, neighbors from the hamlets of Deansboro and Marshall in New York ("Old Brothertown") enlighten us with details about landscape features, contemporary area history, and unique local flora and fauna. This context, often missing in books, brings our readings to life. Scholars enrich our understanding by shedding light on areas of their expertise (e.g., early American history, religious studies, musicology, English, archaeology, anthropology, and Indigenous studies, to name a few). Members from other Native communities deepen the conversation by sharing individual and tribal memories, experiences, and history. Last but not least, Brothertown Indians round out our Wednesday evenings with ancestral and community knowledge and family lore.

We have discovered that exploring Occom as a group allows natural relationships to develop and strengthen. Sharing experiences and listening to various perspectives brings a deeper understanding of individuals and the subjects we are reading about, even if we have differing opinions. Questions, especially unanswerable ones, help us examine our own assumptions and challenge us to consider new possibilities. The book club has become a gathering place where, supported by mutual respect and love, people come to learn more. We converse, as our ancestors did, and "brighten the chain of friendship."

The club's focus has expanded to include not only books but also articles, letters, photos, current events, videos, and virtual field trips. We have enjoyed presentations from the librarians and curators from the Special Collections and Archives of Hamilton College and the William L. Clements Library at the University of Michigan.

It is through this reading group that we have gotten to know Ryan. He has been a regular participant since our first book, the 1899 publication *Samson Occom and the Christian Indians of New England* by William DeLoss Love. Ryan had already begun researching and writing a manuscript on Occom. Over the next several years, he shared excerpts from this work. It was always a treat to break up our readings with his chapters. Together, our group explored thoughts, ideas, and mysteries about Occom and the people, places, and circumstances surrounding him.

When Ryan asked us to contribute a foreword, we were simultaneously intimidated and delighted. *Samson Occom: Radical Hospitality in the Native Northeast* is a compelling piece. Ryan weaves academic rigor with his humor and wit, leaving behind a tapestry of new and interesting ideas about Occom. He challenges us to think more deeply about Occom's own choices and fierce love—for not only his brethren but also strangers. At the same time, he asks us to broaden our understanding of early Christian Indians.

While this book may be important to scholars of American history, Indigenous studies, and other areas of academia, it also carries Occom across a new threshold and brings a greater dignity to his Brothertown "children." Through Ryan's careful detective work, thoughtful analysis, and approachable style, Occom becomes less a shadowy figure of history and begins, again, to take on a bit of substance.

Ryan taps into a new perspective, showing the kind of critical thinker Occom really is. At last someone has taken the time to delve into Occom's mind, looking not only at his historical circumstances, background, and primary writings but also at his sermons, marginalia, letters, and conversations with his "children" and other amateur historians. This book speaks at length to the Reverend's intelligence. It follows his thoughts along until they blossom into unique concepts that prove to be wholly Occom's. We witness, without a doubt, that he does not simply parrot teachings fed him by Eleazar Wheelock. Rather, Occom has agency. While he was a willing participant in ideas that promoted Indian causes, he was nobody's puppet. Occom worked in service of God *and* his people.

At the same time, this book carries meaning for Occom's Brothertown "brethren in the flesh." Ryan takes great care to ensure that Occom is not plucked from his tribe and examined like an unmoored specimen. Instead, he remains firmly rooted in *both* his tribe of origin (Mohegan) and the tribe he helped form and became a part of (Brothertown). Of all the contributions this study offers, this may be the most novel. Rarely has Brothertown been included on the same level with Mohegan when describing Occom. Now, there is a new meeting point for community reconnections and scholarship.

When Mark unexpectedly "walked on" in April 2021, our Sunday evening circle was reduced to three. We still meet weekly to discuss our responsibilities as Brothertown Indians, organize events, and explore ways to encourage our community.

Calumet and Cross and its book club also continue. Calumet and Cross's community-building mission was developed from our original group of four before we considered Occom's "stranger-love." The overlap is not surprising however, as consideration for others has been a core value of our people long before our journeys out west. Eeyawquittoowauconnuck!

Megan Fulopp, a Brothertown Indian descended from the Narragansett Hammer family

Amy Besaw Medford, a Brothertown Indian descended from the Mohegan Brushell family

Acknowledgments

Something I never expected, when I set out to write this book focused on one single person, is that doing so would put me into contact with so much kindness from so many people and communities.

I want to begin by acknowledging the guidance, feedback, and support I have received from Occom's tribal nations, the Brothertown Indian Nation and the Mohegan Tribe. At Brothertown, Megan Fulopp was the first to take an interest in this project and to introduce me to conversations about Occom happening beyond academia. I am especially grateful to Megan and Amy Besaw Medford for their close involvement with the project, for their detailed comments on the entire manuscript, and for contributing the foreword to this volume. Brothertown Historic Preservation Officer Courtney Cottrell also provided key feedback at a crucial stage. At Mohegan, my research received a massive boost from Tribal Historian Jason LaVigne, who more than anyone else helped me understand that Occom means different things in different communities, and from David Freeburg, who answered a barrage of questions and made it easy for me to access Occom's manuscripts shortly after their repatriation. The long afternoon I spent with Jason and David talking about Occom in September 2022 enriched this book immensely. Thank you to all these friends, and to the Brothertown Tribal Council and the Mohegan Council of Elders for facilitating this collaborative work.

Over the past few years I have also received tremendous support, encouragement, and friendship from the Brothertown community members, friends, and allies who make up the Calumet and Cross Historical Society Book Club. Thanks to all of you, especially to Brad Dubos for facilitating, to those who came to the meetings devoted to Occom, and to Amy Buchholz, Janet Dangler, Lawrence Gilley, Gabriel Kastelle, Roy Paul, Heather Law Pezzarossi, and Kelly Wisecup for their written comments on the work I shared with the group.

I first read Occom closely when I was a graduate student at Yale studying early American literature with Caleb Smith and Michael Warner. Michael and Caleb, and also Kim Benston at Haverford College, taught me most of what I know about literature and how to interpret it. Their influence on my whole intellectual outlook has been immense, and their support has been constant for well over a decade now. A special thanks, as well, to my fellow ex-grad student and committed New Havenite Khalil Anthony Johnson for his comradeship and hospitality over many long years and for talking about Occom with me on innumerable occasions.

After graduate school, the idea of undertaking this project grew out of a series of conversations I had with Scott Lyons, whose approach to Native American literature, and intellectual bravery more generally, have been a major source of inspiration to me. This book would not exist without his kindness and encouragement. I am also grateful to Robert Warrior for his more recent feedback, and especially for helping me think through and better articulate this book's contribution to the field of Indigenous studies.

At Columbia, I have had the immense good luck of being able to discuss the project with both Akeel Bilgrami and Audra Simpson—both of whom have been major influences on my thinking since before this project even started—and with Matthew Engelke, to whom I owe a special debt of gratitude for seeing the merit in the project and its interdisciplinary approach. Thanks to Matthew, Courtney Bender, and the staff of the Institute for Religion, Culture, and Public Life for taking me under your wing; to Wendy Lochner and Lowell Frye at Columbia University Press for their editorial guidance; and to Gregory McNamee for the tremendous copyedit.

For assistance in accessing and understanding Occom's unpublished writings, I thank the Mohegan Tribe, the Brothertown Indian Nation, Peter Carini and Ivy Schweitzer at Dartmouth College, Andrea Meyer at the Long Island Collection of the East Hampton Library (whose collection of books bound and annotated by Occom represents a significant opportunity for future scholarship), Sierra Dixon at the Connecticut Historical Society, Kenneth Minkema at Yale, and the staff of the National Records of Scotland. Thanks also to Alex Leven, Earl of Leven and Melville, for permission to reprint the letters by Susanna Wheatley that appear in the appendix. I am also grateful to the incomparable Paul Grant-Costa of the Native Northeast Portal, who patiently answered a flurry of last-minute queries—about archives and about Northeast Native history more generally—that arose as I was bringing the manuscript to completion.

Major financial and institutional support for this project came from the Fox Center for Humanistic Inquiry at Emory University, where I was a postdoctoral fellow in 2019–2020. Keith Anthony, Celeste Barlow, Amy Erbil, and Walter Melion immediately made me feel at home at Emory and gave me the brainspace to get this book off the ground. Thanks also to Tonio Andrade for his invaluable help in shaping this project, and to Brooks Holifield for his detailed input on the parts of the book that concern Occom's interventions in eighteenth-century New England theology. Seeing Brooks's eyes light up when, over lunch, I showed him Occom's hymns and asked him if they counted as "New Divinity" was a turning point in my research.

Other colleagues and mentors who have read portions of the manuscript and/or provided moral or professional support along the way include Grey Anderson, Jacob Collins, Chris Cox, Christian Goodwillie, John Riggs, Scott Stevens, and Mandy Suhr-Systma. Thanks also to audiences at Princeton University, Haverford College, Baruch College, Northern Arizona University, and Columbia's Seminar on Material Texts for feedback on parts of the manuscript I presented as talks; and to my students at Columbia, where I have been finding ways of teaching Occom even in unexpected classes.

Last but not least: thanks to my friends and family for their love and support, to Yufka, and above all to my partner, Lina, for support that goes way beyond words.

> # SAMSON OCCOM

Introduction

On the Occasion of Samson Occom's Three Hundredth Birthday

Samson Occom was born on an unknown day in 1723. As I write these words in early 2023, preparations are well under way for celebrations of his three hundredth birthday at Mohegan and Brothertown, the tribal nations that Occom called home. This book would not be what it is without the support, instruction, and friendship I have received from the people of these communities and their nontribal friends and allies. These friends are much in my thoughts as I write these words today. So I would like to begin this book by adding my voice to the chorus of the people, wherever they may be, wishing Occom happy birthday.

The place of Occom's birth was Mohegan, an Indigenous nation whose homelands are located near the Thames (or Pequot) River in the present-day state of Connecticut. "I was brought up in Heathenism," he wrote in his 1768 autobiography, which recounts how he spent his childhood immersed in tribal customs that had been passed down among his Northeast Native ancestors for centuries. In his autobiography, Occom's discussion of Indigenous tradition focuses on themes of subsistence, mobility, and hospitality to strangers. "My parents lived a wandering life," Occom wrote, and he himself grew up acquainted with people from other nearby Coastal Algonquian tribes (Occom's mother was of Pequot descent, and he would eventually marry a Montaukett woman) and perhaps also with people from the Mahican, Munsee, Abenaki, and Haudenosaunee peoples who

Figure 0.1 Samson Occom, as captured in a lithograph published by Williams & Smith, Stationers (London, 1808), after a lost oil painting (1766–1768) by Mason Chamberlain.

lived farther to the north and west. Even before the arrival of Europeans, the "Native Northeast" was a robustly transnational space. Occom's life would come to reflect that in a profound way.[1]

Both of Samson's parents, Joshua Occom and Sarah Wauby, had a major impact on his life. Joshua was a councilor to the Mohegan sachem Ben Uncas II, whose tribal council Samson joined at the age of nineteen, around the time of his father's death. Sarah encouraged Samson's education and his interest in Christianity.[2] This interest, which Sarah shared with her son, coincided with an upswelling of religious revivalism in the area around Mohegan. George Whitefield, the eminent Anglican minister who played a major role in the formation of transatlantic evangelicalism, visited America for the first time when Occom was a teenager. Whitefield encouraged a more experiential (or "experimental") kind of religiosity than New Englanders had previously been accustomed to, including bigger meetings for worship, often held outdoors, where people from various backgrounds could set aside their social differences in a shared experience of the Word.[3] Taking inspiration from Whitefield, Anglo-American ministers began leading revivals all over southern New England, some of which Occom may have attended. By the early 1740s, Occom had immersed himself in the study of the Bible, of ancient languages, of early modern religious literature, and (it seems) of anything he could learn about in books, or from his tutors Eleazar Wheelock and Benjamin Pomeroy. Once Occom's talents in reading and writing became apparent to his teachers, an opportunity arose for him to attend Yale, but he missed it, having temporarily ruined his eyesight through excessive reading.

In 1749 Occom accepted a position as a schoolteacher among the Montaukett tribe of eastern Long Island, where he wound up living for more than a decade. During his years at Montauk, Occom continued his own education even as he taught others. He also married and started a family with Mary Fowler, the daughter of a prominent Montaukett family. In 1759, at a ceremony convened by the Suffolk Presbytery in East Hampton, Occom became the first Native American minister ever to be ordained by a Protestant church. One of his first ministerial posts was a missionary trip to the Oneida people of the Haudenosaunee Confederacy. In the early 1760s he traveled widely across New York and southern New England, where he was increasingly in demand as a visiting preacher. In 1765, he ventured even farther afield to England, Scotland, and Ireland as the leader of a fundraising mission for Moor's Charity School, operated by his former tutor

Eleazar Wheelock. Across the Atlantic, Occom raised roughly £13,000 for the school and made himself into an international celebrity among English-speaking evangelicals, but this came at great personal cost to himself and his family. While he was abroad, Wheelock had promised to support Mary Fowler Occom and the Occom children, but he failed to do so, to the entire family's dismay. On top of this, Wheelock took the money Occom had raised abroad—for the purposes, he had been told, of Indigenous education—and disappeared up the Connecticut River to found Dartmouth College instead, whose first six graduating classes were entirely white.[4]

Wheelock's betrayals coincided with a time of turmoil for the Mohegan people. For decades there had existed a factional dispute between two different groups of Mohegans about how properly to manage tribal affairs. One party, Ben's Town, advocated a unitary form of sovereignty under the leadership of a hereditary sachem, who would manage tribal finances and external relations with other nations. This was the party Occom was born into. But amid increasing mismanagement of tribal finances and collusion with Connecticut Colony by Ben Uncas II and III, he switched to the other party, John's Town, whose members tended to be less enamored of the idea of a hereditary sachemship and more committed to collaborating with other tribal nations and with non-Indigenous stakeholders who could help them defend Mohegan sovereignty against Connecticut Colony.[5]

It was during this time of increasingly acrimonious disputes between these two factions that Occom involved himself in the planning of the Brothertown movement. In 1773, a group of Coastal Algonquian families from across the region convened at Mohegan to discuss the idea of a new Indigenous nation where families could live together at a geographical remove from the colonial chaos of the Eastern Seaboard. By 1774, Occom's son-in-law, Joseph Johnson, had negotiated a grant of land for the new community with the allied Oneida Nation near present-day Deansboro, New York. Migration to Brothertown began shortly thereafter but was suspended following the onset of the American Revolution. In the mid-1780s it resumed, and Occom relocated there in 1785 at the age of sixty-three.

Occom retained close connections to Mohegan and, despite suffering from debilitating hip pain, overcame massive financial and logistical challenges to visit Mohegan and other coastal communities on at least two trips in the late 1780s. At his new home in Brothertown, he preached, taught, and advocated fiercely for his people's sovereignty even amid further

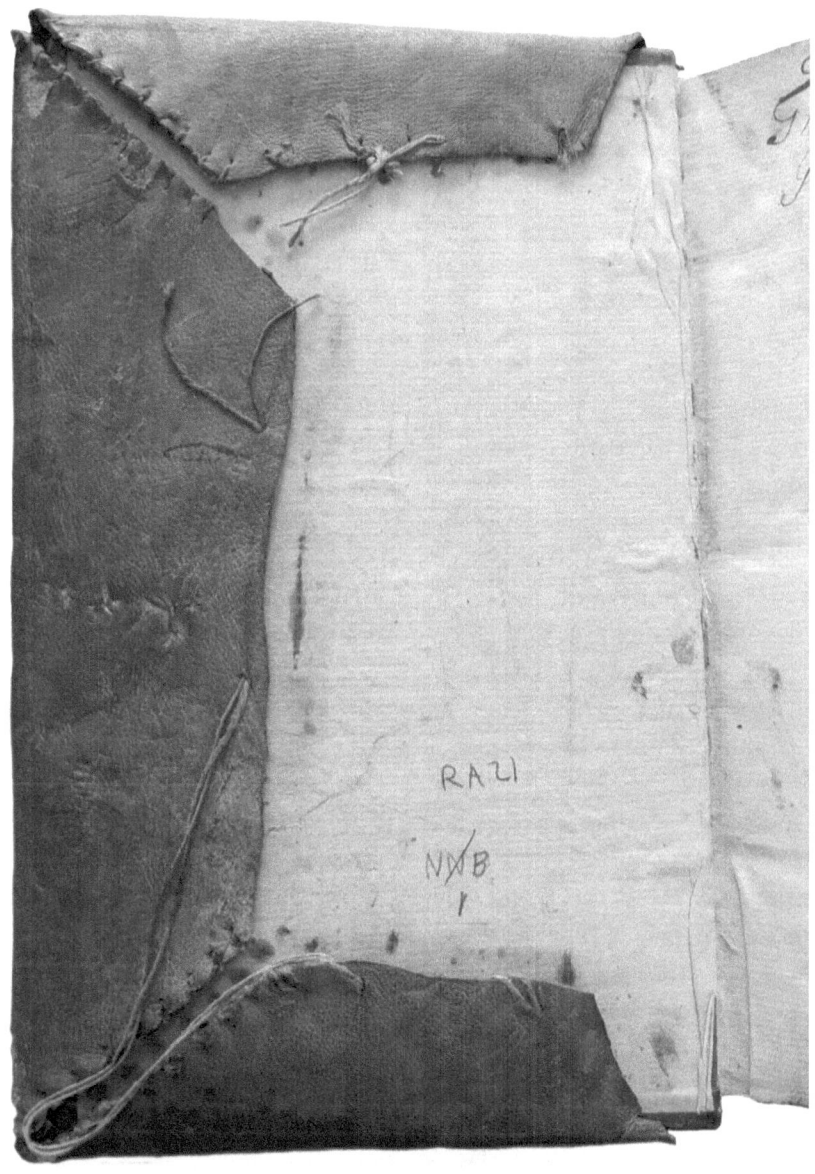

Figure 0.2 A volume of pamphlets hand-bound by Occom.
Long Island Collection, East Hampton (New York) Library. Photograph by the author.

colonial aggressions and new factional disputes. In 1791, perhaps seeking respite from these conflicts, Samson and Mary Occom moved house one last time to the neighboring Indigenous community of New Stockbridge, where he had been preaching for several years. Even still, he remained deeply involved in Brothertown political affairs, drafting a series of petitions and policy agreements that helped guarantee the nation's survival down to the present day. In Occom's last years, he also found time for gardening, handicrafts (he was especially skilled at binding books and making buckets and other household utensils), and reading. He died at home on July 14, 1792.

Samson Occom looms large in the history of the colonial North America. In academic and tribal circles alike, he is among the best known and most studied Northeast Native individuals of his era. Some have even suggested that Occom looms *too* large in the historical literature, that the perennial scholarly focus on his life has foregrounded a set of historiographic themes—conversion, migration, literacy, outreach—that may not have been so important to most Native Americans of his day, even within his own tribes. I take this concern seriously and wish to emphasize here at the outset what many scholars have said before: Samson Occom's life was extraordinary, and thus not necessarily representative of eighteenth-century Mohegan, Brothertown, or Native American experience more generally.

One of the things that made Occom extraordinary was how much he wrote. He was probably the most prolific Indigenous writer of the eighteenth century, and by sheer volume his surviving oeuvre is larger than that of any Native American until the second half of the nineteenth. Yet Occom's writings—and more, his life *as a writer*—have thus far remained largely unstudied. This is partly because most of Occom's surviving writings do not seem (at least superficially) to address specifically Indigenous concerns. Like many other Native writers living in "New England," as the colonists called it, Occom was educated in literacy by white people so that he could read and preach the Gospel. Much of what he wrote accordingly falls into religious genres: sermons, spiritual autobiographies, ministerial diaries and correspondence, and the like. On the surface many of Occom's writings in these genres look a lot like writings by non-Indigenous people from the same era, which can make them seem uninteresting for people who approach his work seeking to learn something about his experience as an Indigenous person. If one looks closer, however, and reads Occom's writings with an awareness of the historical and political contexts in which he created them, it turns out that almost all of them have something to say about Northeast Native sovereignty and self-determination.

In this book I offer a broad interpretation of Occom's entire body of surviving writings: an argument about what his works mean, based mostly on close readings of individual texts. While this interpretation is far from exhaustive and leaves many questions unanswered, I hope to provide readers with a sense of what Occom was usually up to when he put pen to paper. My guiding assumption throughout is that Occom's words are expressive of agency: his own agency as a person, as well as the collective self-determination of the tribal peoples to whom he belonged. Occom's commitment to his communities ran very deep. Indeed, it went "all the way down," defining his identity at the most fundamental level. In this sense, this book is a study not just of Occom's words but also of "literary sovereignty," or the textual mediation of Indigenous power in a world shaped by settler colonialism.[6]

Reading Occom's words as expressive of literary sovereignty means acknowledging that his writings have a special kind of authority as historical evidence. To say that Occom's words are "expressive" of sovereignty, rather than simply being "about" sovereignty, locates agency in the act of enunciation itself. The words he committed to paper manifest his agency in a way that words by others do not. It follows from this that *all* of Occom's words should be examined as expressions of literary sovereignty, even those that do not seem to be about topics typically recognized as "Indigenous."[7] As any reader of Occom knows, many (if not most) of his writings are not about Native Americans *thematically*. But it would be a mistake to think that, when he wrote texts on non-Native themes, Occom did so without concern for the welfare of his people. It can be difficult to appreciate that concern, however, when Occom's texts are abstracted from the historical context in which he wrote them. This context was shaped by what was happening in his Native communities, but also by global developments in geopolitics, religion, and Anglophone literary culture. Occom was very much a creature of this broader eighteenth-century world, and his textual interventions (and innovations) become more apparent the more one knows about the transcultural, transnational spaces in which he moved. One of my main goals in this book has been to supply some of this context for readers who may be unfamiliar with the period.

The portrait of Occom that emerges in these pages emphasizes Northeast Native traditions. Occom valued his communities' culturally distinctive lifeways as they had been passed down from precolonial times, and he sought to preserve those lifeways amid the welter of settler colonialism. He particularly valued his ancestors' customs of hospitality toward strangers, or what I sometimes refer to as "stranger-love," customs practiced by Native families even at the cost of impoverishing themselves. "They will yet Divide what little they have if there is but a mouth full a Piece," he wrote in his unpublished sermon on the Good Samaritan, an indispensable text for anyone seeking to grasp the full complexity of Occom's approach to Indigenous lifeways.[8] Occom's traditionalism formed the bedrock of his religious and political life. In the 1730s and 1740s, when Christian revivalists began visiting the area around Mohegan, Occom initially wrote them off as just another wave of colonial intruders. Over time, though, he started seeing a deep commonality between the Gospel as preached by the revivalists and his ancestors' traditions of hospitality. Eighteenth-century English evangelicals presented themselves as "stranger ministers" whose mission was to unite far-flung peoples in a transnational communion of love.[9] Unfortunately, Occom saw, this mission of love was usually derailed by colonial ministers' inability to see Indigenous peoples as culturally, politically, and morally autonomous. Nevertheless, Occom was impressed by the astonishing communicative techniques the stranger ministers used to preach the very Gospel that they so often failed to live by: the heartrending sermons with their promises of awakening; the books and pamphlets; the transatlantic speaking tours and networks of correspondence; the endless pavement-pounding on behalf of the spiritually dead. It was "religion" as expressed through these new forms of social interaction—what historians today describe as the beginnings of "evangelicalism"—and not Christianity *per se* that got Occom's attention and changed the course of his life. He wrote in 1765 that "the Religion which I heard *at this Time* [i.e., around 1740] was a new thing among mankind," a highly revealing statement given that Occom's people had been acquainted with Christianity for more than a hundred years.[10]

For the most part, the brand of New England Christianity Occom's Mohegan ancestors had known (and almost universally declined to practice) was staid, village-centered, and stridently anti-Indigenous. The "new" religion of evangelicalism, by contrast, was better aligned with Northeast Native traditions that emphasized hospitality, kindness to strangers, and what Occom called a "wandering life."[11] For some reason having to do with the workings of the Word and Spirit, it seemed to Occom that

New Englanders were becoming more extroverted in their religiosity, more welcoming of strangers, more public-spirited, and more encouraging of mobility.[12] Evangelicals taught that life on earth was a "pilgrimage," and reframed theological discourse as an inquiry into perception (hence the emphasis on "awakening") and rebirth, or "regeneration." By the 1750s, Occom was convinced that his people needed all of these things if they were to survive settler colonialism, and he dedicated the rest of his life to the work of political and spiritual "reformation" among his Indigenous kin.[13]

Occom's evangelicalism was never anything other than a way of expressing his traditionalism, since it reflected his abiding commitment to his people's ancestral customs of kindness to people of all nations: what Lisa Brooks describes as the ethos of the "common pot."[14] But for people who read Occom today—especially, perhaps, people like me who read him from a nonreligious perspective—his traditionalism can be hard to relate to, or even see, because of the peculiarly evangelical way he chose to live it out. This book is an attempt to explain why Occom made that choice, and thus why his evangelicalism mattered not just in a religious sense but also *culturally and politically* for his Northeast Native communities and for contemporary readers who care about those communities and about the social purposes of reading and writing more generally.

In the course of writing this book, I have benefited at numerous junctures from feedback, support, and cultural perspectives shared with me by people from Occom's tribal communities. This input from Brothertown and Mohegan has profoundly shaped my understanding of the benefits and limitations of a study like this one. It has helped me realize, for one thing, that it is both inevitable and potentially useful that my perspective on Occom differs from that of his kin. There are several ways of describing this difference, but no way does so accurately without saying something about settler colonialism and its asymmetrical effects on Native and settler populations.

Settler colonialism has been the source of innumerable ills for Mohegan and Brothertown communities, many of which are well documented in the scholarly literature.[15] Settler colonialism also bears in many ways on the practice of scholarship about Northeast Native peoples, not least because of the emphasis settler societies place on the politics of *recognition*. Following Glen Coulthard, Audra Simpson, and other scholars in Indigenous and settler colonial studies, I understand the politics of recognition as a repertoire of legal and political protocols initiated by settler nation-states to adjudicate Indigenous sovereignty and cultural authenticity.[16] Colonial protocols of recognition have often put Brothertown and Mohegan in the position of having to prove their authenticity and sovereignty according to criteria invented by settler states.[17] In doing so, they have drawn support from academic experts purporting to speak with authority about, and hence to *recognize*, what "indigeneity," "Nativeness," or "Indianness" amount to. These forms of academic recognition permeate modern disciplines of knowledge production that take Indigenous peoples as their object of study. The first time I learned about Occom, for instance, was in college, in an anthology of American literature, where he was presented to me as a "Native American" author from the eighteenth century. This anthology was created to serve an educational system in which students and teachers, mostly non-Native, understood themselves as progressing in their educations and careers by producing what *academics* recognized as knowledge about "Native Americans." A version of that system still exists today, and I would not be writing these words if it did not.

In the two decades or so since I was an undergraduate, some things have changed. Thanks largely to the efforts of Indigenous scholars and activists, a growing number of academics are at least aware of the deep disconnection (and often distrust) that exists between Native communities and scholars purporting to make knowledge about them. Yet despite this growing awareness, there remains much disagreement among and between scholars in Indigenous studies and settler colonial studies about how (and whether) the problem can be fixed—and in particular about how knowledge produced in academic institutions relates, or should relate, to the knowledge produced within Native communities, particularly in nonacademic contexts.[18]

In recent years, this disagreement has generated three distinct approaches to the question of how scholarly knowledge about Indigenous peoples relates, or should relate, to Indigenous knowledge outside the academic context.

One group of scholars takes the divide between "colonial knowledge" and "Indigenous knowledge" as their starting point and argues that decolonizing academic research on Indigenous communities requires methods that remake scholarly knowledge as Indigenous knowledge. Indigenous knowledge, on this view, is a methodological *sine qua non* of Indigenous studies research.[19]

A second group acknowledges the desirability of academic knowledge being more closely aligned with Indigenous knowledge but does not think it is reasonable or even desirable to make Indigenous knowledge a precondition for Indigenous studies scholarship. These scholars advocate a multidisciplinary, multimethodological approach to Indigenous studies and argue that the disconnect between academia and Indigenous communities should be resolved through the cultivation of an "ethical research relationship," rather than the inculcation of a particular epistemology.[20]

A third group is skeptical about the term "Indigenous" itself—and, thus, by extension, the project of aligning scholarly knowledge with Indigenous knowledge—because the very idea of indigeneity is, after all, an artifact of colonialism.[21] From this vantage, scholars who hope for or insist on the alignment of Indigenous knowledge with Indigenous studies risk minimizing the overdetermining effects of settler colonialism and related structures of oppression on academic knowledge production in general.

In this book I take the second of these three approaches. My reason for this has mainly to do with my understanding of the term "knowledge." Unlike scholars who take the third approach just mentioned, I have no problem with the idea of Indigenous knowledge in general, assuming this term refers to the kind of knowledge that members of Indigenous communities possess and recognize as Indigenous. On the other hand, I do not claim to actually be *conveying* Indigenous knowledge in these pages for the simple reason that, to my knowledge, no satisfying explanation has ever been offered of how non-Indigenous people (like me) are supposed to acquire Indigenous knowledge in the first place. More generally, as Robert Alexander Innes argues, the claim that Indigenous studies should be based on Indigenous knowledge often elides epistemological complexities and problems of subject positionality that scholars in the field have not yet settled.[22] The second approach appeals to me because it acknowledges that these unresolved questions remain open. Of the three approaches, it is the least dogmatic about issues of epistemology, and I think that's a good thing.

What I have to offer in these pages is not, on my understanding, Indigenous knowledge *per se*; rather, it is a series of interpretations that show that a broad range of Occom's writings—much broader than scholars have previously supposed—are relevant to Indigenous communities and concerns.

As mentioned earlier, this largely involves situating Occom's words in their historical context. Occom composed most of his surviving writings in a "common, plain, every-day" style that he thought would be easy for most people to understand.[23] But three hundred years is a long time! (To put it in chronological perspective, *less* than three hundred years separated Occom's lifetime from Joan of Arc's.) Because Occom lived so long ago, not all of what he wrote in his "plain" style is readily intelligible to most twenty-first-century readers, be they located in academia, in Native communities, or anywhere else. With that in mind, this book answers Chris Andersen and Jean O'Brien's "appeal for methodological promiscuity" in Indigenous studies by drawing on the scholarly know-how that I actually have.[24] This derives from a long (if imperfect) education in the humanities that has acquainted me with a broad swath of colonial and transatlantic literary and religious history, as well as various techniques of textual interpretation that I have found helpful in thinking through what Occom meant when he wrote what he wrote. My hope is that putting these interpretive techniques into practice will be useful both to Indigenous communities and to readers interested in Occom's place in the history of the Native Northeast and in eighteenth-century transatlantic history more broadly.

This book is deeply indebted to previous research on Samson Occom, primarily in the fields of literary and religious history. Before going any further I would like to acknowledge, above all, the tremendous scholarly debt I owe to Joanna Brooks, who painstakingly (and very accurately) transcribed most of Occom's unpublished manuscripts and published them in a single volume in 2006 along with extensive editorial commentary.[25] Scholarly readers will find that I am in agreement with Brooks on most things, above all on the fundamental point that Occom's religious practice furthered his peoples' political and cultural autonomy, rather than compromising that autonomy for the sake of cultural and/or political assimilation.[26] I am also deeply indebted to Lisa Brooks's account in *The Common Pot* of how Occom and his kin used language to welcome non-Indigenous newcomers into a "Native space" of social interaction; and to literary scholars including Matthew Cohen, Philip Round, Kelly Wisecup, and Hilary Wyss for their archivally inspired work situating Occom in broader histories of reading, literacy, books, and other media.[27] This book has been influenced by these predecessors' work in crucial ways, but it also paints a new picture of Occom that differs from interpretations by previous religious and literary historians in a few important respects. Three of these, in particular, may be helpful to note here at the outset.

First and perhaps most important, this book defends the claim that Occom was a traditionalist who sought to perpetuate rather than abandon Indigenous lifeways passed down to him from his Coastal Algonquian ancestors. Today, this proposition may not seem especially controversial to scholarly readers, who widely agree that Occom was a traditionalist. Yet there persists a tendency, particularly in the historical literature on the Brothertown movement, to cast Occom as an "Indian Moses" who sought to deliver Northeast Native communities into a new era in which collective life would be defined by a new relationship to the land (defined by farming) and a new understanding of peoplehood (defined by race and the biblical notion of "chosenness"). This "Mosaic" interpretation of Occom and Brothertown is right to focus on problems of land use, race, and religion. But it has often mischaracterized exactly *how* Occom's ideas on these topics diverged from those of other Coastal Algonquians who declined to join the movement, since it tends to describe that divergence in terms of Occom's willingness to leave behind traditional forms of belonging, subsistence, and cohabitation with the land. Instead of measuring Occom's traditionalism against that of other Northeast Natives who did not emigrate, I argue that there were multiple traditionalisms among Coastal Algonquian communities in the second half of the eighteenth century. Occom's particular style of traditionalism may have been different from that of other Coastal Algonquians, but his commitment to the carrying forward of ancestral lifeways was no less radical for that.

A second way this book differs from previous scholarship on Occom is that it contests the mistaken assumption, first propagated in 1899 by William DeLoss Love in *Samson Occom and the Christian Indians of New England*, that Occom's writings on religious topics were conventional, conformist, and/or derivative in their relation to Anglo-American ideas and ways of talking, particularly the rhetoric of so-called New Light Christianity. It is this assumption more than any other that has prevented readers from appreciating Occom's efforts to reinvent and revitalize precolonial Indigenous lifeways by appropriating evangelicalism.

One of the things I have learned over many years teaching Occom in undergraduate classrooms is that when people use words like "typical" and "conventional" to describe his writings, what they usually mean is that his writings are *boring*. I have also found that when I am able to make Occom's writings seem unboring to students, they almost always come to the realization that his writings are not conformist at all. There are a couple ways to make Occom unboring that I use in my classes and to some extent in this book. One is to emphasize that Occom was very often speaking from a traditionalist place even when he wasn't talking *about* Indigenous traditions specifically. This emphasis reflects my training in the discipline of literary studies, and in particular my commitment to the basic literary-historical premise that the meaning of any text comes not just from its theme or content but also from its form. As Angela Calcaterra and Kelly Wisecup argue, thinking about the form of Occom's writings, as well as their content, opens a new vista onto his traditionalism.[28] My approach to interpreting Occom builds on these scholars' work by construing "form" as a term designating not only syntactic, poetic, and generic features of his writings, but also *forms of interaction*. In most of his surviving writings, Occom used what anthropologists call "metalanguage" (language about language) to provide explicit guidance about how he wanted his words to be used and interpreted by those with whom he shared social space.[29] That metalinguistic guidance was profoundly shaped by Native tradition *and* by evangelicalism; and that's reason enough to study Occom's religious writings closely.[30]

The other way to make Occom's religious writings unboring is to situate them amid the internal complexity of Christianity in the eighteenth-century Atlantic world. Even in colonial (and provincial) New England, Christianity was never monolithic; and by Occom's time it certainly wasn't monolithically "Puritan," as one sometimes hears in classrooms and even in some academic publications![31] The distinction between "Old Lights" and "New Lights," which has become commonplace in more recent Occom scholarship, is more helpful, but only a little. In Occom's milieu, these terms were used—almost always polemically—to distinguish between two different attitudes toward the itinerancy and revivalism that erupted in New England in the 1740s.[32] To be sure, Occom was deeply and lastingly affected by the revivalism of this period. Yet he lived a long life and changed with his times. Occom was not ordained as a minister until 1757, and most of his surviving writings date from the 1770s and 1780s, a full generation after the contretemps between Old Lights and New. So why is this terminology still so prevalent in the scholarship on Occom and, to some extent, other eighteenth-century Americans of color who happened to be Protestants?

One reason is that, for many readers of Occom, the term "New Light" bears with it connotations of "democratic identity," "political autonomy," and triumphant "eloquence" in defiance of "social hierarchies."[33] This way of using the term—which conveniently downplays New Lights' neo-Augustinian obsession with the corruptibility of the human will—became commonplace only in the second half of the twentieth century, when U.S. historians, most famously Alan Heimert, reinterpreted the Great Awakening as a precursor to the American Revolution.[34] The "Heimert thesis" was always highly tendentious and is defended by very few historians today, but it made a major impact on the historiography of eighteenth-century American literature around the turn of the twenty-first century, when the canon was expanding to include previously overlooked writers.[35] For present purposes, the problem with the term "New Light" is not merely that it is misleading to use it in this "democratic" way, but also that it tends to present eighteenth-century religious history as a prehistory of U.S. nationalism, which seems quite unhelpful (to put it mildly) to understanding Occom and the sovereign non-U.S. nations to which he belonged.

Bearing this in mind, and taking inspiration from Indigenous studies internationalists like Jace Weaver and Nick Estes, I propose that it is time to deprovincialize Occom by setting the Old Light/New Light dichotomy aside and resituating him instead as part of the increasingly global religious movement known to present-day historians as "international Protestantism," "transatlantic evangelicalism," and "Protestant popular religion."[36] These terms better describe the historical context in which Occom's religious thought and practice will be presented in the pages that follow. By setting aside the flattening caricature of Occom as a typical New Light and emphasizing how his ideas about religion diverged from those of his colonial teachers, a much different picture of Occom's religious writings comes into focus. Indeed, the more time I have spent reading Samson Occom's writings alongside the religious literature he was reading and arguing with, the more I have come to understand that he was creatively, self-consciously, and often brilliantly heterodox in his Christianity. As demonstrated in the elaborate annotations Occom made in his copy of Jonathan Edwards's *Freedom of the Will* (which he personally hand-bound in leather, along with several other volumes held today at the East Hampton Library), Occom was steeped in Edwards's thought and in the pamphlet literature generated by his followers.[37] Occom knew exactly what was at stake in Edwards's attempt to resacralize the Anglophone philosophical discourse of "moral sense," and he derived from Edwards and his students a theology of awakening that sought to retrain Indigenous communities how to perceive the sacredness of Creation in the way they had prior to the advent of colonialism. Occom also bent the hoary and by his time largely moribund New England discourse of covenant theology toward a purpose for which it was never before intended: Indigenous sovereignty. He did this, in part, through new readings of Paul's letters to the Romans and Galatians, on the basis of which he likened the "Indian Heathen" to the Gentiles of the New Testament. This interpretation of Native Americans as an *unchosen* people, which Occom worked out in his sermons from the 1770s and 1780, was hardly conventional in theological terms; and my hope is that showing this will reignite interest in Occom and other Native Christians as *intellectuals* who appropriated theology and other learned discourses imported by Anglo-Europeans as part of their repertoire of anticolonial practice.

A third difference between this book and previous studies of Occom is that it underscores how Occom used evangelical discourse as a way of practicing his traditionalism *in public*. The public aspect of Occom's traditionalist practice can be a little hard to appreciate from the perspective of recent Indigenous studies scholarship, which has rightly raised concerns about the injustice done to Native communities when tribal knowledge and patrimony are publicized involuntarily.[38] I share these concerns and take them on board in these pages while also arguing that Occom's *aspiration to be public* is something that should be acknowledged and analyzed historically. To an extent that has not quite been appreciated previously, Occom's career ushered in what I refer to in chapter 2 as the "broadcast era" of Indigenous cultural expression. The highly "publick" ways Occom talked about Native tradition and sought to communicate it to the masses prefigured the style of plain speaking found in much later works like Vine Deloria's *We Talk, You Listen* (1970) and *God Is Red* (1973).[39] For Occom, as for Deloria later, broadcasting indigeneity meant deploying specific techniques of addressing strangers that were designed to make words easy to understand, so that those words could have an impact on as many people as possible—all for the purpose of bettering life for Native communities. Occom's traditionalist appropriation of these broadcast-oriented forms of address, rather his use of particular "media" of communication, is what best explains his already widely acknowledged stature as a foundational figure in the history of Native American public culture.

Outline of Chapters

The six chapters that follow are arranged in pairs. The first of these is devoted mainly to methodological and historiographical questions and is addressed primarily to scholarly readers in the fields of Indigenous studies, literary studies, and religious studies. The second deals mainly with Occom's religious thought and practice. And the third explores Occom's writings on perception and on the act of reading, which he came to understand as a practice that trained people to *see* the world anew.

Chapter 1 offers a characterization of Occom's traditionalism, which I argue was one of many traditionalisms that characterized Mohegan life in the eighteenth and nineteenth centuries. Here I am particularly interested in the simultaneously methodological and historical question of how Occom's traditionalism relates to his religion. Whereas there has been a tendency in recent scholarship to collapse the latter into the former (to speak of "religious traditions" but not religion as distinct from tradition), I argue that it is important to keep these ideas separate, just as Occom did.

Chapter 2 poses a very basic question—what does it mean to say that Occom's writings are "about" Indigenous communities?—and develops a response to that question in a way that seeks to reconcile the disciplinary demands of Indigenous studies and literary studies. I argue for an interpretive approach to Occom's writings that eschews practices of literary-historical *recognition* in favor of reading Occom "obviously." This turns out to be more complicated than it may sound, due to complexities arising from the "addressivity" of Occom's texts and from the historical gulf separating the eighteenth century from the present day.

Chapters 3 and 4 focus on Occom's theological views and his practices of piety, respectively. The central claim of chapter 3 is that Occom rejected the idea that Native peoples had been "chosen" by God for some special national destiny that required them to adopt lifeways unlike their Indigenous ancestors. Chapter 4 characterizes Occom's piety as (1) a style of public self-presentation designed to secure others' deference and (2) a micropolitical practice of speaking truth to power.

Chapter 5 offers a reading of Occom's 1768 autobiography informed by new archival research I conducted in 2021–2022 in collaboration with members and friends of the Brothertown and Mohegan nations. This research uncovered some surprising facts about the manuscript and its history. It turns out, for instance, that Occom may have taken the manuscript with him when he moved to Brothertown, which raises the possibility that the document had a hitherto unknown "social life" in Native space.

Chapter 6 explores Occom's writings on perception as a way of shedding new light on his understanding of a religious "awakening." From Occom's point of view, what was at stake in the idea of a religious awakening (and, indeed, in religion more generally) was the recovery of a nonalienated way of seeing the world. Colonization, Occom came to believe, had transformed not merely the external forms of Northeast Native social and cultural experience but also the way he and his kindred perceived one another and the natural world. A religious awakening, for him, was a way of getting back to his ancestors' older way of seeing.

In the conclusion, I bring these various threads together in an overview of Occom's shifting attitude toward the theory and practice of reading. The appendix reproduces two fascinating letters about Occom (one of which transcribes a hitherto unknown letter by Occom himself) that I discovered over the course of this research and that have not previously been published.

PART I

CHAPTER I

"Asylum for Strangers"

An Approach to Occom's Traditionalism

Susanna Wheatley just could not understand why Occom kept letting them in. They came from all over, mostly Native people, a few white people, too—*and he didn't even know them.* He had laid it all out to her in a letter from March 5, 1771, amid the depths of a hard winter at Mohegan:

> I am in greater Straights and Necessities than ever, we had but little Corn last year and Consequently little meat, it was Dry Season with us. . . . I am oblig'd to Sell any thing I have to get meat and Corn with, & my Family Consists [of] ten Souls Constantly, and a great Number of Visitors Continually from all quarters[. T]here has not been one Week nor 3 Days I can remember in the Year past, but that we have had Some Stranger or other—My being acquainted with the World in Some Measure, has made my House a Sort of an Asylum for Strangers both English and Indians, far and near.[1]

Wheatley implored Occom to start saying no. She knew as well as he did that he couldn't afford it. The previous year Occom had fallen out with his former tutor and collaborator, the Connecticut minister Eleazar Wheelock, with whom he had been working for half a decade on a project to found a new academy for Northeast Native children. Most of the fundraising legwork had fallen to Occom, who had managed to raise £13,000 for the new venture during a whirlwind preaching tour of England, Scotland, and Ireland in 1766–1768. Then, in 1770, just as Occom was getting settled back into daily life in Mohegan, Wheelock disappeared up the Connecticut River to Hanover, New Hampshire, to found Dartmouth, a college built for white boys, taking away with him any promise of future financial support for Occom and his family.[2] Thanks in part to the backing of the influential Wheatleys, Occom still managed to collect a monthly salary of £60 from the London Board of the New England Company, as well as an occasional check from his and the Wheatleys' mutual friend John Thornton, the second-richest man in England and leader of the "Clapham Sect" of English evangelicals.[3] After all Occom had been through, Wheatley hated to see him spend what remained of his income on strangers.

Somewhat exasperated, Wheatley eventually picked up her pen and wrote to Thornton in London: "tho he has a salary of £50 sterlg it seems he has but little benefit of it: for his house is almost always full of Indians, 30 of whom come and reside with him several days together. I told him I did not think it his duty and that the salary was given for the support of his family which is very large. But he said he tho't he was doing his duty to let as many come as would."[4]

These letters reveal a clear discrepancy between Occom's sense of "his duty" and Wheatley's. In receiving ten, twenty, or thirty visitors at a time in his Mohegan home—which was bigger than some, to be fair, but not *that* big—Occom was acting according to Native traditions passed down through generations. When times were hard, his people shared things equally: "When there is Scarsity of Food amongst them," he explained in one sermon, "they will yet Divide what little they have if there is but a mouth full a Piece . . . and when anyone is destitude of a Blanket, he that has two, will freely give him one."[5] This generosity transcended boundaries of nation and tribe: "the Indian Heathen . . . are very Compassionate one to another, very Liberal among themselves, and also to Strangers," a trait which manifested Native communities' shared belief that "we Should have the Same Love to other Nations as we have to our Nation."[6] Such practices reflected common human decency, Occom recognized, but they were ones that had been uniquely cultivated by Northeast Native communities for centuries.[7] "We freely Entertain all visitors," he explained in his 1768 autobiography, not just because it is the right thing to do but also because it is "our custom," something that marked "our" lifeways as different from those of outsiders.[8]

Occom was carrying forward these Indigenous customs of stranger interaction when he wrote to Wheatley that his "House [was] a Sort of an Asylum for Strangers both English and Indians." But Wheatley, who cared about Occom and wanted the best for him, couldn't see that. In her letter to Thornton, she put Occom's conduct in the most charitable light she could. She explained that Occom took in strangers because "he had an Opportunity of Preaching and conversing with them, and they are very attentive to his instructions," further reporting that "he says he does not preach for gain, for if he had nothing he would still go on preaching[;] his view is the good of souls."[9] Wheatley was clearly impressed by Occom's willingness to suffer for his faith: "I love him for his humility," she declared to Thornton in another letter.[10] Nevertheless, Occom's extravagant hospitality made her uneasy.

One of the most telling differences between Occom's letter to Wheatley and Wheatley's letter to Thornton is that, whereas Occom reported taking in "both English and Indian" strangers, Wheatley told Thornton that "his house is almost always full of Indians." This implies that she saw something distinctly "Indian" about the hospitality Occom was offering in his home, just as Occom did. Wheatley's assessment of this Native social space, however, did not align with Occom's traditionalist understanding of "our custom" of "freely Entertain[ing] *all* visitors," both "English and Indian, far and near." What she saw instead was a turn of events that threatened to derail one of colonial America's greatest success stories. Her friend Occom, who in 1759 had astonished enlightened observers by becoming New England's first-ever ordained Native American minister, only to rise to still loftier heights of fame and success during his travels abroad, was getting sucked back into penury owing to an exaggerated sense of "his duty" to "Indians." This was the narrative, at least, that found its way back to Occom in a letter from Thornton which he received in November 1771. "I would recommend your writing the Trustees [of Wheelock's new school] & set forth meekly mildly & humbly your many Indian Visitors that have so frequently lived upon you," Thornton wrote, convinced that the trustees would send him more money.[11] Thornton was trying to help, but he too was oblivious to Occom's effort to sustain Native traditions of hospitality to people of all nations. Then again, how could he have known? In passing from Occom to Wheatley to Thornton to Occom, a perfectly clear affirmation of generosity to "English and Indians" had been garbled and twisted into a complaint about "Indians" freeloading or "liv[ing] upon" you." Sometimes settler colonialism was like a game of telephone. No matter how lucidly Occom spoke, the world he lived in was shaped much more than he wanted by what English people were prepared to hear. Still, he thought, he had a "duty" to keep trying.

In December 1772, Occom published a sermon which he had delivered that September at the execution of Moses Paul, a Wampanoag who had been found guilty of murder and sentenced to be hanged on the New Haven town green.[12] In his preface to the sermon's printed version, Occom bemoaned the task of having to explain yet again what everyone in his audience was already supposed to know: that, as per the book of Romans, "the wages of sin is death, but the gift of God is eternal life through Jesus Christ our Lord."[13] What was the point of printing yet another discourse on this familiar topic? After all, Occom wrote in his preface, "the people of God are abundantly furnished with excellent books upon divine subjects." Nevertheless, Occom claimed, his book had the capacity to reach readers in a way that these other books could not. There were two reasons for this. The first was that his book was easier to understand. "The books that are in the world are written in very high and refined language," he explained, but people "can't help understanding my talk; it is common, plain, every-day talk—little children may understand it; and poor Negroes may plainly and fully understand my meaning; and . . . again, it may in a particular manner be serviceable to my poor kindred the Indians." The second reason for publication hinged on Occom's indigeneity: "as it comes from an uncommon quarter, it may induce people to read it, because it is from an Indian."[14]

What was the relationship between these two features of Occom's book——its being easily understood and its coming "from an Indian"—that figured so prominently in his decision to publish it? Superficially, the two explanations might seem to be at odds with one another, since writing as "an Indian," "from an uncommon quarter," conjures up notions of novelty and exoticism, familiar features of eighteenth-century literature that were often used to market new publications.[15] Occom, however, was not interested in being exotic. What he offered instead from his "uncommon quarter" was "common, plain, every-day talk" that everyone could understand, regardless of their age, class, race, or nationality. What was "Indian" about this was that, like the extravagant hospitality Occom had described to Wheatley the previous winter, it carried forward Northeast Native traditions ("our custom") of being welcoming and generous toward people "far and near," regardless of their origin. Language itself, in Occom's hands, was becoming an "asylum for strangers."

The idea of using language to practice hospitality across vast distances may bend the mind somewhat, since it delinks the practice of hospitality from the physical space of the home. Occom knew he was expanding the ambit of tradition by seizing upon new communicative methods, such as printed sermons, to practice his peoples' customary kindness toward strangers. But for him there was no contradiction between hospitality and mobility. In his 1768 autobiography, Occom writes that "my Parents Livd a wandering life . . . follow[ing] their Heathenish Ways, Customs & Religion"; then, a few paragraphs later, he refers proudly to "our Custom" of "freely Entertain[ing] all Visiters." It is no wonder that Occom, later in life, drew a parallel between Native hospitality and the conduct of the Good Samaritan, who in the biblical parable saved the life of the Jewish man, burgled and bleeding in the road, even though he was merely passing through Judea. "He that was a Neighbour in Deed, was a Stranger": for Occom, this held true both the Samaritan and (as he wryly put it) the "Savage Indians, as they are so calld, [who] are very kind to one another, and they are kind to Strangers."[16] For Native Americans, as for the Samaritan, hospitality didn't stop at home.

Two Traditionalisms

Occom was neither the first nor the last of his people to take such an expansive view of Northeast Native customs of hospitality. Mohegan medicine woman Melissa Tantaquidgeon Zobel affirms that "as Mohegans, we have an extraordinary legacy in Occom's eighteenth-century work. But his success stems from the philosophy of our seventeenth-century leader, Chief Uncas," who in the 1630s formed an alliance between the Mohegans and English that forever changed the course of Northeast Native history. Uncas, Zobel says,

> created a relationship with the outside community that we believe bonded us permanently into good relations with our non-Indian neighbors. We take this promise very seriously. We believe that this approach helped us survive the colonial era, but we also see it as a positive force for good in the world. Everything we do, we look at in two ways: How does it help the people within, and how does it help the people without?[17]

As Zobel argues, Occom *was* very much like Uncas in his commitment to being kind toward "non-Indian neighbors." Like Uncas, too, his emphasis on Indigenous customs of hospitality was not only an inheritance from the past, but also a response to political conflicts: conflicts between colonists and Northeast Native peoples, and within tribal communities themselves. These conflicts made Indigenous customs of hospitality and stranger interaction all the more important to Occom; but they also shifted the meaning of these customs in subtle but important ways.

Before the arrival of the English, Northeast Native peoples were highly mobile. Though firmly rooted in specific regions in ways that were both political and cultural, their residences tended to shift seasonally, a pattern referred to by anthropologists as "conditional sedentarism."[18] This was partly for reasons of subsistence. When family groups shifted locations, men would often go on hunting and fishing expeditions while women managed horticultural plots. But mobility was also part of tradition. Well into the eighteenth and even the nineteenth century, for instance, Uncas's descendants maintained a "summer cabin" in the forest south of the main village.[19] Occom's ancestors followed seasonal mobility patterns, as well, as he attests both in his 1768 autobiography and, perhaps, in one of his first pieces of writing, a journal entry from January 1745 where he speaks of visiting "Mothers at bozrah," about ten miles northwest of Mohegan.[20]

Over the course of the seventeenth and eighteenth centuries, these Indigenous mobility practices came into increasing conflict with colonial "expectations about fixity and order."[21] During this period, as historian Jean O'Brien has shown, customs of mobility that Northeast Native communities had been following for centuries came to be seen by English townspeople as a form of "vagrancy," a concept that the settlers used to justify further acts of dispossession.[22] The people of Mohegan and other Native communities responded in various ways to these English expectations (and accusations). Many stopped moving between seasonal hunting grounds and settled down on farms, a choice which had a dramatic impact on both subsistence practices and gender norms.[23] Others, like the Tunxis people of Farmington, doubled down on ancestral traditions of hospitality and welcomed newly dispossessed families into their communities.[24] Still others found common cause with the nascent evangelical movement within transatlantic Protestantism, which revived Augustinian forms of piety that encouraged believers to see themselves as "strangers" or "Pilgrim[s] here in this world."[25] And still others, in an effort to sharpen boundaries of tribal belonging amid dwindling economic resources, appropriated the colonial technique of stigmatizing "strangers" as a means of political exclusion.[26]

These various ways of responding to the changing landscape of Indigenous mobility were not mutually exclusive, and Occom (as we shall see) participated in all of them at various periods of his life. Like other Native people growing up in the first half of the eighteenth century, his upbringing was shaped by intense colonial pressure on tribal resources, populations, mobility and subsistence patterns, cultures, and existence in general.[27] Occom's youth was also a time of dissensus for the people of Mohegan and other nearby communities, as opposing viewpoints on tribal culture and government came into increasingly sharp conflict.

At Mohegan, a new factionalism had emerged at the turn of the eighteenth century around the issue of the Mason land case, a complex legal dispute between the Mohegan nation and the colony of Connecticut over who had right to lands (and the revenues they generated) that had been entrusted by Uncas to the guardianship of the English soldier and settler John Mason.[28] By Occom's childhood, one group of Mohegans had come to see this agreement as a threat to the political autonomy of the tribe as vested in the person of the sachem: this came to be known as "Ben's Town," after Uncas's successors, Major Ben Uncas, Ben Uncas II, and Ben Uncas III. The other party defended the agreement between Uncas and Mason, which theoretically gave them a firmer legal footing in British courts, empowering them to bring suit against Connecticut Colony for various acts of legal and administrative overreach. This group came to see the sachems in the Ben Uncas line as co-opted by the rulers of Connecticut Colony. They thought Major Ben Uncas had usurped the sachemship from Uncas's more direct descendant, John Uncas, and thus came to be known as "John's Town."[29]

Samson Occom was born into Ben's Town. His father Joshua had been on the tribal council of Ben Uncas II, and around the time of his father's death in 1743 he stepped into that position himself. But by the time of Ben Uncas III's funeral in 1769—at which Occom, a pallbearer, reportedly dropped the sachem's casket and stormed out of the church, followed by most of those attending—he had switched allegiances. This was largely due to what he saw as egregious mismanagement by Ben Uncas II and III of tribal lands and revenues. But it also had to do with tradition. While John's Town, in its early years, had coalesced around a candidate for the sachemship who belonged to Uncas's family, its members tended to be suspicious of the notion that tribal leadership (or membership) was best assessed as a question of descent.[30] Before colonization and the precipitous rise of the Uncases, Coastal Algonquian sachemship had been "based on personal charisma and the establishment of wide networks of obligation and support, rather than on heredity"; and, conversely, the families who selected and paid tribute to a sachem could be considered part of that sachem's people.[31] According to historian Paul Grant-Costa, John's Town conformed more closely to these nonhereditary understandings of sachemship and belonging. Among its residents were people descended from the "Pequots, Niantics, and Shoutuckets, all tribes that had at one time been closely allied with and subject to Uncas [I]."[32] Amid the bitter factional acrimony that followed Ben Uncas III's funeral in the early 1770s, Zachary Johnson, the leader of Ben's Town, wrote a series of memorials to the General Assembly of Connecticut complaining about these "Interlopers from other Tribes" and "Strangers living on said Land."[33] Johnson penned these memorials during the very same years when Occom was writing to Susanna Wheatley about how his house had become an "Asylum for Strangers." That is not a coincidence. Although Wheatley might not have seen it, he was taking a strong, politically motivated stand on what it meant to be "Indian" traditionally.

Another reason why Occom took his stand on Northeast Native traditions of hospitality was that he saw that those traditions made Native communities different from people who were not Indigenous. I mentioned earlier how Occom affirmed in his 1768 autobiography that it was "our custom" to "freely Entertain all visitors." But a close look at the original manuscript reveals another intriguing passage, a few pages before, where Occom wrote that he "used to go to my English Neighbours freequently for Assistance in Reading, but went to no School, and my Neighbours were very ready to help me." At some point during the composition of the autobiography, Occom went back and struck out the words "and my Neighbours were very ready to help me"—perhaps (though one can only speculate) after writing the later passage about it being "*our* custom" to be kind to strangers.[34] The point we should take away from this is not, I think, that Occom changed his mind about whether his "English Neighbours" were kind to him or not. Many English individuals were kind enough: Wheelock gets particular credit in the autobiography for "receiv[ing] me with kindness and Compassion" when Occom wanted to study with him, and there is no reason to doubt the sincerity of this. Yet, in his act of crossing-out,

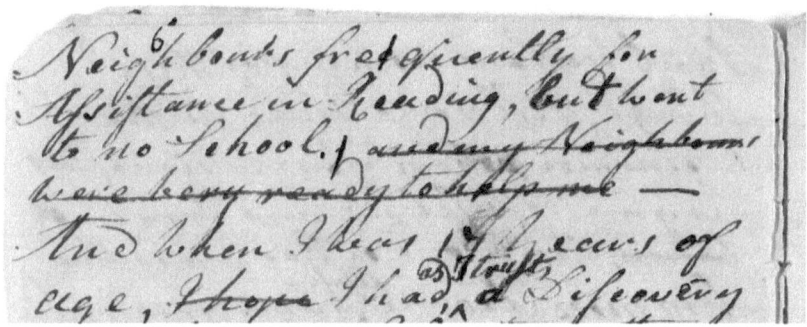

Figure 1.1 Second thoughts about English hospitality in Occom's 1768 autobiography. Samson Occom Papers, Mohegan Tribe. Photograph courtesy of Dartmouth College Library.

we witness Occom deciding not to speak of the kindness of his "English Neighbors" as a group, for the simple reason that kindness toward Native neighbors wasn't something that made his English neighbors culturally "English."[35]

In one sense, then, Occom was even more of a traditionalist than Uncas himself, at least from what the surviving sources indicate. In addition to expanding the scope of ancestral traditions of hospitality, he polemically and self-consciously *publicized* those traditions as a marker of cultural and political autonomy. Yet one of the puzzles Occom's writings present is that, even as he pursued this traditionalist agenda, he also interpreted Native peoples' "neighborly" lifeways in ways that were remarkably universalistic. Informed, no doubt, by his experience of Mohegan factionalism, Occom was avowedly opposed to what he called, in the eighteenth-century idiom, "a party Spirit." He would have preferred that Native peoples' kindness toward people from other nations be emulated by non-Indigenous people everywhere in the world. In principle, he argued in the Good Samaritan sermon, "there is no party in this love," either in who practices it or who receives it.[36]

Occom's understanding of what constitutes a "neighbor" was similarly expansive—unusually so, as he conceded in the Good Samaritan sermon. "Now it is generally understood, that Neigh[bors] are those who Live Near together," Occom observes there; but notice, he says, that "if he that lives further of, is kind and obliging, we Say such a one is Neighbourly." He concludes, "Well then he that is Neighbourly, is a Nei[ghbo]r and from What we have Said amounts to this People that are Loving, Kind, obliging, and Tender to one another are Neighbours let them live together, or at a Distance, of one & Same Nation or not, it makes no odds."[37]

This neighborliness, Occom argues, was in his time exemplified by unconverted Indigenous people, the "Indian heathen," who make "no odds" of national difference in their hospitality: "they are very Compassionate one to another, very Liberal among themselves, and also to Strangers."[38] This assertion is of a piece with Occom's proud avowal elsewhere of "our custom"—meaning, Northeast Natives' ancestral custom—of being kind to strangers. But, it is fair to ask, if neighborliness ultimately boils down to being "Loving, Kind, obliging, and Tender" toward people from all nations, then what exactly does Native peoples' "custom" amount to? After all, as Occom well knew, it was not just Indigenous people who thought it was virtuous to be "Loving, Kind, obliging, and Tender" toward all God's creatures; these principles were espoused throughout the wider colonial world, however rarely they were honored. Moreover, if the point of the parable of the Samaritan is that "he [i.e., the Samaritan] that was a Neighbour in Deed was a Stranger," then it's unclear what the point is of distinguishing between "neighbors" and "strangers" at all.[39] One might be forgiven for wondering whether Occom's expansive idea of neighborliness wasn't *so* expansive, so synonymous with simply being kind to others, as to undermine his claim that Indigenous people were kind to strangers in a culturally distinctive way. Or, to put the question more sharply: given that English and other non-Indigenous people said it was important to "love one's neighbor," wasn't there something safe about the way Occom emphasized those parts of Native tradition that best aligned with the traditions of outsiders—as in the parallel between Native Americans and the Good Samaritan—since this was less likely to upset Anglo-Americans who wanted Indigenous people to assimilate to the dominant culture? Wouldn't it have been more courageous for Occom to celebrate *all* of his people's precolonial traditions with equal zeal, not just the ones that non-Indigenous people were most likely to approve of?

These questions are not unreasonable, if one thinks about them in a historical vacuum. It takes courage to be different from others, especially when those others are seeking violently to impose sameness. But my sense is that the more you know about the history of settler colonialism, the harder it gets to sympathize with the idea that Occom was uncourageous. Living under colonization did not give Native people a lot of options. My guess is that if Occom could have waved a magic wand, he—like almost everyone in eighteenth-century North America who was not a settler—would have made the colonists go away, leaving Indigenous people in control of their homelands and their affairs. Failing this, he and other Native leaders of his era (and other eras) devised various ways of reasserting Indigenous sovereignty against colonial power, none of which could be implemented by people lacking courage.

The courageousness of sovereignty in the Native Northeast took different forms. In collaboration with many leaders from the region, Occom devised a plan for reasserting the sovereignty of Coastal Algonquians as "one people" belonging to the new nation of Brothertown, on the eastern border of the Six Nations. Given that the Brothertown founders had to build up a population base from scratch, it was imperative for Native people to revitalize their ancestral traditions of "freely Entertain[ing] all Visitors"; these newcomers would be taken in with "Benevolence & Favour" and given the opportunity to become part of the new "body politick," so long as they belonged to "the Tribes, to whom this Land was given," an important qualification that I will return to shortly.[40] Yet the new path of Indigenous belonging Occom envisaged was bound to be difficult, not just because of the material sacrifices involved, but also because—at least according to Occom—the reawakened community needed to buffer itself from any "Superstitions" that might be "oppose[d to] the True Religion of Jesus Christ, which Consists in the Power, as well as in form, and produces Love to God and Man."[41] And many of the Northeast Natives who heard Occom's appeal simply refused to do this.

In a book like this one, which is primarily dedicated to reading words written by a single person, this point cannot be emphasized often enough. Many, likely most, members of Brothertown's founding tribes decided *not* to move, for a variety of reasons.[42] This also took courage, including the kind of courage that empowers people to confront the unknown; after all, with so many families leaving—and, in many cases, selling land and other possessions in order to fund their migration—coastal communities could hardly stay the same. Among the challenges faced by those who stayed at Mohegan was the task of figuring out an alternative relationship to Christianity. Occom's brand of evangelicalism emphasized *movement*. As he wrote in his 1774 hymnal, human life was a "pilgrimage" in which one was always heading somewhere else, geographically or spiritually.[43] At Mohegan, in the decades after Occom's departure, there arose a very different configuration of religious belief and practice that sought to reintegrate Christianity with some of the elements of precolonial Mohegan tradition that Occom and his movement had set aside. This process was well underway by 1860, when the Mohegan tribal council, in collaboration with the Mohegan Church, built a wigwam in the churchyard so that the tribe could practice its precolonial Green Corn ceremony of thanksgiving to the Creator.[44] And it was full swing by the early twentieth century, when leaders like Fidelia Fielding and Gladys Tantaquidgeon worked to reassemble tribal traditions, and the Mohegan language itself, in a durable written form that could be used and passed down to future generations.[45]

In summary, eighteenth-century Brothertown and nineteenth-century Mohegan both witnessed courageous new approaches to reconciling Christianity with pre-Christian Indigenous tradition. In fact, when comparing Occom's ideas about Native lifeways to the ones that rose to prominence after his death at Mohegan, it is probably most helpful to think of two traditionalisms. Occom's traditionalism traveled relatively light, drawing on the deep vein of stranger-love that he associated with his ancestors' "wandering life." The traditionalism that emerged in nineteenth-century Mohegan was more about staying put and picking up everything that had fallen by the wayside during the Brothertown movement, but also before and after that, through centuries of colonial repression and forgetting.

Both these traditionalisms took courage. Both insisted on the cultural distinctiveness of Native lifeways (recall Occom crossing out "my [English] Neighbours were very ready to help me" from his autobiography). And both were expressions of Indigenous sovereignty and self-determination. As a non-Native historian, I cannot imagine saying one was better or more "traditional" than the other. They were just different.

I want to make clear that in distinguishing between these two traditionalisms, I am not trying to make a general claim about what most people at Mohegan or Brothertown believed in the eighteenth or nineteenth centuries. In comparing Occom's conception of Native tradition to Fielding and Tantaquidgeon's, I am talking about more or less "official" theories of tradition: positions that important leaders endorsed, but that individual tribal members may or may not have agreed with. On the other hand, official positions on topics like these matter, even among those who disagree with them, because they set the terms of what agreement and disagreement mean.

It is also important to acknowledge that the difference between the two traditionalisms I have described is less sharp today than it was in Occom's time. A lot of things have happened since the 1770s, when Occom's traditionalism emerged as a historical force in the Native Northeast: more migration and more staying in place; transformations of federal Indian law; world wars that Brothertowns and Mohegans fought in; the Cold War; Red Power; the BIA's recognizing the Mohegan Tribe as a sovereign nation; the BIA's waffling on but withholding (so far) the restoration of that status to Brothertown. Amid all these changes, the paths of Brothertown and Mohegan have converged in new ways and diverged in others. Talking about "two traditionalisms" cannot possibly make sense of all these complex changes; all it can do is highlight part of what made Occom's—and, to some extent, Brothertown's—attitude toward Indigenous tradition distinctive during his lifetime and the years that immediately followed it.

Yet I hope this is enough to correct, or at least clarify, the historical record about the type of traditionalism that Occom advocated. For a variety of reasons that I will begin unpacking now, scholars have often claimed that to whatever extent Occom was a traditionalist, his traditionalism must have been just the same as that of his Mohegan forbears and contemporaries. Thus, according to Joanna Brooks, "Samson Occom was first a Mohegan and second a founding member of the Brothertown tribe. His thought-world was rooted in tribal territories, tribal histories, kin networks, political responsibilities and obligations, ceremonial and planting cycles, and understandings of space, time, and personhood he learned first from his father, Joshua; his mother, Sarah; their relatives; and their broader tribal community."[46] Here the traditionalism of Occom's Mohegan ancestors is presented as the only yardstick by which his own (or that of the Brothertown movement) can be measured. But just because the traditions of Occom's ancestors came "first" chronologically doesn't mean that his whole "thought-world" was "rooted" in the lifeways of his parents. As we have already seen, Occom was profoundly committed to carrying forward his parents' way of life in certain key respects; and in the chapters that follow, it will become clearer just how and why Occom wanted to revitalize his ancestors' traditional way of life in defiance of settler colonialism. In order to get clear about this, however, it is important to acknowledge that traditionalism is not synonymous with the celebration of tradition in general. Occom's scholarly readers have sometimes been inclined to portray Occom as a traditionalist whenever he talks about *any* precolonial Indigenous custom—even when he does so disapprovingly—as if his goal as a writer was to create a repository of Northeast Native tradition in order to document and celebrate what his ancestors understood to be the "truth" of the world.[47] Superficially, this makes Occom sound more like Fielding and Tantaquidgeon and less like himself. But on a more profound level, it stems from a caricatured and overgeneralized understanding of tradition as something Native people are "stuck" to, as opposed to something that they "stick to" through their own agency, commitment, and self-determination—which is a better way of thinking about Occom, Fielding, and Tantaquidgeon alike.

Problems of Causality

I have suggested that, in contrast to some Northeast Native traditionalists who have celebrated a comparatively broad range of Northeast Native customs, Occom was more selective about the Native traditions he sought to carry forward. Why was Occom's traditionalism different in this way? This is a difficult question that admits of no straightforward answer. Explanations that rely on a single cause—religion, political necessity, colonial indoctrination, Occom's personality—are unlikely to be successful, since all of these things were intertwined with one another. It may be helpful, however, to begin with a thought experiment and, just for the sake of argument, entertain the hypothesis that Occom's peculiar traditionalism was caused primarily by his Christianity. I should say that I don't think this is true; nevertheless, it is a hypothesis worth considering in some detail, given the widespread assumption that Christianity is historically and/or essentially hostile to Indigenous outlooks and traditions.[48]

Let's suppose, then, that the selectiveness of Occom's traditionalism was caused by Christianity. This might seem like a reason to doubt the seriousness of his commitment to his people's precolonial customs, given that many other Mohegans did not allow Christianity to affect their attitudes toward tradition in the same way. Yet one can also follow this chain of causality one step further and what "caused" Christianity itself, together with its universalistic social ethic. It seems reasonable to ask here whether whatever caused Christianity and its social ethic also caused the Indigenous lifeways toward which so many Christians showed such hostility. What about human nature, supposing such a thing exists? If Christians and Native Americans, at the time of their first contact, both had social customs that encouraged people to be kind to strangers, then maybe this was because of some common tendency toward hospitality present in all human beings. Or, alternatively, perhaps it is the case that in all human societies there exist at least some people who incline toward being unkind toward strangers, which makes it necessary for all societies to have some sort of ethical norm mandating the opposite.

Yet, even supposing any of this to be true, so what? Pursuing this thought experiment just a little further, let's accept—again, for the sake of argument—that whatever caused Occom's traditionalism was something nonhistorical: something like human nature, or the evolution of the so-called social brain, or some other cause explaining the development of both Indigenous traditions and Christianity. Who cares? That sort of explanation is totally irrelevant to anyone whose purpose is to read Samson Occom in a serious way, which means taking the history of colonialism and Indigenous sovereignty seriously.

This objection is a valid one: we really don't need to get into DNA when discussing Occom's traditionalism (which is not to deny that DNA is an important issue in Indigenous communities today).[49] But if this is right—if, in other words, what I am calling a "serious" reading of Occom is distinct from an inquiry into what *caused* his traditionalism—then why is it such a problem if Occom's idea of traditionalism was caused by his exposure to ideas imported by the dominant culture? Here we might point to any number of instances wherein people oppressed by empire have seized upon the intellectual weapons of the oppressor and directed them against the centers of power. Gandhi turned Ruskin and Carlyle against Britain in *Hind Swaraj*. Phillis Wheatley turned the book of Exodus against the slaveholding "modern Egyptians" in her poems and letters, including her famous letter to Occom.[50] Frantz Fanon turned European philosophy against European empire in *Black Skin, White Masks*. Frederick Douglass turned the U.S. Constitution against the people of the United States in his Fifth of July speech. And Samson Occom, in a substantial portion of his surviving writings, turned Christianity against "those who are Calld Christians."[51] It would be a little odd to suggest that the achievements of Gandhi, Wheatley, Fanon, or Douglass were somehow vitiated by their contact with "foreign" traditions. So what makes it legitimate to fault Occom's vision of Indigenous liberation because it was informed (or even, if you like, caused) by foreign influences?

The question is not rhetorical. This is a living, open issue about which reasonable people disagree, and there may well be multiple "right" answers.

As you have probably surmised by now, my own inclination—which is informed by my own cultural upbringing and academic training—is to be skeptical of the idea that traditions, in order to be worthy of the name, must be sealed off from foreign influences. But even if my skepticism is justified, that is not the end of the story, because the issue of causality is just one way of approaching what makes Occom's traditionalism seem problematic.

One of the questions I raised earlier was whether or not it made sense to think of Christianity as a kind of filter that led Occom to celebrate Indigenous customs of "freely entertain[ing] all Visiters," but not other aspects of Northeast Native tradition. I think it probably does, but notice that there is a bit of a chicken-and-egg problem here, since it is no less plausible that this "filtering" worked instead in the opposite direction, meaning that Occom chose Christianity—or, to be more precise, a certain version of Christianity that prioritized social ethics—because of his prior commitment to Indigenous forms of "neighbourly" living.

This reversal of my earlier hypothesis has much to recommend it. For one thing, there is the obvious but hugely important fact that Occom was immersed in Indigenous traditions before he was a Christian. Therefore we need to affirm the *chronological* priority of his traditionalism at the outset and try to figure out how he made sense of everything else in light of that unbroken commitment.

Another reason why it is plausible to think of Occom's traditionalism as "filtering" his Christianity, and not the other way around, is that his religious views were highly idiosyncratic, sometimes verging on heretical. For instance, as I have already suggested, Occom thought that the "Indian heathen" were lovers of God even before Christians arrived in North America. *Very* few people in eighteenth-century Anglophone America agreed with him about this, if any.[52] It was also compatible with Occom's traditionally filtered Christianity to encourage women to work as missionaries, another view that practically no one in eighteenth-century New England endorsed except the widely reviled Quakers.[53] Occom's traditionalism also informed his increasingly abolitionist interpretation of the Gospel: by the 1780s he had decided that people who "keep Slaves against their own Light" are "not Neighbours to anyone, and Consequently they are not Lovers of God."[54] In addition to these unorthodox ethical and political positions, Occom's traditionalism informed surprising innovations in covenant theology and protology (the theory of beginnings), which I will be saying much more about in chapters 3 and 6.

So did Occom's Christianity "filter" his traditionalism, or did his traditionalism filter his Christianity? As I have said, the chronological priority of his traditionalism should always be kept in mind. But having reiterated that, I also think that it is worth lingering with the idea that the filtering process worked in both directions—that there really is a chicken-and-egg problem here, in other words. And as with other chicken-and-egg problems, there comes a point when it becomes unproductive to obsess over whether the egg or the chicken deserves more credit, so to speak. We need to step back and ask why the chicken-and-egg problem presents itself in the form that it does. And that means saying more about settler colonialism.

As scholars in Indigenous and settler colonial studies have been arguing for many years now, the conceptual dichotomy between "authenticity" and "assimilation," which is very often used to measure "Real Indian"-ness, has a long colonial pedigree.[55] This pedigree does not necessarily invalidate these concepts in every case. But it is undeniable that they are applied asymmetrically in settler society, and in ways that often prove highly disadvantageous to Indigenous communities. Colonial histories of early America have grown especially notorious for propagating what Jean O'Brien calls the "myth of Indian decline": the fallacy that Native communities entered a period of irreversible cultural and political decay after their first encounter with Europeans.[56] Such narratives have an air of inevitability because of their assumption that contact with foreign peoples can only lead to the corruption of Indigenous cultures (but not non-Indigenous ones). As the late Patrick Wolfe argued, one way of sidestepping this ruse of colonial reason is to think of settler colonialism as a "structure" that changes the way *everyone* in colonial society understands one another, rather than simply an "event" in which one civilization corrupts another.[57] J. Kēhaulani Kauanui further develops this point by emphasizing the double meaning of the phrase "enduring Indigeneity," which implies (1) "that Indigenous peoples exist, resist, and persist," but also (2) "that settler colonialism is a structure that endures indigeneity, as it holds out against it."[58] This second sense of enduring Indigeneity—of Native people giving settlers *something to endure*—provides a way of seeing stranger-love as something more than a bland humanitarianism masquerading as Indigenous tradition. By pinning

Native peoples' cultural identity to their kindness to outsiders, Occom carried forward an aspect of Northeast Native tradition that was structurally inassimilable to settler society. If his people recommitted themselves to their ancestors' practice of loving strangers as themselves, in other words, they would be doing the one thing that settlers would never be able to do by virtue of their colonial project, which was inherently hostile to Indigenous lives and interests. Occom may well have been gesturing toward this structural "binarism" between Native and settler societies when, in his Good Samaritan sermon, he said that "to Love our Neighbours and Enemies" the way the "Indian Heathen" do "is Loving them as ourselves, *and doing more than others*."[59] Why "doing more than others"? It would be quite out of character for Occom to insist that outcompeting other people in love (or anything else) should be seen as a goal in and of itself. I think he means that "others"—Occom is being tactful—simply cannot love their enemies, no matter how much they might want to. This would certainly apply to settlers, some of whom might aspire to love their enemies on an individual level. But individual settlers could never disentangle themselves from the structural violence of colonialism, which was antithetical to "national love."

Speaking as an evangelical made it possible for Occom to compel colonists to "endure" Indigeneity in a way they could not fail to understand. But it is important not to let the structural analysis of settler colonialism overstep its bounds and degenerate into a crude instrumentalism. For instance, it may be tempting to construe the language of stranger-love as a form of "camouflage" that allowed Occom to sneak behind settlers' ideological defenses so as to attack their worldview from within. From that perspective, Occom's emphasis on kindness to strangers might be seen as a tactic subservient to a broader geopolitical strategy, something akin to the "'secret weapon' of outer agreement and inner disagreement" that, according to ethnohistorian James Axtell, Northeast Native proselytes deployed in their interactions with seventeenth-century missionaries.[60] Yet at some point, this type of analysis is going to run afoul of the perennial social-theoretical problem of structure and agency: meaning, the analysis of structural social forces (in this case, arising from settler colonialism) is going to displace Indigenous agency as an object of study.[61] This structure/agency problem has recently obtruded itself into debates in the fields of Indigenous studies and settler colonial studies in ways that are deeply relevant to the analysis of Occom's traditionalism. In a special issue of *Postcolonial*

Studies from 2021, Alice Te Punga Somerville, Robert Warrior, and J. Kēhaulani Kauanui take up a question posed by Lorenzo Veracini: "Is settler colonial studies even useful?" What is largely at stake in this question for Veracini and his respondents is whether or not the structural analysis of settler colonialism is "useless" or even "detrimental to Indigenous struggles"—that is, to Indigenous people *acting* collectively against the constraints of settler colonialism.⁶² The upshot of this recent flood of autocritique on the part of settler colonial studies scholars is, in my view, that while settler colonialism is undoubtedly a structure, *structuralist* approaches to Indigenous peoples and their histories often wind up minimizing the capacity of Indigenous individuals and communities to act on their own behalf. If this is right, then it may make sense to think of Indigenous studies and settler colonial studies as having arrived, for good or for ill, at a division of academic labor whereby scholars in the latter field prioritize the analysis of settler colonialism as a social, political, and economic structure, while those in the former prioritize the study of Indigenous agency—or, at least, remain open to a "methodological promiscuity" in which that agency can be openly celebrated.⁶³

As the reader has probably guessed by now, I agree with scholars who think that the structural analysis of settler colonialism can and often does obscure the reality of Indigenous agency.⁶⁴ In order to understand Occom aright, it is imperative to draw on insights from both settler colonial and Indigenous studies, which means avoiding the kind of unnecessary methodological overreach that reduces agency to structure, or vice versa. When it comes to studying Occom's traditionalism, in particular: if we understand Indigenous traditions (and traditionalism) as being subject to structural causation, then it is not going to matter much when traditionalists, including Occom, say they value their traditions for their own sake, independent of any instrumental or "structural" explanation. Yet this is in fact what Occom said, and his saying that matters, not just in some vague ethical sense, but also historically and politically.⁶⁵

To recall Zobel's statement about what it meant for Uncas and Occom to maintain "good relations with our non-Indian neighbors": "We believe that this approach helped us survive the colonial era, but we also see it as a positive force for good in the world."⁶⁶ These words acknowledge that there was a structural or strategic rationale for Mohegans' customary practices of stranger-interaction ("this approach helped us survive the colonial era"), but they also insist that survival wasn't the only rationale:

"but we also"—not *and we therefore*—"see it as a positive force for good in the world." It matters that this other rationale is noninstrumental. There is no ulterior motive that needs to be brought in to explain why "we" see things that way. Tradition arises out of a common commitment to contributing to the good of the world in a self-determined way.

Occom would have agreed with this, although he might have phrased it slightly differently. He would have said that the custom of the "Indian Heathen" of being "very Liberal among themselves, and also to Strangers," was Indigenous peoples' way of "Discover[ing]" their love to God: "for this is the very fruit of it, if you Love God, it will naturally lead you to Love your Neighbour."[67] Occom's way of describing stranger interaction as a "force for good in the world" is, obviously, more theistic than Zobel's. But they both describe treating strangers well as a way for Native people to put themselves in touch with something genuinely outside themselves. And they both conceptualize that "something outside" as being really good in and of itself, not merely according to some kind of instrumental, strategic, or structural calculation. The conception of Indigenous agency they bring to light, in other words, is not about projecting value onto the world, but rather finding value there.[68] It is about being committed to what is really there, because what is there matters.

It is because I think this kind of commitment is so important that I have coined the slightly cumbersome term "stranger-love" to talk about Occom's traditionalism. The term may sound romantic, but I do not mean it in a sentimental way. I use it, rather, to connect Occom's traditionalism to the idea that when people care for one another, they put themselves in touch with the world in a way that may not lend itself to easy explanation.

Benefiting from the power of hindsight, scholars who study colonialism often make it sound as if everything happened for a reason. This may well be true, if one looks at the world from a sufficiently detached point of view. In practice, however, life would be unlivable if we had to provide coherent explanations for all the commitments we make. The term "love"—which is often described as something that people do *without* a reason, or "just because"—is useful as a reminder of that.[69] Time and again, Occom's writings testify to love's power to motivate people to do extraordinary things. It was through his own "very Remarkable" acts of "national love" that Occom sought to carry forward the legacy and tradition of his great ancestor Uncas, even though he knew (as Uncas must have known) that many would find his actions unreasonable.

Traditionalism and Iconoclasm

Occom did strange things for love, and those things came at a cost. Perhaps the hardest thing to understand about Occom's traditionalism is why it was so selective: why it had to be the case that, in celebrating Indigenous customs of stranger interaction, he looked upon other traditions critically and, at times, dismissively. I have hinted at a couple different answers to this question: first, that Occom espoused a "lightweight" traditionalism that was purpose-built for mobility and migration; and second, that he did it for love. On their own, however, these interpretations are incomplete: the first is too "functional," and the second is less about explaining Occom than about how love imposes limits on structuralist reasoning. In this final section, I want to tie these two threads together into something more complete and—I say this to alert the reader—more unsettling: an account of how Occom came to feel justified in criticizing certain Indigenous traditions because, according to him, they obstructed the affective and political power of love. I acknowledge that this account may not be easy to accept, but I hope it has value as a way of clarifying what Occom thought he was doing and, what's more, what he thought he *had* to do in order to help unite Coastal Algonquians as "a body politick."[70]

Critical comments about one specific subset of Indigenous traditions recur throughout Occom's writings, and the basic thrust of these comments is almost always the same: Native customs are bad when they involve idolatry. To be truly religious—or, as Occom revealingly put it, "reformed"— Native people had to renounce "heathenish idolatry and superstition."[71] What exactly did this renunciation amount to? Occom's most detailed discussion of Indigenous idolatry occurs in his "Account of the Montauk Indians of Long Island" (1761), where he associates the phenomenon with the Montauketts' use of ritual objects he calls "images": "As for their images, they kept them as oracles. The powwaws consult these images to know the minds of their gods; for they pretend these images tell what the people should do to the gods, either to make a dance or a feast, or give something to the old people, or sacrifice to the gods."[72]

Note here how Occom associates "images" with the act of "pretending": the powwaws (an Algonquian term sometimes rendered as "priest" or "shaman") "pretend these images tell what the people should do." The implication, obviously, is that the images do not do that, and that there is some element of fantasy in the powwaws' soothsaying and in the Montauketts' use of images as "oracles." This commentary on Montaukett "idolatry" is an instance of *iconoclasm*: a "denial of the power of material things to mediate divine actions."[73] This denial on Occom's part was not universal. Under certain conditions, he thought, the material world could be a locus of divine activity, and this divine activity could even take the form of "images." This was what happened during God's act of Creation, which culminated in the creation of "man," "for Whom he made this World,—he was the Crown, the Glory, and the Excellency and the Beauty of the Whole Creation. For God made him in his own Image and Likeness."[74] Having been made "in his own Image," human beings enjoyed lesser versions of God's supreme powers, including the power of creating images. But owing to the fallibility of human nature, the images they created did not "mediate divine actions" in the same way that humans themselves did at the moment of creation; human beings merely "pretended" they did.

Occom's critique of idolatry focused not just on human-made "images" themselves, but also on human beings' capacity to create images in the first place, a capacity he refers to as "imagination." Occom's use of this term in his description of Montaukett religion is pejorative.[75] The Montauketts, he says, "imagined a great number of gods"; and their powwaws insisted that their "poison," which they used (Occom says) in order to communicate with the devil, "is no imaginary thing, but real."[76] For Occom, all of these beliefs and practices fell under the umbrella of idolatry, because all of them were concerned with the misuse of "images" and the dangers of "imagining." Rather than worship images of their own design, Occom argued, Native people (and all human beings) should reciprocate the love of the divine Creator, of whom they themselves were actual (not "imaginary") images: this, he argued, was the "restoration of soul from sin to holiness, from darkness to light . . . it is being restored to the image of God."[77] As long as "man . . . has lost the Blessed Image of God he is gone from his love to god."[78] Idolatry, which directed human attention toward human creations, was a distraction from what Native Americans needed, which was a reciprocal, loving relationship with the "one, Great good Supream and Indepentant Spirit" who created them.[79]

Always attuned to Native peoples' inner capacity to love God in this way, Occom thought he discerned the seeds of reform, even amid the Montauketts' image-making and polytheism. True, they believed in many gods, "but," he went on, "they had a notion of one great and good God, that was over all the rest of the gods, which they called CAUHLUNTOOWUT, which signifies one that is possessed with supreme power."[80] Deep down, Occom thus suggests, the Montauketts understood that there was one God to whom they should be directing all their devotion and attention. His role as a minister, as he understood it, was teaching them to embrace that truth, with all its implications.

Acknowledging Occom's iconoclasm, and the broader theory of "images" that underwrote it, helps account for why the Northeast Native customs he celebrates in his writings tend to focus on social interaction, and in particular on the creation and maintenance of loving relationships among human beings, the only real "images" of God. Occom's theory of images is also relevant to his focus on the love of *strangers* in particular, as fostered by Indigenous customs of hospitality and diplomacy. As he observes in the Good Samaritan sermon, human beings find it relatively easy to act kindly toward people who "are either of their own nation or party," since doing so is typically in their own self-interest.[81] Yet when people act lovingly toward strangers, self-interest is less likely to be the motivating factor. The Samaritan, for instance, helped the wounded man in the street with no expectation of reciprocation: "he Brought him to an Inn, and took care of him and on the morrow, when he departed, he took out two pence, and gave them to the Host, and said unto him, Take care of him; and Whatsoever thou Spendest more, when I come again, I will repay thee."[82] The Samaritan settled his debts to the host, but he did not expect repayment from the person he helped; nor, even, did he expect ever to see the wounded man again. He did all this because he was fully conscious of the divine love that was *immanent in creation itself,* and particularly in "man," who embodied the "the Glory, and the Excellency and the Beauty of the Whole Creation[,] For God made him in his own Image and Likeness."[83] When human beings acted lovingly toward strangers as the Samaritan did, it could *only* be because they saw other human beings for what they most truly were: not members of a "party"—parties, for Occom, were vehicles of human self-interest—but images of the Divine. When the "Indian Heathen" acted lovingly toward strangers, it was because they were attuned to God's love in the same way. The customs that fostered this attunement were immune from the charge of idolatry.

Thinking about Occom's iconoclasm inevitably raises anew the question of where he learned to approach Native tradition in this way. Iconoclasm has been famously associated with Protestantism, and the Reformed Protestantism that prevailed in New England undoubtedly had a big impact on him. Yet here, as with other dimensions of Occom's Christianity, we are definitely not dealing with a straightforward case of colonial indoctrination. As recent scholarship has demonstrated, iconoclasm refers to a wide range of cultural practices that go far beyond the Christian tradition; as a broad category of social behavior, we might expect to find it any time there is a "struggle to define the proper relationship between signs and what they can signify," and it is probable that Occom and his ancestors dealt with such struggles long before Christianity came to Mohegan.[84] It is also worth noting that Occom often turned his iconoclasm against Reformed Protestantism itself. Over the course of the next few chapters, we will explore various passages where he describes the Bible itself as an object of idolatry (or "bibliolatry"). And in one sermon on Genesis he even accuses the English of having such corrupt "imaginations" as to turn Christ himself into a kind of false God. "Before the flood," Occom observed, citing Genesis 6, "god saw that the Wickedness of Man was great in the Earth, and that every Imagination of the Thoughts of his was only Evil, Continually; and I think," he continued, "without misapplying this Pasage of Scripture; You See now that the Wickedness of the Professors of the Religion of J[esus Christ] is very great and that every Imagination of the thoughts of their Hearts are only evil."[85] If the "Religion of Jesus Christ" was what its "Professors" said it was, in other words, it was a mere invention, a product of the "imagination" that had to be debunked like any other idol that distracted from the Divine. I will be returning to several of these counter-Christian forms of iconoclasm in future chapters.

But before concluding this introduction to Occom's traditionalism, I want to acknowledge (and try to address) a question that some readers may have about the argument I have been developing so far: that Occom was both an iconoclast and a traditionalist who held fiercely to the belief that ancestral Native customs needed to be carried forward. This both/and claim goes against the grain of some prominent modern scholarship on Native American religion, which has tended to emphasize that "Native Americans' response to Christianity was syncretic over the long run," meaning that Native Christians typically approached their "religious choices . . . in terms of testing, sampling, and appending to existing customs and practices."[86] In contrast to these familiar arguments, I have argued that if we want to be clear-eyed about Occom's traditionalism, we need to acknowledge that he did not see Native religion simply as a matter of "appending"; it also required taking a hard look—which never amounted to a wholesale dismissal—of the way Native people "imagined" the relationship between their existing customs and the "one, Great good Supream and Indepentant Spirit" who created all things. And it might seem to some like I protest too much by insisting that Occom could do this and still be a "traditionalist." Why not just concede, as many have, that Occom's experience wasn't "typical" of Northeast Native traditionalism and move on?[87]

The reason I am pressing the point is that I think acknowledging Occom's traditionalism for what it was (and not measuring it by the yardstick of what it was not) helps advance Indigenous studies and settler colonial studies scholars' ongoing critique of colonial reason as it applies to Indigenous religion and traditionalism. But in order to see how, it will help to broaden our focus a little bit and think about the relationship between iconoclasm and empire more expansively.

It is a truism of the historiography of Native American religion that Anglo-American colonists misunderstood Indigenous traditions owing to their "Protestant" understanding of what counted as "religion." Hence, in standard scholarly practice, a critique of Protestantism is presented as a precondition for seeing Native traditions for what they really were, including what was "typical" about them.[88] The problem with this type of argument is that it risks presupposing what it seeks to explain: that there exists such a thing as "typical" Native American religious experience, and that such experience is non-Protestant. This circularity raises the question of how successfully the standard scholarly practice succeeds in extricating itself from Protestant thinking. After all, the assumption that we can get to the "truth" of religious experience by attacking the core assumptions of Protestantism is itself rather "Protestant"—or, to be more precise, iconoclastic.

Scholarly iconoclasm isn't necessarily a problem, in and of itself. As Christopher Hill famously argued, "history has to be rewritten in every generation, because although the past does not change the present does."[89] And the demands of the academic profession (to say nothing of human psychology) very often place history's rewriters on a footing of iconoclasm with respect to their own intellectual background. When we are talking about the historiography of Indigenous religion, however, anti-Protestant (or, if you like, crypto-Protestant) iconoclasm is a problem, insofar as it helps sustain an image of Indigenous religion as "Other," in the sense of *transcending the practice of iconoclasm itself.* Yet, speaking as a member of the scholarly community, it seems to me that if we want to be iconoclasts about Protestantism and its intellectual legacies, we should push that methodology all the way and ask how we know (or "imagine") that there exists such a thing as a "typical" Native American tradition, religion, or anything else. Here is where it helps to consider the phenomenon of Occom's iconoclasm in a broader historical context.

Those of us who study Indigenous religion in colonial New England are not the first to wrestle with the question of how "paganism" and "tribal religion" are portrayed by people who believe in one true God. In his notorious classic *The Religion of Israel* (1937), the biblical scholar Yehezkel Kaufmann drove an analytical wedge between monotheism and "paganism" by focusing on the issue of transcendence. What distinguished ancient Israelite religion from that of the Canaanite pagans, Kaufmann argued, was the belief that the God of Israel, who created the universe and everything in it, inhabited a transcendent realm beyond nature itself. According to the "pagan" religion of the neighboring Canaanites, in contrast, the gods were not the top layer of the cosmological layer cake. Whereas the God of Israel was uncreated, transcending space and time, the pagan gods were born, just like human beings, and sometimes even died. This, Kaufmann argued, implied that the pagan gods were part of nature rather than transcending it; hence the forces of nature, to which both gods and humans belonged, were from the Canaanite perspective "metadivine."[90] According to Kaufmann, the Canaanites believed that if they could master the forces of this "metadivine realm" through magic, they could "coerce the gods to [their] will."[91] From the Israelite perspective, this was the essence of idolatry.

The relevance of Kaufmann's account to Occom—and the historiography of Northeast Native Christianity—has to do with the way Kaufmann distinguishes between "indigenous" religion on the one hand and monotheism on the other in a seemingly "Protestant" way. In an important essay on ancient Canaanite ritual, Naomi Janowitz shows that Kaufmann's account of Canaanite magic (their "trust in temples, sacrifices, and priests as if they were innately effective") implicitly imputed to them a "pagan trust in human work," in place of which Israelites cultivated an inward, "ethical" relationship to a transcendent God over whom they disavowed any coercive power.[92] But, as Janowitz argues, we cannot take *any* distinction between "indigenous" and monotheistic religions "at face value" because such distinctions are typically motivated by a "continuing, almost unavoidable" drive to define Indigenous religion as "other"—and, in particular, as averse to the very idea of divine transcendence, owing to Indigenous peoples' supposedly "pagan" belief in a metadivine realm.[93]

Refusing to accept dichotomies between "Indigenous" and monotheistic religions at face value—whether the latter are Israelite or Protestant—does not necessarily mean throwing those distinctions out altogether; it just means understanding who is drawing those distinctions and what agenda they have when doing so. Part of Kaufmann's motivation for drawing the distinction had to do with his desire to define the religion of ancient Israel as the "original creation of a people" and indeed the "fundamental idea of a national culture."[94] Occom was up to something similar.[95] His iconoclastic version of Northeast Native traditionalism went hand in hand with his nationalism: his plea to Coastal Algonquians to "collect the remnant of their scattered Tribes to one place and *become a people*."[96] This is not to suggest that Occom was an "Indian Moses" who understood Native Americans to be a "chosen" people (though this view is widespread in the scholarly literature, I think it is deeply mistaken, as I argue in detail in chapter 3). What made Occom's analysis of Indigenous religion similar to Kaufmann's, rather, was that he thought the political mobilization of his people would be helped along by their renouncing "idolatry" for the sake of a loving relationship with a transcendent Creator.

Occom's monotheism, like his iconoclasm, was clearly influenced by Protestantism; and these views, together with the vehemence with which he asserted them, may well have made him "atypical" among Native people. Be that as it may, I hope this brief detour into ancient Palestine has been sufficient to show that it is not necessarily an anti-Protestant gesture to insist that Indigenous religion, in its "typical" form, is averse to transcendence. Yet this is precisely the gesture that is often made when Occom's style of religiosity is deemed aberrant relative to a more typical form of Indigenous syncretism.

Among historians of Native Northeast religion, syncretism is usually described as a resilient religious outlook according to which non-Indigenous beliefs, practices, and even deities can be incorporated into preexisting Native tradition without threatening the basic outlook that make Indigenous religion distinctive. Thus, according to Fisher, "Indian approaches to religion were incorporative, and Christian beliefs could [be] appended in provisional and incomplete ways, without intellectual or religious discomfort."[97] Julius Rubin, arguing along such lines, sees Occom's "ritual practice" as "foster[ing] a sacramental and magical coercion of the other-than-human persons, Jesus and God, to bring good fortune to the people."[98] James Merrell makes a similar argument about Santee religion in his most recent history of Anglo-Catawba relations; he relates how "the Santee," having to some degree accepted the Gospel, "had not converted to alien ways or shed his own; the foundation of priestly prestige still lay in special access to the mysteries of the cosmos. But now those mysteries included European as well as native secrets, a blend that at once acknowledged important changes yet left Indians firmly grounded in their own cultural traditions."[99]

There is a striking parallel between these descriptions of Indigenous syncretism and Kaufmann's description of the ancient Canaanites' "metadivine realm," where gods came into and passed out of existence without threatening the basic cosmological outlook of paganism. Indeed, there is a way in which the prevailing scholarly understanding of Indigenous religious syncretism *requires* the category of "tradition" to be effectively "metadivine." How else could foreign ideas and practices pass in and out of Native belief systems with so little "discomfort" if there weren't some durable sphere of "cultural tradition" in which Native people remained "firmly grounded" through all the religious changes they went through?

In a further development of this syncretistic argument, Tisa Wenger has recently suggested that the *concept of religion itself* made its way into Native communities through an "incorporative" process that preserved inviolate Native peoples' "traditional" outlook. As Wenger notes, it is "often observed that the indigenous cultures of the Americas did not traditionally conceive of 'religion' as a separate sphere of life." But "the claim that traditional Native cultures had no concepts of religion and the secular . . . elide[s] the historical processes, impositions, and accommodations through which these concepts have entered into Native traditions."[100]

Wenger here brings out into the open an assumption that remains widespread in the scholarly literature: the assumption that, for Native Americans, the category of "the traditional" transcends the category of "the religious"—a perfect mirror image of the worldview of the colonists, for whom God provides the last word on everything. This binaristic view of Native and settler societies is sometimes presented in the guise of anticolonial critique, but in order for such an approach to be truly critical, it would have to scrutinize its own most basic concepts, including the concept of "tradition."

In popular culture and scholarly discourse alike, Indigenous self-determination is typically associated with a fundamental commitment to tradition, while colonists are thought to understand religion in terms of abstract or transcendent truths. Or, to put it another way: people often assume that Native peoples' religious beliefs are part of their traditions, whereas colonists think that religion requires a commitment to something "higher" than tradition alone. These assumptions might be valid in certain cases—even most cases!—but I agree with Janowitz that we cannot take them at face value. Their colonial legacy is too deep; indeed, it probably stretches back to antiquity. This legacy goes a long way toward explaining scholars' relentless drive to map different rankings of these concepts (religion, tradition) onto Indigenous and non-Indigenous peoples. More to the point, it explains why Occom may seem to some atypically "Indigenous" because his traditionalism coincided with iconoclasm and a commitment to divine transcendence. Meanwhile, the real-world history of Occom's communities reveals that religion and tradition, and the concepts thereof, have had different resonances among different Native communities at different times, even within relatively close-knit groups.

CHAPTER II

Occom Obviously

Literary Studies and the Problem of Indigenous Knowledge

Samson Occom communicated with the people in his world in an astonishing range of media, genres, and contexts: through idle chitchat and more serious "holy conversation"; through the ceremonial exchange of wampum; through sermons, lectures, and petitions delivered both orally and in print; through painted and printed images of himself; through school lessons and parlor games; through marginalia and inscriptions in books, some of which Occom bound himself with decorative leatherwork (another form of communication); through letters and diaries; through singing and hymn-writing. By Occom's own account, some of his most affecting communication took place without words, in face-to-face encounters that were "not noisy, but very deep; Solemn and Silent, with flow of Tears."[1] When Occom did use words, he sometimes opted for English, but he also spoke and occasionally wrote in the Mohegan language of his ancestors. Less frequently, when the occasion called for it, he communicated in Latin (in which he was proficient enough to deliver an oral "Exegesis" at his ordination), Greek, or Hebrew.[2]

Given the extraordinary range of communicative practices he engaged in, one can only get so far by "reading" Samson Occom, that is, by considering him as a person who is somehow embodied in his writings, as this book sometimes implies. Occom wrote a lot, much of which survives, but not nearly enough to provide anyone with a complete picture of him or his world.

[50]

On the other hand: Occom wrote a *lot*, more than all but a few scribes and literati of his day, and probably more than any other Native American writer until the late nineteenth-century careers of Charles Eastman, Carlos Montezuma, and Zitkala-Ša.[3] Samson Occom's surviving writings comprise roughly a quarter-million words, which is in the same neighborhood as *Jane Eyre* or *Moby-Dick*. Most of these writings have been widely available since 2006 in Joanna Brooks's edited volume *The Collected Writings of Samson Occom, Mohegan*. But relatively few have been the subject of any serious scholarly attention: the 1768 autobiography, the sermon for Moses Paul, the "Account of the Montauk Indians," "Herbs and Roots," a few letters and journal entries, and selected hymns. These are all important texts that are well worth the attention they have received, but together they comprise just a fraction of what Occom wrote. When it comes to exploring Occom's total literary output, the scholarly community is still at the beginning.

For anyone who is interested not merely in what Occom wrote but also in the history of how he has been read, it can be helpful to understand the principles of selection that have led readers to focus on some writings by Occom, but not others. Here I would submit that the subset of Occom's writings that has been most read, by far, consists of texts that concern explicitly Native themes. This makes sense, since it seems fair to say that almost everyone who reads (or has read) Occom's writings is interested in Native American history, literature, religion, or politics. This diverse population of readers includes, but is not limited to, academics in various disciplines, members of Occom's communities, tribal historians, theologians, colonial chroniclers and antiquarians, cultural anthropologists, literary scholars, historians of early New England, ethnohistorians, lawyers, college students, and so on. It also seems fair to say that most of these readers, who begin from the (perfectly correct) premise that Occom is an *Indigenous* writer, have found little interest in those of his writings that do not explicitly discuss Indigenous communities or topics thought to concern them.[4] This includes most of Occom's sermons, which tend to be preoccupied with scriptural interpretation, Reformed Christian doctrine, and pastoral themes like sin, death, awakening, and salvation. It also includes large parts of more widely read texts that drift away from Indigenous themes toward matters of theology or scriptural interpretation. For instance, a great many academic papers, from the undergraduate level on up, have been written about the opening and closing paragraphs of Occom's execution sermon for Moses Paul, where he discusses various issues of Indigenous history and identity; but none to my knowledge have explored the intricacies of Occom's interpretation of Romans 6:23, which takes up the remaining fifty or so paragraphs, for the simple reason that they are not—or do not seem to be—*about* Native communities, cultures, or concerns.

In a sense, this book is no different from previous scholarship on Occom, in that it too cares about what Occom's writings have to say about Indigenous communities. Yet I am also interested in the question of how readers come to decide that a text by Occom (or anyone else) is "about" one thing as distinct from another. This question is of fundamental importance to literary scholars like me who are trained to think that the meaning of texts is a question not merely of theme but also of form.[5] Accordingly, in some of the best recent scholarship on Occom's writings, literary-formal analysis is brought powerfully to bear. In *Literary Indians*, for instance, Angela Calcaterra devotes a chapter to a letter Occom wrote to his sister-in-law Esther Poquiantup, in which two different messages are inscribed on alternating lines:

> What is the Reason, that I dont hear anything at
> Our Friendship I believe is grown old and Rusty
> all from you, is our Friendship, which use to
> We Use to Write to each other once in a While but . . .[6]

Beginning from the observation that this text "require[s] the recipient . . . to engage with the letter's form as much as its content," Calcaterra shows how the letter conveys Occom's sensitivity to the "formal requirements" for speech between members of different Indigenous nations, a sensitivity Occom had honed during his work as a missionary to the Six Nations. Occom's verbal facility with "Haudenosaunee figures and structures," Calcaterra argues, set him apart from Anglo missionaries like Eleazar Wheelock and David Avery, who cared primarily about transmitting the content of missionary discourse. These literal-minded missionaries saw no value in Indigenous forms of speech, except insofar as they made it possible to "translate" their own pedagogical "message" into an idiom Haudenosaunee students could understand.[7] By recovering the link between Occom's "chain" letter and Haudenosaunee conventions of transnational communication associated with the "Covenant Chain," Calcaterra deploys literary-formal analysis as a way of expanding our sense of what Occom's writings are about, while also showing how his writings furthered Native communities' cultural and political survival.[8]

Putting literary studies to one side for the moment, the question of what Occom's writings are "about" can also be posed from an Indigenous studies perspective. Such a perspective is not necessarily incompatible with a literary-studies one, but neither are these necessarily the same. Here I understand an "Indigenous studies" perspective to be defined by three priorities laid out in an important essay published by Robert Alexander Innes in 2011:

1. To access, understand, and convey Native cultural perspective(s).
2. To conduct research that benefits Native people and/or communities.
3. To employ research methods and theories that will achieve these goals.[9]

For anyone trying to do scholarship that fulfills all of these priorities, using literary-formal analysis to describe Occom's engagement with Indigenous communities more expansively seems both valid and important, since this "research method" helps "convey [a] Native cultural perspective." But in order for such analyses to meet Innes's second condition, it also needs to "benefit Native people and/or communities." I have no doubt that Calcaterra and other literary scholars' work very often does this. As Innes and others have argued, a variety of scholarly methods can be used to fulfill the aims of Indigenous studies. "Methodological promiscuity," write Chris Andersen and Jean O'Brien (following Innes) has always been one of the field's greatest strengths, since it helps sustain a transdisciplinary conversation between scholars who have different competencies and different sorts of relationships with Indigenous communities.[10] Work like Calcaterra's provides just one example of how tried and true methods of literary analysis can shed new light on what Native-authored texts are about. In the pages that follow, accordingly, I rely a great deal on the formal analysis of Occom's writings, studying not just what he wrote but also how he wrote it, in an attempt to "understand and convey [a] Native cultural perspective."

Yet formal analysis of the kind I have been describing is not the only technique that literary scholars have used to challenge readers' assumptions about what Occom's writings (or Indigenous literatures more generally) are about. According to Joanna Brooks, Drew Lopenzina, Kelly Wisecup, and other scholars influenced by postcolonial studies, presupposing that Indigenous literatures are "about" Indigenous communities and concerns risks "underestimating the globalizing reach of European systems of thought and language," which treat "colonial archives" as places for "stabilizing and authorizing [non-Indigenous] interpretations of Indigenous literatures and histories"; to treat the colonial archive as a "purely neutral information bank," as Lopenzina puts it, is tantamount to "unwitnessing its lineage to power."[11]

I agree with these scholars up to this point. However, I find myself unable to take the further step they recommend, which is to predicate noncolonial knowledge production upon the recovery of Indigenous knowledge. Indeed, while these readers follow postcolonial theorists in reframing "the archive" as a nontransparent locus of colonial hegemony, they also propose moving beyond the "overstated skepticism" that often characterizes postcolonial approaches to the archive in order to recover the "Indigenous knowledge," or "substratum of suppressed memory," that lies overlooked within.[12] From this perspective, the task of Native American literary studies is not, in the first instance, making new knowledge *about* Indigenous people—that, after all, was just what the colonists sought to do. It is, rather, the liberation of Indigenous knowledge and Indigenous "ways of producing knowledge" that already exist, "unwitnessed," in the colonial archive.[13]

While I admire these scholars' prioritization of Indigenous knowledge, I have often found myself puzzled by their claims to have recovered unwitnessed knowledge from within the colonial archive. It is not that these claims are inherently suspect. I agree that the deconstructive skepticism that characterized much postcolonial studies scholarship often went too far in insisting that the "subaltern does not speak," which sometimes amounted to a denial of the very possibility of studying Indigenous knowledge. So when Lopenzina interprets Occom's 1768 autobiography as part of the same history of Mohegan traditionalism that found expression in the nineteenth-century Mohegan Church, or Wisecup reads Occom's herbarium in the context of Coastal Algonquian medical traditions, I nod my head and say, yes, these sound like accounts of Indigenous knowledge, because these discussions are grounded in the experience of Indigenous *knowers*—that is, Indigenous agents knowing the world in a distinctively Indigenous way. But for the very same reason I find myself befuddled when I find Indigenous knowledge linked to specific literary forms and genres (the compilation, diplomatic speech, the hymn) and delinked from other forms and genres (the sermon, historical and ethnographic writing, conversion narratives, and so on) that have historically been more closely associated with the "colonial archive" and colonial ways of reading.[14] If Indigenous *knowers* found uses for these imported genres within their communities, then I see no reason to doubt that these genres should also fall under the scope of "Indigenous knowledge." If that is right, though, it calls into question the whole literary-historical project of linking Indigenous knowledge (or Indigenous agency more generally) to specific literary forms.[15] If any textual form can be "Indigenous," in other words, what's the point of formal literary analysis in the first place?

This question about formal analysis points to a problem of recognition. Literary scholars' critiques of the "colonial archive" have either relied upon or claimed to discover some formal criterion that makes it possible to repeatedly distinguish ("re-cognize") instances of Indigenous knowledge from instances of colonial knowledge. But it's not always clear how this qualifies as a *method* for achieving the disciplinary goals of Indigenous studies as I, following Innes, characterized them earlier. Here I use the term "method" in a (I hope) straightforward way to refer to a repeatable technique of knowledge-production that can be relied upon to achieve the goals of a given academic discipline. If I understand their position correctly, the literary scholars I have been discussing seek both to recover Indigenous knowledge and to interrogate "the archive" as a locus of colonial knowledge-power; and they do this out of a conviction that scholarship should be more closely aligned with "Indigenous knowledge" as opposed to "colonial knowledge." If this realignment is understood as a goal of Indigenous studies, I think it makes sense. But as a *method*, it seems unduly exclusive since, as Innes, Andersen, and O'Brien argue, not everyone who practices Indigenous studies has Indigenous knowledge, at least, not in the same way.[16]

In my view, any viable account of "Indigenous knowledge" has to ground that knowledge in the lives of specific Indigenous knowers: meaning, you can't just see it there on the surface of a text. This understanding of Indigenous knowledge is informed by the "process"-based understandings of indigeneity advocated by scholars such as Scott Lyons and Robert Warrior, who argue that indigeneity is always changing because Indigenous people are always changing.[17] From this point of view, indigeneity (the indigeneity of texts, for instance, but also anything else) is not a formal characteristic that can be reliably recognized across historical or cultural contexts, but rather a process of self-definition. Thus, as Lyons concisely puts it in *X-Marks*, "Indians [are] people seen as Indians by other Indians."[18]

This approach to indigeneity has much to recommend it as both theory and methodology. For one thing, it refuses to pin indigeneity to any determinate criteria of recognition and is therefore resolutely anti-essentialist. For another, it acknowledges and foregrounds the subject-positionality of knowledge as an activity grounded in specific peoples' lives. The significance of such subject-positionality is a familiar theme in scholarly theories of identity, Indigenous or otherwise. By now, it is a well-established (if not universally respected) view that having such and such an identity gives the people who have it a distinctive "first-personal" authority to determine what that identity means—whence what Linda Alcoff, in a pathbreaking 1991 essay, called "the problem of speaking for others."[19] If I, as a non-Indigenous person, say that "Indigenous identity is x" and an Indigenous person tells me I am wrong, then that is going to be awkward for me. My interlocutor and I will be on justifiably unequal argumentative footing because I do not have the same authority as they do to determine what Indigenous identity amounts to. Yet this asymmetry applies to Indigenous knowledge as well as Indigenous identity. The justifiable presumption of first-personal authority that generates the "problem of speaking for others" also gives rise to a problem of *knowing* for others. If, following Lyons, "Indigenous knowledge" is defined as knowledge identified as "Indigenous" by Indigenous knowers, then non-Indigenous knowers are not going to be the best people to explain what Indigenous knowledge is. That's why, as a non-Indigenous person, I am puzzled by the proposal that recovering Indigenous knowledge is the method literary scholars should reach for when striving to meet the disciplinary demands of both literary studies and Indigenous studies.[20]

In advocating the alignment scholarship with Indigenous knowledge as a "goal," but not necessarily a "method" of Indigenous studies research, I am taking inspiration from Innes, and other Indigenous studies scholars following him, who have argued that Indigenous studies is not the same thing as Indigenous knowledge. As Andersen and O'Brien write, "distinguishing between the two and not losing sight of their key differences is . . . important to building the legitimacy of Indigenous Studies in the academy *and* in Indigenous communities."[21] One problem with conflating Indigenous studies with Indigenous knowledge is that, if they were identical, then the former wouldn't be an academic *discipline*, with all the "epistemological prescriptions" and institutional constraints that this term connotes.[22] Another is that it undermines the "methodological promiscuity" that has historically been one of the field's greatest assets.[23] A third is that doing so is unduly exclusive, since not everyone who practices Indigenous studies *has* Indigenous knowledge.[24]

When Innes, Andersen, and O'Brien argue that Indigenous studies is distinct from Indigenous knowledge, they are not trying to give people carte blanche to disregard the latter. I agree with these scholars that "Native studies scholars should have a connection to a Native community"; that "as a person becomes better acquainted with Native culture, his or her skill in interpreting Native cultural perspectives will improve"; and, finally, that "in certain cases and under the right conditions [Indigenous studies] can be broadly allied with . . . Indigenous knowledge, particularly as situated and practised outside of the academy."[25] I hope that the work I have done on Occom bears all this out, although it is ultimately up to people who belong to Indigenous communities (especially Occom's own) to decide.[26] For me this work has entailed further unpacking the deceptively simple question of what Occom's works are "about," but not in the way you might expect.

Occom, Obviously

So far I have been exploring the possibility of arriving at a method for reading Occom's writings that fulfills the disciplinary goals of both literary and Indigenous studies, and I have indicated why—in light of my own subject-position as a non-Indigenous knower—it seems to me that this method cannot *rely on* aligning my practice of knowledge production with Indigenous knowledge, however desirable such alignment might be as a goal. But aside from the (admittedly) vague pronouncement that I am committed to finding out what Occom's writings are "about," I have yet to clarify why this is a desirable goal, or what *kind* of knowledge I am proposing to produce. I want to say something about this latter question now before moving on, in the next section, to an explanation of what I think the "aboutness" of Occom's writings amounts to.

Let me begin by saying a bit more about what I understand to be problematic about the kind of knowledge that recognition produces. My understanding of this is informed by anthropologist Audra Simpson, who in

Mohawk Interruptus analyzes various ways in which Kahnawà:ke Mohawk people have refused to be recognized by the U.S. and Canadian governments. In a crucial passage from this work, Simpson makes the following two-part assertion:

[1] Refusal [is] a political and ethical stance that stands in stark contrast to the desire to have one's distinctiveness as a culture, as a people, *recognized*.

[2] Refusal comes with the requirement of having one's political sovereignty acknowledged and upheld, and raises the question of legitimacy for those who are usually in the position of recognizing: What is their authority to do so? Where does it come from? Who are they to do so?[27]

At the core of this claim is a distinction between (1) "recognition," which takes as its object a people's "distinctiveness," and (2) "acknowledg[ment]," which takes as its object "sovereignty" and entails a "question[ing]" on the part of the acknowledger of who they are and where their "authority" comes from. One of the problems with recognition, as distinct from acknowledgment, is that the former is motivated by what Simpson calls an "anthropological need" that is deeply engrained in settler states and the institutions of knowledge production that they sponsor. In academic discourse, this need takes the form of a disciplinary imperative to be the "voice of the colonized."[28] It sustains colonial scholars' belief that Indigenous people *want to be known by them* and want them to relay that knowledge to the rest of the world. And Simpson's claim is that this type of disciplinary practice presupposes non-Indigenous "authority" over the recognition or "adjudication" of indigeneity, while reproducing a scholarly subject-position that leaves settler identity unproblematized. In contrast, "acknowledgment" has the potential (at least in principle) to go beyond these limitations because it can perceive and "uphold" Indigenous peoples' sovereignty.

How can acknowledgment achieve this? Simpson's discussion of the topic aligns closely with that of the political theorist Patchen Markell, whose *Bound by Recognition* serves as an important theoretical touchstone for Simpson's broader argument. Here Markell argues that the demand for acknowledgment (but not recognition) "aims to change our understanding of the relevant 'knowledge' itself: of what it means to know, and of what kind of knowledge we need to have in order to take the further step of acknowledging others."²⁹ Following the philosopher Stanley Cavell, Markell insists that acknowledging others is not merely a "supplement" to knowing them. What is involved, rather, is a "shift in . . . the direction of that knowledge."³⁰ Acknowledgment (but not recognition) challenges the knower's own "self-relation" by forcing them to grasp the inadequacy of their former way of knowing. This is also a goal of "ethnographic refusal" as theorized by Simpson, which seeks to redefine "what you need to know" and to make that redefinition central to Indigenous studies practice. The point of ethnographic refusal, then, is not necessarily to keep knowledge about Indigenous communities secret or, still less, to reorient Indigenous studies around the "centrality of esoteric and sacred knowledge."³¹ It is, rather, to interrupt the scholarly recognition of Indigenous peoples—including their traditions, cultures, and/or knowledges—according to any criteria that are not established by Indigenous agents themselves.

As a literary scholar, I take this to imply that I cannot just pick up a Native-authored text, read it, and claim to be *acknowledging* Indigenous sovereignty. Even if that text is literally about Indigenous sovereignty, I will acknowledge its author's "literary sovereignty" only when I see the text itself as an assertion of "jurisdiction and authority" that has the capacity to change "what kind of knowledge [I] need to have."³² This does not necessarily mean that as a non-Indigenous person I need to acquire Indigenous knowledge; that could be the case, but if I *assumed* it were, then I wouldn't be in a position to acknowledge "literary sovereignty," since I would already know (or thought I knew) what kind of knowledge I needed.

So how does this apply to reading Samson Occom in the context of Mohegan and Brothertown sovereignty?

In an essay published in 2020 in *American Indian Quarterly*, Brothertown tribal historic preservation officer Courtney Cottrell details her efforts to repatriate a ceremonial pipe from the Peabody Museum at Yale. Cottrell reveals various ways in which the provisions of the Native American Graves Protection and Repatriation Act (NAGPRA), which she had hoped would facilitate the Brothertown claim, "coerce Native peoples to recognize themselves using federal terms and often in comparison to other tribes"—particularly, in Cottrell's case, in comparison to the Mohegan Tribe, which in the 1990s had explored the possibility of including the pipe in a larger repatriation request they had submitted to Yale. "In trying to prove the Skeesucks pipe's affiliation to the Brothertown and not the Mohegan,"

Cottrell writes, "I fell into this paradox as I tried to recognize us based on federal criteria for what it means to be American Indian." These criteria, Cottrell argues, fail to account for "the complicated and intertwined relationships eastern tribes," especially "agglomerated" eastern tribes like Brothertown, "have faced through colonial entanglements."[33] What NAGPRA's politics of recognition overlooks above all is what Occom, in a passage cited by Cottrell, calls "our *reformation*," a process initiated in the eighteenth century through the Brothertown movement's "promotion of survival, endurance, and revitalization of the Algonquian communities and Algonquian traditions through the use of certain Christian ideals—an ethnogenesis that ensured stability, as well as the ability to not have attention drawn to themselves as Natives during uncertain times."[34] This "re-forming of tribal communities," Cottrell claims, "works against the perceived notion within the United States and elsewhere that Indigenous communities need to be distinct, continuous communities (i.e., stagnate) to prove legitimacy, supported by documentary proof of unchanging demographics, traditions, and lifestyles."[35]

I cite Cottrell at length here because she expresses much more powerfully than I can the incommensurability between what she and Occom call "re-forming" and what the U.S. government calls "recognition." Morphologically, these two terms seem connected: both are "re-" words, and as such imply an awareness on someone's part of what came before and is happening now again. But whereas "recognition" implies going back to a prior idea ("cognition") or mental representation, "re-forming" evokes a continuity of agential change, of someone or some group of people giving themselves a new shape without negating their prior existence. In the present context, it means looking at an individual or collective agent and saying, this is still the *same* person (or people) even though, and in some sense because, they have made themselves different from what they were "known as" before; they are the same, in other words, but they have stayed the same by making themselves hard to recognize.[36] As Cottrell emphasizes, "reforming" Indigenous communities like Brothertown can still be "traditional." But acknowledging the traditionalism of such a community requires a more expansive understanding of tradition than the politics of recognition—with its emphasis on "unchanging" criteria of Indigeneity—typically entails. Acknowledging the traditionalism of a reforming people means asking, what is it in this agent's background that could possibly be giving them the strength to change in these circumstances? It also requires asking—per Simpson, Markell, and Cavell—how do the people of this community demand either *not* to be known, or *to be known, but differently*?

From the perspective of modern literary theory, knowing Occom the way he *wanted to be known* almost necessarily means knowing him differently. In the discipline of literary studies, we are taught as students that analyzing literary texts means setting aside authorial intention: we're supposed to study what authors wrote, not what kind of people they were or how they wanted to be read. Yet Occom wanted and expected to be known in specific ways, by people from his tribal communities, and also by outsiders, and it seems to me that this *has to* matter for anyone trying to "acknowledge" his literary sovereignty, as opposed to merely recognizing it. Acknowledging Occom's literary sovereignty, in other words, requires taking seriously his intentions about how interactions between himself and his readers should go—even if this type of acknowledgment entails overriding disciplinary norms about the objectivity of the literary "text."

Given that I read Occom as a nontribal and non-Indigenous outsider, I have a particular interest in the question of how he wanted to be known and read by people who occupy that position. The claim I have been advancing so far in this book is that Occom wanted nontribal readers to know him *as strangers*: he expected them to have a surface-based (though not necessarily superficial) knowledge that took seriously the way he presented himself to non-community outsiders. In chapter 1, I argued that there was something deeply traditional about this expectation of Occom's, given his immersion in Northeast Native customs of mobility, diplomacy, and hospitality. Occom's communities had cultural knowledge about how to talk to people who did not share their tribal identity. He celebrated that cultural competency and carried it forward into his own writing, which he celebrated for its capacity to connect with a broad swath of humanity. As he wrote in his sermon for Moses Paul, "people . . . can't help understanding my talk; it is common, plain, every-day talk. . . . Further, as it comes from an uncommon quarter, it may induce people to read it, because it is from an Indian."[37] Occom's great innovation as an Indigenous writer was to use new media and speech genres to extend the scope of Northeast Native hospitality.

Given that Occom's interactions with strangers were so deeply informed by Northeast Native tradition, it would be incompatible with his intentions to "read between the lines" of his writings to find some hidden, occult indigeneity that his public, stranger-facing persona concealed. Occom's writings were painstakingly written in order to be easily understood. By offering "common, plain, every-day talk," he continued his ancestors' tradition of being "liberal . . . to strangers."[38] What he expected of these strangers, in return, was that they take him as he came to them. He expected that his readers would read him *obviously*.

Reading Occom obviously is one way, this book's way, of acknowledging his literary sovereignty. This type of reading takes inspiration from the thinkers I have been discussing in the previous pages—Simpson, Markell, Cavell, Cottrell, and Occom himself—and also from literary-studies ideas of "surface reading." As Stephen Best and Sharon Marcus argue in their famous essay on the topic, "surface reading" describes a broad repertoire of literary-critical techniques that take written words for "exactly what they appear to be," as distinct from *symptomatic* reading, which works on the assumption that "what a text means lies in what it does not say."[39] Surface reading, Best and Marcus argue, typically goes beyond appreciating a text as a material surface ("paper, binding, typography," etc.) to encompass what they call an "affective and ethical stance" toward what might be called, following Erving Goffman, the *self-presentation* of texts as objects that wear a certain "face" in their interactions with readers.[40] To "embrace the surface," they write, "involves accepting texts, deferring to them instead of mastering or using them"; conversely, it entails a certain skepticism about the sometimes seductive notion that "the surface of the archive" conceals a buried "repository of latent voices and 'hidden transcripts.'"[41]

Best and Marcus's allusion, in the sentence just cited, to anthropologist James C. Scott's *Domination and the Arts of Resistance: Hidden Transcripts* has a special relevance to the study of Native American literature, and particularly to the developing scholarly conversation on Occom. This is because several of Occom's recent interpreters have appealed to Scott by way of justifying various forms of the assertion that his surviving writings *cannot be* what they so obviously seem to be: an extensive and at times overwhelming record of "salvationist discourse" and evangelical piety.[42] Those who read Occom for the "hidden transcripts" of resistance concealed behind his evangelical discourse typically construe the latter as a symptom of colonial power-relations whose true nature Occom was forced to repress; on such a reading, Occom belongs to what Scott describes as the mass of unnamed "millions who spend most of their waking hours in power-laden situations in which a misplaced gesture or a misspoken word can have terrible consequences."[43] Such an approach seems tailor-made to diagnose the colonial power-relations impinging upon Occom's textual performances. But Scott's methodology has serious shortcomings for anyone seeking to acknowledge Occom's literary sovereignty in the way I have been describing in this chapter.

Before proceeding further, I want to be very clear that, in reading Occom "obviously" instead of symptomatically (that is, for "hidden transcripts" of resistance) I am not trying to minimize the dangers he faced by practicing his traditionalism in public. It is a benefit, rather than shortcoming, of Scott's approach that he foregrounds the dangers faced by colonized thinkers. The problem, rather, has to do with way Scott's notion of "hidden transcripts," and the basic philosophical-anthropological premises that support it, run afoul of the critique of "anthropological need"—the need to "hear" and even "be" the "voice of the colonized"—that Simpson persuasively levels against scholarly methodologies that seek to "recognize" Indigeneity as something "esoteric," accessible only to expert human-scientific knowledge.[44] Scott's approach is premised, above all, on a seemingly universal psychological likeness shared by people living in "political environments" where they cannot speak openly, a likeness which Scott recognizes in his own experience when, at various times, "I had to choke back responses that would not have been prudent" when speaking "before those who had power over me." As Scott relates, "I often found someone to whom I could *voice* my unspoken thoughts," but this opportunity was not typically available to the oppressed peoples he studied.[45] Accordingly, Scott offers the idea of "hidden transcripts" as part of a research program for liberating the "choked back" "voice" of the repressed. This research program is to be pursued through a reading practice which address itself to an imaginary archive where "unspoken thoughts" are recorded and *recognized* across time, space, and culture by a select group of "readers" who understand and sympathize with the repressed in a way that those in "power" do not.

It is in this latter respect that Scott's interpretive methodology follows most closely in the footsteps of Leo Strauss, whose essay "Persecution and the Art of Writing" inspired *Domination and the Arts of Resistance* (whence the similar title) to an extent that interpreters who rely on Scott may not always realize. What Scott borrows from Strauss is a reading practice purpose-built for "esoteric" texts "in which the truth about all crucial things is presented exclusively between the lines."[46] Strauss's esoteric reading practice, like Scott's, evinces a sympathetic attitude toward the plight of oppressed writers and an awareness of the chilling effect of political persecution, attributes which are, in a way, perfectly commendable. But the reason so many people have found Strauss's esotericism unpalatable is its further supposition that only a privileged cadre of readers has the wherewithal to engage in the kind of reading "between the lines" that texts by persecuted writers demand. "The fact which makes this literature possible," as Strauss puts it, "can be expressed in the axiom that thoughtless men are careless readers, and only thoughtful men are careful readers."[47] The implication is that reading obviously, or surface reading, is an affliction of the *hoi polloi* who are oblivious to the operations of power upon discourse. And this implication, in turn, gives rise to the unapologetic literary elitism with which Straussian esotericism has become practically synonymous. Scott, to be fair, roundly rejects this elitism. Yet the reading practice he advocates is nevertheless one whose interpretive and political payout comes only when one acknowledges that the "political environment" in which persecuted individuals write "seldom permits a transparency in meaning."[48] In order to read for "hidden transcripts" one has to abjure the "hegemonic public conduct" of ordinary life—the domain of what Occom called "common, plain, every-day talk" that people "can't help understanding"—in order to enter into a different interactional "environment" where "hidden" meanings can be transmitted esoterically.[49]

To be sure, not everyone who studies Occom takes inspiration from Scott, and it seems safe to presume that few if any of those who do would identify themselves as Straussians. Yet I think it is fair to say that esoteric reading practices similar to the ones I have been discussing have long held, and continue to hold, a powerful allure for many readers of Indigenous-authored texts. Indeed, I would go somewhat farther than this and submit that the prevalence of esoteric reading practices goes a long way toward explaining why culturalism remains a dominant paradigm in the study of Native American literature, even though most scholars in the field would probably agree on a purely theoretical level that culture is not what exclusively or even most importantly defines Indigenous communities as self-determining entities.

This linkage between esotericism and culturalism can be illustrated with reference to two different interpretations that literary scholars have offered of Occom's 1768 autobiography. In the introduction of that text (discussed at much greater length in chapter 5), Occom states that "it is against my mind to give a History of myself and publish it," but goes on to explain that he has decided to do so anyway "to do Justice to my Self, and to those who may desire to know Something concerning me—and for the Honor of Religion."[50] This opening does not mention Indigenous traditions, but that has not prevented scholars from interpreting it as expressive of traditions that Occom leaves unmentioned in both the introduction and the autobiography as a whole. Joanna Brooks, in her edited collection of Occom's writings, proposes that this opening "may reflect a traditional proscription against storytelling that privileges the self over the community."[51] Literary historian Dana Nelson, by contrast, argues that the text can be read as continuing a tradition of what David Brumble calls "preliterate autobiographical narrative[s]" which took the form of "'self-vindication' . . . structured by charge, self-vindication, and countercharge."[52] It is hard to see how both of these interpretations could be true, and even harder to imagine how one would go about finding out, especially since neither of the traditions on which the readings are based—"a traditional prescription against storytelling" that privileges the self and a "preliterate" genre of "self-vindication"—are discussed by Occom in any of his surviving writings. One can only find them "between the lines."

In contrast to these esoteric readings, the interpretive practice I advocate privileges how Occom intended to present himself on the surface of his writing. The way to address the puzzle Occom raises in his introduction—why write and "publish" a "History of myself" when it is "against my mind" to do so?—is by looking at the text itself, and if necessary at other writings by Occom that shed light on the question. There is, for instance, Occom's earlier autobiographical sketch of 1765, which he circulated among his missionary bosses before his trip to England in the hopes of correcting "great miss Representations by Some Concerning my Life."[53] The fact that this earlier effort was, basically, a failure goes a long way toward explaining why Occom might not have wanted to repeat the exercise.[54] Another relevant text from around the same time, which substantially clarifies what Occom meant when he said he wrote his autobiography "for the Honor of Religion," is the sermon for Moses Paul. Here Occom warns his listeners not to let their religious observances get contaminated by "self-love, like the Pharisees of old," who "loved to pray in open view of men, that they might have praise from them."[55] Maybe Occom's qualms in writing his second, longer autobiography stemmed from his uncertainty about whether or not he could do so without falling prey to the sin of self-love. Does either of these alternative explanations align with Brooks's and Nelson's esotericist hypotheses about the "traditional" or "preliterate" customs which may have "proscri[bed]" or encouraged Occom's performance? I am not really sure, but who wants to know? And why? That doesn't seem what these texts are about, at least not in any obvious way.

To be clear, my argument here is not that esotericism is bad in general, as a reading practice or as broader way of life. The question I am pursuing, rather, is what methods make sense for reading Occom now, at this historical moment. And my claim is that esotericism works against "acknowledgment" in Simpson and Markell's sense because it presupposes "what kind of knowledge we need to have"—in this case, hidden Indigenous knowledge—without giving Occom the authority to determine what kind of knowledge he wanted to hide or reveal.

Acknowledging Occom's "literary sovereignty" in the way I am proposing here, then, means not publicizing things he kept secret. Instead, it begins with the observation that Occom opened a channel of communication with readers about what he wanted them to know. When Occom said that everyone should be able understand his words "because I am an Indian," he was pursuing a very specific cultural and political agenda, grounded in Indigenous custom, about how he wanted his words to circulate in the world.

To put this in more technical language, what I am advocating is a method of reading Occom that is attuned *both* to his words' surface or "denotational" meaning *and* to his literary sovereignty as this found expression in his writings' "metapragmatic regimentation." I borrow the latter term from the field of linguistic anthropology, where it is used to analyze the control ("regimentation") of interaction through the use of language about ("meta-") how language is supposed to be used ("-pragmatic").[56] In Indigenous studies, the concept of metapragmatic regimentation has been particularly useful for anthropologists studying tribal language revitalization programs—which, for obvious reasons, tend to entail a whole range of suppositions about how (and by whom) Indigenous languages are supposed to be used.[57] I use the term here in a slightly broader way, since I am interested not in the formal properties of tribal languages *per se,* but rather in the question of how Occom asserted literary sovereignty by seeking to "regiment" the use of his words by the people who read and heard them. And one of the things that becomes clear, when one looks at Occom's surviving writings with metapragmatics in mind, is how often he made it explicit that he intended his words to be intelligible, without searching for hidden meanings, to a broad range of people whom he did not personally know. To bring together just a few examples:

> the books that are in the world are written in very high and refined language . . . so that the common people understand but little of them. But I think they can't help understanding my talk; it is common, plain, every-day talk—little children may understand it; and poor Negroes may plainly and fully understand my meaning; and it may be of service to them. Again, it may in a particular manner be serviceable to my poor kindred the Indians . . .

> Here I present you, O Christians *of what Denomination soever*, with cordial Hymns, to comfort you in your weary Pilgrimage

> every one of us is placed in the world according to gods pleasure So all from the Highest of mankind to the lowest have Something to do for god in the World, & every one of us know Something of the Work or Duty he requires of us

> Christianity ought to be the Greatest and universal Concern of all Mankind of all Ranks and Degrees

> The grand Question occurs again, is man, a Rational Man . . . [able to] become a Chaste Creature? I imagine to hear an Answere Universaly from all Rational Men, Saying, O! Yes O!

> every one, who is grown to Years of Some understanding, will readyly own, that this Command ["love thy neighbor as thyself"] is to them

> The errors and mistakes in People, in their Rel[igious] Concerns, either in Principle or Practice . . . does not at all alter God. . . . [The] Commandments to every one are the Same, Heaven [is the] Same, the Bible is the Same.[58]

In each of these examples, Occom communicates a certain vision about how his listeners should use the words he is telling them. And in each case, his vision is that the words in question should be seen as making an ethical, spiritual, and/or political claim on anyone who might happen to hear them. It is a vision of his language as *public*.[59]

I want to underscore that I am using the term "public" here primarily in a metapragmatic sense, and only secondarily to describe the media or material networks through which Occom's utterances were transmitted. This differs from the way the term has been used by some historians of Native American literature who define publicness primarily in terms of media and literacy.[60] While this approach has yielded valuable insights, it also has certain limitations, the most important of which is that conceptualizing publicness as a disposition of media often puts media in a fungible, means/ends relationship to extrinsic moral, spiritual, and political priorities.[61] Thus, in the scholarship on early Native alphabetic literacy, Native students are often presented as starting off with an antagonistic relationship to a colonial "literacy complex" that defined writing in terms of conversion and assimilation; Native literary history, on this understanding, is a story of how Indigenous writers repurposed written media for their own political and cultural ends.[62] From Occom's point of view, however, public discourse was not some foreign tool that he and his people figured out how to make use of—not, that is, if we understand publicness from a metapragmatic perspective, in terms of a set of linguistic cues through which Occom sought to direct his words to the attention of strangers. Disaggregating the history of publicness from the history of media, and in particular the stadial history of media *shift*—a shift from orality to literacy, or from "Indigenous" nonalphabetic literacy to "colonial" alphabetic literacy—makes it possible to see that his practices of public address were *always* grounded in Northeast Native customs of stranger sociability.

The metapragmatic approach I am describing can be illustrated by briefly examining a circular letter that Occom addressed in 1784 "To all the Indians in this Boundless Continent." This letter is divided into three paragraphs. The first and shortest of these is a greeting and plea for his listeners to pay attention. The second paragraph begins by asserting the main tenet of monotheism—"There is but one, Great good Supream and Indepentant Spirit above, he is the only Living and True God"—and moves from there into an elaborate recapitulation of the first three books of Genesis. The last paragraph recounts how God expelled Adam and Eve from Eden, and how He "Discoverd his Love and Designs of mercy to Adam & to his Children" in the person of the "the Son of God, his name is Jesus Christ." The text's final sentence emphasizes that God only created humankind once:

"this one man and Woman, is the Father and Mother of all Nations of the Whole World."[63]

Borrowing a semiotic distinction first formulated by anthropologist Michael Silverstein, I propose that this letter can be read as two texts in one: a "denotational text" and an "interactional text."[64] The denotational text—a rough approximation of which can be found in the previous paragraph—is what the text refers to: "the 'content' in the primary sense of reference-and-predication."[65] This denotational text encompasses the meanings of the words on the page (the "text artifact") as these might be looked up in a dictionary, as well as other referential phenomenon associated with "indexical" or pointing signs such as "I," "you," and "here." In short, the denotational text comprises everything we can reasonably say a given text-artifact is "about" when we analyze its content solely in terms of the message the sender put there.

When we read Occom's letter with its "interactional text" in mind, we gather information about what kind of social situation the text-artifact is trying to "map out" for the people reading it.[66] As Silverstein (citing J. L. Austin) puts it, an interactional text is "a co-participatory 'doing things with words.'" Most of the interactional "mapping" that takes place in Occom's letter comes in the first, framing paragraph, where Occom provides a series of vivid metapragmatic cues: "let nothing Croud into your Ears whilest I am Speaking, and prepare your hearts. Let there be Room for my words & keep them there Choice and loose them not, awake your Understanding and Call home all your Roving Thoughts, and attend Diligently."[67]

This brief passage tells us quite a lot about how Occom thought his listeners would "co-participate" in the social exchange occasioned by the delivery of his letter. For one thing, it tells us that he imagined them participating in the act of communication with their "hearts" as well as their "Ears." He also says that "prepar[ing]" the heart to listen requires a certain mental discipline, "Call[ing] home all your Roving Thoughts." Intriguingly, having all one's thoughts back at "home"—rather than trying to banish all distractions from one's mind—seems to be a precondition for making "Room for my words" in one's mind and/or "heart." Above all, the sentences convey Occom's desire that the parties to the interaction should *take care* of language as if it were a person, or perhaps an animal belonging to one's herd or flock: "Let there be Room . . . and loose them not." This warning presupposes that, once admitted into the heart/mind,

Occom's words and the "thoughts" they represent will be apt to go "Roving" off again. And who will be there to call them back? Occom emphasizes that he is old and that he put off this interaction longer than he wanted to: "I have had a great Desire to Write to you a long While, but I have put it off from Time to Time, to This Time, I am now Sixty one years of Age." And his hope seems to be that, even in his absence, his words will have a lasting impact on his audience. It is almost as if he wants his hearers to *adopt* them and thereby to sustain a "co-participatory" encounter with Occom's words that outlasts the moment of the letter's reading and perhaps even the lifetime of its sender.

These are some of the "metapragmatic" cues Occom embedded in his letter, but it is important to realize that they do not paint a complete picture of how Occom thought the interaction would go. As an Indigenous person—"I am an Indian also," he says in the opening line—addressing other Indigenous people, Occom took for granted that the parties to the interaction would share certain cultural understandings about how social interactions were supposed to play out. His metaphor of adding new words into the already crowded "home" of one's mind, for instance, sounds a lot like what he elsewhere refers to as "our Custom" of "freely Entertain[ing] all Visitors."[68] Such social norms, which we know about only from Occom's other writings, not from the specific "text artifact" at hand, also gave shape to the historical interactional event to which Occom's letter provides a partial metalinguistic "map." We might think of the metapragmatic signals from the letter's opening paragraph as being akin to cue cards used to help actors remember their part. They can be helpful for those who already know their lines, but they don't contain the entire script.

It would be reasonable for the reader to wonder at this point whether the kind of metapragmatic analysis I have just demonstrated conflicts with my earlier proposal to read Occom "obviously." I take this objection seriously. I also acknowledge that the reading I have just offered may be wrong in its conjecture that the metapragmatic cues in Occom's letter can be understood as continuous with Indigenous customs of hospitality. If the conjecture *is* wrong, however, it is not because I am reading the colonial archive for a "hidden transcript" of Indigenous knowledge that is not explicitly stated. Rather, as I have tried to show, Occom's concern for strangers lies right there on the surface of his writings, in almost everything he wrote. All I have done is to reemphasize what Occom himself emphasizes, that being "kind to strangers" was something his people did long before him, and conjecture that Occom's public and exoteric manner of talking to strangers extended those ancestral lifeways. This conjecture could be wrong. It could be the case that there was no relationship whatsoever between Indigenous customs of hospitality and Occom's plea to "let there be Room for my words." But is it really plausible that he compartmentalized his world in this way?

It seems to me much more likely that Occom's traditionalism afforded a more deeply integrated perspective on things. Occom described his community as one where people were proud of their social customs. As I argued in chapter 1, he recognized a deep commonality between Native traditions of hospitality and the kind of neighborliness described in the Gospel, where Jesus taught that "if we are true Neighbours, we are so to all."[69] Taking inspiration from this teaching, Occom took it upon himself to put his own "neighborliness" into words. Saying that Occom was an "evangelical" is just another way of saying that he used language to put his traditionalist social ethic on display for strangers to pay attention to. What Occom said of Jesus's ministry applied just as well to his own: "his Preaching was now also Publick to every mans Consideration."[70]

Public Space and Native Space

> When I look about me, and see such a crouded Assembly, I am ready to say within myself, what shall I observe to such a People? Such a vast Number, that have been brought up under the Gospel all their Lives: You are the happiest among the Nations! . . . But as God has brought me amongst you at this Time, an obscure Stranger, from an obscure Place, I shall speak to you in few Words at this Time. Every Thing shews forth the Goodness of God, that we see before us and round about us; but I shall make a few Remarks upon the Words that I . . . now read.—This People have I formed for myself; they shall shew forth my Praise. (Untitled sermon delivered by Occom in Bristol, England, on August 10, 1766)[71]

When people talk about what one another's words are "about," they usually have in mind what those words refer to. But the term "about" can also be understood spatially, as in the quotation above from a sermon Occom delivered during his fundraising tour of England. "When I look *about* me," as Occom put it, who do "I" "see?" What, we might imagine him asking, is the best way to respond to those others, their needs, their expectations? The "aboutness" of Occom's writings thus has to do not merely with *referring* but also with those writings' (and Occom's) *positionality* in social space. What they are about is partly a function of who is "around and about," and of how Occom used words to give a certain shape to the social interactions he initiated.

In drawing attention to his use of metapragmatic discourse to structure social space, I take inspiration from Lisa Brooks's account of Occom's involvement of the "recovery of Native space in the Northeast."[72] In *The Common Pot*, Brooks shows how Occom and his kin used language as a way of welcoming newcomers to the Native Northeast while also encouraging them to live according to the social norms of Indigenous communities. The argument I have been developing in this chapter is a variation on this Brooksian theme. By carrying forward Indigenous customs of hospitality through the expressive outlet of evangelicalism, Occom found a way of staying traditional even in a transatlantic world of strangers.

This argument raises a question: what about people who read Occom today? Do they (or, if you like, "we") belong to Occom's public and thus to the Native space he created? This is not an easy question to answer. Often, but not always, Occom explicitly addressed his words to a broad public and even to posterity.[73] Be this as it may, however, the idea that "we" (whoever we are) enter Native space whenever we read Occom's writings may seem a little too convenient, since it suggests that "we" can experience his traditionalism simply by reading his words. Let me work my way toward a response to all of this by putting Occom's relationship to his audience(s) in a broader historical perspective.

While Occom never described himself in these precise terms, it seems uncontroversial in hindsight to say that his career marked the beginning of what might be called the "broadcast era" of Indigenous cultural expression. He understood that language, when it circulated promiscuously among strangers, had the power to crystallize new publics and new possibilities for Indigenous liberation; and he took advantage of this power to *be culturally Indigenous* for the benefit of as many people as he possibly could. More straightforwardly: Occom was proud to belong to Mohegan and Brothertown, and he wanted to show the world why.

The transatlantic communications networks Occom used to broadcast his words were a forerunner of what we now call "the mass media," in the sense that they used broadcast-oriented forms of address and metalinguistic cues: "to all the Indians," "for all sincere christians," "this word . . . is to every one of us," et cetera. Yet Occom was not particularly fixated on print, or any other medium (as we use that term now), as a way of getting his message across. Only in subsequent decades and centuries would Native American writers and intellectuals begin to associate broadcast forms of address with specific material channels like print, radio, and TV.[74] In the 1820s, for instance, Elias Boudinot orchestrated an international philanthropic campaign on behalf of the Cherokee Nation that turned print technology into a hallmark of Cherokee nationalism.[75] At the turn of the twentieth century, Indigenous writers such as Zitkala-Ša, Charles Alexander Eastman, and D'Arcy McNickle began reaching truly massive audiences by partnering with commercial publishing firms such as Harper Bros., Little, Brown, and so on. This was also the era of the Society of American Indians (SAI), which made mass-circulating print central to its vision of furthering "the highest good of all classes and divisions of the Indian race and for the uplift of humanity." As Arthur Parker wrote in 1913 in the first issue of the society's *Quarterly Journal*, "the publication of this Journal marks a new departure in the progress of the Society of American Indians and, indeed, in the history of the race. . . . This venture is therefore more or less an experiment based . . . [on] the essential pride of the race in its position as the native race of America. . . . [SAI] is organised for the uplift and adjustment the Indian race, thus is of directly benefiting every individual Indian and all humanity."[76] By using broadcast forms of address to make the "uplift" of "the Indian race" an issue of concern for "all humanity," the leaders of the SAI were following in footsteps trod by Occom and other Indigenous evangelicals a century and a half before. But the real high point of the broadcast era of Native American cultural expression came in the aftermath of the American Indian Movement, with the publication of international bestsellers by writers including Vine Deloria, N. Scott Momaday, Leslie Marmon Silko, and Louise Erdrich. Like Occom, all these writers supposed that *some* (not all) Indigenous lifeways were of broad human significance and deserved to be publicized to an audience of strangers; and they all sought to effect the metapragmatic regimentation of public space in order to bring that space into better alignment with Indigenous ways of being and communicating. Vine Deloria's *We Talk, You Listen* (1970) is a spectacular document of Indigenous publicness in its deepest, metapragmatic sense: in its very title, it takes control of the way language circulates in order to get a big, chaotic society to pay attention to the demands of Native communities.

What I am calling the "broadcast era" of Indigenous cultural expression was characterized by an enduring optimism about the emancipatory power of public discourse. This can be a little hard to relate to now, given the increasing awareness among scholars and the broader public that Native communities do not always want their cultures and traditions to be publicized. To a certain extent, the broadcast era of Indigenous cultural expression was as a victim of its own success. The Trail of Broken Treaties, for instance, was a public relations triumph; but precisely because it drew so much non-Native attention to Indigenous communities, it helped breathe new life into the "anthropological need" that, as Simpson shows, migrated out of Orientalism into scholarly discourse about Indigenous peoples over the course of the nineteenth and twentieth centuries.[77]

In this book, I side with Simpson's critique of "anthropological need" and Deloria's insistence that "knowledge for knowledge's sake becomes an irrelevant assertion . . . [when] it does not directly contribute to the elevation of [Indigenous] people."[78] Yet precisely because the "broadcast era" of Indigenous culture seems a bit remote from present-day concerns (especially in academia), it seems to me all the more important to acknowledge Occom, and other Indigenous intellectuals like him, who sought to communicate with the world in an exoteric, public way. As I have tried to show, reading his words for their surface meanings, rather than esoterically, just *is* reading them as expressive of Indigenous tradition, and thus seems like a good way of working toward the Indigenous studies goal of "access[ing], understand[ing] and convey[ing] Native cultural perspective(s)."[79] Reading Occom obviously, as a public-spirited Indigenous evangelical, is also a way of giving him and his people the authority to determine "what kind of knowledge we need to have." And it is for this reason, if for no other, that my answer to the question I raised earlier—can people living today be considered members of the "public" whom Occom thought he was addressing?—is and I think has to be: yes.

I acknowledge that this reasoning might seem bizarre (or worse) to some of my fellow literary scholars, since it frames textual interpretation in terms that are, basically, interpersonal. One of the oldest precepts of literary theory is that approaching literature in this way is "romantic" and undisciplined, since making knowledge about literary texts requires bracketing questions of authorial personhood and intention.[80] But it is not obvious to me how one could hew to this precept *and* read Indigenous authors in a way that acknowledges their literary sovereignty. In fact, from my point of view, one of the most exciting things about bringing Indigenous studies and literary studies together is that it makes it possible, and indeed urgent, to raise again the very basic question of whether the "intentional fallacy" was ever really that fallacious in the first place. Since space prevents me from going too deep into this issue here, I will simply say that I don't think it was, although I am also not "against theory" like some have argued that you need to be if you take authors' intentions seriously.[81]

Without compromising disciplinary integrity, the study of literature can and should be somewhat intentionalist some of the time, because the study of literature—often, but not necessarily always—involves the study of people(s): not just individual human beings, or humanity in general, but also specific "peoples," that is, groups of people who belong to one another in such a way as to constitute a collective agent. *One* perfectly valid way of characterizing literature with peoples in mind is advocated by Jace Weaver in *That the People Might Live*: "I define literature broadly as the total written output of a people."[82] This definition does two things: (1) it posits a connection between literature and peoplehood and (2) it identifies the former as an "output" of the latter. The second of these two subclaims serves an important purpose for Weaver's broader argument that Indigenous peoples are chronologically, causally, and analytically *prior* to the literatures they create. I agree with this, but I also agree with Scott Lyons that literature is often an *input* of peoplehood as well as an output.[83] As Lyons argues, and as several examples from this chapter attest—for instance, Occom's insistence that Indigenous people "make room" for the Gospel in their hearts and minds—texts have the power to recruit people into new forms of belonging, even while they are reproducing old ones. This seemingly paradoxical fact may be the most complicated and fascinating thing about literature in general. It also matters politically, particularly when it comes to the history of Indigenous literatures and their reception. On the one hand, Indigenous literatures (like other literatures) have the power to recruit preexisting peoples into forms of textually mediated belonging that are at once new and old: new ways of being what they always were. On the other hand, this power of literature to "recruit" people also affects the relationship between Indigenous communities and outsiders, since Indigenous literatures also have a power of "speaking to" readers who do not belong to Indigenous communities. Some Indigenous writers and intellectuals—Occom and Deloria, for instance—have described this latter power of Indigenous writing as a source of strength for Native communities; but it can also be a liability, since sometimes the non-community readers who feel most strongly that Indigenous literatures "speak to" them are not actually being spoken to. This type of unsolicited and often unwelcome overhearing can be a serious problem for Native peoples, as Simpson's work on ethnographic refusal makes abundantly clear.

One way of further elaborating this problematic relationship between Indigenous literatures and outsiders (who may or may not be friendly) is with reference to what Mikhail Bakhtin termed "addressivity," which, according to Bakhtin, is an intrinsic feature of any utterance. Addressivity describes the peculiar way in which utterances "turn to someone" and pick that someone out as an "addressee." That addressee, Bakhtin writes,

> can be an immediate participant-interlocutor in an everyday dialogue, a differentiated collective of specialists in some particular area of cultural communication, a more or less differentiated public, ethnic group, contemporaries, like-minded people, opponents and enemies, a subordinate, a superior, someone who is lower, higher, familiar, foreign, and so forth. . . . All these varieties and conceptions of the addressee are *determined by that area of human activity and everyday life to which the given utterance is related.*[84]

For Bakhtin, *how* a text addresses people is a function of *where* in society that text circulates. It is only in some social spaces ("area[s] of human activity") that utterances have the capacity to address people who identify themselves as "readers," an identity that can, in turn, be characterized in terms of the expectation that some utterances will address readers as "literature." One important question raised by Bakhtin's account of addressivity is how the intrinsic addressivity of any utterance relates to human beings' historically conditioned *expectations* that certain utterances address them in certain ways. When people feel like a text is "speaking to them," we might ask, under what circumstances is it possible to determine that they are wrong?[85]

This problem of addressivity, as it pertains to the academic study of Indigenous literatures, is both urgent and extremely difficult. One of the reasons Simpson's work on ethnographic refusal has been so important for scholars of Indigenous literatures, or so it seems to me, is that it puts the problem of addressivity front and center by relating the problem of "literary sovereignty" to the question of what (as Simpson puts it) "maybe I will tell you to your face."[86] Whomever Indigenous literatures might be thought to address "in theory," it is imperative to acknowledge Indigenous communities' collective agency in determining how their cultural patrimony circulates and whom it addresses. Perhaps some Indigenous literature "belongs to the public," as the New Critics liked to say.[87] But not all of it, and not all in the same way.

From Addressivity to Answerability

Because our books belong to the public . . . do our persons? Do our lives?
—ELIZABETH BARRETT BROWNING, LETTER TO MARY HOWITT (1856)

"Now let us listen to the Text," Occom says in the Good Samaritan sermon,

> Thou Shalt Love thy Neighbour as thy Self,— Harke ye! Who is this, that Speakes? . . . It is the Eternal Jehovah, that Speekes. But who, does he Speak to, is there anyone in this g[rea]t Congregation, that he is Speaking to? has he any business with any of us? has he any Power or Authority so to speak to us? take notice of that Word, Thou: it is in the Singular Number, it is to every individual of us, to one as much as nother. . . . Thou Shalt Love thy Neighbour; thou old man, thou old woman, thou middle Aged man, thou middle aged Woman, thou Young man, thou Young Woman, thou Boy, thou Girl . . . and who dares to Say? that this Command does not include me, I am out of the Question, he is not my God, I do not own him, and therefore he has no Business with me; but I take it for granted, that every one, who is grown to Years of Some understanding, will readyly own, that this Command is to them, from their God, and will approve it as most Reasonable Command.[88]

I still remember the moment I first read these words. They made me feel involved with the language of scripture in a way that I—a nonreligious person eating a salad, at the time, in a midtown Manhattan cafeteria—was not prepared for. I was struck in particular by Occom's rhetorical question: "Who dares to say . . . I do not own him?" If you like the idea of loving your neighbor as yourself, in other words, then how can you not also like the person who came up with that idea, or at least gave it new life—which in this case, it occurred to me, meant Jesus; but didn't it also mean Occom himself?

Occom, a sort of Bakhtinian *avant la lettre*, was an astute observer—and manipulator—of language's remarkable power to find addressees. But he was also sensitive to how utterances' addressivity, their way of "turning to someone," can create new power dynamics on an interpersonal level. In the passage just cited, Occom describes a situation in which those who find themselves addressed by an utterance ("*Thou* Shalt Love thy Neighbour . . .") become newly accountable, ethically and/or spiritually, to that utterance's speaker, someone who *wanted* to address them. Yet, as I have suggested, while a Bakhtinian approach to addressivity can help specify the kind of problem we are dealing with when we ask to what extent Occom's writings "belong to the public," such an approach has a harder time accounting for the impact of intentionality on interpersonal relations. It *mattered* to Occom that Jesus intended to address all human beings when he said "Thou shalt love thy neighbor as thyself"; and, it seems to me, it should matter to Occom's present-day readers that he himself intended to be "neighbourly" to humankind at large; again: "Every man & woman that we have any Knowledge of, is our Neighbour, yea them that we never had any acquaintance with are our Neighbours, and we are their Neighbours or ought to be."[89]

Since it mattered that Occom wanted to be "Neighbours" with everyone, and since Bakhtin doesn't have much to say about whether (or how) addressivity can be thought of as contingent upon intentionality, more theoretical resources are needed in order to specify the ethical and political implications of the way Occom's writings address modern readers. Here I find it useful to expand the analysis of addressivity to accommodate what Stanley Cavell called "answerability." Cavell—who in the second half of the twentieth century developed a distinctive approach to ordinary language philosophy, and who is perhaps most widely admired today for his essays on Shakespeare and black-and-white romantic comedies, and who wrote nary a word about

Indigenous peoples—might seem like a strange person to invoke in this context. But he shouldn't be. After all, as I showed earlier, the idea of "acknowledgment" that Cavell developed in a series of important essays in the 1960s and 1970s has already made a significant impact on political-theoretical discussions of the politics of recognition; and these political theoretical discussions overlap in important ways with efforts by Indigenous studies scholars to theorize refusal, and other everyday practices of social interaction, as assertions of Indigenous sovereignty.[90] More to the point, Cavell is relevant to people who analyze Indigenous-authored texts, and the way those texts mediate relationships between Indigenous writers and the people who read them, because Cavell developed a rich albeit idiosyncratic philosophical vocabulary for discussing how interpersonal relationships transform participants' lives. Cavell's writings on acknowledgment, which influenced Markell's distinction between acknowledgment and recognition, exemplify this vocabulary: thus "acknowledgment goes beyond knowledge," he writes, "in its requirement that I *do* something or reveal something on the basis of that knowledge."[91] So do his comments on "answerability."

In *The Claim of Reason*, Cavell uses the term "answerability" to analyze the relations of interpersonal obligation that get created or reproduced when one person identifies themselves as *belonging* to some person or thing (or vice versa). Cavell illustrates how this happens when he identifies himself as belonging to a nation:

> I recognize the society and its government, so constituted, as mine; which means that I am answerable not merely to it, but for it. So far, then, as I recognize myself to be exercising my responsibility for it, my obedience to it is obedience to my own laws; citizenship in that case is the same as my autonomy; the polis is the field within which I work out my personal identity and it is the creation of (political) freedom.[92]

Cavell's idea of answerability has a good deal in common with the Bakhtinian notion of addressivity, that feature of an utterance which gives it the power of "turn[ing] to someone" in the context of a determinate "area of human activity." But it comes built in with a bit more ethical texture. Merging these two concepts together, we might say that the addressivity of texts has the power to make people "answerable for" others or "answerable to" them, or both.

Note how, in Cavell's example, the person identifying some nation's laws as "theirs" (we might think of someone who feels themself "addressed" by a given state's Constitution, say) becomes answerable both to and for those laws. There are other cases, however, in which finding oneself addressed by someone or some text does *not* make one answerable both to and for that person or text. In the passage from Occom's Good Samaritan sermon that I cited a moment ago, the addressivity of scripture creates answerability relations that are universal, but only in one direction. Occom's claim is that no human being can deny being answerable *to* God, once they have experienced the addressivity ("*thou*") of his Word. But, on his understanding, no human being can be understood as answerable *for* God, unless that human being happens to be Jesus (who happens to be God, anyway).[93] Be that as it may, Occom's sermon powerfully points toward a hypothesis about addressivity that I find very helpful in thinking about the scholarly interpretation of Indigenous-authored texts: there is *no addressivity without answerability* (if you hear God's word, per Occom, you are bound to become answerable to God) but just because someone feels addressed by a text, that doesn't make that person answerable *for* the person who wrote it. Let me make this hypothesis, and its bearing on literary-interpretive method, more concrete by considering another example.

One way of describing Edward Said's *Orientalism* is as a critique of the scholarly fantasy of "owning" texts written in another society, in precisely Cavell's sense of owning: of making oneself answerable both to and for the "Other." Orientalists believed that a reader could unpack a text so assiduously—fulfilling all the scholarly obligations entailed by being "answerable to" one's source—as to become "answerable for" that text. Hence the "Orientalist ability to reconstruct and reformulate the Orient, given the Orient's inability to do so for itself."[94] Although Said himself did not put the point in quite such polemical terms, it seems fair to me to say that the Orientalist philologists whose work he so patiently unpacks were utterly mystified about who they were answerable to and for. They were answerable to empire and the academic institutions it supported (and vice versa), but the way they read "the Orient" led them to forget that. They convinced themselves that they were answerable in the first instance to the texts they were reading, and that they had achieved a mind-meld with the Orient that empowered them to answer for it—or, as Cavell puts it, to "own" it.

This book is a *reading,* written by a reader for other readers to whom I know (or suppose) I am answerable. I also feel answerable to Occom in a complicated way that has been shaped by colonialism; and I hope my response (or answer) to his writings encourages other readers to reflect on the way Indigenous literatures create and reproduce relations of answerability that might or might not involve them. I am answerable for everything I have written here, but not for Occom or his people, who have always spoken for themselves.

PART II

CHAPTER III

A Theology of Land and Peoplehood

The question of how Samson Occom reconciled his religious beliefs with his commitment to Indigenous self-determination has long been something of a puzzle. The puzzle can be posed most sharply in terms of sovereignty. In his struggles for justice, liberation, and cultural revitalization as a member of the Mohegan and Brothertown nations, Occom was clearly a defender of Indigenous sovereignty. But Occom also believed that God was the "great Sovereign of the Universe"; he wrote in his execution sermon for Moses Paul that it was "altogether of God's sovereign good pleasure" or "free grace" to give "mercy *in this life*" or in the hereafter, a sentiment that recurs throughout his writings.[1] How did the sovereignty of Native nations relate to God's sovereign authority over human beings? Occom spent many years thinking about this question and eventually arrived at a way of answering it that focused on Native peoples' relationship to land.

The Mohegan nation where Occom grew up was and remains a sovereign Indigenous people with its own intellectual traditions respecting land and peoplehood. Even as Occom identified strongly with these traditions and sought to preserve them, his surviving writings also discuss Indigenous politics from a broadly Christian vantage. Like other Christians of his era, Occom saw the Bible as an important source of historical knowledge and moral guidance about nations and their destiny. He was especially interested in what the Bible had to say about the relationship between peoples and the territories where they resided. Like other Christians of his era, too, Occom had to engage in a certain amount of theological conjecture (and sometimes speculation) in order to gain clarity on this matter. After all, the Bible says nothing explicit about the Americas or the Native peoples living there. In order to make the Bible relevant to the various white, Black, and Indigenous peoples of colonial North America, its eighteenth-century readers, no matter what nation they came from, had to do some creative interpreting.

The interpretation most often advanced by white New Englanders focused on the book of Exodus and the idea of a "chosen" nation. A chosen nation was one picked out by God, from among all the peoples of the world, and appointed to live in a specific place. From the seventeenth century through Occom's lifetime, white New Englanders argued that God had chosen *them* to live along the Eastern Seaboard of North America. English ministers read Exodus, in which God leads Israel out of Egyptian bondage into a new life in the "promised land" of Canaan, as a foretelling of their own godly mission to the New World, or the "New English Israel," as they sometimes called it.[2]

This interpretation of Exodus as a foretelling of New England chosenness seemed deeply problematic to Occom. For one thing, the idea that New England was a "promised land" akin to Canaan put Indigenous people in a subordinate political position akin to that of the Canaanites in the book of Exodus: they were bit players at best, relevant to history "only as the people Yahweh removes from the land in order to bring the chosen people in," as Robert Warrior puts it.[3] But the deeper problem was with the idea of national "chosenness" itself. Just because God appointed Israel as his chosen nation in the book of Exodus, Occom observed, that did not mean that any chosen nations existed in the present day. On the contrary, "where ever the Gospel of Jesus Christ is receivd by any People," as he put it in one sermon, "they are the People of God."[4] That English people fancied themselves "chosen," therefore, was a human fiction with no biblical basis. Moreover, Occom argued, it was a *gratuitous* fiction, since the history of Native nations proved that a political community did not need the idea of "chosen" peoplehood—or even the Bible itself—in order to have either sovereignty or a divinely appointed relationship to a specific homeland.[5] From the beginning of his life to the end, Occom refused to appropriate the concept of chosenness as a biblical basis for Indigenous sovereignty. He opted instead for a noncovenantal conception of Indigenous nationhood whose central premise was that God "planted" Indigenous peoples on the North American continent and intended for them to thrive there as autonomous communities. The traditional understandings of land and peoplehood that they had developed prior to colonization remained valid, no matter what the New England colonists said about chosenness. Native peoples' special relationship to "this great Continent" was approved by God, and no act of colonization or conquest could abrogate it.

Reconstructing Occom's theological views and the reasoning behind them is not a small task. For one thing, since Occom did not write systematic discourses on theology (very few eighteenth-century ministers did), his arguments on these topics are spread out across a wide range of writings: mostly sermons but also petitions, letters, and even hymns. For another, Occom's theological arguments about national sovereignty and chosenness (what is known today as "covenant" or "federal theology") can be appreciated only if they are properly contextualized as interventions in specific intellectual debates taking place among religious thinkers in New England. When Occom's scattered theological arguments are properly contextualized, however, a remarkably coherent picture emerges: a theology of land and peoplehood purpose-built for Northeast Native communities trying to reassert their sovereignty against English (and later U.S.) Zionism and exceptionalism—claims made by Anglo-Americans, in other words, that North America belonged to them and they to North America in a cultural, religious, and/or political sense.

Before providing an overview of Occom's peculiar approach to covenant theology, there are some scholarly misconceptions that need to be dealt with: above all, the notion that Occom did actually think of Native nations as "chosen" by God. According to the historians who take this view, Occom was a kind of "Indian Moses" who sought to liberate Coastal Algonquian communities from colonial oppression by advocating a new, ethnonational identity defined by "racial exclusivity," English-style agriculture, and an "otherworldly" piety focused on salvation in the hereafter.[6] Like the Exodus narrative itself, this "Mosaic" interpretation of Occom's life stresses the cultural, political, and religious *discontinuities* between the forms of life that obtained among God's "chosen" nation before migration (along the Eastern Seaboard) and after migration (at Brothertown). Ultimately, however, this Exodus-inspired way of describing Occom and the Brothertown movement rests on shaky historical foundations. Occom never called Brothertown a "chosen" nation, and the forms of racial exclusion, land cultivation, and religion practiced there were not as discontinuous with prior Coastal Algonquian practices as historians have made them out to be. The fact that the Exodus narrative continues to play such a large role in Occom scholarship says more about the continued preeminence of that narrative in Anglophone culture than it does about Occom or his people.

Methodologically speaking, this chapter approaches Occom's theology from a nonconfessional and indeed nontheistic perspective. Ultimately, I am less interested in what Occom's theology has to say about God than I am in what it tells us about him and his communities. For readers who may be interested in the latter topics but uninterested in theology, it is worth remembering that in the eighteenth century the line between theology and what we now call "political theory" was much blurrier than it is today, and much the same can be said about the boundary between theology and "history," understood as a genre of writing or domain of scholarly inquiry. Indeed, Occom's theological writings constitute a rich and largely unexplored repository of argumentation about history and politics. They explain how God's Providence relates to the disposition of political power in colonial North America and clarify, more broadly, Native Americans' unique place in world history.

Reading Occom's theological writings also reveals a lot about the distinctively Indigenous perspective he brought to the act of Bible-reading: how, above all, he assembled a mini-canon of scriptural passages that he found useful for advancing his anticolonial political priorities. This mini-canon, as we will see, focused largely on the book of Genesis and the letters of Paul, especially the parts of those texts that emphasized the abundance of God's unspoiled creation and the innate morality of non-Christian "heathens." Occom was unusual among his ministerial contemporaries in making anticolonial arguments—or, indeed, political arguments of any kind—based on Genesis and the letters of Paul. This fact has been broadly overlooked by historians, among whom Occom has "seldom [been] described as a sophisticated theologian," as Margaret Connell Szasz observes.[7] Before exploring some of the ins and outs of Occom's central theological arguments, more needs to be said about where this stereotype about Occom's "[un]sophisticated" theology came from and how it has survived down to the present day.

This chapter is divided into three relatively free-standing sections. These can be read independently of one another according to the reader's interest; when read in succession, they are intended to provide a reconstruction of the central arguments of Occom's theology of land and peoplehood, his motivations for making those arguments, and their broader historical significance. The first section traces the emergence of the "Indian Moses" stereotype back to the writings of William DeLoss Love, who argued in his 1899 biography that Occom dutifully took on board the widespread colonial assumption that all nations worth taking pride in were chosen nations. This mistaken view has been taken up by more recent historians seeking to shore up the claim that Occom's approach to land-use, political belonging, and religion represented a new departure in the history of Northeast Native sovereignty. The second section explores Occom's rejection of Indigenous chosenness and, indeed, the entire New England tradition of triumphalist covenant theology. The last shows that, insofar as Occom's idea of Indigenous peoplehood was informed by the Bible, it was less by the book of Exodus than by Genesis, particularly that book's depictions of the earth's self-renewing abundance.

An "Indian Moses"?

The assumption that Occom thought Indigenous Americans were a "chosen" nation dates back to his first biographer, William DeLoss Love, who never seems to have entertained the possibility that Occom understood his people in any other way. Occom, says Love, was "neither a logician nor a theologian," but he dutifully "understood and held with intellectual vigor and clearness the principal doctrines of the Christian faith."[8] In the eighteenth-century New England context, one of these "doctrines" was that any nation worth belonging to must be a "chosen" nation—or so Love assumed, not entirely without justification. To be a leader of one's people, colonial ministers widely agreed, was to be like Moses, who had delivered Israel from thralldom under Pharoah. And so, Love concluded, Occom was properly understood as an "Indian Moses [who] brought his people into their promised land."[9]

The thralldom from which Occom delivered his people was, on Love's account, that of being "savage." At stake in Occom's life story was the question of whether his people could share in the American dream of freedom: "whether the Indian is capable of being permanently established in the ways of civilized life; and . . . Christianized, brought into church estate, educated in industrial pursuits, invested with rights in the land which supports him, and trusted with the responsibilities of government."[10] The Occom portrayed by Love is accordingly keen to set aside "old tribal relations" and customs in favor of a more "democratic" collective life based on what Love repeatedly calls "industry."[11] Love, a Progressive-era minister from South Hadley, Massachusetts, believed that a hard day's work was good for the soul, no matter one's calling. He therefore found it quaint but also somewhat bewildering that Occom "seems to have thought" that Indigenous peoples' future "depended in large measure upon [their] relation to the land upon which [they] lived." Love was preoccupied with Occom's inscrutably intransigent commitment to farming—a perfectly valid livelihood, inasmuch it was an "industrial pursuit" that enabled people to "obtain a living from the soil."[12] But why Occom's single-minded insistence on forms of Native economic life that necessitated such strong connection with the land? Love intuited that some other, noneconomic source of value must have been involved for this Indian Moses, but he was not able to put his finger on precisely what it was. For him it was presumably one of the "defects of his race" on account of which "the Indian . . . race itself [was] gradually dying away toward the setting sun."[13]

While Love's racism and "savagism" are upsetting, my purpose in offering the forgoing summary is not to smear a work which has often proved useful to Indigenous communities. It is, rather, to note the way Love uses the image of an "Indian Moses" as a shorthand for Occom's prophetic, law-giving vision of what Indigenous peoplehood would amount to for the unprecedentedly "civilized" and "Christianized" people of Brothertown. A fundamental assumption of his argument is that Occom thought that older Northeast Native understandings of peoplehood and land needed to be replaced, or at least buttressed with a new, biblical rationale. Love made this assumption for very bad reasons having to do with Native Americans' purported savagery, reasons that no modern scholar endorses. Yet the assumption itself has proved surprisingly durable; and it has motivated more recent scholars not just to reproduce the mistaken image of Occom as an "Indian Moses," but also to overstate, as Love did, the extent to which his ideas about Indigenous peoplehood were untribal and untraditional, particularly with respect to ancestral understandings of land. According to David Silverman, the founding families of Brothertown "met almost every demand the whites imposed on them: they adopted Christianity, literacy, the English language, male plow agriculture, fences, and democratic government."[14] They did this under the tutelage of Occom, who "like Moses leading his people out of Egypt," ushered his people into a brave new form of sovereignty in which their daily lives would look a lot like those of the colonists.[15] But even though this new form of life required relinquishing traditional lifeways, Silverman argues, Occom and the other members of the Brothertown movement didn't see themselves as *politically* assimilated. Why? Because the biblical concept of chosenness, or what Brad Jarvis calls the "tenets of Christian brotherhood," furnished new "ideological foundations" for Indigenous peoplehood that set the new community apart *both* from Coastal Algonquian families who stayed behind, and from the Anglo-Americans who continually crowded their borders.[16]

But how much of a departure from pre-Christian forms of Indigenous belonging was this new form of Christian solidarity, exactly? In their descriptions of the new form of peoplehood Occom helped bring about, Silverman and Jarvis train their focus on Occom's ideas about race and agriculture, or what Jarvis (echoing Love) calls "industriousness." According to Silverman, Occom was a law-giver: his leadership centered on a "racial code" that would allow the Brothertown founders to realize the "utopian dream of transforming Native people into God's chosen ones."[17] Jarvis leans less heavily on the Exodus narrative in his account of Brothertown's founding, but, like Love and Silverman, insists that Occom's leadership entailed a radical reorganization of daily life through "the adoption of Anglo-American agriculture, believing that this practice would promote economic self-sufficiency in what had become an English marketplace."[18]

To be clear, both Silverman and Jarvis get a lot right in their discussions of the Brothertown movement. Racial purity was most definitely a preoccupation of Occom and other Brothertown founders, and so was farming. The aim of their arguments, however, is not merely to identify race and farming as important concerns. It is also to show that Occom understood race and farming in ways that *differed fundamentally from Mohegans who did not join the Brothertown movement* and, moreover, that he "saw himself" (per Silverman) as bringing about a new departure in Northeast Native peoplehood because of the innovative way in which he approached these issues.[19] It is by pursuing these two further aims that Silverman and Jarvis inadvertently carry forward Love's assumption that Occom thought traditional Northeast Native forms of belonging were inadequate. Yet a careful reading of the sources calls into question whether this assumption is actually supported by the historical record.

In support of their claims that Occom propagated a new conception of Indigenous peoplehood, Silverman and Jarvis both cite a series of Mohegan petitions and colonial pronouncements drafted in the 1770s concerning a long-running dispute among tribal members about the management of their lands. These documents are the most important evidence that survives attesting to intra-Mohegan disputes over land use and race during the crucial period in which the Brothertown movement coalesced, and they are therefore worth some attention here.

The disagreement in question unfolded between two factions of Mohegans who had taken opposing sides in the Mason land case, a complex, decades-long legal battle over tribal lands that divided the nation in two. The first of these parties sought to defend the claim of Ben Uncas III and his successors to the Mohegan sachemship, on the grounds that they were the legal heirs to authority over tribal lands by virtue of their lineal descent from the seventeenth-century sachem Uncas I. The second party, to which Occom belonged, sought to reestablish sovereignty over territories that had been put under the guardianship of the English settler John Mason in the seventeenth century and accused Ben Uncas III and his supporters of misappropriating tribal land and revenue in collusion with Connecticut Colony.[20] In 1771, after years of delay, a London court finally settled this dispute in favor of the former party. Yet the tribe remained divided and the sachemship remained unfilled, having been effectively "outlawed," according to some historians, by Connecticut Colony.[21]

Amid this turmoil, Zachary Johnson, a supporter of Ben Uncas III, sent a series of memorials, at least seven in the years 1773–1782, to the General Assembly of Connecticut Colony complaining about the conduct of people associated with the Mason party. In the first of these memorials, from May 1774, he wrote that

> since the Death of their late Sachem Ben Uncas, who died about 4 years ago, the Tribe have remained in an unsettled State, and many Difficulties & Disputes have arisen among them both with regard to that internal Policy and also with regard to the Possession and Improvement of their Lands & the Distributions of their Rents and many Interlopers from other Tribes & Straggling Indians & Molattos have crowded themselves in upon said Lands, whereby many Difficulties & Disputes have arisen . . . [22]

In response to various follow-up queries returned to Johnson by the General Assembly, which wanted to ascertain the identity of the "Interlopers" he was referring to, Johnson forwarded to the Colony "A List of Heads of Family now living in Mohegan who are not properly Mohegan" in October 1774. The list consisted of members of the Mason Party including "Samson Occum."[23]

What exactly do these documents reveal about the different approaches to land use and peoplehood that were dividing Mohegans in the 1770s? First of all, they reveal that Zachary Johnson had a strong personal and political animus against Occom, a leader of the Mason party. This implies that his writings on the tribe's internal affairs should be taken with a grain of salt, not as the expression of an unproblematically "traditional" understanding of Mohegan attitudes toward land or peoplehood, as they have been taken by Silverman, Jarvis, and others.[24]

Johnson's memorials also indicate that the tribe's disagreement over land was primarily about (1) *occupancy*, or who was using it, and (2) *revenue*, or who was making money from "Rents," and much less about (3) *agriculture*, or the way the land was being cultivated. Let's explore each of these issues, as they arose at Mohegan in the 1770s, in a bit more detail.

"many Interlopers from other Tribes & Straggling Indians & Molattos"

In response to Johnson's concern about Mohegan being overrun with "interlopers," the General Assembly appointed a committee to investigate; they visited Mohegan in the summer of 1774 and reported that "it is Difficult to find out who they are . . . they having no Records to find out their Genealogy and are very Differing in the Acc[oun]ts . . . and It is very Difficult to Distinguish between the whole blood and the part blood. We cannot find they have any internal civil polity among them but seem to be in a state of nature."[25] As numerous scholars have argued, this back and forth between Johnson and the General Assembly indicates that the determination of tribal membership through "blood"—and, by extension, the allocation of tribal resources along racial lines—was becoming increasingly important to both tribe and Colony from the 1770s forward.[26] This was largely a consequence of the crisis of legitimacy and political authority precipitated by the Mason case and the factional dispute over Ben Uncas III's succession. It is particularly telling that the racialization of intra-Mohegan politics, as reflected in these exchanges from the 1770s, coincided with Johnson's solicitation of closer supervision by Colonial authorities. Johnson's expectation was clearly that representing intra-Mohegan disputes as racial disputes *to* Connecticut Colony would work to the advantage of his faction; later, Occom himself would make a similar calculation when he complained to New York Governor George Clinton that "Mixtures or Molattoes" were living at Brothertown illegally.[27] As Amy Den Ouden argues, racializing intratribal politics—and, above all, stigmatizing people who were (or who were associated with) "Negroes" and "Molattoes"—was a way for individuals and groups to "jockey for internal political authority or an 'improved' standing with the Connecticut government" throughout the period in question.[28] Yet colonial authorities could hardly be objective adjudicators of Indigenous racial identity, since the very process of racialization worked to the settler state's advantage. This is apparent in the report by the committee appointed to look into Johnson's 1774 complaints. As Den Ouden observes, what most clearly proved to the Colony that the Mohegans were living in a "state of nature" was their lack of administrative oversight over their own "blood."[29] The petition thus reflects the increasing centrality of racial categories to the governance of Indigenous lives, at the tribal level as well as that of the settler state, not just at Mohegan or Brothertown but throughout the British Atlantic.

With all this in mind, Silverman's proposal that political belonging at Brothertown, but not Mohegan, was defined by what he calls a "race code" is somewhat obscure.[30] The phrase may refer to the final sentence of the 1774 deed by which the Oneida Nation granted the original Brothertown tract to the "New England Indians and there Posterity for Ever Without Power of Alienation . . . with this Particular Clause or Reservation that the same shall not be Possessed by any Persons Deemed of the said Tribes Who are Descended from or have Intermixed with Negroes and Mulattoes."[31] But this deed, with its condition respecting racial exclusivity, was penned by Guy Johnson, the British superintendent of Indian affairs, not Occom. It may well be that Occom assented to this provision, at least tacitly. His letters indicate that he sought to enforce it on one occasion in the 1780s—although it is unclear whether this reflected his own preferences, his acquiescence to the terms of the Oneida deed, or some combination of the two.³² But there is no evidence that Occom sought to introduce further racial restrictions of his own, let alone a new regime of "racial exclusivity" that (per Silverman) this "Indian Moses" devised for Northeast Native communities when he saw that "customary practices . . . were unable to meet their needs."³³ In fact, as I argued in chapter 1, Occom's writings from this period reflected a profound commitment to Indigenous social customs, a claim which finds further support in the documents under present consideration.

We have seen how, in their report responding to Zachary Johnson's 1774 memorial, the committee appointed by the Connecticut General Assembly was unable (or chose not to) corroborate his claims about Mohegan being overrun by "Interlopers" and "Strangers." As the committee's earlier-cited allusion to "Differing . . . Accounts" suggests, it was hard to gather accurate information about who, exactly, was living at Mohegan at the time. The committee's findings were was likely biased by the fact that, during their visit, they had a long talk with Occom, who probably gave them a very different point of view on things.³⁴ In fact, as Occom's correspondence from the period indicates, he was personally hosting many of these "Interlopers" in his home. As he wrote to John Moorhead in April 1773, "I have had a great Number of Visiters Since I got home from Boston I had forty at once in the beginning and I have now 12 with me from Long Il"; and again, to Susanna Wheatley in September, "My Visitors Continue as thick as ever . . . I expect a great Company of Indians this Week from Several Tribes."³⁵ It is apparent from these letters that Occom was working hard to encourage mobility among Coastal Algonquian communities surrounding Mohegan. Why he was doing this is not entirely clear. One possible explanation is that he wanted families from across the region to come to Mohegan in order to discuss the Brothertown movement.³⁶ Another is that many Native people in southern New England and Long Island were struggling to make ends meet, and he thought it was his duty to take care of them. In any case, his hospitality was consistent with his commitment to the customary practices of the "Indian heathen in this great Continent," who are "very Liberal among themselves, and also to Strangers," and who "will yet Divide what little they have if there is but a mouth full a Piece."³⁷ This was clearly a time when Occom himself was putting these traditional lifeways into practice.

To be sure, Occom's extravagant "neighborliness" during the early 1770s did require him to do some extra work on his farm. "I am obliged to

Contrive a little about raising Some thing on the Land," he wrote to the Moor's Charity School trustees in November 1773, "for I have a Large Family and Constant Visiters as ever."[38] Zachary Johnson surely took notice of all the planting taking place around Occom's house at the top of Mohegan Hill. In petitions sent to the General Assembly after 1774, Johnson made much of the fact that "Strangers" were "plant[ing] corn without paying anything." But there is no evidence that Occom's conduct disturbed him because he was experimenting with nontraditional farming practices. Quite the contrary: "nor," Johnson wrote in another memorial, "do [we] think if said Foreign Indians and white people are allowed to go on in the manner they do at present they will leave your Memorialists an Acre of land to plant or a stick of Wood to Make a Fence."[39] Johnson's complaint was not that Occom and the "Strangers" he countenanced were planting and improving the land, but rather "that they take up more land than they have right to."[40] To be clear, there is no reason to doubt the sincerity or veracity of this claim. In fact, we have every reason to believe that Johnson's concerns were valid. My aim is to clarify what was at stake in the dispute over land use at Mohegan, not to come down on one side or the other. And what the documentary evidence shows is that both parties saw the dispute as being about the allocation of scarce resources, not about who was using the land in the most traditional way.

"Money is almighty now a Days"

A similar point can be made about rents. In his memorials to the General Assembly, Johnson frequently attested that, ever since the death of the last sachem, rents were not going where they were supposed to. His plea to the Colony was to restore something like the old system, in which the sachem personally managed rent revenues in a manner agreeable to the Colony. "By such Strangers living on said Land," Johnson wrote in a memorial penned during the Revolutionary War, "they Cunningly Evade paying any Taxes, toward the support of Government, or the Expenses of the present war," a thinly veiled suggestion that if the General Assembly followed his advice, it would work out to their advantage.[41] This was a canny line of argument since, as Johnson knew, Connecticut Colony still harbored a grudge against Occom and the rest of John's Town for siding against the

Colony in the Mason case. As the years went by, Johnson grew more assertive of his own side's interest. Writing to the governors of Connecticut (now a state) in 1782, Johnson

> humbly submit[ted] it to the wise Consideration of this Assembly whether the said [Mohegans] . . . should not be Rated according to their Ability for the use and benefit of this State . . . and your Petitioners further inform the Honorable house that most of these Foreign Indians were the greatest Advocates for the Late case Between this Government and the Masons . . . at least make them pay something to keep them more in Subjection, for the benefit of the State and also for the true Mohegan tribe of Indians. . . . Old Councillor Johnson wishes Honble Assembly would be pleased . . . if the Land is to be Let out it may be on Shares that your petitioner may receive half of the profits and not to be any more Leased out as has been formerly practised.[42]

The "former" practices to which Johnson here objects were probably those that had been put in place back in 1774 when the General Assembly had instructed the tribe's overseers to consider "money due for rents of land" as a "Common and undivided interest" of the tribe.[43] This 1774 ruling probably had Occom's support, in light of 1778 Mohegan memorial written in his hand announcing that "it has been agreed Unanimously heretofore once and again . . . that the Money does belong to the Whole Tribe, and it shall be dispos'd of acordingly for the Benefit of the Whole."[44]

As I hope is clear by now, there was in practice very little that was "Unanimous" about Mohegan politics during the pivotal period leading up to the Brothertown migration. The documents that survive from both sides of the disputes of the 1770s reflect fiercely held and long entrenched political positions and thus do not describe events neutrally. But no matter how the disagreements are interpreted in historical hindsight, these documents are the best evidence that exists concerning how the parties involved understood Mohegan affairs at the time. And from both sides' point of view, their disagreement had to do with *money* as much as it had to do with land. As Paul Grant-Costa has shown, members of "Ben's party" including Zachary Johnson assumed that tribal revenue would best be managed by a sachem because they thought "heredity was the most important feature of a leader."[45] This helps explain why, according to research by Melissa Tantaquidgeon Zobel, Johnson was signing documents as "regent" of Noah Uncas as late as 1787.[46] Occom's ideas about what to do with tribal revenues are somewhat harder to characterize. What he said, time and again, was that rents collected from leases on tribal land should be "dispos'd . . . acordingly for the Benefit of the Whole."[47] Yet the very idea of monetizing tribal land in the form of rent also made Occom uneasy. In a 1773 letter to his friend Samuel Buell commenting on the settlement of the Mason dispute on the Colony's side ("I believe it is a pure Favour," he said of the verdict, meaning the English were taking care of their own), he wrote that "Indians will never Stand a good Chance with the English, in their Land Controversies because they are very Poor they have no Money, Money is almighty now a Days, and the Indians have no Learning, no Wit nor Counting the English have all."[48] Until such time as Mohegans should have the same commercial acumen (and access) as white people, the decks were bound to be stacked against them, at least when Indigenous claims to land and revenue were adjudicated by colonial courts.

But even if his people were to acquire the requisite "Learning," "Wit," and "Counting"—even if all Mohegans became the eighteenth-century equivalent of MBAs—it seems doubtful that Occom would have wanted them to lease their lands according to whatever financial incentives could be found on the open market. "We never were ripe yet for Leasing," he wrote from Brothertown in 1792, "even to this Day . . . and when ever we Shall be ripe for leasing, it must be done in Union and good agreament of the Whole Town."[49] The people of Brothertown would be ready to lease, in other words, when they did so *as a community*, not as private individuals, and with the common interest in mind. This hardly conforms to the received scholarly image of Occom as an "industrious" agriculturalist trying to "accommodate Anglo-American notions of private property" and self-sufficiency.[50] The idea that Occom championed "self-sufficiency" as a moral virtue is particularly incongruous with the evidence I have been examining from the 1770s. In his letters from this period, when so many visitors were crowding into his house, he never once expresses a wish that any of them be more self-sufficient. "We are dependent Creatures upon one to another," he said in one undated sermon; "the greatest of men Can't well live without the vulger Sort, and we, as Sotiable and Fellow Creatures, give and receive Benefets, one from another."[51] The idea of self-sufficiency was anathema to Occom's traditionalism and his theological outlook alike.

"and it was not Plowed nor dug up With a hoe"

Finally, there is the question of cultivation, or how Occom thought the land should be worked. For both Jarvis and Silverman, "Anglo-American agriculture" (or "male plow agriculture") features prominently in the list of innovations Occom supposedly introduced to Brothertown as a replacement for "customary" ways of relating to the land.[52] As mentioned earlier, this argument had previously been advanced by Love, whose commitment to the Protestant ethic (and, perhaps, social evolutionism) led him to champion the industriousness of Indigenous individuals wherever he found it. Yet Love also deserves credit for acknowledging that the value Occom assigned to farming was not quite reducible to what he called "industriousness," since it derived more fundamentally from the belief that his peoples' future "depended in large measure upon [their] *relation to the land* upon which [they] lived."[53] Love was also right to wonder whether Occom's not wholly industrious commitment to preserving this "relation" had something to do with his unrepressed attachment to precolonial Indigenous traditions. Unlike his brother-in-law and Brothertown cofounder David Fowler, Occom never actually attended the "charity school" operated by Eleazar Wheelock in Lebanon, whose students got a thoroughly English perspective on the moral and economic value of farming. Because of this, Love noticed (or thought he noticed) a subtle difference between Occom's attitude toward farming and that of Fowler, who spent several years at Wheelock's school and was thus better positioned to understand agriculture as a form of "industry."[54] Yet even the identification of Fowler as an Anglo-style industrialist only makes sense on a one-sided interpretation of the evidence. As Margaret Szasz observes, the teaching of agriculture at Wheelock's school was centered around Wheelock's own relatively well-planted and well-established farm.[55] His pupils learned to cultivate fields in the manner of English husbandmen, but these skills were not particularly useful in the forested settings where the students went to work as missionaries. "I design to come down next year after I have planted Corn and my Garden things come up," Fowler wrote to Wheelock from Oneida in 1766, "so that I may be able to tell my Children [i.e., Fowler's students] how they must manage the Garden in my Absence."[56] Fowler also reports suffering from "much Warry and Fatigue" as well as a "hungry belly."[57] Fowler was working the land for subsistence, not as a market-oriented "industry." Whether or not he learned "male plow agriculture" that could help him (or his students) achieve "economic self-sufficiency" in an "English marketplace" was, in practice, irrelevant.

It's worth reflecting for a moment on the occurrence of the word *garden* in this letter from Fowler; and on that word's absence from existing scholarship on land cultivation at Mohegan and Brothertown from the 1770s forward. By Occom and Fowler's day, horticulture had been part of Coastal Algonquian life for centuries. As a form of cultivation, traditional Northeast Native horticulture resembled "agriculture" in certain respects. Gardeners tended to cultivate the same crops—including maize, which had been grown in the northeast since at least 1100 CE—on the same plots of land for years at a time. What distinguished these planting practices from agriculture, Lucianne Lavin writes, was that "they were only one part of the economy, not its foundation."[58] This remained the case long after colonial contact. As Native peoples became increasingly imbricated in the colonial economy, they took on a range of new jobs, many of which involved wage labor.[59] Yet even as some Northeast Native individuals came to see their labor as a commodity, they did not necessarily think of their land in the same way. This was true even in the eighteenth century. As families like the Occoms and Fowlers found themselves forced to work smaller pieces of land more intensively, they remained "gardeners," both in the technical sense mentioned by Lavin, and according to their traditional self-understanding. On June 30, 1765, during his trip to England, Occom took a sailing trip down the Thames and saw vast tracts of land under cultivation between London and Gravesend. From the river, he wrote, there was "a fine Prospect . . . each Side of the River, flat Land, and very Fruitful, indeed it is like one Continued garden."[60] Occom was not just being fanciful here. His eyes were wide open to the human suffering he saw throughout England, including along this stretch of the Thames, where it was a "Maloncholy Sight . . . to See So many Malefactors Hung up in Irons by the River."[61] Traditional Coastal Algonquian forms of subsistence, not romantic whimsy, predisposed Occom and Fowler to see lands under cultivation as gardens, not farms.

With this in mind, consider Occom's description of the first harvest he witnessed at Brothertown in 1785. Visiting the one-acre plot of his Narragansett neighbor John Tuhy, Occom marveled at the size of the harvest, which had yielded "20 Bushels of good Corn 56 Bushels of Potatoes about 200 Heads of Cabage, and about 3 Bushels of Beans, and about 2 Bushels of Parsnips and Beats together; besides Cucumbers and Watermelons"; most remarkable of all, this abundance all came from "the Same ground, and it was not Plowd nor dug up With a Hoe, only leaves and Small Bushess were burnt on it and great many Logs ly on it now." This, Occom said, was "the best land I ever did see in all my Travils."[62] And that assessment must have had something to do with the fact that Tuhy, as Joanna Brooks observes, was working with the land in a traditional Coastal Algonquian way: burning the fields in the spring ("last May") so that the land could regenerate itself in time for harvest in the fall of the following year *without being intensively plowed*.[63] Occom contrasted Tuhy's techniques with the methods of cultivation being practiced just a few miles away at New Stockbridge, where the harvest had been good, but not quite as remarkable as what was happening on Tuhy's plot: "they Plowed up, and dug up good many Potatoes . . . one man got 3 skipples, and he planted them, and he has raised a fine passel of them."[64]

Although there is a risk of reading too much into this diary entry, it raises important questions about how Brothertown farmers (or gardeners) were actually working the land during the settlement's first years.[65] While historians have yet to ascertain whether there were proportionally more families plowing the land at Brothertown or New Stockbridge, it is apparent that Occom was delighted to find that his people were successfully practicing ancestral techniques of Coastal Algonquian horticulture.[66] As to Occom's opinions about the plowing happening at New Stockbridge, one can only speculate. Certainly he admired and respected the New Stockbridges enough to take up residence among them in 1791, after the renewed eruption of factionalism at Brothertown over the issue of leasing land to white people. But there is no evidence that he ever followed them in taking up—or recommending to others—plowing as a way of making a living. Of course, by 1791, the nearly seventy-year-old Occom, who had suffered from debilitating hip pain for decades, was at a stage of life where plowing was probably not his first choice. Even as a younger person, however, Occom seems to have had apprehensions about plowing and to have avoided doing it himself when possible. When he was living at Montauk in the 1750s, Occom paid someone else to plow his plot every year, despite being desperately short of money.[67] And at the end of his 1768 autobiography, when Occom recounts the story of a "poor Indian boy" who was beaten by his employer for no other reason than "because I am an Indian," he identifies plowing as the form of wage labor the boy had been forced to take up.[68] Perhaps Eleazar Wheelock even had Occom in mind when he wrote in

1771 of "the deep prejudices, so universally in the minds of the Indians, against their men's cultivating lands, or going into the business of husbandry."[69] More often than not, in any case, Occom used plowing to symbolize the various forms of psychological abjection and economic dependence to which Coastal Algonquian communities had been reduced by the settler economy.

When William DeLoss Love wrongly asserted that, according to Occom, Coastal Algonquians' "old tribal relations would [have to] be broken up" in order for them to survive as a "race," he cast a very long shadow over subsequent scholarship. I hope the foregoing analysis dispels some of that shadow, not necessarily by displacing it with a more authoritative account, but rather by demonstrating the need for a less unilinear, more multivocal approach to the question of how Occom and his kin conceptualized relations of land and peoplehood, especially during the pivotal decades of the 1770s and 1780s. Much remains obscure about the various approaches that the people of Mohegan and Brothertown took at this time toward problems of race, rents, and working on/with the land. But understanding these various perspectives requires setting aside the crude cultural dichotomies that get ascribed to Occom's communities when it is assumed that he was trying to deliver his people into a new form of peoplehood and a new relationship between nation and land. The picture of Occom as an "Indian Moses" was a stereotype created during an era when it was assumed that Indigenous Christians passively absorbed colonial conceptions of biblical chosenness. Yet nothing could be further from the truth.

The Never-Chosen

When Occom was growing up, he very likely heard English ministers espouse all manner of demeaning accounts about what the Bible purportedly said regarding Native Americans. In eighteenth-century New England, these accounts fell into two categories: there was the Canaanite interpretation, and the Israelite interpretation. The Canaanite interpretation was the most popular. It held that the Indigenous peoples of America were in a historical position akin to that of the Canaanites occupying the Promised Land on the eve of the Israelites' return. Their destiny, on this view, was to be displaced, eliminated, or colonized. This colonial likening of Native Americans to Canaanites saturated New England religious culture throughout the seventeenth and eighteenth centuries. Occom, presumably, was all too familiar with it.[70]

The Israelite interpretation was more recondite and mainly confined to scholarly circles until after Occom's lifetime, when it emerged in popular religious culture thanks largely to the Irish American historian James Adair.[71] This interpretation also dated back to the seventeenth century, when a minority of English Puritans (including the famous missionary John Eliot) proposed that Native Americans were descended from the "Lost Tribes" of Israel. In the eighteenth century, this Lost Tribes theory found an eminent advocate in the person of Jonathan Edwards. Edwards propounded the view that remnants of the Lost Tribes had been lured to North America by Satan, who was determined that they should never hear the good news contained in the New Testament. When the Lost Tribes got to America, they brought with them vestiges of the religious traditions of the old world: "heathen stories about gods and goddesses [that] were actually distortions of Hebrew counterparts."[72] Edwards's understanding of Indigenous religions was informed by the patristic interpretive methodology known as *prisca theologica*, which construed nonmonotheistic religions as degenerated versions of the "true religion" transmitted in biblical revelation.[73] While Edwards's thought left its mark on Occom in numerous ways (as we shall see), his views on the Lost Tribes were tucked away in manuscripts that were never published in his lifetime. It is unlikely that Occom knew about them, and he never mentions the Lost Tribes in any of his surviving writings.

In his mid- and late-career writings—those composed, roughly, after his break with his teacher Eleazar Wheelock in the late 1760s—Occom developed a unique theological approach to Indigenous history and religion that aligned with neither of these two interpretive camps. On his view, the situation of the North American "heathens" was to be understood from a perspective derived primarily from the Pauline epistles, instead of the Old Testament texts that English ministers tended to rely on when discussing the topic: Exodus, the Hebrew prophets, and the Psalms. According to Occom, following Paul, God reserved a special historical role for heathens or Gentiles in both the ancient and modern epochs, a role that the ministers and ideologues of his "chosen" nations (Israel and, later, New England) were predisposed to overlook. Arguing from his own experience as an Indigenous evangelical who refused to be assimilated to

Anglo-American lifeways, Occom, following Paul, argued that New World Gentiles were perfectly capable of accepting Christ without having to relinquish their preexisting traditions or nationalities. He also held that the purportedly "chosen" status of the New English Israel was much less significant than Anglo-Americans liked to believe and could even be a moral and political liability, insofar as the English took it to warrant the mistreatment and exploitation of people from non-elect communities.

Whether Occom drew on previous theologians in arriving at this highly unusual interpretation of Native Americans' place in history is unclear. The view of Native Americans as unchosen Gentiles was not wholly unprecedented in the Anglophone world, but it had never been more than a fringe position. This may have been because the New Testament, at least the parts Occom favored, made the Gentiles look *too good*. In Paul's letters, "heathens" or "Gentiles" are typically portrayed as virtuous in ways the chosen people are not because the former have the law of God "written in their hearts."[74] In seventeenth-century Rhode Island, this Pauline theme of virtuous heathenism characterizes certain writings by Roger Williams, who marveled at the quasi-Christian behavior of the Narragansetts among whom he lived, contrasting their justice and generosity to the corruption of his "chosen" English countrymen: "I have acknowledged amongst them an heart sensible of kindness, and have reaped kindnesse again from many," Williams wrote, "hence the Lord Jesus exhorts his followers to doe good for evil, for otherwise, sinners will do good for good."[75] Similar arguments were advanced by Quakers like George Fox and William Penn, who found in Native communities confirmation of their fundamental creed that God communicated directly with human beings via the Holy Spirit as apperceived by the "inner light" residing within each individual. In a tract entitled *The Heathens Divinity* (1671), published in London shortly after his first trip to America, Fox asked his English readers: "Now was there not something in these *Heathens* above your selves, who had no Scripture, and yet acknowledged God? Whereas you say, You had not known there had been a God, unless you had a Scripture to declare it to you: Neither indeed do you know him now, though you have Scripture."[76] This appeal of Fox's bears a certain resemblance to Occom's argument, developed in his Good Samaritan sermon and elsewhere, that the American "Heathen in general manifest more Humanity, than such degenerate Christians" as the English, who despite having access to God's scriptural commandments "take almanner of ways to hurt their Neighbours."⁷⁷ There is no concrete evidence, however, linking Occom to these relatively obscure (in New England, at least) Quaker teachings.

One precursor Occom might have drawn on, in comparing Native Americans to the Gentiles of Paul's letters, was his English friend and mentor from Long Island, the East Hampton minister Samuel Buell. Buell preached the sermon at Occom's ordination as a Presbyterian minister on August 29, 1759. At a climactic moment of his sermon, Buell drew attention to the eschatological significance of his friend's call to the ministry. "BEHOLD," Buell announced, with Occom in mind:

> The Wilderness and the solitary Place are glad, the Desert rejoices and blossoms as the Rose! The Gentiles see the Glory of the Lord . . . [while] the Jews train'd up for so many Ages, and by all Kind or Preparations for a Redeemer, reject him; and the Gentiles who were no Way prepared, receive him . . . Without any preparatory Dawn, the Light of the glorious Gospel is darted among the Gentiles, like a sudden Rush of Light in a cloudy and dark Day.⁷⁸

What Occom's ordination made plain was that God's grace had been extended to Native Americans: "heathens," as Buell and Occom both put it, "who were no way prepared" through prior acquaintance with God's law.⁷⁹ Finally, Buell said, "the Love [God] used to keep within Bounds"—that is, the favor that God used to reserve for the people of Israel and, in latter days, England and New England—had begun to pour across national boundaries to become the "Glory of the Universe."⁸⁰ Occom was living proof that the history of redemption had reached a critical new juncture in its progress toward the apocalypse.

Buell's description of Occom as an Indigenous "Gentile" who had "receive[d]" Christ, even as the "chosen" English spurned him, foreshadowed arguments that would later be made by Occom. But Occom pushed the comparison much further than Buell, developing it in ways that his teacher probably would have disapproved of. Buell, a beneficiary of English colonization who had settled into a prosperous living on the eastern end of Long Island, was not interested in using the New Testament to disrupt the secular political order. By the 1770s, Occom was: for him, the Gospel's power to effect spiritual and political change were all but inseparable. In order to see how he expressed this theologically, it is necessary to go back to the early days of Occom's education and say something more about the religious milieu he was brought up in.

"I was Born a Heathen and Brought up in In Heathenism till I was between 16 & 17 Years of age, at a Place Calld Mohegan in New London Connecticut." This sentence from Occom's 1768 autobiography tells us a great deal that is relevant to the way he would come to do theology. Note first the place: "a Place Calld Mohegan in New London Connecticut." This is a peculiar turn of phrase, since Mohegan was most definitely a separate town, roughly twelve miles from New London up the Thames River. It is likely that Occom wanted to play up Mohegan's proximity to New London in order to set his life story against the background of the famous revival of religion that took place there beginning in 1741, not long after Occom got interested in Christianity when he was "between 16 & 17 Years of age."[81]

The New London revival—retrospectively identified by historians as a pivotal episode in the Great Awakening—began in the winter of 1741 when the Pennsylvania minister Gilbert Tennent visited town, delivering "seven sermons in two days." This ushered in a wave of itinerant preaching that culminated in the bizarre bonfires of March 1743, in which the visiting preacher James Davenport burned a variety of supposedly heretical books and a smaller number of luxury goods (including a pair of his own breeches) in an auto-da-fé on the town wharf.[82]

It is worth taking seriously the possibility that Occom, a curious teenager living a few miles away, was personally present for one or both of these widely publicized visits by Tennent and Davenport, but it is impossible to be sure. In any case, the way Occom locates his birthplace indicates that he *wanted people to know* that he on hand for, or at least in the neighborhood of, New London's famous revival. This suggests that Occom was a pro-revival or "New Light" Christian, as commentators have long observed.[83] More than that, however, it indicates his willingness to associate himself with a particularly radical cadre of revivalists who were closely associated with Tennent and Davenport, and thus often disparaged in mid-eighteenth-century Connecticut as "enthusiasts." "Commentators used strong adjectives to describe the New London events," write Harry Stout and Peter Onuf: "they were 'wild,' 'extravagant,' and 'indecent.' The 'thronging multitudes' who participated in the carnage were 'mad men' consumed by their 'flaming zeal' and 'enthusiastic fury.'"[84] Occom was well aware that the New London revivalists had this reputation, but he also believed that revivalism and enthusiasm could be sharply distinguished from one another. He makes this clear later in his autobiography when he describes how, just before he took up the post of teacher to the Montauketts of eastern Long Island in 1751, a group of "Inthusiastical Exhorters from N England" had led his charges astray: "And being acquainted with the Enthusiasts in New England . . . I woud read Such passages of the Scriptures, as I thought woud confound their Notions, and I would come to them [i.e., the Montauketts] with all Authority, Saying, thus Saith the Lord, and by this means, the Lord was pleased to Bless my poor Endeavours, and they were reclaimd."[85] Subsequently, Occom writes, "there was a remarkable revival of religion among these Indians and many were hopefully Converted to the Saving knowledge of God in Jx."[86] Whereas Old Light critics of the New London revivals had decried them as expressions of enthusiasm, Occom here implies that enthusiasm is an obstacle to revivalism, not a cause of it. Those who participate in real revivals do so under the supervision of an "Authority" whose source is "the Scriptures." Occom's commitment to a rigorously disciplined form of hopeful—but not "Inthusiastical"—revivalism aligned him with a very specific theological position in 1760s Connecticut, a school of thought preoccupied with the "linking of a doctrine of divine sovereignty with the revivalist's demand that the sinner had the responsibility and the ability to repent now," as E. Brooks Holifield writes.[87] This was what was just then coming to be known as the "New Divinity."

New Divinity theology was, in many ways, an extension of the work of Jonathan Edwards. Most of the ministers who shaped the movement in its early years knew Edwards personally; most also studied at Yale, where Edwards cast a long shadow following his tutorship there in 1724–1726.[88] Like Edwards, the New Divinity ministers preached a religion of the heart (or "will") and sympathized with the revivals; most were friends and supporters of James Davenport, although almost everyone involved in the movement thought he had gone too far in New London, to the detriment of the New Light cause. One of the primary aims of the movement—an aim pursued in Occom's autobiography, as we have seen—was to specify how revivals could be theologically distinguished from enthusiasm. Another goal was to adapt and reinterpret Edwards's sometimes abstruse arguments for the purpose of public polemic. The most famous New Divinity theologians, such as Samuel Hopkins and Joseph Bellamy, engaged in heated pamphlet wars with such respected New England divines as Moses Mather and Jonathan Mayhew. More often than not, New Divinity polemic hewed carefully to positions staked out by Edwards, although those positions were elaborated in new and sometimes scandalous ways.[89]

Occom's first exposure to Edwardsean theology and the first stirrings of the New Divinity probably occurred between 1743 and 1747. During this period immediately following the New London revival, Occom lived in Lebanon, Connecticut, where he was tutored in reading, religion, and other topics by Eleazar Wheelock, another Yale graduate and a close associate of both Edwards and Davenport.[90] Wheelock himself played an important role in the emergence of the New Divinity, albeit one having more to do with education, publicity, and tireless itinerancy than it did with theological innovation *per se*.[91] During Occom's time in Lebanon, Wheelock was frequently in touch with all of the ministers who would come to be associated with the movement, including Hopkins, who was arguably its intellectual leader, and the Long Island preacher Samuel Buell, who became Occom's most important ministerial mentor after his move to Montauk in 1751.[92] Indeed, Wheelock's most important contribution to Occom's theological education may have been that of introducing him to these two future colleagues, both of whom made lasting impressions on Occom and on New Divinity thought more generally. Ultimately, the connections Occom formed with Buell and Hopkins in Lebanon would prove strong enough to outlast his relationship with Wheelock himself, which fell apart around 1770 following Wheelock's misappropriation of the funds Occom had raised for Moor's Indian Charity School.[93]

Nowhere is Occom's indebtedness to New Divinity theology, particularly the work of Hopkins, more apparent than in the sermon he delivered in 1772 at the execution of Moses Paul. Literary historians have long noted this text's deployment of tropes and themes that had been part of the Reformed sermonic tradition for decades and even centuries: the terrifying "wages of sin," the all-sufficiency of grace, the urgent need for repentance, and so on.[94] But the sermon is also an engagement with New Divinity theology: specifically, with Hopkins's distinctive and highly controversial treatment of the "means of grace" as developed in two tracts published in Boston and New Haven, respectively, in 1765 and 1769: *An Enquiry Concerning the Promises of the Gospel* and *The True State and Character of the Unregenerate*, a riposte to objections raised to the former work by New Haven pastor Jedediah Mills.

The controversy surrounding Hopkins's treatment of the means of grace concerned the question of what could be achieved by unregenerate sinners who knew about the "promises of the gospel" but had nevertheless refused Christ. Hopkins's claim was that short of accepting the gospel promise, such sinners could do nothing to reform themselves in the eyes of God; moreover, as Holifield explains, Hopkins asserted that "the unregenerate became 'more vicious and guilty in God's sight' the more knowledge they derived from the means of grace"—that is, in effect, from preaching, the sacraments, and the Bible itself. If you are a sinner, in other words, and remain "unconvinced" after having read the Gospel and gone to church, then having done those things means you are more likely to be damned.[95] This proposal made Hopkins notorious among the New England clergy. Before long, "Hopkinsianism" became a byword for the "New Divinity," as it was at first pejoratively called. In fact, the claim that knowledge of the means of grace increased one's exposure to damnation was not new *per se*, having been made in passing by Edwards himself, as Hopkins himself observed.[96] But Hopkins "emphasized the point in a way that drew spirited reactions" since "he insisted that resistance from the awakened brought greater blame than resistance from someone who knew nothing of the gospel."[97]

The reactions were spirited indeed. "I appeal to the common sense of mankind, is not this strange divinity?" Jedediah Mills wrote in a 1767 pamphlet responding to Hopkins: "What! is there no possibility that the drunkard, the thief, the liar, the profane swearer, the adulterer, the murderer and blasphemer should become, on the whole, less vicious in God's sight while unregenerate, by reforming all this atrocious wickedness, tho' on no higher principle than that of natural conscience, awakened by the common influences of the spirit, as Ahab was?"[98] Here Mills draws out a surprising implication of Hopkins's argument about the means of grace: that exposure to the Gospel renders "conscience" irrelevant to one's salvation. Surely, Mills retorted, God was sure to look favorably upon any effort to "reform" misdeeds flowing from "wickedness of the heart," regardless of whether the sinner had been exposed to the means of grace. Wickedness was an ineradicable feature of human nature, but so was "natural conscience." Yet Hopkins's position implied that righteous actions governed by the latter were of no account in God's eyes specifically when performed by unregenerate sinners under the means of grace. According to Mills, this view seemed strangely to minimize the sinfulness of people who had not encountered the Gospel. It was almost as if "their sin had been little or nothing, if he [i.e., the savior] had not come and spoken to them." Surely, though, there must be some qualitative similarity among all sins, insofar as they flowed from human "wickedness," whether they were performed with or without access to the means of grace: "Is the fountain," he asked "nothing to the streams?"[99]

Responding to Mills in *True State and Character of the Unregenerate* (New Haven, 1769), Hopkins dug in, reasserting that only those who were acquainted with the means of grace could be held accountable for rejecting Christ, or what he termed "unbelief." Unbelief respecting the promises of the Gospel was on Hopkins's account a higher-order or "meta" sin whose commission "aggravated" all others:

> All the sin[s] men commit under the gospel . . . have their chief aggravation in this, that they are against Jesus Christ, and carry in them unbelief and opposition to him; so that unbelief itself, in all the actings and exercises of it, is unspeakably a greater crime than all this wickedness, considered in itself, and not as implying and expressing unbelief and rejection of Jesus Christ. . . . All the sins of Sodom, and all the abominations that have been committed by the worst of men, or that men can possibly commit, without being guilty of unbelief and rejecting Christ and the gospel, are incomparably less criminal and vile than this sin of unbelief, or not receiving but rejecting Christ, when he is revealed and offered to men.[100]

Rejecting Christ, as one could only do "under the gospel," was a sin of an altogether higher order than any other, since it entailed not only "wickedness of the heart" but also something much worse: the *rejection of the offer of being forgiven* for that wickedness. As Hopkins put it, rather extravagantly, "the devils have never sinned, nor can they sin in such an aggravated manner, because they have no such offers, no such salvation to reject, no such Redeemer to despise."[101] All sins, then, did not really come from the same "fountain" of wickedness, as Mills had supposed.

Occom appears to have made a close study of this controversy between Hopkins and Mills. At the climactic moment of his sermon for Moses Paul, he offers a crystal-clear recapitulation (and pastoral redeployment) of Hopkins's "strange" new arguments about unbelief and the means of grace. Pointing out to Paul that he had been lucky to have had a "good education" that acquainted him with the promises of the Gospel, Occom despairingly explains that his guiltiness for murder has been "aggravated" by the higher-order sin of unbelief:

> Alas! poor Moses, . . . Should God come out against you in strict justice, alas! what could you say for yourself? for you have been brought up under the bright sun-shine, and plain, and loud sound of the gospel. . . . You have sinned with both your eyes open as it were, under the light even the glorious light of the gospel of the Lord Jesus Christ.—You have sinned against the light of your own conscience, against your knowledge and understanding. . . . You have sinned against all the mercies and goodness of God; you have sinned against the whole bible, against the old and new-testament; you have sinned against the blood of Christ, which is the blood of the everlasting covenant. O fly, fly, to the blood of the Lamb of God for the pardon of all your aggravated sins.[102]

Occom's insistence here that Moses Paul had committed "aggravated sins" owing to his exposure to the "bright sun-shine . . . and loud sound of the gospel" is Hopkinsian in both doctrine and diction. He seems to have been particularly impressed by Hopkins's definition of "unbelief," in the above-referenced reply to Mills, as "an impenitent rejecting [of] Jesus Christ now, under the full blaze of gospel light and clear convictions of conscience."[103] It seems likely that Occom read this latter work sometime during the three-year interval between its publication—also in New Haven, where Mills had published his *Inquiry*—and the Moses Paul sermon, which Occom delivered in September 1772 on the New Haven Green. Nor, indeed, would it be at all surprising if Hopkins had shared his views about unbelief and the means of grace with Occom in person. The two ministers had been personally acquainted since at least 1761 and probably much earlier, and we know from Occom's journal that he stayed with Hopkins at least once, and borrowed money from him, during his periods of itinerancy in the 1770s.[104] These biographical clues, together with the textual evidence we have been examining, support the idea that by the 1770s Hopkins had become a major influence on Occom's theological outlook. They suggest, too, that Occom had by 1772 come into his own as a New Divinity preacher. It may be, in fact, that his "bestselling" and oft-reprinted sermon on Moses Paul was (and remains) the most widely read work of sermonic literature that the New Divinity ever produced.[105]

* * *

It took a lot of intellectual creativity for Occom to make New Divinity teachings relevant to the anticolonial political projects to which he devoted increasing attention in the 1760s and 1770s. Indigenous sovereignty concerns the politics of peoplehood and tribal autonomy; but the New Divinity had limited traction on eighteenth-century discussions about colonialism, political self-determination, or the fate of nations. This was largely by design, and it stemmed from New Divinity ministers' insistence on God's sovereignty in dividing humankind into two basic categories: the regenerate and the unregenerate. There was no "middle ground," as Hopkins's arguments about the futility of unregenerate "strivings" implied.[106] Occom himself sometimes spoke about humankind in these dichotomous terms. "Here I Shall endeavour to repre[sen]t two Sorts of People yt are in the World, and Distinguish them one from the other—the one is Believer, and [the other] unbeliever," he wrote in notes for a 1760 sermon; and, in another manuscript from around the same time, "there are but two [sorts] in the world, or only two Families, the Family [of] Christ and the family of the Devil."[107] For Occom as for his New Divinity colleagues, God's division of humankind into believers and everyone else was fundamentally important; and, as a minister committed to the post-Edwardsean ideal of "disinterested benevolence," he saw it as his goal to help as many people into the first category as possible.[108] What made Occom unique among New Divinity ministers was that he pursued this goal in a way that supported a politics of Indigenous separatism and self-determination.

Occom justified his peculiarly Indigenist form of universal benevolence in the idiom of covenant or "federal" theology: that is, in terms of "national election" or promises made by God to certain chosen groups of people.[109] It was here, in this return to covenant theology, that Occom parted ways most dramatically from his ministerial peers and mentors. As Joseph Conforti and Mark Valeri have noted, the New Divinity's commitments to disinterested benevolence, to the preeminence of grace, and to the fundamental binary distinction between believers and nonbelievers led the movement's proponents to cast a jaundiced eye upon the older Anglo-Protestant tradition of splitting the world up into various covenanted and uncovenanted peoples.[110] The title of a pamphlet published by Bellamy in New Haven in 1769 effectively summarized the New Divinity's narrow construal of "covenant" as an agreement between God and the saved: *That there is but one covenant, whereof baptism and the Lord's-Supper are seals, viz. the covenant of grace; (proved from the word of God) and, the doctrine of an external graceless covenant . . . shewn to be an unscriptural doctrine.* In publishing such pamphlets against Moses Mather and other latter-day practitioners of federal theology—a theology of "external graceless covenant[s]"—Bellamy, Hopkins, and other New Divinity preachers continued the attack on the "halfway covenant" that their teacher Jonathan Edwards had reinitiated in Northampton twenty years before.[111]

Occom was no friend of the halfway covenant and he agreed with his New Divinity colleagues that the doctrine of national election was, basically, a dead letter. Yet it is important to remember that these post-federal beliefs put Occom and his New Divinity colleagues in an intellectual vanguard. Because of his position as an Indigenous person who grew up hearing white New Englanders constantly describing themselves as God's "chosen" nation, Occom was uniquely attuned to the continued relevance of covenant theology as ideology, despite the New Divinity's theoretical innovations. More than any of his peers, he presciently saw that covenantalism was deeply entrenched in Anglo-American intellectual and political culture, and that it was not likely to be theologized out of existence any time soon. Even for Anglo-Americans who might have agreed with Bellamy and other Edwardseans that New English "chosenness" had no basis in scripture, it was still possible to remember the myth of national chosenness as part of a shared cultural legacy. Gilbert Tennent makes for an intriguing case study in this regard. Though insistent upon the preeminence of the Covenant of Grace—that is, the nonnational covenant, embodied in Christ, between God and individual believers—Tennent stirred up his congregations with old-fashioned national covenantalism when it suited his purposes. During the Seven Years' War, for instance, Tennent appealed to British North Americans to enlist in the Army by comparing the French to the biblical Babylonians and likening British forces to "Soldiers which were employ'd in recompensing upon the aforesaid Enemies of Israel, the Deeds which they did to them . . . his sanctified Ones."[112] As this example attests, the Seven Years' war saw a major uptick in covenantalist rhetoric during the years of Occom's youth—which were also the years when the New Divinity was getting off the ground.[113] This resurgent culture of covenantalism was not mutually exclusive (at least in popular practice) with the new post-Edwardsean rhetoric of "disinterested benevolence." For white New Englanders who valued covenantalism as a cultural legacy more than as a theological doctrine, universal benevolence could be seen as the next logical step in their people's glorious history.[114]

A THEOLOGY OF LAND AND PEOPLEHOOD

For Indigenous people, though, the situation was different. According to most eighteenth-century interpretations of federal theology, Native Americans were "Canaanites in the Promised Land" or, as the widely cited Ephesians 2:12 put it, "aliens from the commonwealth of Israel, and strangers from the covenants of promise." To put the point slightly differently and in a way that would have better conformed to New Divinity skepticism about the idea of national election in general: Native Americans were not and had never been a people chosen by God. Occom took this idea of Native nonchosenness on board, along with the New Divinity's emphasis on universal or disinterested benevolence. But he also recognized that the latter idea was potentially problematic from the point of view of Native nations. Universal benevolence could not be an ideology of reform for them—not, at least, in the same way it was for Anglo-Americans. Since Native nations had never been chosen by God, there could be no way for them to follow white people in their purported metamorphosis from elect nation to benevolent empire. This, Occom realized, meant that the historical and theological significance of Native nationhood was still an open question. How could the fact of never having been chosen be understood as a feature of Native Americans' collective past? And how could such a collective identity be pressed into the service of Indigenous self-determination *and* universal benevolence in a colonial context? What Occom realized in the 1770s and 1780s was that presenting Native Americans as a never-chosen people made it possible for him to accomplish two theological goals at once: first, to keep faith with post-Edwardsean skepticism about the very idea of national covenants, and second, to retain a heuristic analytical distinction between chosenness and unchosenness in order to gain argumentative purchase on urgent problems of colonial politics.

One relatively easy way of seeing how Occom deploys this heuristic distinction is by considering the form of address he uses in his sermons. It follows from what has been said so far that Occom's sermons are not properly seen as jeremiads. The prophet Jeremiah, after all, belonged to a nationally covenanted people. He was a virtuoso of ancient Israelite religion: aloof from his people and apart from them because of his prophetic calling, but still a member of God's chosen nation. In Occom's time, the jeremiad tradition was still thriving in "the New English Israel," but Occom did not identify with Jeremiah because he did not think his people had ever been chosen.[115]

This nonidentification is particularly apparent in his sermon for Moses Paul, where he addresses his ministerial colleagues as "reverend Gentlemen and fathers in Israel." After speaking to the condemned Paul, Occom begs leave "to speak a few words to you [fathers in Israel], tho' I am well sensible that I need to be taught the first principles of the oracles of God, by the least of you"; nevertheless, he continues, "the providence of God has so ordered it, that I must speak here on this occasion."[116] Readers of Occom sometimes interpret this deferential language as a modesty trope, which is fair enough.[117] But its more serious purpose is to performatively disaffiliate its speaker from the New English Israel. It matters, with this in mind, that Occom does not say, "I am the least among *us*," even though he was an ordained Presbyterian minister in good standing. What he says, rather, is that he has something to learn from "the least of you," and this second-personal pronoun "you" clearly does not encompass Occom's "I." Tellingly, the only time Occom uses the pronoun "we" in his remarks to his fellow ministers is embedded in a quotation of Paul's letter to the Ephesians: "For we wrestle not against flesh and blood, but against principalities, against powers, against the rulers of darkness of this world, against spiritual wickedness in high places."[118] This passage from Ephesians was very widely cited in eighteenth-century sermons whenever preachers wished to highlight the role of ministers in fighting against political and social impediments to religion. I will return to this contest between religion and politics in a moment. For now, though, let's stick with the question of rhetoric. Given that elsewhere in his sermon Occom refers to his fellow ministers as "you," what is it about the Apostle Paul's words that gives him license to address them as "we"?

Occom observes that Paul used the term "we" in Ephesians in the context of his "Apostle[ship] of the Gentiles." In this context, the pronoun "we" bridges the identities of "I"—Paul, a Jewish member of the Jesus movement—and "you," Paul's addressees, a group of ex-pagan Christians in Ephesus, "ye being in time past Gentiles in the flesh."[119] From one perspective, Occom's citation of Paul can be seen as an endorsement of the transnational scope of Christian fellowship, an idea perfectly continuous with New Divinity teachings about there being "but one covenant," namely the Covenant of Grace. But Occom also recognized that he did not approach the question of nationhood in exactly the same way Paul did. Paul could not be a perfect role model for him because the two ministers had different national statuses vis-à-vis God's (supposedly) chosen people. As Laura K. Arnold notes, "Unlike Occom, St. Paul was born an Israelite and was thus an Apostle *to* the Gentiles even though he was not a 'Gentile' himself."[120]

Conversely, Occom, who was not born "in Israel," as he put it, could preach *to* chosen New Englanders, but he could do so only from the standpoint of a people who had never been identified as chosen. As a Jew seeking to bring ex-pagans into the fold of the saved, Paul could ecumenically address the latter *and* his fellow Jews with the pronoun "we." But Occom could not use this rhetoric because he did not share New Englanders' "Israelite" identity. They did not see him as sharing it, because they still understood themselves—historically, or theologically, or both—as being "in Israel" while Native people were outside of it. And Occom did not see himself as sharing it because he did not believe that God had ever made a national covenant with Native Americans. They were party to the Covenant of Grace, but that was all. So even though, as a New Divinity proponent of universal benevolence, Occom endorsed Paul's ecumenicism and moral universalism, he also identified himself rhetorically (and politically) as a Gentile belonging to a never-chosen people.

What about the rest of Occom's quotation from Ephesians, the part about "wrestl[ing] . . . against spiritual wickedness in high places"? Occom's rationale for choosing this passage becomes clearer if we consider it alongside his remarks to Moses Paul about the means of grace, remarks that occur just before Occom's address to the "fathers in Israel." As we have seen, Occom espoused a Hopkinsian line on this topic: because of Moses Paul's knowledge of the means of grace, of "the bright sun-shine, and plain, and loud sound of the gospel," he had sinned in an "aggravated way" against his "own conscience," against his "knowledge and understanding," and "against the blood of Christ, which is the blood of the everlasting covenant." This stern admonition would still have been fresh in most hearers' (or readers') minds when Occom turned to remind his white ministerial colleagues to "wrestle . . . against spiritual wickedness in high places." So also would Occom's rhetorical disaffiliation of himself with the "fathers in Israel," whom he had previously addressed as "bishops" and "rulers of the temples of God." The sermon presents this group as being of much higher status than "me," Occom, who is "lower than the least of you," along with all the rest of "my poor kindred the Indians." The order of Occom's exposition thus invites his audience to draw a connection between Anglo-American "fathers in Israel" and what the Apostle Paul calls "spiritual wickedness" in "high places."[121] The connection seems all the more obvious since the ministers attending Occom's sermon were well acquainted with the means of grace ("the plain, and loud sound of the gospel"), as was almost every other English person in Occom's audience. The same could hardly be said about Native people, however, as Occom notes by drawing attention to Moses Paul's exceptional status as one who has had "a good education" and who "can read and write well."[122] Occom does not connect all the argumentative dots here—to do so in New Haven in 1772 would have been unthinkable—but it hardly seems a stretch to read him as intimating that "aggravated" sin, or "unbelief" of the Hopkinsian kind committed by Moses Paul, was very likely *more* pervasive among the English than it was among Indigenous people, especially in "high places" like the ministry.

Reading the Moses Paul sermon in this way becomes much more plausible if we consider it alongside a slightly later sermon by Occom on Isaiah 58:1, "Cry aloud, spare not, lift up thy voice like a trumpet, and shew my people their transgression, and the house of Jacob their sins." This sermon survives only in manuscript and is undated, although text-internal evidence suggests that it was written in the early 1780s.[123] Here Occom continues his earlier reflections about the meaning of unbelief, which he describes, in terms echoing the pamphlet war between Hopkins and Mills, as "the Root of all Sins or a fountain from which Streams all Wickedness." In this sermon on Isaiah Occom is particularly interested in exploring the connection between unbelief and the idea of national election, a link that is much more vividly highlighted here than had been possible on the occasion of Moses Paul's execution. Midway through the sermon, Occom has this to say about the identity of the "Covenent People" who, according to Isaiah, are guilty of unbelief and various other "transgressions":

> the Jews were the first People of God, but they have . . . Sinned away their Blessings and Inesteemable Priviledges and have been long Since un Peopled and un Churchd. . . . Has God no Covenent People then in the World Since the rejections of the Jews, Yet Blessed be God, where ever the Gospel of Jesus Christ is receivd by any People, they are the People of God,—and the English People are the Covenent People of god, they have enjoyd the Gospel Priviledges for a long Time, and they are now greatly Degenerated from the Purity and Simplicity of the Gospel and therefore they are the Very People that the Eternal Jehovah is Speaking of Speaking to in [the] Text.[124]

This remarkable passage weaves together two distinct covenant-theological themes that were becoming increasingly central to Occom's understanding of colonial politics. At the heart of Occom's argument is a clear statement of New Divinity suspicion regarding the very idea of a national covenant: "where ever the Gospel of Jesus Christ is receivd by any People, they are the People of God." When it comes to the ultimate question of salvation, the theological bottom line is that there is "but one covenant," as Bellamy had put it: the Covenant of Grace between God and those who have "receivd" Christ. Wrapped around this central claim is a discussion of national election as manifest in the "Covenent People" of Israel (the "house of Jacob") and England. Occom's argument here is typological, in that it "describe[s] the way an event in the Old Testament foreshadowed one in the New Testament, or the way a biblical happening presaged one in believers' lives."[125] The text of Isaiah talks about the "house of Jacob," whom Occom calls "the Jews," "the first people of God"; yet on Occom's reading this Old Testament narrative foreshadows the history of the English, who "*are* the Covenent People of god" in present times.

What made Occom so sure the English were God's modern-day "Covenent People"? Well, for one thing, they said they were. Wheelock himself frequently said so, for instance in his *Plain and faithful narrative of the original design, rise, progress and present state of the Indian charity-school at Lebanon, in Connecticut*, where he wrote to an English audience about "the great Obligations lying upon us, as God's Covenant-People, who have all we have better than they in a Covenant Way"—"they" referring here to the "Heathen Natives."[126] A second reason Occom gives for identifying the English as God's chosen or "Covenent People" is that they, as a nation, had long been favored with the means of grace, having "enjoyd the Gospel Priviledges for a long Time" (though, as we have seen, Occom saw this as a mixed blessing since it exposed the English to the "aggravated sin" of unbelief). So far, so good; but Occom was willing to entertain the view that even this was not quite enough to pin the identity of chosenness on the English: "Some may query and say, Why may not this Text be more Sutable to the Roman Catholics than the English?"[127] After all, the Roman Catholics also identified themselves as God's "People"; and they, like the Jews, had long enjoyed the "Priviledges" of scripture. Be that as it may, Occom argues, the reason Isaiah's words do not apply to Catholics is that the "Roman Catholics are left to themselves . . . already they are unchurchd the Lord dont own them as his People."[128] Occom here presupposes general agreement among his Protestant audience that the ascendency of the Catholic "People" was a thing of the past, whereas the English were still on the rise and had everything to lose.¹²⁹ Indeed, what really clinched England's identity as the present-day "house of Jacob" was that they were "now" at a stage in the process of *losing* their chosen status similar to that of the Jews when Isaiah addressed them. Occom is quite clear on this point: "they are *now* greatly Degenerated from the Purity and Simplicity of the Gospel and *therefore* they are the Very People that the Eternal Jehovah is Speaking of."

Thus, while it might seem at first that Occom is engaging in covenant theology in his sermon on Isaiah, what he says actually leaves no clear place for national election in the historiography of redemption. Chosen individuals will be saved, since ultimately "they are the people of God." Chosen nations, on the other hand, are born only to die, to become "un Peopled and Un Churchd." By Occom's time, all the national covenants entered into by God had been annulled except for one, and the days of this last one appeared to be numbered because England (like the Catholics and, earlier, the "house of Jacob") was clearly incapable of living up to the terms of the agreement. This "Degenerated" covenant between England and God was an atavism, something grotesque, even vaguely undead.

Where did this leave Indigenous people? Occom addresses their status in relation to God's last "Covenent People" a little later in the sermon, in the course of his enumeration of the specific sins of the English as these flowed from the "fountain" of "Unbelief." Here, Occom clarifies the connection between English chosenness and English sinfulness by contrasting these with the relative lack of sinfulness among Native American "heathens." Following Paul's enumeration of the sins of the flesh in Galatians 5:19, he begins with adultery. Occom finds adultery "abounding" in this "degenerate Age," but observes that in North America

> the Heathen Abominate this Sin, and they punish it [with] most Ignominious Punishment, The man, Whose Wife has Playd the Whore, will bite off her Nose, that She may bear the Shamful mark all the rest of her Days, Wherever She goes,—yet this Sin is Committed by Christians. What abominable this must be in the Sight of God and Christian man What? to have the light of the Bible, and Committ this Beastly Sin What? . . . What a Cursed Sin this must be in the Sight of God, this Sin upon Baptized Persons, may be Seven times Worse than the Heathen.¹³⁰

A THEOLOGY OF LAND AND PEOPLEHOOD

Occom makes similar points about murder and fornication. The last of these, he claims, is seen as so "abominable and Shameful among Some Heathen Indians" that its perpetrators, upon being discovered, "woud voluntarily Banish themselves from their own Country and never to [be] Seen there again," yet it is "hardly esteem'd as Sin" by "those that are calld Christian People."[131]

In drawing these pointed contrasts between the chosen people's immorality on the one hand and "heathen" justice on the other, Occom is following Paul, who drew analogous distinctions between the Jews and Gentiles in his first letter to Corinthians ("It is reported commonly that there is fornication among you, and such fornication as is not so much as named among the Gentiles, that one should have his father's wife") and in the letter to the Romans, both of which Occom preached from frequently.[132] Paul's analysis of Gentile morality in Romans is especially noteworthy here, for this is where he famously identifies "the law" as the causal mechanism that explains why Gentiles act with more "righteousness" than the people of Israel. As Paul controversially argues, it was precisely because God had chosen Israel to receive his law that the chosen people had "not attained to the law of righteousness. Wherefore? Because they sought it not by faith, but as it were by the works of the law." In contrast, the Gentiles, who lacked access to God's revealed Word, nevertheless acted with "righteousness": "For when the Gentiles, which have not the law, do by nature the things contained in the law, these, having not the law, are a law unto themselves: Which shew the work of the law written in their hearts."[133]

In his sermon on Isaiah, Occom draws on this Pauline argument in order to expand the scope of his scripture-based interpretation of eighteenth-century colonial politics. What he clearly means to do in the sermon is not merely identify biblical Jews as forerunners or "types" of present-day English people but also to point to the Gentiles, as described in the Gospels and the letters of Paul, as prefigurations of present-day Native Americans. Whether or not this reading of the New Testament Gentiles amounts to a typology in a strict sense might be debated, since the source of the type is in this case the New Testament rather than the Old. Moreover, whereas types were typically thought to be abolished or transcended by the advent of the antitype that they foretold—such that the Old Testament rules respecting circumcision, for instance, could be seen by Paul as noncompulsory since that rule was a foretelling of the "circumcision of the heart"—Occom thought that the nonchosen identity of the New Testament Gentiles was something that latter-day Native "heathens" shared and sustained rather than abolished.[134] On the other hand, the precise definition of typology has always been difficult to pin down, and by Occom's time there already existed a long tradition of literary and theological experimentation that adapted typological methods for new argumentative purposes. Occom, who used the term "types" on other occasions but rarely practiced typology in the strict sense, belongs to this tradition of experimentation.[135] In any case, Occom's writings on Gentile morality entail a significant departure from traditional New England typology and covenant theology alike, both of which most often likened the situation of Native Americans to that of Old Testament Canaanites.

One important advantage Occom gained from construing Paul's Gentiles, as opposed to Old Testament Canaanites—or, even less plausibly, Jews—as types (or at least prefigurations) of Native Americans was that doing so could be a way of according the latter more historical agency. As we have seen, the contrasts Occom draws between "heathen" virtues and chosen unrighteousness follow Paul's arguments in Romans and elsewhere about the ability of Gentiles to avoid the pitfalls of seeking salvation "by the works of the law." Yet Occom also supplements this Pauline reasoning with a more comparative and ethnographic mode of argumentation than the apostle had undertaken. I already mentioned one example of this in the sermon on Isaiah, where Occom adduces specific penal practices (corporal punishment, voluntary exile) that were customarily assigned by Native peoples to the crimes of fornication and adultery. By submitting these Native traditions to a comparative analysis alongside the lax or nonexistent penal practices of the English, Occom sought to demonstrate that Native culture and history were critically relevant for anyone who would seek to diagnose the ills of colonial political life or, more broadly, to understand the unfolding fates of the world's nations.

Beyond this methodological point, however, Occom also drew an eschatological lesson from the recent history of Northeast Native life under Anglo colonization. This lesson differed markedly from the one propounded by the majority of his teachers and colleagues. Eleazar Wheelock, for instance, understood the conversion of the Native Americans as fulfilling Isaiah's "prophecy of the enlargement of the church of *God* in the days of the *Messiah*." But Wheelock interpreted this extension of the "*Messiah's* kingdom" in decidedly imperialist and assimilationist terms.[136]

In his *Plain and faithful narrative*, he argued that civil and religious authorities should work together to educate Native peoples in order to bring them—and, no less important, their lands—under the jurisdiction of Great Britain: "how much the Interests of His Majesty's Dominions, especially in *America*, would be promoted hereby, we can hardly conceive."[137] Educating Native people, according to Wheelock, would cost less than half what it would cost to subdue them militarily; and it was sure to "provoke them to Emulation" of English customs and English agriculture, thus leading to a glorious cultural homogeneity in the domain of the Messiah (and "his Majesty").[138] Occom understood the national fate of his people in the "days of the Messiah" very differently. Whereas Wheelock saw Native Americans as being in the early stages of an inexorable slide toward political and cultural assimilation, Occom underscored the eschatological significance of the Indigenous conversions that had already taken place. To be sure, only a few Native people in his day had really "receivd" Christ, and some of these, like Moses Paul, had already fallen away. Even if just a few of his people were regenerate, though, that meant that God's work of redemption had burst the boundaries of the old federal covenants, if those ever really existed. (Here is where Occom may have been picking up on the point about his own "Gentile" identity that Buell had made in his ordination sermon.) Whereas Wheelock persisted in speaking of Great Britain as a "Covenant-People" well into the 1760s, Occom's interpretation of colonial history was much more consistent with the post-Edwardsean, New Divinity doctrine that there was "but one covenant."[139] In fact, Occom's own theological arguments demonstrate quite effectively—by design, it seems reasonable to suppose—that Wheelock's imperialism and assimilationism were incompatible with both scripture *and* the anti-"Federalist" thrust of the New Divinity.[140] At the same time, Occom's arguments raised an urgent political question that other New Divinity theologians generally avoided: given that national covenants were obsolete but that nations themselves were clearly not going away, what did it even mean to belong to a nation? What history demanded, Occom thought, was not (or not only) an abandonment of covenantalism for the sake of universal benevolence, but rather (or additionally) a *positive* theological account of how the meaning of nationhood had to change in the "days of the Messiah" for the benefit of his own colonized people and for the world at large.

Occom's attempt to formulate such a positive theological account of nationhood finds its clearest expression in his sermon from the 1780s on the parable of the Good Samaritan. Picking up where he had left off in the sermon on Isaiah, Occom draws a Pauline contrast between the virtues of Indigenous Gentiles and the vices of the English, focusing in this case on the particular virtue of being generous toward foreigners. Whereas English people treat foreigners badly, especially the foreign Africans whom they enslave, "the Indian Heathen in this great Continent . . . are very Compassionate one to another, very Liberal among themselves, and also to Strangers."[141] As I argued in chapter 1, Occom's argument here appeals to a kind of moral universalism: the Good Samaritan shows that, when Jesus told his followers to "love thy neighbor as thyself," what he had in mind was a feeling of "Commiseration to all Without respect of Persons." This was the sort of feeling or "love" that "the Samaritan Showd to a Stranger and to a man Who was quite of another Nation, Yea of a Nation Who dispisd him."[142] The national likeness between the Samaritan and the "Indian Heathen in this Great Continent" is clear: all are outsiders to chosen nations, and their kindness to strangers "Who dispisd" them proves that they have a "native" sense of universal benevolence despite (or perhaps because of) not being favored by God with his Word.

Here, again, Occom appears to be reading scripture in a loosely typological way: the unchosen Samaritan is the type or prefiguration of Native Americans; and the Jewish "Priest" and "Levite," who decline to help their own wounded countryman, are figures for the English. Occom may have found inspiration for such a reading in his favorite Bible commentary, the *Exposition of the New Testament* by "the great Mr. [Matthew] Henry."[143] Henry, too, had glossed the parable of the Samaritan in Pauline terms, as an expression of the above-mentioned causal mechanism linking national election to unrighteousness: "if they [the Israelites] saw a Gentile in *danger of death*, they thought themselves under no obligation to help to *save his life*. Such wicked inferences did they draw from that holy covenant of peculiarity which God had distinguished them by, and by abusing it thus they had forfeited it."[144] Occom follows Henry this far, but he also goes beyond him in assigning a name to the virtue that the Samaritan and (per the typology) Native Americans display in their dealings with strangers. Whereas chosen people like the ancient Israelites and modern English ignore the sufferings of foreigners owing to what Henry described as the "wicked inferences . . . they draw from that holy covenant of peculiarity," nonchosen people exhibit the virtue of what Occom calls "national love":

> if we are true Neighbours, we are so to all; tho it is very natural for every Nation to have a National Love, and I believe it is not forbid in our Text, but then we Should have the Same Love to other Nations as we have to our Nation; and if this took place, there woud be an End of Wicked Wars and Blood Shed among the Nations, O How happy the Nations of the World [would] live if they were all Neighbourly to one another.[145]

Nations matter, on this argument, because they provide a space for the cultivation of moral and political affections: specifically, for the kind of love that the truly righteous will practice toward humankind as a whole. This much is intuitively grasped by Native Americans, who are "Compassionate one to another . . . and also to Strangers," and who thus practice a righteous "National Love" even in their "Heathen[ish]" state, unlike their professedly Christian English neighbors. If the "Nations of the World" want to comport themselves righteously in their internal dealings and their dealings with foreigners, Occom shows, then they would do well to follow Indigenous peoples' example.

In holding up Northeast Native peoples' "national love" as a moral example for the world at large, Occom in the Good Samaritan sermon conveys a message that is both evangelical and nationalistic. In the Good Samaritan sermon, these two themes are woven around one another as part of the same unfolding dialectic. The sermon addresses itself to a sinful world and casts Native people as "heathens" who stand in desperate need of conversion. But it also presents them as possessed of a national culture that is both autonomous and exemplary. This dual identity is reflected in Occom's emphasis on Indigenous hospitality toward strangers as the example *par excellence* of how people ought to love their neighbors as themselves. By practicing such hospitality, Native people demonstrated to the world at large what it meant to practice "national love." But Indigenous hospitality had a soteriological significance as well as a moral one for Occom, because Christ was a stranger too: "he said the Foxes had holes and the Birds of the air had Nests but he had no where to lay his Head."[146] Native peoples' receptiveness to foreigners was sure to make them receptive to Christ, if only their political situation could be improved.

Robert Warrior brings out this soteriological dimension of Native openness toward strangers (though not with reference to Occom specifically) in an important essay, first published in *Christianity and Crisis* in 1989, where he describes the nonchosen tribes dwelling in Israel's promised land as an "indigenous people" who "trusted in the god of outsiders."[147] Reexamining the Exodus narrative with "Canaanite eyes," Warrior observes that, from a Native perspective, the God of Israel has historically been associated with imperial intruders, but that Native Christians have not seen that as a reason for rejecting him. This is not to say that Native people, or anyone else, should read the Exodus narrative of Israelite redemption the way European colonizers read it, as a warrant for the conquest and subjugation of Indigenous peoples. On the contrary, "keeping the Canaanites at the center" requires constantly interrogating "America's self-image as a 'chosen people,'" which has for centuries "provided a rhetoric to mystify domination." There can be no easy answer to the question of whether "Native Americans and other Indigenous people dare trust the same god [as the colonizers] in their struggle for justice." Warrior seems to think the answer is yes, but he does not wish to impose that answer on others. The broader aim of the essay is to offer a political and theological perspective on Native life that transcends the Exodus narrative, "in which Indigenous people put their hope in a god from outside" but "saw their story of oppression revised out of the new nation's history of salvation."[148]

Roughly two hundred years before Warrior, Occom arrived at substantially the same position. He would have heartily endorsed Warrior's assertion that "the Exodus is an inappropriate way for Native Americans to think about liberation."[149] And he would have further agreed that, from a Native point of view, colonization entailed a catastrophically asymmetrical breakdown of relations between nations: Native people had extended hospitality to a foreign people and a foreign god, but their generosity had not been reciprocated by the settlers. At the same time, there are instructive differences in emphasis in the way Warrior and Occom express their respective nonchosen perspectives on colonial politics. For instance, Warrior's discussion of Indigenous nonchosenness draws primarily on Old Testament sources, whereas Occom tends to discuss the nonchosen from a perspective that merged the New Divinity with the writings of Paul. Warrior and

Occom also differ in that they use very different interpretive methods in their approach to scripture. Warrior, equipped with all the tools of modern textual-historical scholarship, is primarily interested in teasing out the various historical and literary meanings of the Old Testament Canaanites in order to contrast how Exodus has historically been read with how it might be read "with Canaanite eyes." Occom, on the other hand, reads the Exodus narrative in a broadly typological manner, as a proleptic description of events that would happen later in the New Testament or later still in historical time. While he would have agreed with Warrior that the Exodus narrative is "inappropriate" as a model for Native politics, the reason he gives for this is not that Exodus was a narrative of conquest and dispossession (although he would probably not have denied this), but rather that the whole analytical framework of national election has been transcended in the Covenant of Grace: "where ever the Gospel of Jesus Christ is receivd by any People, they are the People of God." Whereas Warrior talks about redressing the actual crimes of colonialism, Occom argued that generosity toward foreigners, even hostile ones, was fundamental to true "national love."

Perhaps the relative historical remoteness of Occom's theological-typological outlook helps better explain why so many scholars continue to mistakenly think that he wanted Native Americans to "become a chosen people."[150] Those who defend this interpretation often point to an uptick in Occom sermons on Old Testament texts during the years of the Brothertown migration.[151] Yet the fact that Occom preached about the Hebrew Bible hardly proves that he thought Native nations were themselves chosen, as the aforementioned sermon on Isaiah demonstrates.[152] Such arguments often wind up corroborating the stereotype of Occom as an "Indian Moses," which misrepresents his separatism and traditionalism, flattens the rich texture of his theological views, and assumes the universal appeal of the Exodus narrative as what Warrior calls a "fundamental model for liberation."[153]

Not only were Native Americans *not* the beneficiaries of national election, Occom thought; it was imperative for them to understand their political and cultural inassimilability to God's "Covenent People." If Native people had never been chosen, then they were not susceptible to the causal mechanism identified by Paul in the letter to the Romans, whereby Israel had failed to attain the "law of righteousness . . . because they sought it not by faith, but as it were by the works of the law." So there was a clear scriptural basis for thinking that Native Americans could actually be morally superior to English—provided, as Occom came to believe in the 1770s, that they could buffer themselves politically and geographically from the latter's corrupting influence.

More than this, even, Occom's reading of the New Testament convinced him that scripture also provided a warrant for cultural revitalization. To be a chosen nation, according to scripture, was to be favored by God with his revealed Word—that is, his law. The fact that Occom's people had never been chosen implied, conversely, that God had never provided them with a set of rules about how to live, until he brought them the Gospel. The Gospel commanded people of all nations to worship the God of Israel; but Jesus warned his followers that this did not necessarily mean that everyone should emulate Israelites in their outward behavior. Paul emphasized this feature of Jesus's ministry in his letter to the Romans in a passage from which Occom preached more than once during the final decade of his life: "For he is not a Jew, which is one outwardly; neither is that circumcision, which is outward in the flesh: But he is a Jew, which is one inwardly; and circumcision is that of the heart, in the spirit, and not in the letter; whose praise is not of men, but of God."[154]

In this part of Romans, Paul is addressing the Jews in his audience. His message to them is that they should not expect Gentile Jesus-followers among them to circumcise their children just because that is what Jews do, even though Jews do so because scripture tells them to. The object of true faith is "in the spirit, and not in the letter" of the moral law. True, Paul likens the Gentile who has such faith to "a Jew, which is one inwardly"; but his point is not necessarily that such individuals should think of themselves as trading in their Gentile nationality for the superior nationality of Israel. Paul can also be read as saying that the Gentiles should retain their nationhood and keep to their own cultural ways; there is no need, in other words, for them to act like Jews, or "judaize." Unfortunately, none of the manuscripts for Occom's sermons on Romans 2:28–29 survives, so we can only speculate about what he himself said about it. But many commentators throughout history have read Paul in this way, and I believe that Occom would have been among that number.[155] This would have been consistent with Occom's broader theological perspective as I have been reconstructing it here, particularly his New Divinity–inspired arguments against the idea that national covenants play any role whatsoever in salvation.

Reading Occom as a Gentile opponent of judaization further clarifies the theological rationale behind his commitments to Mohegan and Brothertown sovereignty and his opposition to his peoples' assimilation to

Anglo-European culture. While these commitments are widely attested in the secondary literature on Occom, scholars have had a hard time connecting them to his sermons and other religious writings. It is certainly true, as Jarvis writes, that for many Northeast Natives "Christianity reinforced a common identity for communities atomized by colonialism."[156] But Occom was also up to something even more politically and intellectually ambitious than shoring up a threatened identity. He wanted to proclaim to the whole world, with the backing of the Bible, that humankind in general would be better off if Northeast Native communities persisted as self-determining peoples with their own land and their own culture. Casting Native people as chosen was never going to suffice for Occom, who understood that doing so would merely model Indigenous nationhood on "another people's identity."[157] Occom thought a more robust justification of Indigenous nationhood was needed, and he found it in the New Divinity, in Paul's teachings on the Gentiles, and in his own remarkable mind.

"very much like the garden of Eden, Which was the garden of god"

Occom's theology of Indigenous self-determination, I have been arguing, was singularly and spectacularly Pauline. (To me, at least, it hardly seems like an exaggeration to say that Occom was one of the most careful and creative readers of Paul's letters anywhere in the eighteenth-century Anglophone world.) As much as he took inspiration from Paul, however, Occom parted with him in one crucial respect: on the question of apocalypticism.

As Paula Fredriksen argues, Paul's ministry to the Gentiles was characterized by his "tireless and wide-ranging efforts at pagan recruitment; his insistence on maintaining ethnic distinctions between Gentiles and Israel; his defiance of pagan gods; [and] his empowerment by spirit."[158] These were all priorities that Occom shared; but for Paul these commitments were articulated in the context of a "vivid apocalyptic expectation" that he had taken over from a centuries-old Israelite tradition of "eschatological messianism."[159] Occom, for his part, was not wholly averse to thinking about the apocalypse. As a young person, he did his fair share of dabbling in apocalyptic numerology in the endpapers of his Hebrew grammar-book.[160] Over time, however, Occom became less and less preoccupied with the end of the world, and less stridently convinced than some Edwardseans that it was right around the corner. In his one surviving sermon on the topic, Occom opens by calling "this Book of Revelation very misterious and Dark [to] us, Yet they will be all made plain to God's People either in this World or in the World to Come."[161] The last phrase here, "either in this World or in the World to Come," reveals something important about Occom's understanding of the relationship between sacred and secular history: he thought the relationship was murky. The book of Revelation was something worth puzzling through, but it did not provide unambiguous guidance about how to act "in this World." Here, as in many of his sermons, Occom displays an abiding concern with what to do *now*, and a willingness to admit that the Bible, which is often "misterious and Dark," cannot always answer that question.

Occom's demurral from Paul's apocalypticism is all the more remarkable given the prevalence of apocalyptic thought in his own theological milieu. In his *History of the Work of Redemption*, Jonathan Edwards recast all of human history as a prelude to the Last Judgment and explicitly linked the coming of the Christ's Kingdom to the "propagation of the gospel among the heathen here in America."[162] A similar connection between Native "heathens" (understood as remnants of the "Lost Tribes") and the apocalypse would later be taken up by the famous Pequot minister William Apess. In an appendix to his millenarian tract *Increase of the Kingdom of Christ*, Apess described Native Americans as a "nation, peculiarly and emphatically blessed of God, his own highly favored and chosen people . . . brought up out of Egypt and their cruel bondage by miraculous means."[163] Yet whereas Apess, following a long line of Exodus-inspired theologians, saw God's deliverance of Israel "out of Egypt" as a prefiguration of the Last Judgment, Occom tended to relate the Bible more to the historical present. And the book of the Bible he most often turned to, when seeking insight on the historical situation of Native Americans and their relation to their homelands, was not Exodus but Genesis.

From the time he moved to Brothertown in 1785 until his death in 1792, Genesis was (according to his ministerial diary) Occom's favorite book to preach from. The whole of Genesis seems to have preoccupied him, but in the writings that survive it is the first two chapters—which recount how God created the world, "planted a garden," and "created man in his own image"—that he refers to most often.[164] One of Occom's most remarkable discussions of Genesis comes in a petition he wrote on behalf of

Brothertown to the United States Congress some time in or after 1785. Reworking Genesis 1:6 ("And God said, Let the waters under the heaven be gathered together unto one place, and let the dry land appear"), Occom tells Congress how "the Spirit above . . . saw fit in his good pleasure, to Divide this World by the Great Waters, and he fenced this great Continent by the Mighty Waters, all around, and it pleased him, to Plant our fore Fathers here first."[165] This passage sums up Occom's late-career understanding of what the Bible had to say about Indigenous land and peoplehood: Native people belonged to "this great Continent," and vice versa, from the "first." Occom is careful not to describe this as a covenantal relationship, like the ones God formed with Abraham and Moses. In Exodus, God gives Israel sovereignty over the land of the Canaanites on condition that they obey his rules and build him a sanctuary "that I may dwell among them."[166] In contrast, according to the Brothertown petition, the relationship "our fore Fathers" enjoyed with America was unconditional: "he gave them this Boundless Continent, and it was well furnishd, and Stored with all Necessaries of Life for them, and here they have livd and Spread over the Face of this Wilderness World."[167] It was also more historically continuous. "Here they *have* lived," the petition pointedly states, a clear indication that Native peoples' sovereign connection with the land remained unbroken.

How did Occom reconcile this understanding of his ancestors' past with what Genesis actually says about humanity's origins? In many of his writings, after all, Occom defends the conventional view that Adam and Eve were "the Father and Mother of all Nations of the Whole World"; and it is not immediately obvious how Occom thought God's placement of these ur-humans in Eden related to his "plant[ing]" of "our fore Fathers" on Turtle Island.[168] This is another instance where it helps to remember that Occom read the Bible typologically, not simply as a chronological record of empirical historical facts.

Occom reveals his typological approach to Genesis in an undated sermon on Galatians 5:1: "Stand fast therefore in the Liberty wherewith Christ has made us Free." Here Occom explains that "the People of God of Old" had a different experience of the Word. God spoke to them through "figures[,] modes, Types, and Shadows, and even by Dreams, Visions and Voices."[169] As a record of God's purposes in his dealings with humankind, the Old Testament remained mostly obscure until the "perfect day" when the Divine "actually & personally appeard in the World" as Jesus. Only then did it become clear what all these "Types, and Shadows" were hinting at.

Reading Genesis typologically, Occom derives the familiar lesson that Adam's expulsion from Eden foretold humankind's "Bondage to Sin." He also says, intriguingly, that having "lost the knowledge of God, and Consequently lost Communion with God," Adam was a "vacaband."[170] This term would surely have gotten the attention of Occom's listeners given the increasing cultural and political salience of what colonists called "Indian vagrancy." In Occom's time, Jean O'Brien writes, Northeast Natives were increasingly a "diasporic population defined by the complex transformations and dislocations brought about by English colonialism."[171] From Occom's perspective, Adam's vagabondage gave him a special typological significance for Native communities specifically: his "lost Communion" with God was, preeminently, a "biblical happening [that] presaged one in believers' lives."[172]

Yet Adam's vagrant status was not merely a prefiguration of settler colonialism's dispossessive power. Out of his vagabondage, a new kind of freedom emerged. This is what Occom, following Paul's letter to the Galatians, calls "Stand[ing] Fast in Liberty."[173] *Standing fast*, for Occom, meant being like "Jesus Christ," who defied the wiles of all the hypocrites and tempters the ancient world could throw at him: as he says in the sermon, "there is none that Can Stand in Competition with him."[174] Here Occom was probably alluding to the episode from the Gospels, where Jesus, in defiance of Satan's injunction to fling himself off the roof of the temple as proof his divinity, utters the words, "Thou shalt not tempt the Lord thy God."[175] This scene was especially familiar to English-speaking Protestants because of its famous reinterpretations by authors such as John Milton and John Bunyan, both of whose works Occom knew well.[176] At the climax of *Paradise Regain'd*, Milton embellishes just *slightly* on the Gospel account of Jesus's temptation, in a way that Occom would have liked. Following Satan's eloquent plea to "Cast thy self down," Milton picks up the dialogue in this way:

To whom thus Jesus: also it is written,
Tempt not the Lord thy God, he said *and stood*.
But Satan smitten with amazement fell . . . [177]

It is likely but far from certain that Occom knew this passage from Milton. However he almost definitely knew about the character "Mr. Standfast" from Bunyan's *Pilgrim's Progress*, a work whose female protagonist became the namesake of Occom's daughter Christiania. In Bunyan's poem, Mr. Stand-fast personifies resistance to temptation (his rebuking of the lascivious Madam Bubble makes him "certainly a right good pilgrim").[178] But the real point of Stand-fast's piety is to prepare him to enjoy the earth in a more profound and more collective way.

In chapter 10 of *Pilgrim's Progress*, Christiana and her family of pilgrims meet Mr. Stand-fast in the Land of Beulah, just across the river from the Celestial City: "Here, because they were weary, they betook themselves awhile to rest. And because this country was common for pilgrims, and because the orchards and vineyards that were here belong to the King of the Celestial Country, therefore they were permitted to make bold with any of His things."[179] In Beulah, the final meeting between Christiana and Stand-fast takes place on land that was "common for pilgrims," a land of "gardens" where the "children of the town would . . . gather nosegays for the pilgrims, and bring them to them with much affection." This was a place where "stand[ing] fast in liberty" meant dwelling on communal ground where the earth's abundance was available to all.

The resonance of such words for a Northeast Native leader like Occom, raised in the tradition of the "common pot" and seeking to manage land for "the benefit of the Whole Tribe," must have been profound.[180] In his sermon on Galatians, Occom finds a similar promise of abundance prefigured in the Genesis account of Eden, where Adam "had free Liberty from his God to injoy the garden of Paradise or Eden, his gracious god freely gave him every thing that grew in the garden, except one Tree. . . . God more over gave him the Whole World besides and all Creatures and things therein and he had uninterrupted injoyment of God with all his Creature injoyments, this was his Superlative Glory and Happiness."[181] Yes, Occom observes, Adam spoiled his freedom by eating from the "one Tree" he wasn't supposed to eat from, thus necessitating Christ's redemptive sacrifice. But, on Occom's reading, that did not mean that the *land* was spoiled for the "injoyments" of Adam's successors. The same land that God had created still existed: the "upstart earth," as "the great Mr. Henry" described it in his *Exposition of the Old Testament*, which "was no sooner made, than it became fruitful and *brought grass* for the cattle, and *herb* for the service of man," and "several kinds of vegetables, which are numerous, and all curious, and every one *having its seed in itself after its kind.*"[182] This last phrase, a direct quotation of Genesis 1:12, may have been ringing in Occom's ears when he saw the cabbages David Fowler was growing at Brothertown in 1785:

"Brother David Fowler told me and his Wife and others Confirmd it that he had one Cabage Stomp Stood three Summers and it headed every year, the last it Stood, it [had]three Heads."[183] At Brothertown, Occom found that the earth's abundance was inviolate. Now it was just a question of the people getting right with God: "if the People were as ingagd in Religion as they are in their Temporal Concerns this Settlement woud be very much like the garden of Eden, Which was the garden of god."[184]

In the mid- to late 1780s, an Edenic existence at Brothertown seemed to Occom almost within reach. The "upstart earth" was as good as could be imagined, and in Occom's more optimistic moments he caught glimpses of his people sharing in the land's vitality, partaking of what he had called in 1772 the "active principle within" that "breathes towards God, a living breath, in praises, prayers, adorations and thanksgivings."[185] In these moments, Occom saw his people "planted here" on the land, just like their "fore fathers." Bunyan, riffing on Genesis, had described something similar in a widely reprinted memoir that Occom likely read at some point: "When Christians stand every one in their places, and do the work of their relations, then they are like the flowers in the garden, that stand and grow where the gardener hath planted them, and then they shall both honour the garden in which they are planted, and the gardener that hath so disposed of them."[186]

On October 24, 1785, Occom found himself on a horse, riding with David Fowler through a rainstorm ("extreemly bad muddy riding . . . and some Places very Mirely") on the way to "our Indians new Settlements":

> we travild about a mile in the Dark, and then we arrivd at Davids House as we approach'd the House I heard a Melodious Sin[g]ing, a number were together Sin[g]ing Psalms hymns and Spiritual Songs, we went in amongst them, and they all took hold of my Hand one by one with Joy and Gladness from the Greatest to the least, and we Sot down a While, and then they began to Sing again, and Some Time after, I gave them a few words of Exhortation, and then Conclude with Prayer—and then went to Sleep Quietly, the Lord be praised for his great goodness to us.[187]

At last, Occom's people had arrived at a place where they could honor the garden and the "gardener" alike. Surely this must have been one of the best nights of sleep he ever had.

* * *

Historians who study radical ideas in early modern political and religious thought sometimes use the term *protology*, literally "the study or science of origins," to refer to theological discussions of the creation of the world.[188] Protology is often described as a foil or counterpart to eschatology, the study of end-times. By the end of his life, Occom was much more likely to be drawn to the former. The reasons for this have everything to do with the Indigenous standpoint from which he practiced theology. By retelling early Northeast Native history as protology—"the Spirit above . . . saw fit . . . to Plant our fore Fathers here first"—Occom aimed to supply his people with a theological rationale for "stand[ing] fast in liberty." True, in order to continue growing where God had planted them, some Northeast Native people would need to transplant themselves, as it were, to a slightly distant plot of ground. But Occom did not see the migrations he lived through as an Exodus *redivivus*; and he certainly didn't see himself as an "Indian Moses" sent to liberate his people into a new way of life governed by a new law in a new country. Occom's protology was about getting back to the way things were, before colonization, when his people were able to enjoy the earth's self-renewing abundance.

Occom's late-career turn toward protology forced him to confront difficult questions about the utility of scripture in Indigenous communities. If true religion, for Northeast Native communities, was about "standing fast" where God had planted them, then what purpose did it serve for ministers like Occom to school those communities in the "figures, modes, Types, and Shadows" in which scripture abounded? Did Native communities even need to know about the old "national" covenants God formed with once-chosen people like Israel and, in latter days, England? What about Jesus? If the moment of creation set the standard for what Indigenous communities could hope to achieve, and if there was a promise of recovering an Edenic existence in the here and now, then why exactly did Native communities need to know about Christ's redemptive sacrifice? The rest of this book works its way toward answers to these questions and confronts them head-on in chapter 6. For now, having explored the main tenets of Occom's theology, let us consider in greater detail some of the nontheological dimensions of his religious and political practice.

CHAPTER IV

Piety and Placemaking

Styles of Strangerhood Among Occom and His Kin

On the rainy morning of October 9, 1785, a farmer in the upper Hudson River Valley answered a knock at his door to find a man he had never seen before. The man was elderly, drenched to the bone, with long gray hair and dark skin, English-style clothes, a splendid gold-headed cane, refined manners, and a proud, even magisterial air.[1]

The farmer invited the man in, gave him a seat by the fire, and tried making small talk. It was Sunday, and there wasn't much time before he would have to head up the road to attend church, where today's sermon was to be delivered by a celebrated preacher from out of town. He asked his guest if he was on his way to hear this minister too.

"I suppose I should hear him," the visitor replied, vaguely. This was not especially pleasant small talk. The man must have been very tired.

Then, breaking an awkward silence, he spoke up again: "The people could not see that strange creature till I get there."

The stranger gave this a moment to sink in. Then, suddenly, the farmer sprang into action, as if suddenly finding himself in the presence of a god. Looking around frantically, he noticed, back out on the road, a group of churchgoers passing by and yelled at them to stop and see the celebrity who had come into his home: the Reverend Samson Occom.

In a matter of minutes, Occom, surrounded by his new entourage, was on the road again, now mounted on a villager's cart as if it were a parade float. At 11:30 he arrived at the Stillwater meetinghouse where, according to his diary, "there was a prodigious large Congregation, the biggest that was ever See[n] in the place." He preached one sermon in the morning and another one in the afternoon, and "the People attended with great and Solemn attention and with many Tears." After church Occom got on another wagon and rode out of town to a "Small Log meeting House . . . crowded like a Bee Hive" where he delivered yet another sermon to families who hung on his every word "like Criminals at the Bar." At last, "much spent," he collapsed in sleep.[2]

This was a day in the life of Samson Occom, the itinerant preacher. The identity of his farmer host remains unknown to us, and so it seems to have remained even to Occom himself, judging at least from the diary entry in which he recorded this episode. Occom was apparently content for this farmer to remain a stranger to him. Yet this is part of what makes the episode, as retold by Occom, so powerful. In addition to being a record of his ministerial activities and a place to tell a joke, this diary entry from October 1785 is a sophisticated reflection on what it meant to be a stranger, or "strange creature," in Occom's strange eighteenth-century world.

Occom's diary, in this entry and elsewhere, shows that interacting with unknown persons was a routine, yet also unpredictable part of his everyday life. The entry I have been examining begins as follows:

> Sabbath Octor 9 [1785]—got up very early and Sot of to go Still Waters to preach in Mr Campels got to the River about 9, and Sent the mare back by James Waucus for he Came down with me; got over Soon and I on a foot and tryed to get a Horse at the first House, But I Coud not and went on foot, and two or three Places and all in Vain, a wagon came by me going to meeting and I Desired him to help me a long, but he woud not, at last I gave up, and Sent Word forward to have Horse Sent me and I went into a House, told the man of the House of my difficulties

Note how utterly mundane it seems to Occom to ask for things from people he does not know. In endeavoring to "get a Horse at the first House," to hitch a ride on a wagon and, finally, to take refuge indoors while waiting for help, Occom finds nothing remarkable in the way strangers behave: the diary conveys no feelings of ill will or recrimination toward those who refuse to help, but neither does Occom let loose any effusions of joy and gratitude regarding the "man of the House" who eventually takes him in.

Instead, Occom implies that when it comes to asking strangers for help, one has to play the odds. Some will be receptive, and some won't. This sort of unpredictability would have been unremarkable to anyone who traveled frequently across the countryside of eighteenth-century North America.[3] And in his vocation as an itinerant preacher, Occom had by 1785 been a frequent traveler for well over thirty years. When it came to strangers' hospitality or lack thereof, he had seen it all.

Occom's familiarity with strangers is apparent, as well, in his narration of his conversation with the farmer who finally takes him in: "he asked me Whether I was going to hear the Strange Mister." The topic of this "mister" first arises as a form of small talk, which is among the most common forms of conversation for strangers to engage in. Strangers practice small talk largely because it is safe: a way for unacquainted individuals momentarily to share social space by focusing together on objects of low-level mutual interest—the weather, the traffic, the celebrity touring the area—while simultaneously avoiding more substantive topics whose discussion could bring the parties into conflict.[4] It is in this spirit that, on Occom's account, the unnamed householder "asked me Whether I was going to hear the Strange Mister." At first, Occom plays along: "I told [him] I Suppose I Should hear him." For a brief moment, Occom and the householder remain routinized strangers enjoying their minimal degree of solidarity. "And then" Occom tells his joke: "[I] told him, the People Could not See that Strange Creature till I get there."

The joke, at first, seems innocent enough, a passing display of folksy humor of the sort that people often use to leaven banal interactions. But the joke also has the more serious consequence of disrupting the flow of stranger-interaction that he and the farmer had earlier entered into. "And then he asked me whether it was I that they expected I told him Yes,—and he was Surprised." What, exactly, is the nature of this "Surprise"? Clearly it is, at least in part, a result of the artful way in which Occom presents himself to the farmer. After all, Occom could have simply announced himself as the celebrity "mister" at the outset, when the farmer first opened his door. This could have saved the farmer (and Occom) some trouble and time. After his long morning of sodden travel, Occom sounds genuinely glad, if not relieved, when the farmer offers him a warm resting place indoors and some nonthreatening small talk to pass the time. Yet engaging in small talk is also a way of setting the farmer up to be "Surprised" when Occom reveals that he is entitled not merely to everyday respect, but also to reverence and obedience: "and he was Surprised, and there were then Several People going by, he Calld to them and told them I was in the House and wanted help." The householder's actions grow frantic as it dawns upon him just how mistaken he was. He seems anxious to repair any affront he may have caused by treating Occom as just another traveler. All this could have been prevented if Occom had simply said who he was at the outset. Is there not something gratuitous about the delayed revelation of his true identity?

Perhaps. But we misunderstand Occom if we read this revelation as a mere stage-effect. From his point of view, there *was* a real transformation in the kind of strangerly relationship he bore to the householder, a transformation over which Occom himself was only partly in control. After his wagon ride to church, Occom relates that he preached a sermon that was met "with great and Solemn attention and with many Tears." It hardly seems like a coincidence when Occom writes that the "short discourse" he gave on this occasion came from the book of "Jona," the Bible's quintessential tale of a prophet coming into his divinely appointed authority, after initially masquerading as an ordinary traveler. It is unclear from this diary entry which passage from Jonah Occom focused on that day, but a look at Occom's other entries from the mid-1780s indicates that when he preached from Jonah it was almost always from Jonah 3:5.[5] This passage relates how, after "Jonah began to enter into the city . . . the people of Nineveh believed God, and proclaimed a fast, and put on sackcloth, from the greatest of them even to the least of them." It is not hard to imagine why Occom might have found inspiration in this passage about Jonah who, just like him, was a traveling preacher gifted with the ability to inspire total strangers to unprecedented works of repentance. He may also have been drawn to the passage because it takes place in Nineveh, the capital of the Assyrian empire, which God had lately promised to destroy.

Occom's diary from October 9, 1785, brings into view complex interconnections between strangerhood, piety, and politics, three topics whose interrelation in Occom's writings is well worth untangling. In the entry we have been examining, Occom's revelation of himself as a "Strange Creature" is crucial to his assertion of interpersonal authority over the people he interacts with, and to his quasi-prophetic self-presentation as a latter-day Jonah warning of the collapse of earthy empires. Yet these themes of power and authority are dealt with in an extremely pious way. How then are we to understand the relationship between piety and politics in this diary entry, and in Occom's writings more generally?

The question is not an easy one, since from a modern, secular perspective the notion of piety often connotes conformity, obedience, and even an "otherworldly" attitude aloof to worldly concerns.[6] And, of course, piety does involve an element of conformity with respect to established norms of religious behavior. Yet piety can also be understood as a means of social transformation in two distinct yet interconnected ways that I'd like to explore further in the present chapter. Piety can change the way people *perceive* the world, and it can transform their relationship to *place*.

People who engage in practices of piety often (not always) do so in order to change the way others see the world. In recent scholarship on piety, this perceptual dimension is perhaps most often associated with the work the late Saba Mahmood, whose *Politics of Piety* (2005) theorized piety as a *display* of personal agency in contexts of face-to-face interaction. Mahmood's ethnographic work focused on the women's mosque movement in 1990s Cairo, a groundswell of Islamic piety whose participants brought into view "sharp lines . . . between those who conduct themselves in an 'Islamic manner' and those who ground their sociability in what may be glossed as 'Western-liberal' lifestyles."[7] Through the practice of piety, the women Mahmood worked with sought to effect a wide range of social transformations ("changes in styles of dress and speech, standards regarding what is deemed proper entertainment for adults and children, patterns of financial and household management, the provision of care for the poor, and the terms by which public debate is conducted") through forms of "embodied sociability" that sought to bring about the "*retraining* of ethical sensibilities so as to create a new social and moral order."[8] On Mahmood's account the politics of piety in the Cairo mosque movement had less to do with "religious indoctrination" than with "micropractices of persuasion" that sought to transform the world through acts of public self-display.[9]

Mahmood's theorization of piety as a practice of "retraining . . . sensibilities" can be immensely helpful for thinking through Occom's own self-presentation as a "Strange Creature," as I attempt to show in the pages that follow. It also has important implications for understanding Occom's relationship to *place*, and in particular to his Northeast Native homelands. If, following Mahmood, Occom's piety was as a technique for retraining people's perception of social space, then it becomes urgent to ask how this retraining contributed to (and also complicated) the processes of "placemaking" described by Christine DeLucia, Heather Law Pezzarossi, and Patricia Rubertone in their recent work on the Native Northeast.[10] As these scholars show, placemaking is a complex and sometimes contentious process within Indigenous communities; to be a "placemaker," writes Rubertone, is to take a stand on "questions about what happened here (or there), how it was formed, who was involved, and why it should matter."[11] Occom's piety reveals a lot about the distinctive way he approached these questions, in ways that require careful unpacking. While it has sometimes been suggested that his style of piety was "otherworldly," in the sense of being focused on the salvation in the hereafter, understanding Occom's piety in terms of "micropractices of persuasion" allows a somewhat different, more this-worldly picture to emerge.[12] Irrespective of how we define Occom's piety, however, it is clear that it was not to everyone's taste in the Native Northeast. Even at Brothertown, which is sometimes represented (not very accurately) as a latter-day "Praying Town," there was room for multiple styles of "embodied sociability," not all of which were pious.

Before diving deeper into these issues of perception and place, however, I want to make the case that, in coming to terms with Occom's piety (and its attendant politics), it helps to understand more about what it meant to him to be a *stranger*. As religious historians have amply demonstrated—and as Occom's aforementioned references to Jonah indicate—there existed in the eighteenth-century Anglophone world a rich textual culture in which the notions of piety and strangerhood were very closely connected. This textual culture mattered to Occom, but from his point of view, being a stranger was not primarily about acting out some pre-scripted religious or cultural role. Indeed, reintegrating the concept of strangerhood into the foregoing discussion of perception and place can help us move beyond the narrowly culturalist perspective through which the term *stranger* has usually been interpreted in the scholarship on Occom and his communities.

Styles of Strangerhood

In order to understand the transformative power of Occom's piety, I have suggested, it is helpful to appreciate how the avowal of stranger-identity in everyday social interactions reproduces deference and social status. But it is also important to bring a more historical perspective to bear on Occom's strangerhood, since the persona of the stranger had rich religious, cultural, and literary connotations in Occom's world. These connotations made it possible for Occom to insinuate to unknown persons that, as a stranger, he was a person of unusual authority on a divinely appointed mission. They also gave him (like other eighteenth-century evangelicals) a way of signaling his abjection before God and his solidarity with other "Christians" whom he sought "to comfort . . . in [their] weary Pilgrimage," as he wrote in the preface to his 1774 hymnal.[13] In all these ways, the persona of the "stranger" belonged to a rich field of cultural reference, or what literary scholars call "intertextuality," in which Occom had been immersed from the 1740s onward.

To grasp the real importance of strangerhood for Occom, though, it is important to break him out of this narrowly culturalist framing and think about his strangerhood in terms of *performativity*. Getting other people to acknowledge him as a "Strange Creature" was not just a means of encouraging them to see him as belonging to a certain culture, but also a way of producing "social distance." This notion of social distance has a deep and complex history in social theory (and, as more recent history attests, in the public-health literature as well). In the present discussion I use the term, following Erving Goffman, as a way of linking the idea of strangerhood to the phenomenon of "deference."[14] A classic Goffmanian example of deference between strangers is the crowded elevator where every new passenger, upon entering, immediately turns around to face forward. What explains this behavior is not just culturally determined "manners," although those certainly have a part to play, but also passengers' need for personal space.[15] People do not always want to be known, Goffman and other theorists of social distance have argued, and they routinely communicate this not just to strangers but also to people they know well. When a partner in an intimate relationship tells their counterpart that they "need space," to take another relatively banal example, that is a demand for deference.[16] The fact that people make and accede to such demands says something important about the relations of power that inform everyday social interactions. There is a truism dating back to antiquity (at least) that "knowledge is power"; but people also assert their authority over others in their social environment by telling them, in one way or another, "you don't know me." This is part of what Occom was communicating when he identified himself to the New York farmer as a "Strange Creature," or when he told the people of Bristol that he was "an obscure Stranger, from an obscure Place."[17] What statements like these say, among other things, is *you don't know me, and that gives me power over you*—the sort of power, at least, that demands deference, or what Occom in his journal entry from Stillwater calls "a great and Solemn attention."

The connection identified by Goffman between strangerhood and "social distance" seems to me especially pertinent for thinking about Occom's self-avowed identity as an *Indigenous* stranger. This is partly because being a stranger is about setting limits to what other people know, which is something that also happens in the practices of ethnographic refusal discussed by Audra Simpson and others.[18] Another way in which the avowal of stranger-identity connects to recent discussions of Indigeneity has to do with *expectations*. If asserting one's strangerhood is a way of demanding deference from others, then the particular techniques by means of which such demands can be asserted and acknowledged (on an elevator, or in a stranger's house) vary according to how people expect one another to behave in particular interactional contexts. Yet, as Philip Deloria argues in *Indians in Unexpected Places*, "expectations" about how Indigenous people act "are both the products and tools" of "colonial and imperial relations of power and domination."[19] Two features of the expectations discussed by Deloria are worth underscoring here: they tend (1) to be "cultural" in nature and (2) to presuppose cultural otherness, or what Deloria calls "Indian difference."[20] Deloria's argument here is not merely that expectations about Native people are informed by cultural biases, although that is obviously true; his key point is that "expectations" about Native Americans tend to be biased *toward culture itself* as a privileged domain in which people (non-Native people, in particular) expect Indigenous "difference" to express itself.

Deloria's discussion of "expectations" is particularly important for present purposes because it helps explain the curious historical (and historiographical) fact that when the term "stranger" is applied to Indigenous people, it is almost always used to refer to cultural difference, even in the scholarly literature. This narrowly culturalist understanding of strangerhood is perhaps most obvious in the field of ethnohistory, whose practitioners have often foregrounded attempts by Indigenous and non-Indigenous people to communicate with one another across lines of cultural difference. This is the way the term "stranger" was used, for instance, by Alden Vaughan and Daniel Richter when they wrote in 1980 that "Indian culture incorporated strangers far more thoroughly and enthusiastically than did Puritan New

England"; or by James Axtell, who wrote in *The Invasion Within* that "when it became clear . . . that the strangers . . . sought to compromise the autonomy of the natives in nearly every sphere of life, the Indians . . . harden[ed] their resistance to the cultural blandishments of the Christians."[21] In more recent Indigenous studies scholarship there has been a shift away from the culturalist assumptions of this ethnohistorical work; yet it is a mark of ethnohistory's lasting impact that, even today, the word "stranger"—even when it comes in for criticism—is almost always assumed to designate a relation of "foreignness" or cultural otherness.[22]

While culturalist conceptions of colonial strangerhood can be highly illuminating, understanding "stranger" in exclusively culturalist terms has tended to obscure the fact that Indigenous people often have noncultural reasons for identifying themselves as strangers to others. This point is driven home by Simpson's analysis of ethnographic refusal as a sovereign commitment to *remaining unknown*. It is made in a slightly different way by Elizabeth Povinelli, Mark Rifkin, and other Indigenous studies scholars influenced by queer theory, whose work troubles the assumption that Indigenous sociality is always and only about interpersonal "closeness."[23] In Occom's historical context, the importance of stranger-identity has been demonstrated most lucidly by Jean O'Brien, who describes how settler colonialism forced Northeast Native communities to reimagine long-standing patterns of mobility and subsistence. Women accustomed to horticultural work, O'Brien argues, found themselves "divorced from the land" and, under the pressure of colonialism, "expected to sever the vital connection they had to the soil as its principal cultivators and nurturers." This pressure "went well beyond a simple shift in the gendered organization of labor," forcing women to adapt "ideologically" by rethinking "deeply rooted cultural values."[24] After centuries of seasonal mobility, Native women and men alike found themselves pressured to settle down and live like "normal" colonial householders. If they were going to stay traditional, they were going to have to practice their traditionalism "in unexpected places" and unexpected ways.

Perhaps the most marvelous example of how traditionalism (and social distance) got reimagined in Occom's own household comes not from Samson Occom himself, but from Mary Fowler Occom, the Montaukett woman who married him in 1751 and lived with him until his last days.[25] In a diary entry from June 1772, the Anglo-American minister David McClure reported after a visit to the Occoms' house that Samson "wished to live in english style; but his Wife who was of the Montauk Tribe retained a fondness for her indian customs. She declined, evening & morning sitting at table. Her dress was mostly indian, & when he speake to her in english, she answered in her native language, although she could speak good english."[26]

What is this anecdote about, exactly? It is impossible to be sure from McClure's brief discussion exactly how Samson or Mary interpreted their interpersonal divergences in language use and dress. But McClure's description of those divergences as a difference of "style" is telling, since style is one of the most prevalent ways in which people reproduce social distance in the space of everyday interaction. When people adopt a personal style—by dressing, talking, or writing in ways they make their own—they give themselves "freedom of movement," writes Jeff Dolven, by creating "distance between interlocutors." Having a style is a way of saying "I am like you but not." This seems a plausible characterization of what Mary Occom was up to when she wore traditional Montaukett garb in the house she shared with her black-clad husband.[27] Her traditionalist style was a way of asserting her nonconformity vis-à-vis her husband and her expectation of "deference" in the Goffmanian sense. It was also, perhaps, a way of creating room for freedom and play within their relationship. While not much evidence about the Occoms' domestic life survives today, what little there is points toward the fact that each of them made a point of showing off for the other their peculiar personal styles. In one of the first letters Samson wrote to Mary after he arrived in England in 1776, he adopted a comically mannered persona, probably modeled after the polite bourgeois he was meeting in and around London:

My dear Mary & Esther

Perhaps you may Query whether I am well; I came from home well, was by the way well, I got over well, am received at London well, and am treated extreemly well, yea I am Caress'd too Well,—And do you pray that I may be well; and that I may do well; and in time return Home well,—And I hope you are well, and wish you well, and as I think you begun well, So keep on well, that you may end well, and then all will be well: And so Farewell,

Samson Occom[28]

The letter is a joke, but it reveals something serious, which is that intimacy for Samson and Mary Occom was not incompatible with the assertion of social distance. They acknowledged themselves as different from one another, and in doing so devised a new way of living together with different styles of strangerhood. Mary was a Montaukett traditionalist, and Samson was a polite and pious sort who traveled a lot for work—an odd couple, in a way, but perhaps not that uncommon in the eighteenth-century Native Northeast.

I acknowledge that it might seem bizarre and perhaps somewhat anachronistic to suggest that Occom's piety should be thought of as a "style of strangerhood." Historians of the Native Northeast have not often connected the ideas of piety, style, and strangerhood in the way I am trying to do here. There is, however, at least one well-known precedent in the Anglo-American literary tradition for seeing these things as closely related; and this precedent (while not, perhaps, to every reader's taste) is an instructive one. In Nathaniel Hawthorne's famous short story "The Minister's Black Veil" (1836), a New England preacher named Mr. Hooper decides to wear a black veil over his face for the rest of his life as an emblem of his sinfulness. At first the townspeople take this seriously as a manifestation of piety, but over time they find it increasingly comical and eventually scary. At the climax of the tale, by which point he has become something of a pariah, Hooper has a fight with his fiancée, Elizabeth, who presumes that as Hooper's betrothed "it should be her privilege to know what the black veil concealed." The minister piously disagrees, declaring that "I am bound to wear it ever, both in light and darkness, in solitude and before the gaze of multitudes, and *as with strangers, so with my familiar friends.* No mortal eye will see it withdrawn. This dismal shade must separate me from the world: even you, Elizabeth, can never come behind it!"[29]

This is a splendid send-up of earlier generations of pious New Englanders. As a nineteenth-century secularist of sorts, Hawthorne wanted to show that all the outward trappings of colonial piety were nothing more than style, despite their bearers' spiritual pretensions. Nevertheless, Hawthorne's story is remarkably acute in its depiction of how piety, as a style, creates social distance by addressing "familiar friends" as if they were "strangers." Here I apply a similar set of terms to Occom not to belittle or demystify his religiosity but rather, following Mahmood, to show how he used "micropractices" of piety to assert his personal authority in specific social situations where macro-level forces did not afford Indigenous agents much room for maneuver. For Occom, piety was a style, a way of being, and even a form of freedom: "a freedom," as Dolven puts it, "not of founding nor of starting over, but a freedom to keep going, the freedom we already have."[30]

Signs Against Hypocrisy

In the Samson Occom Papers at the Connecticut Historical Society there is an undated and unsigned manuscript that may be the earliest surviving text written in Occom's hand. The document, which appears to be an academic exercise written in response to some now-lost prompt, is a reflection on what the writer calls "the school of Christ": "The Church of Jx has also been called, by some the school of Christ, but I should choose to cal it the College of Jesus Christ, in which the Disciples Learn Spiritual knowledge or Wisdom."[31] This is an intriguing formulation, especially given that Occom may have written it as part of a college-preparatory education. But what did this "Spiritual knowledge" consist in? The author emphasizes three main points. First is the primacy of the Bible as the basis of all true knowledge respecting religion: "in this Book, is every writing that is necessary for his Disciples to know whereof they are here in this world," including "the knowledge of our Relation to god, and his Relation to us." Second is the importance of "Lov[ing] and Esteem[ing] him who is the Lord our god . . . and if we thus love him, we Joyfully resign and give over ourselves unto him, and cheerfully and pleasurably obey him in al[l] his Holy Commands." Last—and most important when it comes to the practice of piety—is the idea that "they that worship him must worship him in Spirit and in Truth . . . not only with our Spirits, but with a Divine Spirit, and with Sincerity and uprightness of Heart, in truth, not in Hypocricy and falsehood."[32] From the beginning of his ministerial career, Occom understood piety as a way of manifesting "Truth": not just propositionally, by reciting a catechism or the Ten Commandments, for instance, but also corporeally, at the level of pious practice and "worship."

The nonpropositional, corporeal dimensions of evangelical truth-telling were an important, if not exactly central theme in the religious milieu in which Occom was educated. In the sermon Samuel Buell delivered at Occom's ordination in East Hampton, New York, on August 30, 1759, he offered a spectacular discourse on what it meant to embody the truth of scripture in one's words and behavior. As we saw in the previous chapter, Buell's ordination sermon presented Occom as a living witness to the divine "Glory of the Universe," as the first Indigenous person "covenanted" to preach the Gospel. Buell knew that Occom would be conducting his ministry from an unusual—and unusually perilous—social position and took his sermon as an opportunity to instill courage in his friend.

To be a "Gospel Minister," Buell said, was to be "prepared to declare the Word of GOD powerfully and faithfully," to be "saved from the ensnaring Fear of Man," to "lift up the Voice like a Trumpet, and . . . not spare to declare important Truth, whether People will hear or forbear."[33] The kind of "truth"-telling Occom would be engaging in, Buell foretold, was not the recitation of bland religious dicta. Rather, it was a carefully orchestrated rhetorical practice of what Buell, in the sermon's preface, called *parrhesia*, an ancient Greek term usually translated today as "freedom of speech" or "speaking truth to power":

> When pernicious Errors are advanced and disputed for, and important Truths rejected and disputed against; with Zeal awaken'd to Flame we will to speak our Opinions, with the Reasons of them, with an undaunted *Parrhesia*, with a noble Boldness, whilst we plead the precious Cause of God. . . . We speak as in the Sight of GOD:—We have the Testimony of JESUS to keep us in Countenance, and are not ashamed of his Gospel,—which giveth Boldness against that universal Fire, which shall melt the Elements, and shrivel upon the Heavens like a Roll of Parchment.[34]

Given the risks Occom faced as an Indigenous minister, it doesn't seem like a coincidence that Buell spoke at such length about parrhesia, the kind of speech that is unafraid of the "universal Fire." This passage contains two interrelated descriptions of what Buell thought parrhesia amounted to. On the one hand, it meant "speak[ing] as in the Sight of God," the ultimate judge, who before long will bring the world to an end. God knows the truth, in other words, and he is listening to see if his ministers know it too. On the other hand, parrhesia meant speaking freely before other human beings, including those who might wish to harm you, on behalf of "important Truths" that are "rejected and disputed against." The parrhesiast or free-speaker thus has to be mindful of two different audiences at the same time, one divine and one worldly: one speaks "in the sight of God," but also "against" other humans. According to Buell, these two audiences gave shape to the interactional environment in which Occom's ministerial career would unfold.

Parrhesia was a powerful idea, but also a dangerous one, especially for a young Indigenous person who was familiar, to be sure, with all manner of "pernicious Errors" in the religion of colonial America. Speaking courageously against "spiritual wickedness" was nevertheless Occom's ministerial duty, Buell suggested, even as he warned that parrhesia could easily degenerate into enthusiasm, or illicit mouthing off unmoored from scriptural restraint. In counselling courageous speech, Buell emphasized that "we pretend not thereby to immediate Revelations and Inspirations of new Truths, no; there is an exact Agreement between the Works of the Spirit, and the Word of GOD; and therefore all Impulses, Revelations, or pretended Operations of the Spirit, which are contrary to, or have no Foundation in the Scriptures; are to be rejected as enthusiastic Fancies, or satanical Delusions."[35]

As people who lived on the shores of the Long Island Sound in the aftermath of the Great Awakening, Buell and the people he was addressing (including Occom) were all too familiar with such "Fancies" and "Delusions." There were, for instance, the Quakers, who from the perspective of many Presbyterian and Congregational clergy had long been a menace to the towns and cities of England and America. Not only did the Quakers allow women to preach, they were also notorious for outrageous displays of piety like "going through the streets 'as a sign' naked or in sackcloth . . . or with ashes or a pan full of fire and brimstone on their heads."[36] In 1725, Quaker leader George Whitehead commented on early Friends' infamous practices of public nudity, describing such displays as "Signs to those Hypocrites who covered themselves under an empty Profession of Religion, and not of the Spirit of the Lord. . . . The Shame of whose Nakedness, the Lord's Truth made more and more appear, even in those Days; and therefore I believe he set some as Signs and Wonders against them . . . to make themselves such Spectacles to the World."[37] By turning themselves into "Signs and Wonders," Quakers sought not just to manifest the Holy Spirit in their very persons but also to follow the scriptural example of the early apostles who in Acts found themselves waylaid by unbelievers in the Anatolian city of Iconium: "Long time therefore abode they speaking boldly in the Lord, which gave testimony unto the word of his grace, and granted signs and wonders to be done by their hands."[38] It is no accident that this passage was a *locus classicus* not only for early modern discussions of pious acts as "signs and wonders" but also for parrhesia, a term that appears in the original Greek text of this verse and is rendered in the King James translation as "speaking boldly in the Lord." It was, after all, a central aim of the early Quakers to recreate in England and America the vibrancy of the apostolic days and the "primitive church," where piety and parrhesia were one and the same.[39]

While Quakerism was a byword for illicit piety throughout the British empire, Friends did not have a monopoly on outrageous displays of religiosity. In Occom's milieu, the practice of pious nakedness was perhaps most strongly associated with James Davenport, who (as discussed in chapter 3) torched his undergarments in 1743 at a New London prayer meeting that Occom may well have attended.[40] None of the reports of this episode mention that Davenport actually got naked as a Quaker might, though like the Quakers his aim was surely to expose "those Hypocrites who covered themselves under an empty Profession of Religion." The main charge leveled by Davenport's critics, correspondingly, was the same one that had long been associated the Quakers: his purported "signs and wonders" had nothing to do with scripture—which is to say, with truth. His supposed piety was a form of hypocrisy.

In 1742, the Boston minister Charles Chauncy published a sermon denouncing Davenport and other itinerant preachers who "leave their callings . . . wandring about from house to house, speaking the things they ought not."[41] Chauncy was obliged to concede there was some scriptural precedent for displays of piety that took the form of public spectacle: the "*inspired Paul*," for instance, "made it evident to the world, that he was a *prophet*, and *spiritual*, by signs and wonders which he did before the people, by the power of the SPIRIT of GOD." Still, Chauncy warned, "those are *enthusiastical*, who pretend to the SPIRIT, and at the same time express a disregard to the scripture."[42] Chauncy's charge against Davenport's "enthusiastical" conduct (that it seemed intent on severing "spirit" from "scripture") was a familiar one; but his allusion to the early Apostles' displays of "signs and wonders" shows how even among the antirevivalist clergy it was perfectly commonsensical that the human body could be turned into a "sign" if the Holy Spirit empowered it.

It was against the backdrop of this controversy of iterancy that Occom's own style of piety took shape. Following the prudent course recommended by Buell and other preachers in the wake of the Davenport scandal, Occom took a clear stand against enthusiasm in the 1740s and 1750s.[43] But he also learned a lot from the unusual displays of religiosity advocated by less mainstream groups like the Quakers, whose countenancing of female preaching he endorsed in the "extraordinary case" of Phillis Wheatley.[44] By the 1780s, Occom was openly associating with Quakers, ex-Shakers, and others whose religious practices would have been deemed "enthusiastical" by the likes of Chauncy, and perhaps even by his younger self. This probably reflected his shifting religious commitments, as well as shifts in the broader religious landscape of New England. It is also important to acknowledge, however, that an uncommonly broad-minded and, indeed, parrhesiastic understanding of piety was forced upon Occom in some sense, since in his very person he was something the Anglophone Protestant world had never seen: an *Indigenous* minister, whose deeds and preaching were bound to seem remarkable since they came "from an uncommon quarter," as Occom tactfully put it.[45] To borrow Saba Mahmood's terminology, he had no choice but to engage in practices of "embodied sociability" that were bound to challenge others' "ethical sensibilities."

Be that as it may, Occom cultivated and even leaned into his peculiarly Indigenous way of being pious. There was, he thought, a great deal of work to be done to contest hypocrisy and spiritual deadness, since most of the people he encountered in his ministry were astonishingly skilled at finding ways of being "stupified" by sin, or what he called "the death of the soul."[46] This soul-deadness, Occom said, made human beings "ignorant of God" and of "themselves." It "blinded their eyes" and made them "deaf as adders" to the "gospel sound" and "correspondence with heaven." It even prevented them from appreciating the pleasures of human society: sinners, he said, "are totally ignorant of the agreeable and sweet intercourse there is between God and his children here below . . . they know nothing of that love, that the children of God enjoy."[47] Truth-telling, for Occom, was thus largely about waking people up, getting them to sense the world anew.

Occom honed his practices of piety—his skills at "retraining . . . ethical sensibilities"— during his fundraising trip to England, Scotland, and Ireland in 1765–1768. Scholarly discussions of Occom's trip abroad often emphasize its darker side: how his fundraising efforts on behalf of Moor's Charity School were coopted by Eleazar Wheelock; how he failed to bring home a victory in the Mason land case; how his wife and children struggled without his economic contributions; and how Occom resigned himself to becoming "a Gazing Stock, Yea Even a Laughing Stock, in Strange Countries," as he wrote to Wheelock in 1771.[48] But it is also worth acknowledging that, to a remarkable degree, Occom's truth-telling campaign in the British Isles—his effort to instill in strangers a new religious and ethical sensibility—*worked*. This much is clear from the letters Occom received, during the period 1766–1770, from people in England and Scotland who had been able to hear him preach. "We have just cause to believe that God hath sent you hither to this Island by the power and Divine Grace of his holy Spirit," wrote one English person who saw Occom speak, "as an Instrument in his Hand for the awakening calling & conversion of Dead dark & lost Sinners to believe in."[49] Others wrote even more specifically about the strange experience of *seeing* Occom: "Mr Occom I cannot Express to you in word what exult[ation] and joy my Soul was filled with at your first appearance," reads one letter from Yorkshire. "After I heard you first in Tuckersfield and saw you I return'd to my house with my soul filld with joy and my heart with the love of God."[50]

To be fair, not everyone in England appreciated the way Occom sought to rouse people from the spiritual and perceptual numbness he saw in the world. "I say many of us were surprized that . . . you should positively tell us that we were all by nature as blind & dead as a stone, and stood in need of the same kind and degree of the assistance of the spirit of God as the apostles did," wrote one "Jos. Green" to Occom in 1767. Occom's spirit-focused brand of piety, Green argued, placed excessive emphasis on the sensory experience of religion, to the neglect of the cognitive faculties that made humans "rational & free agent[s]." Green tried to persuade Occom that "it is not *sound, or words*, but *sense*"—that is, ideas or intellectual sense—"that must be taken from the Gospel or Scripture."[51] This was the sort of argument often made in the eighteenth century by theological liberals who disdained the sensuality and alleged anti-intellectualism of evangelical piety. It is unknown if Occom replied to Green's letter. If he did, it is plausible to imagine him retorting that there is no reason why a minister could not appeal to the senses and the intellect at the same time. In any case, Occom's richest and most politically well-connected friends—particularly those associated with the Countess of Huntingdon and the so-called Clapham Sect presided over by future Moor trustee John Thornton—were often the most supportive of the way his style of truth-telling appealed to people on a visceral, perceptual level. Thornton, who would later write to

Occom that he found some of his sermons *too* cerebral, told him when he was in England that there was a galvanizing energy in the way he embodied piety, which gave people a concrete example of the workings of the Holy Spirit. He encouraged Occom to keep practicing a "personal exemplary obedience" that would inspire others to live as he did. Thornton saw himself and Occom as members of a new vanguard of evangelical piety comprising those "few living witnesses at this hour who are the Epistle of Christ known & read of all Men."[52] Thornton's figuration of the collective body of true believers as a living "Epistle of Christ" is an excellent illustration of how mid-eighteenth-century evangelicals sustained Protestant radicals' aspiration to exist in the world "as a sign." What he is almost (but not quite) saying is that he and Occom were themselves the "Word made flesh." The culmination of piety was to be like Christ.

The written feedback Occom received in Britain about his preaching there, whether supportive or critical, points to a central assumption that informed the "experimental" way he lived his religion—namely, that it is impossible to experience the sacredness in other people if you lock yourself indoors and try to understand the world with only your mind. While Occom agreed with theological liberals like Green that human reason deserved to be glorified as a God-given means of understanding scripture, he disagreed with the increasingly pervasive idea that scripture was the *only* place where religious knowledge was accessible to human beings, at least in modern, postprophetic times. This latter idea was a favorite of rationalists like Green for the very reason that it desacralized or disenchanted the natural and social world, thereby expanding the range of phenomena that science could study naturalistically; but it had no place in Occom's ministerial agenda. His priority was putting people in touch with what he referred to in the Moses Paul sermon as the "spiritual life," or the quasi-mystical experience of being touched by the Holy Ghost. Such a life, Occom explained, consists in "a real participation of the divine nature, or in the Apostle's words, it is Christ formed within us; I live says he, yet not I, but Christ liveth in me."[53] This apostolic experience of channeling Christ in one's person had been sustained "in all ages with true Christians," including by "many of the *fore-fathers* of the English, in this country."[54] Who these apostolic Anglo "fore-fathers" were is not entirely clear. (Based on the general tenor of Occom's religious views, candidates might include William Tyndale, John Knox, Richard Baxter, John Milton, Matthew Henry, George Fox, Margaret Fell, John Bunyan, and John Cotton.) But the real point of the comment is to suggest that the apostles among the *present-day* English were few by comparison. Yes, "there is the same life in true christians now in these days," but one has to look much harder to find it.

Among the "true christians" Occom had in mind were undoubtedly his friends Susanna Wheatley, John Thornton, and George Whitefield. These friends, together with Occom himself, belonged to what Susan O'Brien and other historians have described as the eighteenth century's "transatlantic community of saints": a small but expanding social network built on letter writing and other forms of circulating discourse that enabled far-flung layfolk to revitalize the Protestant dream of a priesthood of all believers.[55] In the 1760s and 1770s, a remarkable correspondence emerged between Occom, Thornton, Wheatley, and Whitefield (until his death in 1770), which focused largely on the theme of what it feels like to be estranged from God. Exchanging letters about this estrangement seems, perhaps paradoxically, to have brought these friends closer together, with each new letter expressing greater abjection than the last. "Looking at our own failings & the excellencies of others is the most effectual method to cure self love & self importance," wrote Thornton to Occom in February 1773,

> These things should teach us our nothingness & convince us that the whole of success ought to be attributed to the almighty power of God.... You may perhaps remember Bunyans very expressive & instructive Riddle
> He that will kill must first be overcome
> Who live abroad would, first must die at home[56]

Certainly Occom knew the riddle. In 1757, the year he was ordained, his second daughter was born. Occom named her Christiana, after the main female character in Bunyan's *Pilgrim's Progress*. He would also allude to the riddle mentioned by Thornton in his own March 1771 letter to Susanna Wheatley: "I Pray God to kill me to the World, and that he woud Kill the World to me—that I may be Dead to the World and the World to me."[57] Wheatley's letters, meanwhile, took up a similar rhetoric of self-mortification: "How sweet and at the same time how mysterious is this love of God to man, who is in perpetual rebellion against him in thought word and action," she wrote to Thornton in October 1771. "Let us strive earnestly then to lay aside the weapons with which we have been daring him ever since the fall, for the whole armour of God to fight against his and our enemies. . . . I beg you to carry me to God as a Sinner, who am made sensible that I have no Righteousness of my own: that I might be invested with the perfect Righteousness of Christ."[58] Formally, this letter is particularly notable for the way Wheatley shifts back and forth between addressees. She begins by addressing Thornton in the second person ("Hon'd Sir, I received your agreeable and instructive favor . . ."), then starts talking to Jesus ("I beg you to carry me to God"), then turns back to speak with Thornton again, asking for "the continuance of your prayers for my Husband and Son." This interruptive style of address seems calculated to signal that friendship isn't just about comfort and intimacy, that feelings of calm and security may in fact be an *obstacle* to salvation, and that true friends take it upon themselves to challenge those feelings. More generally, this correspondence typifies the way evangelical "conversation" in Occom's circle created social distance between practitioners while attempting to foster a "regulative sensibility" that constantly reoriented addressees toward the Divine.

Today, Occom's correspondence with his evangelical friends can make for challenging reading. As a nonreligious reader I find it difficult to avoid the thought that the piety displayed in the letters is excessive yet also somehow banal—in any event, not to my taste. Yet to levy a literary judgment against this correspondence would miss its real point. As I have been arguing, following Mahmood, the central aim of evangelical piety in Occom's circle was, precisely, to be abrasive to the senses so as to propagate a new "regulative sensibility" among the world at large. Piety was about waking people from their spiritual deadness by challenging their all-too-human tendency toward numbness. As Occom explained in numerous sermons, sin has the insidious power of rendering humankind insensible to the appeal of religious truths: it makes people "ignorant of the agreeable and sweet intercourse there is between God and his children here below" and even "dead to the holy bible. . . . When [sinners] read the book of God, it is like an old almanack to them, a dead book."[59] It was this ever-present threat of human numbness toward the Bible, and indeed language more generally, that sustained the need for a form of truth-telling that went beyond the mere rehearsal of propositions: for a practice of piety that performatively *embodied* the truth in the very act of "holy conversation and godliness." In the extravagant displays of abjection they engaged in with one another,

Occom and his correspondents sought to practice just this kind of godly conversation.

Yet just as sin itself was inescapable, so too was there always a risk that the godly "intercourse" between Occom and his friends would become merely mundane, a "dead almanack" of empty sayings. Occom felt this problem acutely. Like other evangelicals of his era, he was an experimentalist on behalf of the Gospel, always looking for new ways to draw each individual's attention to God's Word. Occom's diary records extensive "exercises" with his "Christian Cards," individual Bible verses written out on pieces of cardboard which Occom distributed to the members of the households he visited during his various preaching tours. "After they had Chosen each of them a Text," he would help each person understand how the verse applied to them.[60] This was usually an "agreable exercise" but it could also be quite upsetting. In one household, Occom reported, "two women" were thrown into a state of great "Solemnity and affection"; in another, he recalled how "the minds of many were much Bowed down and [it was] a Night I believe they cannot forget Soon."[61]

Yet, for all his innovations in piety, there were limits to how much Occom, as an Indigenous person, could purport to "retrain" the sensibilities of his unregenerate world. Under settler colonialism, opportunities for manifesting a "spiritual life" were distributed unequally. When James Davenport lit his breeches on fire in New London, he was forced to issue an apology, but not to abandon his ministry.[62] If Occom had done such a thing it would have meant the end of his career or worse. As a minister to his people and the world at large, he wanted to present his body to the world as a "sign" of the spirit and a living "Epistle of Christ." Yet, in order to confront the ministerial challenges he faced, he needed evangelical allies, and that required not getting ostracized from the "sweet intercourse" he enjoyed with non-Native Christians like Thornton and the Wheatleys. Even still, as we have seen, Occom thought these allies needed to be constantly roused from the besetting numbness of sin, just like every other human. Accordingly, in his interactions with his non-Native associates Occom devised tactics of fostering a "regulative sensibility" that were often surprisingly subtle. His white friends suffered from perceptual "deadness" and often needed to be jostled back into "spiritual life," but in doing so Occom had to be careful not to spoil the friendships. This was not a matter of communicating secret messages "between the lines," but rather of saying things that had the potential to provoke and irritate without being totally alienating.

At the very end of the "asylum for strangers" letter to Susanna Wheatley with which this book's first chapter began, Occom writes something that seems calculated to engender the kind of subtle irritation I have in mind. Whether or not this intervention was intentional is impossible to determine—although there are enough such moments in Occom's writings to make one think they cannot all be accidental. (The following figure reproduces the relevant part of the manuscript, so that the reader can see what I mean.)

Occom's sign-off in this letter occupies three short lines aligned on the right side of the page:

>   your most unworthy and most
>   obliged Humble Servant
>   Samson Occom

Immediately under these lines, Occom asks that his greetings be sent to the enslaved and indentured members of the Wheatley household: "PS:

Figure 4.1 Repetition of "servant" at the end of Occom's March 5, 1771, letter to Susanna Wheatley.
Samson Occom Papers, Mohegan Tribe. Photograph courtesy of Dartmouth College Library.

please remember me to Phillis and the rest of your servants," with the word "me" inserted above the main line of text via a caret. Occom arranged these words on the manuscript in such a way that when one looks at his signature, what one sees is:

Servant
Occom
Servants

The effect of this is strange on multiple levels. For one thing, it deconventionalizes the letter's sign-off, "your . . . Humble Servant," words which would otherwise be so familiar as to be practically meaningless. In this letter, however, signing off as a "servant" cannot be seen as meaningless because the words on the page recontextualize the writer as one "Servant" among many "Servants." This suggests a likeness of identity and subject-position between Occom and the enslaved members of the Wheatley household in a way that seems illicit and even scandalous: both for the way it trivializes the condition of enslavement and, conversely, for introjecting the very problem of slavery into the space of evangelical "holy conversation."[63] Perhaps inadvertently, this display of piety thus manifests deep ideological and material connections among colonialization, Christianity, and slavery, connections that were rarely discussed and only vaguely understood in Occom's milieu.

At the same time, it is impossible to discount the possibility that this seemingly trivial accident of penmanship by Occom was completely intentional: an act of parrhesia calculated both to disrupt the flow of conventionalized language used by the privileged to talk about the oppressed, and to insinuate the hypocrisy of someone (albeit a friend) who claimed to be enlightened in her dealings with Native Americans even as she countenanced the enslavement of Black people in her household. It is difficult to advance such a reading unequivocally, given that Occom himself had, prior to March 1771, sought to exploit slave labor for his own benefit on at least one occasion. "I ext[r]eamly want one of your Negroes and a Yoke of oxen,—my Business is Crouding, and I want to dispatch it as fast as I can," he had written to Wheelock during the fall harvest in 1765, "pray let me have a yoke of oxen, if you cant Spare a Negroe." This letter expresses a belief in the fungibility of Black bodies and labor from which Occom seems to have distanced himself by 1774, when he wrote Phillis Wheatley the now-lost letter "respecting the negroes" containing what she praised as a "highly reasonable . . . vindication of their natural rights."[64] This shift in Occom's attitude toward the rights of African Americans was likely informed by his interactions with Black evangelicals including Wheatley and Lemuel Haynes, and also by his trip to England, where he may have come into contact with the first stirrings of British abolitionism via Thornton and other members of the Clapham Sect.[65]

What is beyond question is that Occom's letter to Susanna Wheatley testifies to the shifting, multilayered meaning of what it meant to be both a "stranger" and a "servant" in eighteenth-century America. In his world, these terms described interpersonal relations of authority and deference that were deeply ambiguous and problematic; when he deployed them in his own writings, he was very often trying to think through how worldly relations of power fit into a broader cosmological outlook in which all human beings were servants and strangers to God. Because of their primordial estrangement from their Creator, human beings had lost touch not just with what God wanted but also with how they were supposed to conduct themselves in their relationships with one another. The people of "all nations," Occom said in 1783, were "all Adamites" who had lost "knowledge of god."[66] This loss of knowledge mattered not only to Occom's understanding of salvation but also to his ideas about slavery, colonialism, and other injustices perpetrated by human beings against one another. When it came to getting properly reacquainted with God, people were going to have to wait until the end of their worldly existence. In his sermon for Moses Paul, Occom presents the condemned as a "creature [who] will in a few minutes know more than all of us, either in unutterable joy, or in inconceivable wo"; "yet," he adds, "we shall certainly know as much as he in a few days."[67] In the meantime, wherever people might find themselves in their "weary Pilgrimage," they needed to figure out how to serve one another in the best way they could, using whatever fallen knowledge they had.

Piety and Placemaking

Well I remember home—O mohegan O Mohegan—the time is long before I Shall be walking my wonted places which are on thee—once there I was but perhaps never again, but Still I remember thee—in you is lodged my father & Mother Dear—and my Beloved Sisters—and brothers—Keep them in thy womb O Mohegan, till thou dost hear the Voice of God—O Mohegan give up thy Dead—then no longer Prisoners Shall they be unto thee—the joyfull hour is Approaching. My Soul Come Meditate the Day and think how near it stands when you must leave—this house of Clay—and fly to Unknown Lands . . . Perhaps in due time I may once more Come on thy borders—but first I have to go, to distant Lands; and far Country—and Differant Nations I have to walk through—before I see thee. Thus O Mohegan I must bid you farewell, and Shut the door of my Heart against thee—for I have a truer friend—to entertain in My Heart—So good night— (Diary of Joseph Johnson, December 17, 1772)[68]

There is no one way to describe the relationship between piety and placemaking in the eighteenth-century Native Northeast. So far in this chapter I have been arguing that, as an evangelical, Occom often organized social spaces through complex "micropractices" of piety and truth-telling. But for other Coastal Algonquian traditionalists, like Mary Fowler Occom, evangelical piety was a primarily a foil that served to elicit other styles of living and dwelling. Occom's son-in-law, the Mohegan preacher and Brothertown cofounder Joseph Johnson, had yet another approach to piety and place. His writings tend to be more inward-looking than Occom's, more attuned to the emotional turmoil attendant upon geographic and spiritual dislocation. Johnson's style of strangerhood turned evangelical piety into something approaching existentialism.

As Patricia Rubertone and Christine DeLucia argue, "social practices of constructing place" have largely to do with memory.[69] When a person or people moves to a new place, they immediately begin "making memories" there, but they also construct narratives about how they got there and what they left behind. For Occom and those of his kin who joined the Brothertown movement, placemaking meant taking some kind of stand on what it meant to relocate amid colonialism, and on how relocation did or did not impact the "network of relations" that linked Coastal Algonquians to one another and to their lands.[70] Occom's approach to placemaking was profoundly shaped by Northeast Native tradition and by his peoples' ancestral relationship to the land where "it pleased [God], to Plant our fore Fathers."[71] It was also shaped by his piety.

When Occom, during his trip to England in 1766, stood on the pulpit at Bristol's Tucker Street Meeting and identified himself as "an obscure Stranger, from an obscure Place," he did so partly by way of explicating the text he had chosen for that occasion, Isaiah 43:21: "This People have I formed for myself; they shall shew forth my Praise."[72] In his sermon, Occom explains how Isaiah's discussion of "God's forming a People" related back to his creation of Adam "out of the dust of the earth" and suggested that this act of creation was replaying itself on that very day: "you," Occom told his congregation, "are all formed by God," and "you may also be called his People, for he hath formed *you* for himself."[73] One of the wondrous things about God, Occom implied, was that he had the capacity to create new "Peoples" through the sheer power of his Word, even when that Word was preached by an "obscure Stranger." Then again, we might imagine Occom asking, given that humankind in general was estranged from God by sin, weren't all ministers "stranger ministers" anyway? Every real church was, from this point of view, a "People" made of strangers.

Occom's characterization of his churches, at least, as places of strangerly belonging had very deep roots in the Christian tradition. As early as the fifth century CE, the notion of a "church of strangers" was being propounded by the African bishop Augustine of Hippo, who declared that Christians were "strangers in this world . . . who fix their hope on a heavenly country"; to belong to the true Church was to dwell in a "pilgrim city" whose inhabitants "know that they are pilgrims even in their own habitations."[74] Over the ensuing centuries, such affirmations of strangerhood became a hallmark of "Augustinian piety" and the "Augustinian devotional tradition," terms that have often been associated with the English Protestants who colonized New England from the 1620s onward.[75] As Charles Hambrick Stowe writes, New Englanders in the seventeenth century tended to see themselves as "geographical as well as a spiritual traveler[s]. The stages of the physical journey often corresponded with the stages of the spiritual pilgrimage."[76] Historians of New England disagree about how much this Augustinian idea of the secular world as a site of spiritual pilgrimage mattered to the increasingly bourgeois colonial élites of the mid–eighteenth century, a period that is perhaps more often described in terms of the Edwardsean theology of "universal benevolence" and/or the "flaccid moralism" purveyed by Cotton Mather.[77] In the domain of popular or "lived" religion, however, the Augustinian metaphor of life as a spiritual pilgrimage remained prevalent. It is no accident that one of Occom's favorite places to preach was Boston's so-called "Church of Presbyterian Strangers," presided over by the Scots-Irish minister John Moorhead. "Good old Mr Moorh was better than all the Rest of the Ministers in Boston to me," Occom wrote to Buell after a trip to the area in 1773; "He was the only Minister in Boston that Invited me to preach in his Meeting House . . . and [I] preachd there four Times."[78] The group of people who attended Moorhead's church was uncommonly mixed by the standards of its day. It was possibly there that Occom first met both Susanna and Phillis Wheatley, both of whom attended Moorhead's church.[79]

Moorhead's idea of founding a church for Presbyterian "Strangers" had a fascinatingly Augustinian backstory of its own. Moorhead had brought this type of congregation with him over the Atlantic from Edinburgh, a city that had been a bastion of Presbyterianism ever since the days of John Knox, who in the 1550s had ministered to a "Church of Strangers" (*ecclesia peregrinorum*) of his own.[80] Knox's church in turn was modeled on the original Church of Strangers, which was founded in England by the Polish reformer John à Lasco, whom King Edward VI had granted permission to worship in an abandoned friary that had fallen into disuse following the dissolution of the English monasteries in the late 1530s.[81] That this Catholic friary—which, fittingly enough, had belonged to the Order of Saint Augustine—became a Protestant Church of Strangers shows how deeply and multifariously Augustinian piety permeated early modern Christianity. Moorhead exemplified this piety in his *ecclesia peregrinorum* in Boston, and Occom kept it going in his own way in sermons like the one from Bristol, when he set about to "form" a new "People" comprised of "obscure Stranger[s]." Indeed, this people-forming power of the Word was a perennial theme of Occom's sermonizing: as he put it in his sermon on Isaiah 58:1, "where ever the Gospel of Jesus Christ is receivd by any People, they are the People of God."[82]

Occom's belief in God's power to gather strangers into "Peoples" mattered greatly to his understanding of Northeast Native placemaking, but it is a delicate matter to describe exactly how. There exists a long scholarly tradition of describing Christian piety (especially in its Augustinian forms) as a form of "worldlessness" through which believers attempt to shed their earthly identities for the sake of membership in the City of God.[83] Julius Rubin has characterized Occom's piety along these lines, as part of "an

Indianized quest for salvation from this-worldly troubles and toward the promise of otherworldly paradise."[84] Yet thinking about piety from Mahmood's vantage, as a set of political "micropractices," brings into view a less one-sided interpretation of Occom's piety and of the "godly community" of Brothertown, as historians sometimes describe it.[85] When Occom and the other Brothertown founders gathered on November 7, 1785, to formally establish themselves as nation, they described it not as a Christian commune but rather as a "Body Politick" governed by norms of "Peace" and "Friendship" whose members, Occom wrote, "desired me to be a Teacher amongst them," not a minister. The people of Brothertown were not required to belong to any church; and given how hard it was to get a critical mass of families to migrate there, such a requirement would probably have spelled disaster.

Brothertown was founded as a political community whose members were left to go their own spiritual way.[86] This is in not to deny the strength of Occom's personal opinion that the people of Brothertown *should* be godly churchgoers. But that opinion was not hegemonic, and Occom knew it. The secular terms in which Occom described Brothertown's founding indicate that he saw the need of managing his own expectations on this matter. Yet while the godliness of Brothertown was far from guaranteed, Occom was prepared to wait. On October 1, 1787, two years into Brothertown's existence, he penned a progress report in his diary: "the People has made a rapped Progress in Cultivating the Land," he reported; now it was just a question of getting them to be "as ingagd in Religion as they are in their Temporal Concerns."[87] Occom's discussion of Brothertown's *worldliness* in its early years provides valuable information about the nation's history, since it suggests the community possessed sources of cohesion that went beyond "Christian fellowship."[88] Indeed, Occom's practices of piety were themselves carefully adapted to this-worldly concerns that were part and parcel of the Brothertown movement.

Here I especially have in mind Occom and Johnson's practices of hymnody, another form of popular (and often Augustinian) piety that Northeast Natives appropriated in ways that might at first seem to be but were not quite "otherworldly." In the preface to his 1774 *Choice Collection of Hymns and Spiritual Songs*, which scholars today agree was written with Brothertown in mind, Occom greeted readers with these words: "Here I present you, O Christians of what Denomination soever, with cordial Hymns, to comfort you in your weary Pilgrimage; I hope they will assist and strengthen you through the various Changes of this Life, till you shall all safely arrive to the general Assembly Above, and Church of the First-Born, where you shall have no more need of these imperfect Hymns."[89] This is pretty Augustinian, and certainly interested in the afterlife, or "Assembly Above." But it is not entirely otherworldly. This world, like the hymns Occom offers, may be "imperfect," but there is still much to do by way of "comfort[ing]," "assist[ing]," and "strengthen[ing]" one another. In the hymns themselves, these practices of worldly care are closely connected with the theme of relocation, which makes sense in light of the hymnal's intended use at Brothertown, as Joanna Brooks has noted.[90] In "A Son's Farewell," Occom begins,

> Honor'd parents fare you well,
> My Jesus doth me call,
> I leave you here with God until
> I meet you once for all.
>
> My due affections I'll forsake,
> My parents and their house,
> And to the wilderness betake,
> To pay the Lord my vows . . .
>
> And if thro' preaching I shall gain
> True subjects to my Lord,
> 'Twill more than recompence my pain,
> To see them love the Lord.
>
> My soul doth wish mount Zion well,
> Whate'er becomes of me;
> There my best friends and kindred dwell,
> And there I long to be.

Like the preface to the hymnal, these verses are conscious of another world without being unequivocally "otherworldly." There is, to be sure, a "long[ing]" for a spiritual resting-place that cannot be attained in this life. But the hymn also describes a more practical way of living with oneself and others. The goal, in this world, is to get others to turn toward God: "to see them love the Lord." This turning toward God entails a spiritual reorientation of "subjects," but from the vantage of the persons voicing the hymn (whoever's saying or singing "I") it also implies a physical redirection toward another part of the earth: "I'll . . . to the wilderness betake." For any Coastal Algonquian person reading or singing this hymn, the referent of these words would have been clear: Brothertown. The hymn also leaves open the possibility of a new form of worldly belonging. "*Due* affections" are to be "forsake[n]," but that doesn't necessarily mean telling everyone one loves that one doesn't love them anymore. What it really means is that social relations are no longer to be understood as being grounded in obligation, or what is "due."[91] In this respect, Occom followed in the footsteps of Jonathan Edwards, who argued that "grace . . . totally eradicates the selfish basis of natural love and refounds love again on a different principle," namely love of God.[92] The prospect of such grace-assisted love was, for Edwards and Occom alike, cause for hope, since those to whom one had formerly shown *merely* "due" affections could also reimagine love in just the same way. The hymn is not about the breakup of families, in other words, so much as the regrounding of existing intimacies on a new spiritual basis.

It is instructive to contrast the style of piety modeled in "A Son's Farewell" to the one we find in some of the more self-critical writings of Occom's son-in-law Joseph Johnson. As I mentioned earlier, Johnson pushed Augustinian piety in a more existential direction than Occom. For Occom, being a "stranger" in a religious sense meant seeing one's life as a "pilgrimage" in which one sought to turn toward God while remaining firmly grounded in this world. Johnson followed Augustine in a slightly different direction, focusing on sin's power to open a fissure within the *inner* domain of the individual soul: "O God of mercy," he wrote in his diary on December 1, 1771, "be pleased in thy infinite Mercy, to Open my Eyes to See my miserable case, whilst I am a Stranger to myself and thee."[93] It is possible, but not very likely, that Johnson learned about the possibility of being a "stranger to myself" from the writings of Augustine, who often spoke in such terms. It is also possible that he picked up the notion from his father-in-law, or that he came up with the idea independently. Most likely, however, Johnson had in mind the famous hymn by Isaac Watts: "My God, permit me not to be / A stranger to myself and thee."[94] It seems telling that this hymn was *not* among the numerous works by Watts that Occom included in the various editions of his hymnal. My sense is that this more self-regarding strain of Augustinian piety was not generally to his taste. Perhaps this was partly because Occom saw its effects on Johnson. Being a "stranger to myself" was an aspect of Johnson's piety, but the phrase seems also to have expressed deep personal pain, much like the diary entry from December 1772 I quoted from at the beginning of this section: "think how near it stands when you must leave—this house of Clay—and fly to Unknown Lands.... Thus O Mohegan I must bid you farewell, and Shut the door of my Heart against thee."[95] My guess is that Occom, who was in close contact with Johnson in the early 1770s, found the despairing and self-critical tenor of his piety worrisome. For decades, Occom had been cultivating a form of religiosity that had a clear social and political *purpose* even, as we have seen, in its most otherworldly moments. But his beloved Johnson often talked like someone who thought he had nowhere to go.

Johnson's surviving letters indicate that Occom worked hard to help him recover his spirits during the trying years of 1771–1773. On April 5, 1773, Johnson wrote from Farmington, where he had been working as a teacher, to thank Occom for

> Your unlimited, kind treatment, towards poor me: during the time I was at Mohegan. Well I remember how chearfully, and libirally, ye administered to my necessities. Ye have been, as it were, the Support of my drooping heart, when Dejection like a Garment covered it; well I remember the trying times which I went through the last summer, forsaken of friends ... yet was thou pleased to Shew me Respects, and consider'd of me, and gave me advice, and Encouraged me.[96]

This letter is another reminder that piety, understood as what I have called a "style of strangerhood," can have serious emotional and existential stakes. For Johnson, spiritual "Dejection" was "like a Garment": something he *wore* like the black veil in Hawthorne's story. But at a certain point, Johnson observes, such guises can take over a person's sense of self and reduce one to "necessities." How exactly Occom helped get Johnson out of his "Dejection" is unclear. Maybe he impressed upon him that piety is not about turning inward on oneself but rather about turning toward God and, in doing so, finding a better direction in the world one shares with others.

Whatever Occom may have said to Johnson in private, it is probably not a coincidence that Johnson's recovery of his spirits occurred just a couple weeks after the initial planning meeting for Brothertown at Mohegan on March 13, 1773, a meeting at which both Johnson and Occom had been present.[97] It also seems fitting that the Algonquian word for Brothertown, *eeyawquittoowauconnuck*, means, according to Mohegan linguist Stephanie Fielding, "he does so like someone looking in a certain direction or a certain way."[98] That is what both piety and placemaking meant to Occom and to some, but not all, of his kin.

PART III

CHAPTER V

Seft at Last

Occom's 1768 Autobiography in Native Space

Samson Occom's autobiographical narrative of 1768 has attained canonical status in the history of world Anglophone literature. Indeed, it seems safe to say that it is the most widely read piece of writing created by any Native North American author prior to the nineteenth century. For all its familiarity, however, Occom's second autobiography is, like its author, a "strange creature" that has lived through multiple relocations. Conceived in 1768 to silence a group of white ministers who were spreading false rumors about his life story, Occom's manuscript was belatedly adopted into Native space after 1770, only to be dragged back into non-Native hands in the early nineteenth century and then, finally, repatriated to Mohegan in 2022, just as I was completing this book.[1] In more recent decades the autobiography has been transcribed by scholars and published widely, but the manuscript that Occom actually created—the physical "thing" as distinct from the text it contains—has been largely overlooked in favor of more recent printed editions. Still, there are many mysterious things about it.

There is, for instance, the last line: "I did not make my seft so."[2] In every edition of the autobiography that has appeared in print to date, the sentence is rendered "I did not make my self so."[3] In the manuscript, the words are difficult to make out because the text is a palimpsest of two hands, but based on comparisons with other instances of the word "self" in the manuscript, it seems clear that Occom wrote "seft." The more heavily inked "self" was a later change, probably by a nineteenth-century editor who tried to "fix" what Occom put there by thickly overwriting the manuscript to turn the "f" into an "l" and the "t" into an "f." But it should be plain for all to see that Occom really wrote "seft," thanks to the excellent reproduction of the manuscript that is freely available on the Occom Circle Project website and the even closer up image I was able to capture in September 2022 with the help of the staff at the Mohegan Tribe's Cultural Preservation Center.[4]

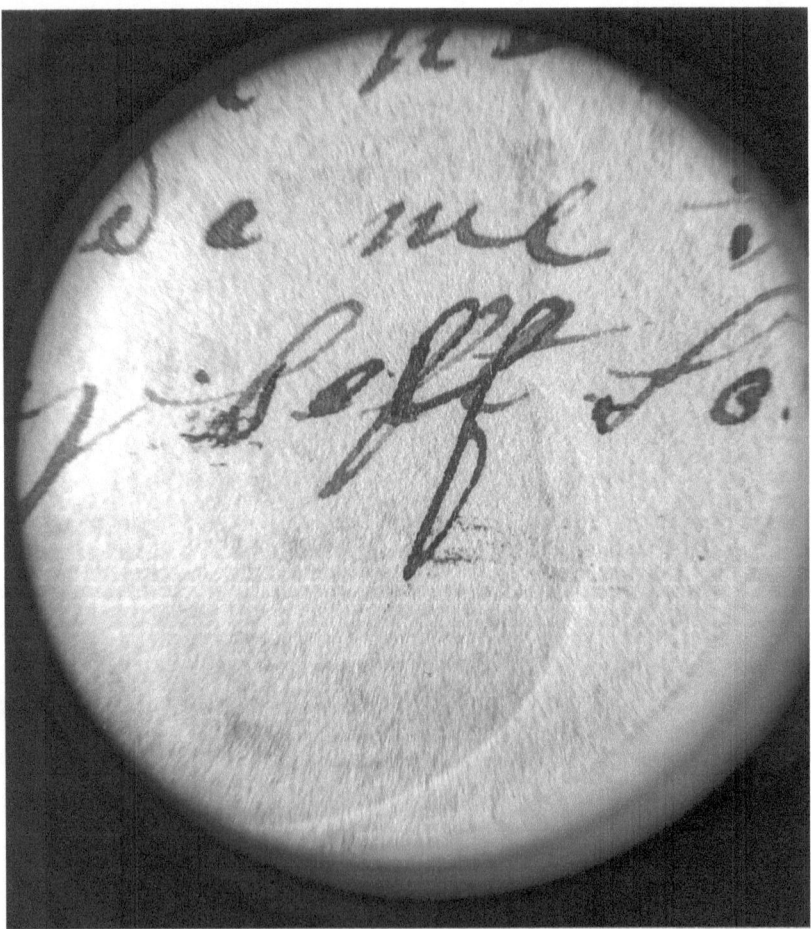

Figure 5.1 Seft becomes *self* at the end of the narrative.
Samson Occom Papers, Mohegan Tribe. Photograph by the author.

I have been thinking about "seft" for years, and I still don't know what to make of it. My first thought, when I realized what Occom had actually written, was that it must be a provincialism. In some times and places in the long history of the English language, "seft" has been used as a past participle of the verb "save," just as "left" is used as a past participle of "leave."[5] It is not impossible that Occom occasionally used the term in this way, but it seems unlikely since "seft" appears nowhere else in his surviving writings or (so far as I have seen) in the writings of anyone who knew him.

Another possibility is that Occom actually wrote "saft" (the black overwriting makes it impossible to say for sure), a word he might have learned on his travels through Scotland and the north of England, where it was used in the eighteenth century to mean "agreement, freedom from strife, peace."[6] So perhaps we should really be reading the last sentence of the text as "I did not make my saved so," or "I did not make my peace/agreement so," a reading that would be compatible with his desire to present himself in the text less as a freestanding and self-sufficient person that as a being whose *relationship* to God gave him a feeling of peace with the world.

In any case, while it is probably not wrong to call Occom's manuscript an "autobiography" (Occom himself referred to it as "a short narrative of my life") it seems telling that the "self" whose history it relates is not, in the end, where one would most expect to find it.

Occom began writing his "short narrative" in the fall of 1768, shortly after his return from the British Isles. The trip had been a huge financial success, with Occom raising £9,497 in England and another £2,530 in Scotland for Wheelock's new school for Native children (in 2023 currency, this would be worth somewhere in the neighborhood of $1.5 million).[7] Personally, however, Occom was not fully satisfied. He wrote the autobiography in the hopes of correcting certain "gross Mistakes" being propagated about him "by Some gentlemen in America," and also, perhaps, of persuading his superiors in the ministerial hierarchy to pay him a fair wage.[8] Within a few years of finishing the autobiography, however, these hopes were dashed. Wheelock disappeared up the Connecticut River to found Dartmouth, and so too did any hope Occom might have had of gainful employment as a teacher in his school. Then the Revolutionary War broke out, throwing transatlantic channels of missionary finance and communication into chaos. Occom's autobiography never had a chance to fulfill the purposes—a better reputation and a decent wage—for which it was originally designed.

What happened to Occom's manuscript in the wake of these upheavals? Up until now, scholars have assumed that Occom gave the manuscript to Wheelock some time before the two had their falling-out in 1770 and that it "languished amongst Wheelock's letters at Dartmouth until the late twentieth century," when it was rediscovered by the German literary historian Bernd Peyer and published for a print readership for the first time since its composition.[9] Today, Occom's autobiography is a mainstay of college-level surveys of American literary and religious history; yet enthusiasm for it among scholars appears to have diminished slightly, relative to some of Occom's other writings, since the first flush of excitement and debate that followed its rediscovery in the 1980s and 1990s. This diminishment makes sense in light of the widespread assumption that the text has always been part of what Drew Lopenzina calls the "colonial archive," having been written in the 1760s for a white audience and possessed by white people ever since.[10] Along these lines, Joanna Brooks argues in her editorial introduction to the autobiography that the narrative "reveals more about the constraints within which Occom worked—his white audiences' prejudicial preconceptions of 'Indianness'—than it does about his own sense of himself as a Christian Indian."[11] The autobiography, on this reading, stands as a testament to Occom's courageous defiance of anti-"Indian" prejudice at one moment in time; but beyond that the text has little to say about more substantive issues of Northeast Native survival and self-determination of the sort that Native communities and their academic allies care most about today.

In this chapter I want to sketch a very different history of Occom's autobiographical manuscript and offer a new interpretation of the text to go along with it. My argument, in brief, is that Occom's manuscript spent most of its existence in Native spaces—in Mohegan and later in Brothertown—at least until the time of Occom's death in 1792, and probably well into the nineteenth century. This argument is based on hitherto overlooked archival materials pertinent to the manuscript's history and provenance, which suggest that Occom took his autobiography with him when he emigrated from Mohegan to Brothertown. I say "indicate" rather than "prove" because the evidence I will be describing is far from overwhelming, and I am mindful that strong claims require strong evidence to back them up. Having registered this proviso, however, I would also observe that it applies equally to the hypothesis (for it is really nothing more than that) that Occom gave his manuscript to Wheelock, who later gave it to Dartmouth. There is very little to prove this assertion, and much about it that is problematic.

The question of how to interpret the text in light of this new information is a complex one. For one thing, it is unclear what Occom did with the manuscript after he relocated to Brothertown. It is conceivable that it remained buried among Occom's own papers, but the more exciting possibility is that he shared it with other Native people in his community. Even if that is true, the fact that Occom took the manuscript with him to Brothertown does not necessarily mean that he changed his mind about anything he wrote in 1768.

The interpretation I will be providing here, accordingly, is in the first instance an attempt to reconcile the autobiography's intended meaning (what Occom wanted to say when he wrote it) with a broader understanding of the manuscript's circulation among different groups of readers. Even though the text wound up circulating in ways Occom could not have foreseen in 1768, his original intentions still mattered; but in Native spaces the text would have mattered in new and different ways, even to Occom, and produced different kinds of effects.

In exploring these shifting meanings, I have found it helpful to conceptualize the manuscript of Occom's autobiography along the lines of Arjun Appadurai's work on the "social life of things": as an object that is value-laden because of the way it circulates socially.[12] Given the very real possibility that the manuscript was passed back and forth within Native communities for decades, what value could it have had for them? This is partly, but not entirely, a question about audience. To say that Occom's autobiography had a different "social life" after it moved into Native space is to ask questions that have not hitherto been asked about what eighteenth-century Northeast Native communities might have made of it.

As important as this question of audience is, however, it is also important to keep in mind, following Appadurai, that *things in general* mean different things (as it were) among different communities at different times. This contextual variability in the meaning of "thingness" is especially pertinent to the interpretation of text-artifacts, like Occom's autobiography, whose "social lives" involve crossing boundaries between settler and Native spaces. As Webb Keane and other anthropologists working in the tradition of Michael Silverstein have noted, one of the defining features of the "semiotic ideology" peculiar to modern "Western" societies—especially those shaped by Protestant reading practices—is that the thingness of written objects tends to get overlooked in favor of the written symbols those objects transmit.[13] Certainly it is the case that in eighteenth-century New England and, for that matter, in academic discourse ever since, the thingness of Occom's autobiography has typically been conflated with, and hence obscured by, its textuality. From this very widespread point of view, the words on the page are what really matter, and the "thing" that is the manuscript is just one vehicle among many others (anthologies, websites, photocopied course packets, and so on) for transmitting those words from Occom to readers.

To some extent, Occom invites readers to look at the autobiography in this familiar "Western" way, to see his manuscript as little more than a vehicle for the valuable textual cargo it contains. In the autobiography's opening he frames his narrative as a juridical performance ("to do justice to my self") in which "gross mistakes" will be overturned by means of argument and evidence and "publish[ed]" for all interested parties to see and assess. Occom hints that this process of readerly judgment could take a while. He addresses the text, in part, to later readers "who may desire to know Something concerning me," words which seem to reflect his expectation that the autobiography would be widely disseminated in print, not manuscript—"perhaps," as Lopenzina plausibly speculates, as "an addendum to one of Wheelock's many promotional narratives concerning the state of the Indian Charity School."[14]

As it turned out, Occom never saw his autobiography in print. For more than two centuries it remained one object, discrete in its thingness: eight sheets of paper stacked on top of one another, folded in half, and stitched into a booklet along the crease with needle and thread. If you had been fortunate enough to meet Occom at Mohegan or Brothertown and told him, "I read your autobiography," he would have said back to you something like, "Wait, how? I never gave it to you." Those people whom Occom *did* show it to participated in a "social life" organized around the manuscript that meant something very different from what the autobiography's text means for contemporary readers. It would have been an uncommon and value-laden experience just to be among those who had held it and pondered it, knowing that the person who created it had been engaged in important work in faraway places. Whatever else the autobiography is, it is most certainly a record of one Native person's "acquaint[ance] with the World," of his birth, childhood, education, relocation, teaching, travels, and struggles.[15] In Native space Occom's manuscript may have been read less like it typically has been since 1982—as a great work of literature, canonized in an anthology—than in the way that wampum belts were read by Occom and his contemporaries: as an artifact that was actually a part of collective memory rather than a mere description of it.[16]

Of course, none of this changes the fact that Occom wrote what he wrote in 1768 not knowing that his manuscript would travel with him from Mohegan to Brothertown. This earlier phase of its social life remains relevant, in part because Occom's social milieu in 1768 bears certain important similarities (including the semiotic ideology mentioned above) with the non-Native or "mixed spaces" inhabited by most people who encounter the text today.[17] One of the goals of the present chapter is to reinterpret the words Occom wrote in 1768 in light of the conjectures sketched a moment ago about the manuscript's social life in Native space. These conjectures foreground Northeast Natives' social competency of using things, passed from hand to hand, to embody the past. Yet my argument here is that this Northeast Native competency was part of Occom's background understanding of his social milieu even in 1768, at a time when he was mainly focused on what he would say to his white superiors in settler space. Even then, Occom understood his autobiography as having a meaning that went beyond the evidentiary function of the conversion narrative genre within which he was working, and even beyond his own desire to prove to his colleagues and the wider world that he was a true and authentic Christian who was also authentically Indigenous. Occom wanted to write a text that would have value for other people irrespective of such proofs by virtue of its power to put readers in a right relationship with one another and with God. "God has made me so," Occom says, and on his understanding the same was true of his words: he wanted them to be seen as "shot through with value because [they were] shot through with the presence of the divine."[18] That value was not a "social construction" or a figment of anyone's imagination, but rather something that lived out there in the world, embodied in a thing—letters and sounds, paper and ink—that God had given people to see, hear, touch, and pass from hand to hand.

Most of the chapter that follows is dedicated to further developing the reading I have just begun to sketch. Beforehand, however, I invite you to follow me as I recount the collaborative journey through the archives that inspired this revisionist interpretation of Occom's most widely read text. This journey began with my realization that Occom had written "seft" instead of "self." And it is still going on today. In a powerful act of justice and reconciliation, Dartmouth College repatriated Occom's manuscripts to Mohegan in April 2022. I write these words in September 2022, a few weeks after paying a visit to the Mohegan Tribe's new Cultural Preservation Center, where I discussed the manuscript and other aspects of Mohegan history and tradition with Tribal Historian Jason LaVigne and archivist David Freeburg. Library staff were able to bring out a range of magnification tools that allowed me, David, and Jason to get a closer look at the manuscript than perhaps any previous researchers. Many questions about Occom's autobiography still remain unanswered, but at least the document has found its way back to the Mohegan homelands where its own odyssey started.

Questions of Provenance

My exploration of the history of Occom's second autobiography began in 2019, when I decided to write this book. I knew the autobiography would feature prominently in my study, and in typical humanist fashion decided I should go back *ad fontes*—meaning, since this was during a global pandemic, to the digital reproduction of the manuscript on the Dartmouth Library website—to see if there were any noteworthy features of the manuscript that previous editors had missed. I was surprised to discover an editorial notice on the Occom Circle Project website indicating that someone other than Occom had attempted to "correct" the manuscript sometime in the nineteenth century, and even more surprised to find that one of those corrections had altered "seft" to "self" in the manner described earlier.

At first I could not believe my eyes. "I did not make my self so" was probably the best-known line from Occom's best-known text, thanks in part to the literary historian Eileen Elrod, who used the sentence as the title of her widely cited book chapter about the autobiography.[19] I looked closely at the manuscript to make sure Occom's letters, still visible under the editor's "correction," really spelled "seft." For some time, I was determined to discover some other letters than "ft," since "seft" didn't seem like a word to me. I asked my partner what she thought (she also saw "seft") and then raised the issue by email with my friends at the Calumet and Cross Heritage Society Book Club, a meeting of Brothertown community members and non-Brothertown allies which gathers each week to discuss readings relevant to the Nation. We discussed the mystery together one evening by Zoom, and while I learned a great deal, no clear conclusions were reached. Most group members seemed to agree that the letters on the page read "seft," but people also agreed widely that Occom had simply made a mistake and meant to write "self." One member suggested that "seft" might be from a non-English language, an intriguing suggestion that was echoed by the people I spoke with during my most recent trip to Mohegan. But no one I have spoken with, from Mohegan, Brothertown, or anywhere else, has been able to identify "seft" as belonging to any Native or non-Native tongue they know of.

One member of the book club suggested that I check in with the staff at the Rauner Special Collections Library at Dartmouth College, which I soon proceeded to do. I first consulted the "Validation" version of the text published on the Dartmouth College website, where the archivists who first transcribed the text for the Occom Circle Project provided a detailed description of their own editorial decisions. The transcription of the word in question read, "Se[illegible] [guess . . . ft]," indicating that Hazel-Dawn Dumpert, who edited the Occom Circle Project transcriptions, had also seen "seft."[20] Dumpert no longer works for the project, so I asked College Archivist Peter Carini for his opinion; he told me he thought the first letter was "s," the second one was undecipherable, the third letter was "s" or "f," and the last letter was a "t." I downloaded as many English word lists as I could find and ran searches to find any words matching these criteria. "Soft" was a possibility, but the second letter clearly was not an "o." Nothing else emerged from my word lists that made better sense than "seft."

Peter also shared with me a very interesting fact about the history of the manuscript, which was that he and other members of the library staff suspected, but could not be sure, that the black overwriting that had marred Occom's manuscript was put there in the nineteenth century by William Leete Stone. Stone, apparently, had donated an Occom-related manuscript to Dartmouth in 1866, and as Hazel-Dawn Dumpert first observed, the handwriting on the donation letter resembled the black overwriting on several Occom manuscripts then held at Dartmouth, including some letters and the autobiography.[21] I looked at the handwriting on the donation letter Peter mentioned and the overwritten manuscripts, and that seemed plausible to me—not proof positive, but worth further investigation. What really interested me, however, was the name William Stone. Back in graduate school I had done some research on the legal struggles of the novelist

James Fenimore Cooper, who in the 1830s and 1840s sued a whole cadre of New York newspaper editors for publishing libelous articles about his novels.[22] One of Cooper's early defendants, I recalled, was the editor and amateur historian William Leete Stone. The William Stone sued by Cooper died in 1844, but he had a son of the same name. This William Leete Stone Jr. turned out to be the person who had sent the Occom-related materials to Dartmouth in the 1860s.

The reason this piqued my interest was because I remembered that William Leete Stone Sr., later known as "Colonel" Stone, had begun his career in Cooperstown, New York, less than thirty miles southeast of Brothertown. As a journeyman editor, Stone worked various jobs across New York and Connecticut in the first decades of the nineteenth century, ultimately settling down in New York City in 1821, where he became the editor of the *Commercial Advertiser*.[23] During his early travels, Stone kept an eye out for old books and manuscripts. A die-hard literary nationalist in the classic nineteenth-century mold, he dreamed of monumentalizing in prose the great Native and English leaders whose exploits in upstate New York had left such an indelible stamp on early U.S. history. "At an early period of his life," remembered William Jr., his father

> formed the purpose of gathering up and preserving what remained concerning the traits and character of the red men of America, intending to connect with an account of these, an authentic history of the life and times of the prominent individuals who figured immediately before the Revolution. . . . The amount of labor thus bestowed, and the success with which he found his way to dusty manuscripts, or gained knowledge of the invaluable contents of old chests and rickety trunks stowed away as lumber in garrets and almost forgotten by their owners, were remarkable.[24]

Colonel Stone was born in 1792, the same year Occom died, and took up his post at the Cooperstown *Federalist* around 1810.[25] Could it be that sometime during the tumultuous period of Brothertown history that followed Occom's death his autobiography had found its way into one of the "old chests and rickety trunks," "almost forgotten by their owners," that would soon come into the possession of the enterprising young antiquarian William Stone Sr.?

The idea was not implausible, but it obviously conflicted with the prevailing scholarly assumption that Occom gave the manuscript to Wheelock who gave it to Dartmouth. So I decided to go back to the secondary literature to find out what evidence the conventional view rested on. My main focus here was Drew Lopenzina's chapter on Occom in his fascinating literary history *Red Ink*, which contains the best-researched account of the manuscript's history to date. In this study Lopenzina reaffirms the received view that the manuscript spent its life post-1768 among Wheelock's papers, but the evidence he uncovered on behalf of this claim seemed to me to point toward a very different conclusion.

One of Lopenzina's most important discoveries was an anonymous 1830 article on Mohegan history in the Norwich (Connecticut) *Courier*, which lifted several passages verbatim from Occom's manuscript and wove them, without attribution, into the flow of the writer's third-person history of Occom's life. In one such passage, Occom describes the difficulty his Montaukett schoolchildren had learning their English letters, writing that "the Way I took to Cure em, was by making an Alphabet on Small bits of paper, and Glued them on Small Chips of Cedar, after this manner A B &c. I put these on Letters in order on a Bench, then point to one Letter and bid a Child to take notice of it."[26]

This is rendered by the writer for the *Courier* as: "He invented the following method of teaching children the alphabet: he glued the letters to small chips of cedar, A B &c. and put them in order on a bench, and then pointed to the letter and bid the child take notice of it."[27]

In light of such evidence, Lopenzina is surely right to conclude that whoever wrote this article for the *Courier* had Occom's manuscript in their possession. Yet it is unclear how this inference squares with his claim that the manuscript "languished amongst Wheelock's letters at Dartmouth until the late twentieth century." Lopenzina's assumption seems to be that the writer for the *Courier* read Occom's autobiography at Dartmouth. If this were the case, however, Occom's narrative would almost certainly have been cited and discussed in the *Memoirs of the Rev. Eleazar Wheelock* published in 1811 by Wheelock's devoted pupil David McClure. McClure made extensive use of Wheelock's papers in his memorial and had unrestricted access to the manuscript archives pertaining to Occom's dealings with Wheelock in the 1760s. He even knew about the existence of Occom's autobiography and was on the lookout for it during the research for his book. In the *Memoir* McClure transcribed the entirety of the September 1768 letter from Occom to Robert Keen in which Occom mentions being at work on the second autobiography. Yet, McClure recorded with evident disappointment, the "narrative of his life, has not appeared."[28] Assuming that McClure did not simply overlook the manuscript, this suggests that it was somewhere other than Dartmouth in 1811. And if it wasn't there in 1811, why should we assume it was there in 1830?

Buried among advertisements near the back of the *Courier* issue discovered by Lopenzina is a short editorial notice: "We would direct the attention of our readers to the brief but full and interesting history of the Mohegan tribe of Indians, on our first page. It is written by a gentleman who, although not resident in this town, has had access to valuable sources of information, the accuracy of which is unquestionable."[29] The notice is obviously filler—why advertise the issue's leading story three pages back?—but nevertheless it usefully supported the conjecture that whatever "gentleman" had "access" to Occom's autobiography and other "valuable sources of information" pertaining to the Mohegans was a private collector, or a close associate of one, rather than a researcher digging around in college archives. Could this have been William Leete Stone?

After 1830, the trail of evidence attesting to the whereabouts of Occom's manuscript goes cold until 1842, when the citizens of Norwich invited an eminent historian to give a speech rededicating a monument to the Mohegan sachem Uncas.[30] A pedestal for the monument had been laid several years earlier, in 1833, upon which occasion a celebration had been convened that was presided over, in a perverse publicity stunt, by U.S. President Andrew Jackson. Finally, in 1842, a new obelisk was procured to install on the still unfinished plinth. Now Jackson was nowhere to be seen. Instead, the "ladies of Norwich" promoted the event with a pamphlet celebrating the virtues of temperance and the "progress of the Gospel" at Mohegan, where the old Congregational church had just been "repaired, enlarged, and entirely remodeled."[31] This time around, Uncas's white friends at Norwich wanted to get their history right. They reached out to some of New England's most learned men to verify the basics of Uncas's biography. Organizer George Perkins wrote to the great dictionary-man Noah Webster, asking him to weigh in on "the best spelling of the name of this ancient Sachem and firm friend of the white man."[32] Perkins and his collaborators combed through local archives in search of information on the Mohegans. Some likely still remembered the 1830 history of the Mohegans published in the

Courier. It would hardly be surprising if this "full and interesting history of the Mohegan tribe" convinced the organizers, after due consideration, that the best possible person to deliver the keynote address at their dedication ceremony was the 1830 article's author: the "gentleman who . . . has had access to valuable sources of information" including the manuscript of Occom's autobiography. In any event, the person they wound up inviting was William Leete Stone Sr.

The speech Stone delivered on July 4, 1842, is not worth detailed analysis here, except insofar as it sheds light on the history of Occom's manuscript. In the speech Stone (I presume) recycles much of the material he had used in his 1830 article for the *Courier* but goes into greater detail and deploys much more florid rhetoric. As historian Jean O'Brien has observed, the speech is a classic example of "firsting and lasting": a self-serving local history deployed by colonial writers to memorialize but also efface the presence of Indigenous peoples in New England.[33] Even in the 1840s, the speech—which was swiftly introduced to the print marketplace by New York City publishers Dayton & Newman as *Uncas and Miantonomoh*—was ridiculed for its exceedingly romantic and one-sided treatment of Uncas, "the white man's friend."[34] "History," Stone pronounced, "presents not a nobler instance of courage united with magnanimity, and a humane desire to avoid the unnecessary shedding of blood."[35] Not long after he delivered his oration, Colonel Stone ran into the Connecticut historian James Hammond Trumbull in the town of Stonington, not far from Norwich. Upon hearing from Trumbull that his speech had minimized the violence that had afflicted Native communities during Uncas's sachemship, Stone retorted with: "See here my young freind [*sic*],—if the ladies of Norwich should send for you, to come and make a speech over Uncas's grave, and they were all present to hear you, do you think it would be well to tell all the truth about him? I couldn't do it."[36] The anecdote was written by a biased party, but it certainly accords with the feel-good (for white people) tone of Stone's brand of Native history—or rather "*blarney*," as Trumbull called it, which Stone had "tried to make . . . pass for *history*."[37]

Irrespective of the historic veracity of either party to the Stone-Trumbull dispute, Stone did make *some* effort to meet the minimum threshold of scholarly respectability in the published version of his speech, where sporadic footnotes provide a useful if incomplete record of his sources. This is where *Uncas and Miantonomoh*'s relevance to Occom's manuscript comes in. In its published form, Stone's speech includes a lengthy appendix titled

"Of the New England Indians in General." In a section of this appendix labeled "Of the Mohegans," Stone reprints, with very slight changes, the *Courier* article from 1830.³⁸ While he did not footnote the *Courier* piece itself—presumably because he had written it and was not worried about citing himself—Stone does provide footnotes for many passages that had gone without them in 1830. Recycled facts from the 1830 article about Mohegan population levels, for instance, are attributed in the 1842 appendix to Trumbull, Ezra Stiles, and Abiel Holmes; and an anonymous third-party description of Occom's preaching lifted from the 1830 article is attributed now to "Allen's Biography."³⁹

These footnotes provide further indication that Stone himself was the author of the 1830 article for the *Courier*. How else would he have known the sources of all the facts that appeared there? It would have been highly bizarre (not to mention difficult) for him to go back and trace all the sources relied upon by some writer other than himself, especially when he could have simply footnoted the Mohegan section as being based on an article from the *Courier*. The most likely scenario is that Stone himself was the writer of the 1830 article and the 1842 appendix, and that he used the latter publication as an opportunity to properly cite his sources in a way that he could not do when writing for a newspaper. Stone, then, was indeed the "gentleman" referred to in the 1830 notice, "who, although not resident in this town, has had access to valuable sources of information, the accuracy of which is unquestionable." He was the person, in other words, who possessed the manuscript of Occom's autobiography in 1830, a text from which he borrowed (to put it nicely) just as extensively in 1842 as he had done a dozen years earlier.

Significantly, the extract from Occom's autobiography that Stone includes in *Uncas and Miantonomoh* is the one place where he is *less* clear about his sources in 1842 than he had been in 1830. In 1830, he had quoted several paragraphs directly from the autobiography, prepending them with the sentence, "He wrote the following brief account of himself." That sentence is gone in the 1842 appendix, and so are the quotation marks. Occom's words still appear, but they are now passed off as if they were Stone's: "His parents, like the other Indians, led a wandering life. . . . He lived in a house covered with mats. . . . He bound old books for the East Hampton people."⁴⁰ Elsewhere in his amply footnoted appendix, we have seen, Stone tries to be a good historian; here, however, it seems like he is hiding something. Why should he have been happy to give Occom credit for his words when writing anonymously in 1830, but loath in 1842 even to acknowledge the autobiography's existence? Possibly Stone felt less obligated in 1842 to give a Native American from the prior century the full measure of literary credit to which he was due. A more likely and not mutually exclusive explanation is that Stone, who still held the manuscript in his private collection, knew that it did not rightfully belong to him, and he didn't want other people to know he had it. It is apparent from Stone's discussion of the Mohegans in *Uncas and Miantonomoh* that he knew full well that the Mohegan nation was still alive and well. Occom's sister, Lucy Tantaquidgeon, had just died in 1830, the appendix reports; and "in more modern times" a new church and schoolhouse had been built on the reservation, with the tribe as a whole "putting forth fruits and buds of promise."[41] The last thing Stone would have wanted was someone from the tribe calling upon him to explain exactly how he had acquired his prized collection of Indigenous manuscripts, back in his youth in upstate New York when he had passed his time rifling through "old chests and rickety trunks" which had been "*almost* forgotten by their owners."[42]

Even though Occom's autobiography is very widely read today, the phrase "almost forgotten" captures something important about the manuscript and the complex "social life" it has led. My hope is that the present chapter will contribute to ongoing efforts among scholars and tribes to recover and remember early Indigenous writings not just as words on a page, but also as "things" that embody histories of Indigenous survival and adaptation.[43] Having said that, I am aware that the foregoing account raises more questions than it answers. William Leete Stone died in 1844, at which time most of his massive collection of manuscripts passed on to William Jr.[44] However, I have not been able thus far to determine which of the two gave the manuscript to Dartmouth, nor can I be sure whether it was father or son who scribbled over Occom's writing with their assiduous editorial hand. Most important, even though the most likely scenario seems to be that Stone Sr. acquired the manuscript somewhere in upstate New York, there is no evidence attesting to exactly how or when that happened, or whether the Brothertown Nation or any other Indigenous community knew about it. Then again, there is to the best of my knowledge nothing in Dartmouth's institutional archives that supports the long-standing assumption that the manuscript came to Dartmouth via Wheelock.[45] As Peter Carini told me, the 1866 letter from William Stone Jr. about Dartmouth's "first Indian Scholar" is the best lead anyone has to go on at present.

Thankfully, Occom's manuscript has been repatriated to Mohegan since I began researching its history. Yet where it lived between 1768 and its acquisition by Dartmouth remains mostly a mystery. Another still-open mystery is what to make of "seft." Yes, it could be a mistake, as Stone, *père* or *fils*, seems to have thought. But that feels to me like the easy way out, an evasion of some challenge Occom wanted his readers to confront, as would befit the complex literary persona Occom adopts near the end of the autobiography when he declares, "I speak like a fool." As scholars have long noted, the latter phrase comes from the Apostle Paul, who adopts the fool's persona in a passage from 2 Corinthians that Occom's autobiography reworks in complex ways, as we will see in greater detail shortly. The fact that Occom had Paul's apostolic ministry in mind when he was writing the autobiography brings to mind the possibility that he was practicing glossolalia, or speaking "in an unknown tongue," as the ancient apostles were famous for doing. In his first letter to the Corinthians, Paul claimed that the phenomenon of speaking in tongues demonstrated the Holy Spirit's power to defeat human beings' cognitive faculties and argued that the strange practice of glossolalia warranted new forms of interpretation: "Wherefore let him that speaketh in an unknown tongue pray that he may interpret. For if I pray in an unknown tongue, my spirit prayeth, but my understanding is unfruitful."[46] Occom, who knew this passage well and cited it at least once,[47] could have written "seft" in hopes that future interpreters would recall Paul's teaching that those words which manifest the sacred most powerfully are very often the hardest to understand, as if belonging to a foreign tongue and time.

"I owe them nothing"

> The whole creation will be consumed and appear infinite and holy, whereas it now appears finite and corrupt. This will come to pass by an improvement of sensual enjoyment. . . . If the doors of perception were cleansed everything would appear to man as it is, infinite. For man has closed himself up, till he sees all things through narrow chinks of his cavern.
>
> —WILLIAM BLAKE, *THE MARRIAGE OF HEAVEN AND HELL* (1790)

Previous interpretations of Occom's 1768 autobiography have read it as an attack against anti-Indigenous prejudice, which makes sense given Occom's statement at the opening of the text that he is out to correct the "many gross mistakes" about his identity that certain unnamed "gentlemen in America" had been propagating. These mistakes, which had been circulating in transatlantic religious and political circles for several years by 1768, had been summarized by Occom in a letter to Wheelock three years before, right before he left for England: "they further affirm, I was bro't up Regularly and a Christian all my Days, Some Say, I cant Talk Indian, others Say I Cant read."[48] The most prominent of the "gentlemen" spreading this gossip were Andrew Oliver and Ebenezer Pemberton, officers of the Company for Propagation of the Gospel in New England.[49] Oliver and Pemberton, whose organization had supported Occom's education and ministry financially, felt that they had never received enough credit from Occom, Wheelock, or their powerful backers in England.[50] They wanted recognition for having educated Occom at the school they ran in Mohegan, but since they could not get it, they set about discrediting Wheelock's claim to have educated Occom at Lebanon.

The "gross mistakes" about Occom did not end with Oliver and Pemberton. Their efforts to besmirch Occom's reputation were part of what Eileen Elrod describes as a corrupt "community ethos," a pattern of anti-Native prejudice that afflicted colonial New England society much more broadly than the phrase "some gentlemen" might seem to imply.[51] This colonial prejudice gave white people a distorted view of Native people in general; yet what Occom's narrative shows, Keely McCarthy writes, is that "his Indianness is a problem only because whites make it so."[52] Occom's goal in writing the autobiography, then, was to bring about a more equal world by changing white peoples' minds about what a Native American could be, in accordance with what Dana Nelson refers to as his "desire to be regarded not as a 'fool' but rather . . . a human and an equal."[53]

While correcting white peoples' "gross mistakes" about Native Americans was undoubtedly part of what Occom was out to do in 1768, my view is that the dilemma he faced in putting pen to paper cannot adequately be characterized in terms of "prejudice." Of course anti-Indigenous prejudice was ubiquitous in Anglo-dominated New England in 1768. Yet one of the reasons that the scholarly critique of prejudice has been largely displaced, in recent years, by more structural approaches to inequality is that the notion of prejudice seems to many too narrowly cognitive and idealistic, tracing the origins of injustice and inequality back to "ideas and beliefs" while overlooking "the systematic entrenchment" of such beliefs.[54] To say that Occom conceptualized his authorial mission in terms of changing other peoples' minds about Native people risks overlooking the fact that he also understood his adversaries (the "gentlemen") to be motivated by causal forces that went beyond the minds of individuals; from Occom's point of view these included structural factors like illicit settler governance (what Occom calls in one petition "arbitrary Power over us") and economic exploitation, as well as the supernatural power that governed human history as a whole, irrespective of what anyone thought.[55]

A further problem with interpreting Occom's autobiography as an intervention against settler prejudice is that doing so risks minimizing Occom's own state of mind in 1768 and the way his thoughts about such prejudice had changed over time. It is important to keep in mind that in 1768 Occom was forty-five years old. He had been fighting against anti-Native prejudice in his teaching, preaching, and writing for a very long time. Nor was this even his first attempt to correct white peoples' mistakes about him via the autobiography genre. He had already written one autobiography in 1765, right before his trip to England. In this earlier text, which was also occasioned by rumors circulated by Andrew Oliver and his cronies, Occom vehemently asserts that he was brought up amid his parents' "heathenish notions" and "customs" and had no inkling of Christianity until he was sixteen. This "true account of my Education" thus conformed quite deliberately to what Wheelock was advertising in his publicity materials about his "Charity School". It was written, in some sense, *for* Wheelock and *against* the commissioners. This was a gesture Occom would have been loath to repeat in 1768, after two backbreaking years working, as he wrote to Wheelock, as "a Gazing Stock, Yea Even a Laughing Stock, in Strange Countries to Promote your Cause."[56] Between his first autobiography and his return from England, Occom learned many valuable lessons about how easily the spectacle of speaking on behalf of authentic identity can be coopted, particularly when the success or failure of the performance hinges on the judgment of a dominant group whose authority goes unchallenged. When Occom started over in 1768, he wanted to go beyond writing against prejudice and try something new.

What Occom set about to confront in his second autobiography was not prejudice so much as tokenization. Whereas prejudice denotes inherited misconceptions afflicting the mentalities of individuals or communities, the notion of tokenization better captures the structural forces through which social inequality is typically reproduced. More specifically, tokenization helps bring into view how structural forces of inequality manifest and reproduce themselves in the form of spectacles of judgment wherein oppressed persons are made to testify on behalf of their authentic identities before members of the dominant culture. I have in mind here something akin to what Rey Chow, in her study of what she calls the "Protestant ethnic," dubs "coercive mimeticism": that is, a pressure internal to modern Western society that drives dominant groups to constantly demand that persons of color attest to their cultural authenticity through quasi-ritual forms of ethnic confession.[57]

So when Occom says at the end of his 1768 autobiography that he has been "usd thus" by his white bosses "because I am poor Indian," he is alluding not merely to his unequal pay relative to "other missionaries" but also to the regime of tokenization that forces him, but not them, to plea repeatedly for justice and recognition, for being "seen" by white people as an "Indian" who is culturally authentic and *ready to perform*.[58] The fact that Occom had to undertake such constant pleading—to write two versions of his autobiography to vindicate his preaching tour of England, for instance, whereas his white colleague Nathaniel Whittaker had to write none—can, of course, be partly explained in terms of anti-Native prejudice, which Occom had to confront in a way that "other missionaries" did not.[59] But his repeated self-vindications also testify to his containment within a colonial structure of language use in which his employers circumscribed his social and political authority by forcing him yet again to submit to the degrading, repetitive, and ultimately useless task of proving his identity for their satisfaction.

This is probably part of what Occom meant when he wrote, near the conclusion of the autobiography, about being "Constraind" to "speak like a fool."[60] The seventeenth-century Anglican divine Matthew Henry, in his *Exposition* of the New Testament (one of Occom's favorite books), drew attention to Jesus's warning in the Sermon on the Mount not to pray with "vain repetitions, as the heathens do," a passage glossed by Henry as denoting "tautology, battology, idle babbling over the same words again and again to no purpose, . . . like that imitation of the wordiness of a fool."[61] In his autobiography, Occom reflects in his own way on the connection between being a "heathen" and the practice of "vain repetitions" and "idle babbling." The text's climactic sentence, after all—"it is, because I am poor Indian"—is itself an act of repetition, having been borrowed from a "poor Indian Boy" who, like Occom, suffered not merely from prejudice but also from the indignity of being "called to answer for him self before his master" in order to render up testimony about "what it was he did, that he was So complained of and beat almost every Day."[62] It was not just anti-Native prejudice but also a whole social and ideological system of tokenization that oppressed Native *speakers* like Occom and the "poor Indian Boy" upon whom he modeled himself, forcing them into a confessional subject-position of "vain repetitions" that could not be seen as anything other than foolish. Occom was well aware of all this, but in identifying himself as a "fool" he also had in mind the Apostle Paul, who in 1 Corinthians had asserted that "God hath chosen the foolish things of the world to confound the wise."[63] Far from conceding to a foolish identity imposed upon him by white people, then, Occom's claim to "speak like a fool" is actually a warning to his readers that he is about to turn the world upside down by leading his readers into a rhetorical hall of mirrors in which "foolish things" are finally seen aright as manifestations of the Divine.

It is imperative that we follow Occom into this hall of mirrors if we want to understand the intellectual, spiritual, and political priorities that led him to write the autobiography; this will better prepare us to make an informed guess as to how his own perspective on the narrative evolved after he gave up on Wheelock and brought the manuscript with him into Native space. Before doing so, however, we should regroup, step back, and reflect for a moment on what kind of interpretive practice we should be adopting if we want to understand Occom's authorial practice without reproducing the regime of tokenization that he was so intent on defying. This is not merely a metaphor. The danger of tokenizing Occom in the present day is very real, especially in academic settings. In many classes on early American history and literature, Occom's autobiography is one of the only Native-authored texts, if not *the* only one, from before the nineteenth century that students are likely to read. This is in a way a mark of literary distinction, but it also goes to show that in many contexts Occom is the token Native American who is being "brought into the conversation" to share his people's unique perspective on American history—or, to put it another way, that he is only being attended to "because I am Indian," as his "poor Indian boy" put it.

Today, I think (or at least hope), most people who teach Occom are aware of such tokenization and careful to guard against it in their teaching.

But the risk of tokenizing Occom in the secondary literature is not always so easy to avoid. This has partly to do with the pressure endemic to scholarly discourse to overturn (or more charitably, "build upon") interpretations that have gone before. Audra Simpson and others have written powerfully about how the academic "construction" of Indigenous peoples problematically objectifies people who are subjects.[64] Literary scholars will also be familiar with the Janus-faced phenomenon of "paranoid and reparative reading" famously diagnosed by Eve Sedgwick, which in the context of Indigenous literary history has often found expression in a juridical mode of criticism that seeks to ferret out "prejudice" in the past so that justice might belatedly be done to oppressed writers' accomplishments in the present.[65] The danger of tokenization here consists in calling forth Occom's autobiographical testimony for no other reason than "because [he is] an Indian," in order to (finally) assess his speech in a non-prejudiced way. If that is all scholarship does, then it will remain trapped within the dilemma of tokenization that Occom himself wanted to escape, since such a method takes Occom's Indigeneity, in the manner of Rey Chow's "Protestant ethnic," as sufficient warrant for calling him to testify.

My claim here, to be clear, is not that attempting to "do justice" to Occom belatedly via scholarship is inherently bad, nor is it wholly unwarranted by the text of the autobiography itself. As mentioned earlier, Occom introduces the narrative by expressing his desire to have "justice" done to him by subsequent readers. Such appeals to the deferred judgment of readers "hereafter" are common to literary traditions from many parts of the globe.[66] Certainly the trope of deferred judgment was a familiar feature of ministerial parrhesia, as discussed in the previous chapter, wherein fearless speech was understood as combating untruths propounded by guilty individuals while simultaneously soliciting the admiration of allies (including, perhaps, God himself) who might do justice to the speaker in after times.

By addressing his autobiography to posterity, as well as individuals present in his own locality, Occom may have been exerting a certain kind of resistance against the regime of tokenization he had been struggling under for years. In a widely cited study of tokenization in the modern workplace, the sociologist Rosabeth Kanter describes a "dynamic of role entrapment" which confines tokenized individuals in "already-established relationships" that perpetuate structural inequality by "minimizing change and stranger-contact in the work situation."[67] By 1768, Occom was familiar with such "role entrapment" and determined to resist it. His appeal to "those who may hereafter wish to know some thing concerning me" can very plausibly be read along Kanter's lines as an effort to foster "stranger-contact" with remote readers capable of "do[ing] Justice to myself" in ways his white contemporaries never could.

Having recognized this, however, I would still maintain that when Occom says, "I speak like a fool," he is challenging his reader to do something more than merely judge him. It was one thing to ask people hereafter to recognize what his ministerial bosses could not: that he was not paid enough, that he was discriminated against "because I am an Indian," and so on. It was something else entirely, however, to train other people in a discipline of perception attuned to what was sacred in the world. Let's follow Occom a little further into his hall of mirrors.

Shortly after claiming to "speak like a fool," Occom conjures up a complex hypothetical scenario whose purpose is to illustrate what he is worth and what he "owes." This hypothetical discussion concludes a long argument about wages—an argument which borrows several tactics from Paul's discussion of the same topic in 2 Corinthians 11:7–12—in which Occom underscores the discrepancy between his salary, "180 Pounds for 12 years Service," and that of a white colleague who received "one Hundred Pounds" for "one years Service in another Mission." Occom writes, "I leave it with world, as wicked as it is, to Judge, whether I ought not to have had half as much, they gave a young man Just mentioned, which would have been but £50 a Year; and if they ought to have given me that, I am not under obligations to them, I owe them nothing at all."[68]

In economic terms, the argument here is perfectly clear: Occom's bosses' unwillingness to pay him even *half* of what they paid his white counterpart proves that the whole system of missionary compensation is broken and that any "obligations" he may once have had to his employers should now be seen as canceled. So, at least, Occom's readers (including you and me) are at liberty to "Judge," if we choose. And yet we are still inside Occom's hall of mirrors. Formally speaking, the passage just cited is a maze, a complex verbal contraption that belies the straightforwardness of its conclusion, "I owe them nothing at all." Fair enough, but grammatically we are still trapped inside a conditional phrase: "I owe them nothing," but only "*if* they ought to have given me" half. So, ought they?

As a reader, it is hard to know what to think, and this seems deliberate on Occom's part. Clearly he wants us to go through the thought experiment of judging that, yes, he "ought to have" received half—much more than half, really—of what his white counterpart received. But he also wants us to recognize that such an exercise is one that he himself would prefer to abstain from and leave instead to the "world, as wicked as it is." Why should this be the case? After all, such a judgment would seem perfectly fair, as well as eminently gratifying to Occom (even in the conditional mood Occom's assertion "I owe them nothing" conveys an unmistakable sense of pride) and to those among his readers who recognize the justice of his plea, since we get to experience the self-satisfaction of not being prejudiced in the way Occom's bosses were. From Occom's point of view, however, this sense of gratification is precisely the problem, because it furnishes a psychological and affective motivation for judging Occom "rightly" that has *nothing to do with God*. The judgment of the "world" is "wicked," even when it seems to arrive at the right conclusion, because it is tainted by the kind self-love Occom would later diagnose in his Moses Paul sermon: "if they have any pleasure in it, it is not out of love to God, but out of self-love, like the Pharisees of old," who made an ostentatious display of their righteousness merely in order to gratify themselves and impress other people.[69] This toxic combination of self-love and righteousness, which unavoidably enters into the judgments of the "world, as wicked as it is," can be summed up in one word: pride. If we really want to understand what Occom was trying to do when he wrote this narrative of his life in 1768, we need to ask what it would mean to read Occom's words in a non-prideful way.

Pride has been a central theme of the autobiographical genre since at least as long ago as Augustine of Hippo. It takes a certain kind of autobiographer, however, to make pride a problem for their readers as well as themselves. Occom was one of these. He knew that readers who judged him prideful for writing his own autobiography probably suffered from pride as well. In this respect he was a kindred spirit of his very near contemporary Jean-Jacques Rousseau, who in the 1760s began his own autobiographical narrative with a paragraph which ends in the following way: "let them listen to my confessions, let them shudder at my unworthiness, let them blush at my woes. Let each of them in his turn uncover his heart at the foot of Thy throne with the same sincerity; and then let a single one say to Thee, if he dares: '*I was better than that man.*'"[70] Rousseau found a way of coping with his authorial pride by foisting upon his readers the burden of confronting their own depravity. This rhetorical tactic had deep roots in Reformed Christian piety and may call to mind some of the writings by Occom that were surveyed in the previous chapter. But in his 1768 autobiography Occom approaches the problem of pride, as it impinges upon both reader and author, in a different, more theologically nuanced way.

Much more than Rousseau, Occom is concerned in his autobiography and elsewhere to show that the presence of pride in human affairs testifies to human beings' alienation from God. This, ultimately, is why he casts aside (rhetorically, at least) the judgments of the "wicked" "world" in the passage discussed a moment ago. As we have seen, the "wickedness" of such judgments can be diagnosed an effect of self-love as opposed to love of God. But self-love in this context is just one symptom of a much deeper human failing that is Occom's real polemical target in the autobiography: that of giving credit to human beings for actions and events that were actually caused by God. The failure here is one of accountability, but not of the kind we are most likely to think of today when we talk about a "lack of accountability" in organizations or governments. Occom's target here is a "Sin of Commission" rather than "omission," an excess, rather than lack, of human accountability and judgment.[71]

In an undated sermon in which Occom delves deeply into the morphology of sin, he crystallizes the phenomenon of pride with the help of an anecdote:

> I have heard of a Certain Minister, who was Sensible of the Workings of his Pride he Said, If I preach, and find the People are well pleased, I am also pleas'd, and from Whence this pleasure, Why I find it Sprung from Pride, and if I dont preach Well, I am asham'd, and from Whence is this Shame, Why find it from Pride . . . yea Says he, I am proud of every thing—and this is the very Case of all men by Nature, they are proud of every thing, they are proud of that, which Shoud bring them to Shame and Confusion of Face—and this is a great Sin in this age of the World—Another grt Sin in the World is Loving the World above god.[72]

This anecdote conveys a complex argument about the relationship between affective experience and moral accountability: we find ourselves here in the domain of what Occom's Scottish contemporary Adam Smith famously called "the theory of moral sentiments." Smith's argument in his treatise of that name was grounded in the eighteenth-century tradition of philosophical sensationalism, which held that human judgments about whether a thing is good or bad are ultimately explicable in terms of whether that thing causes pleasure or pain. If Occom's "certain minister" had been a sensationalist, he might have said that the "pleasure" or "Shame" he experienced after different sermons had some causal relationship to the *moral value* attached those sermons; for instance, he might have argued that, over time, repeatedly preaching in a way that caused "Shame" would naturally cause him to deem that way of preaching "evil." Occom's anecdote is designed to illustrate the perils of this sort of thinking. The feelings of "pleasure" and "shame" that the minister attaches to his various preaching performances say nothing at all about whether his preaching was good or bad in a moral sense. His feelings of pleasure and pain are *themselves* morally bad, however, since they both stem "from Pride"—that is, from an inflated sense of his own accountability when it comes to causing good or bad outcomes in the activity of preaching. As a minister, he should have known that it was ultimately up to God to determine whether his sermons went well or poorly. This was something about which Occom constantly reminded himself (and his readers) when it came to his own preaching, as we have already seen.[73] In practically every passage from his letters and journals where Occom says that he preached well, he says it was because of the presence of the Holy Spirit: because the "Lord was pleased to Bless my poor Endeavours," as he puts in the 1768 autobiography.[74] God's active participation in successful preaching explains why there could be no good reason for any minister to ascribe any moral significance to the feelings of pleasure or pain that they might get from any given sermon. Only an inflated sense of human accountability, which is really one and the same thing as "Loving the World above god," can lead to such an error.

It might seem strange that Occom faulted ministers who gave themselves too much credit for their preaching, given how much effort he spends in his autobiography working through the question of his wages, which are, after all, a way of holding people accountable for their labor. There can be no doubt that part of Occom—the self-loving part, he would have said—thought he deserved better and wanted the "World" to know it. If one looks closely at the way he talks about his pay, however, it is apparent that he is trying to achieve something beyond persuading other people to make the right judgment about what he deserved for his work. I suggested earlier that the critique of "prejudice" is a relatively unhelpful framework for analyzing Occom's text, since it focuses too much on the contents of people's minds. Occom, too, thought there was something naive and even counterproductive about trying to make the world a better place by helping other people make more informed judgments. "I Cant Conceive how these gentlemen would have me Live," Occom says at one point, exasperated; "I am ready to impute it to their Ignorance, and would wish they had changed circumstances with me but one Month, that they may know, by experience what my case really was, but I am now fully convinced, that *it was not Ignorance.*"[75] The ministers knew full well what Occom's work was worth, since they paid his white counterpart a perfectly fair wage for doing the same exact job. What made Occom's case different from his white colleague's was not that they were oblivious to his work's value, but that they took an additional factor into account when determining his pay: his "Indian"-ness. This was not prejudice, exactly—not at least in the typical sense of "pre-judgment," of some inherited yet misguided misconception about what Native Americans were like. The wrong committed by Occom's bosses was more akin to the prideful judgments of the "certain minister" from the anecdote described a moment ago. Just as that preacher praised and blamed himself for outcomes that were not, in fact, his responsibility, Occom's bosses overestimated the extent of his accountability. The fact that they paid him less than the white minister for the same work, Occom shows, entailed the assumption that he was less deserving because of his Indianness. But how could Occom's Indianness make him deserve less unless it were somehow his fault? This is the point Occom drives home at the end of the autobiography when he triumphantly declares, "God has made me so." Occom's Indianness is not his doing but rather a fact about the world that "God has made." It is not, therefore, the sort of thing for which he can be blamed.

The sentence brings to a close an argument that is perfectly obvious yet somehow astonishing: in paying Occom less than he deserves, Occom's bosses are blaming God for his creation. How could they have gone so awry? The "gross[ness]" of their "mistake" makes it impossible to reason with them, and ultimately explains why Occom consigns the whole matter of his wages to the "judg[ment]" of the "world, as wicked as it is." Occom knows that if he tries to argue in good faith with his bosses about who owes what to whom, they will merely accuse him of being greedy. That is why he makes his case for better wages in the guise of a fool. In this respect, he follows closely in the footsteps of the Apostle Paul, whose claim to "speak like a fool" in 2 Corinthians 11:23 also occurs in the context of a discussion of wages. Paul had refused to accept payment from the church in

Corinth for his missionary work there in order to prevent competing missionaries from accusing him of being a false apostle. Paul's backstory is, of course, very different from Occom's, but the two reach the same conclusion: in Occom's words, "I owe them nothing at all." Paul puts the point slightly differently, asserting that "what I do, that I will do, that I may cut off occasion from them which desire occasion."[76] But his goal and Occom's are the same. As Occom's trusted glossator Matthew Henry put it in his commentary on 2 Corinthians, "He would not give occasion for any to accuse him of worldly designs in preaching the gospel, or that he intended to make a trade of it, to enrich himself."[77]

By disclaiming any "obligation" to the people he is criticizing, Occom (like Paul before him) frees himself to take on the mantle of a fool, someone whom it is absurd to blame for speaking out of turn. As Ryan Schellenberg notes in an essay comparing Occom's autobiography to 2 Corinthians 11,[78] speaking as a fool for both Occom and Paul involves boasting, as in the following passage from Paul:

> Are they ministers of Christ? (I speak as a fool) I am more; in labours more abundant, in stripes above measure, in prisons more frequent, in deaths oft. Of the Jews five times received I forty stripes save one. Thrice was I beaten with rods, once was I stoned, thrice I suffered shipwreck, a night and a day I have been in the deep; in journeyings often, in perils of waters, in perils of robbers, in perils by mine own countrymen, in perils by the heathen, in perils in the city, in perils in the wilderness, in perils in the sea, in perils among false brethren; in weariness and painfulness, in watchings often, in hunger and thirst, in fastings often, in cold and nakedness.[79]

In his 1772 sermon at the execution of Moses Paul, Occom describes this passage from 2 Corinthians as "an amazing account"—and he would know, since he had put a similarly boastful catalog of labors into his second autobiography: "In my Service, (I Speak like a fool, but I am constrained) I was my own Interpreter I was both a schoolmaster, and minister to the Indians, yea I was their Ear, Eye and Hand, as well Mouth."[80] The whole question of what Occom was trying to achieve with his autobiography in 1768—and, I would suggest, what he would have wanted it to achieve even after taking it into Native space—comes down to how he wanted readers to interpret these lines, lines that *look* boastful but are not supposed to be judged that way, since they are uttered by someone speaking "like a fool."

Henry, in his gloss on Paul, describes Paul's boasting in a way that can help illuminate Occom's meaning too: "here the apostle gives a large account of his own qualifications, labours, and sufferings (not out of pride or vain-glory, but to the honour of God, who had enabled him to do and suffer so much for the cause of Christ)."[81] This description calls to mind Occom's claim at the opening of the autobiography to be writing the narrative "for the honor of religion," despite it being "against my mind to give a history of myself and publish it." So how does speaking as a fool—or, from a reader's perspective, attending to the speech of a fool *without passing judgment*—redound to the "honor of religion"?

The answer comes down to perception. The boasting of a fool, when one is acting as a "fool for Christ's sake," honors God because it is, as Occom put it, "amazing."[82] There is no reason to praise or blame it, nothing in it that warrants holding the speaker to account. The only reaction is awe. There is value in the performance, but it is beside the point to say it is good or bad. "Yea I was their Ear, Eye and Hand, as well Mouth": such strange and "fool[ish]" language, which "God has made" (or made happen) just as he surely as he has "made" Occom Indigenous, is there to be marveled at. Of course, judgments of praise and blame will come, eventually. But if you cannot suspend those judgments and simply acknowledge what is happening as a "strange Providence," then you are missing the point.[83]

It is tempting to say that here, finally, we have in front of us a summary of Occom's argument, but I hope by now to have convinced you that Occom is not ultimately trying to affect his readers via argument, but rather by making an impact on the world by simply *being there for them*, by inviting them to share with him an experience of seeing the world as shot through with sacredness. I acknowledge that this conclusion may sound somewhat vague and even mystical (or mystified) to some, but it is firmly grounded in Occom's historical moment and in the way he and other people understood what he was up to. As we saw in the last chapter, Occom was accused of a kind of irrationalism more than once during his career, of being too preoccupied with the "sound" of religion instead of its intellectual "sense."[84] In truth, however, Occom was in excellent theological company in his efforts to instill a discipline of perception that was distinct from the faculty of judgment and the self-love that tended to go along with it.

In his sermon *A Divine and Supernatural Light* (1734), Jonathan Edwards had argued that, just as

> there is a Difference between having a rational Judgment that Honey is sweet, and having a sense of its sweetness . . . so there is a difference between believing that a Person is Beautiful, and having a sense of his Beauty. The Former may be obtain'd by hear-say, but the Latter only by seeing the Countenance. There is a wide difference between meer speculative, rational Judging any thing to be excellent, and having a sense of its Sweetness, and Beauty. The Former rests only in the Head, Speculation only is concern'd in it; but the Heart is concern'd in the Latter.[85]

Whether or not Occom read this particular passage by Edwards is unclear (though, as we shall see in the next chapter, Occom undoubtedly read more than his fair share of Edwards's writings on perception) but, in any case, he would have agreed with it. The goal of his autobiography was to present for his reader a "narrative of my life" that was just as beautiful or, as he put it, "amazing" as honey, even though he knew that by typical standards of judgment his language was bound to seem ugly or "fool[ish]."

This was an aesthetic project, but it was one Occom carried out with an aim that went beyond creating a great work of literary art or making a name for himself as an author. His broader goal was to get those who encountered his narrative to feel a sense of closeness to him and to divine creation by reveling in what "God has made." The way to bring about this goal was not to convince his readers with arguments—why should they listen to his arguments?—but rather to get himself *acknowledged* by getting up close to them, slipping past the defenses erected by prejudice and the human faculty of judgment more generally, which tends to hold people at arm's length and view them from the vantage of a spectator.[86] In this respect he was putting into practice one of the fundamental principles of Edwardsean theology, which valorized "spiritual perception" as a faculty through which human beings participate in a sacralized world. "What makes the honey passage in *Divine Light* so memorable and so effective," Michael McClymond writes of the lines from Edwards cited a moment ago, "is that it appeals to perhaps the most intimate of the five senses. The visible object remains at a distance; the tasted substance touches our very tongue."[87]

The word "intimate" captures something important about Occom's autobiography: about the way it tries to reach readers up close, on a sensory level, while also bringing about a momentary change in one's whole way of being in the world, of the kind that is often associated with the experience of love. As an expression of love, Occom's biography is meant to heighten the senses, opening a new perspective on what is valuable in the world by unlocking what William Blake, following Maimonides, called the "doors of perception." Occom often described such quickening of perception as an awakening from sleep, from a state of "Stupidity and Deadness" into an awareness of the "Astonishing Love of God."[88] In 1784, after he had made a home for himself (and his autobiography) in Native space, he sent a letter to the Connecticut minister Solomon Welles in which he declared, "I think it is high Time for the People of god to Stir up one another and Provoke one another to Love and to good Works."[89] This language opens a window onto the form of sociability Occom was trying to cultivate at Brothertown, and onto the "social life" his autobiography may have had there. In September 1784, when Occom wrote his letter to Welles, the Revolutionary War had abated and migration to Brothertown was resuming.[90] Occom's hope was that life there would bring about a reawakening, or "stirring up," after the long spiritual darkness that colonization had ushered in. Perhaps Occom also imagined his writings as belonging to that collective life.

If, as the preponderance of available evidence indicates, Occom took his autobiography with him to Brothertown and shared it within the community there, I think he probably did so in the hopes that it would inspire his people, after all they had been through, to "Stir up one another and Provoke one another to Love." As I have been arguing, the autobiography—despite its origins as a polemic—*was* an act of love addressed to the senses. Once it had been transposed into Native space, one can also imagine Occom offering it to his people as an embodiment of what he calls in his Good Samaritan sermon the "Noble Human Self Love" that Indigenous people show within their communities: to "one another . . . and also to Strangers."[91] Like a "Wampum of Friendship," we might imagine Occom's manuscript as an enchanted object that was also an "intimate object of the everyday" symbolizing a newly constituted community "reforming" itself in a new home.[92] By memorializing the trials one of Brothertown's most celebrated leaders had been through, Occom's manuscript was a concrete manifestation of political and social continuity amid change. Perhaps

Occom even intended for his manuscript to play a role in bringing Brothertown together by catalyzing new intimacies among strangers united in the admiration of Occom's "amazing" narrative. Many of the Mohegan, Montaukett, Narragansett, Niantic, Groton Pequot, Stonington Pequot, and Tunxis families who founded Brothertown left their ancestral homes because of conflicts engendered by colonialism.[93] These families could have been the right readers at the right time for a text which, as we have seen, models a way of being in the world in which judgments about prior actions are suspended in order to reveal the value in other people as fellow children of God. From this perspective, the text might be seen as not merely a testament to Occom's devotion but also a celebration and carrying forward of "our custom" of "freely Entertain[ing] all Visitors."[94] It teaches readers—who are themselves, after all, "Visitors" in the space created by the text—the importance of experiencing the strangeness of creation, as manifest in other human beings, without having to venture far from home.

In the introduction to *Our Beloved Kin*, her 2018 history of King Philip's War, Lisa Brooks describes her own historical work in a way that resonates deeply with my sense of how Occom imagined readers experiencing his autobiography. Brooks writes,

> if you hold this book in your hands or are viewing it on a screen, I am asking you to follow these strands and storylines with me. I am saying, "Welcome," although I will warn you that, for some readers, this landscape may seem unfamiliar and unsettling. Others, of course, may find it strikingly familiar. I acknowledge that it may be difficult to follow me at times. Yet, if you come in the manner of a guest to the "place-world" I've created. . . . I hope your participation may be rewarded with the gift of seeing a world we all inhabit with greater insight and clarity.[95]

How did the meaning of Occom's autobiography change when he gave up on Wheelock and adopted his text into Native space? The question gets things the wrong way around. The origins of Occom's manuscript *were* in Native space. How it got displaced, on the other hand, is a question whose answer remains just beyond the horizon.

CHAPTER VI

"Time to Awake"

Occom on Perception, Alienation, and "Pure Religion"

"Here I Shall endeavour to represent two Sorts of People that are in the World, and Distinguish them one from the other," Occom declared in a sermon at Montauk in 1760, "the one is Believer, and [the other is] Unbeliever, Yet Both are a Sleep." At this early stage of his ministerial career, just a year after his ordination, Occom was already busy thinking through the cultural, religious, and political significance of perception. People who are asleep, he wrote, are "Sinceless of all the Carryings on [in] the World"; they lack any "Rellish for Divine Things." These people needed to wake up! "First then examine yourself and if thou art Sleeper . . . Arise and Trim your Lamps, and [Christ] shall give you light."[1]

Occom's message in this sermon is straightforward. Human nature inclines toward sleepiness, but the Gospel can wake you up—this is a pretty common evangelical theme. Yet behind this simple teaching lay a deeper philosophical interest in the variety of ways in which human beings perceive the world. This interest of Occom's had relatively recent sources in evangelicalism, and even deeper ones in Northeast Native tradition, including the traditions Occom observed at Montauk, where he marveled at the lengths powwaws went to in order to access altered states of consciousness.[2] The project of perceiving the world anew, or in unfamiliar ways, was a common concern of precolonial Northeast Native religions and eighteenth-century evangelicalism alike; and in Occom's writings these two traditions come together, with some surprising results.

In 1760, the same year he delivered his sermon at Montauk, Occom "bought of the Rev. Mr. Brown of Bridge Hampton" a copy of the Massachusetts theologian Jonathan Edwards's *Careful and strict* ENQUIRY *into the modern prevailing Notions of that* FREEDOM *of* WILL, *Which is supposed to be essential to Moral Agency, Vertue and Vice, Reward and Punishment, Praise and Blame* (1754), more commonly known today simply as *Freedom of the Will*. In all likelihood this was not Occom's first exposure to the work of Edwards. The eminent New England theologian was a friend and mentor of many of Occom's own teachers, including Samuel Buell, Samuel Hopkins, and Eleazar Wheelock, who kept Edwards apprised of Occom's educational progress and even asked at one point if the elder minister might be willing to help pay the bill.[3]

As the full title of Edwards's book suggests, *Freedom of the Will* was a rejoinder to the "moral sense" philosophers of his day, who associated human freedom with an innate perceptual faculty that allowed people to *feel* whether something was right or wrong. To make a long story short, Edwards denied that moral sense, unaided by divine intervention, could reliably guide human beings toward right action; but he still thought perception mattered.[4] In 1760, this was cutting-edge philosophical theology, and Occom devoured it—although, as we will see, he ultimately disagreed with some of its most important conclusions.

Occom's copy of *Freedom of the Will* is copiously annotated throughout, but most densely in the opening pages where Edwards announces his (partial) agreement with the sensationalist doctrine that "nothing can induce or invite the Mind to will or act any Thing, any further than it is perceived . . . for what is wholly unperceived, and perfectly out of the Mind's view, can't affect the Mind at all." In the margin of this passage, Occom wrote a big, approving "X." He did the same thing next to a passage a few pages later where Edwards seems to elevate humans' perceptual powers over the mental faculties of reason and imagination: "My Idea of the Sun, when I look upon it, is more vivid, than when I only think of it. Our Idea of the sweet Relish of a delicious Fruit is usually stronger when we taste it, than when we only imagine it." This passage got two "X"s of approval from Occom *and* a star, as well as a marginal note: "A lively sense in the mind of the object has great influence in causing volition."[5] Maybe Occom

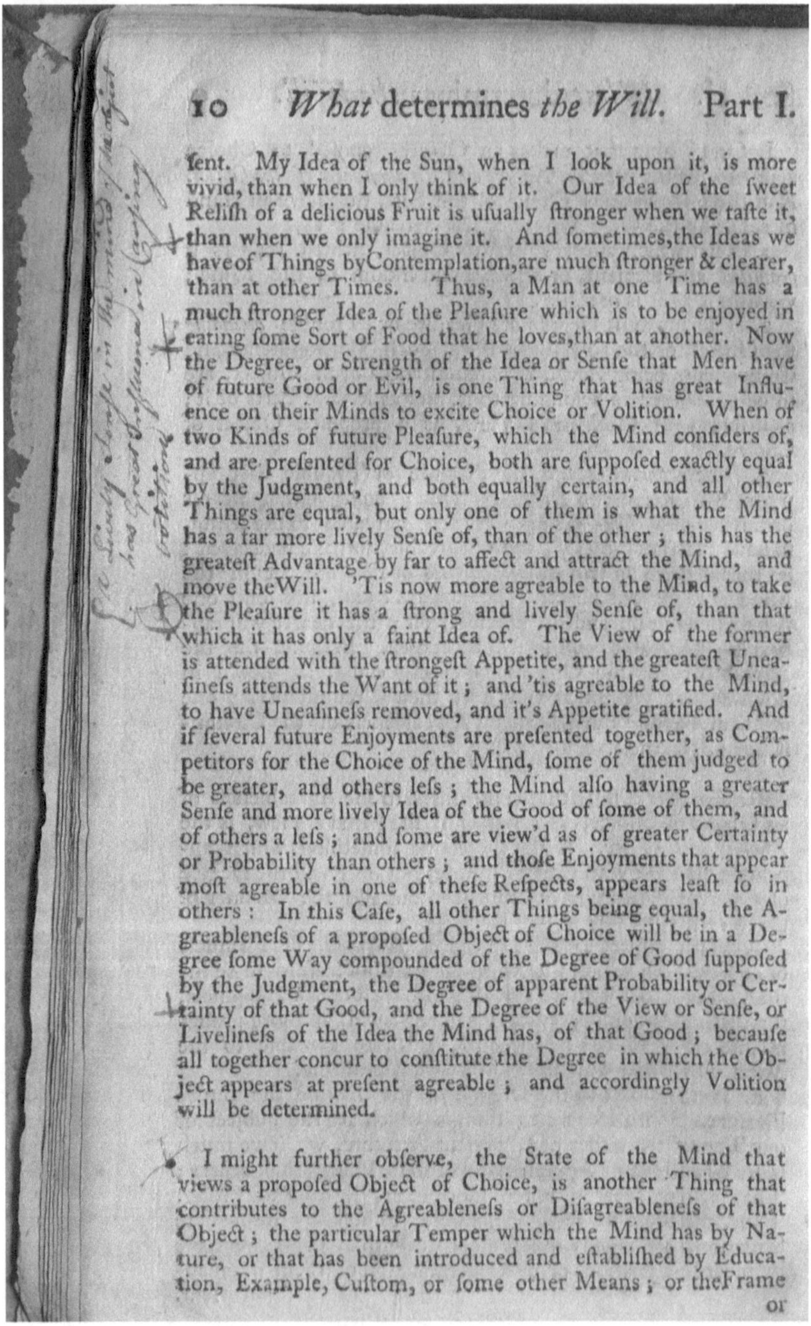

10   *What* determines *the Will.*   Part I.

fent. My Idea of the Sun, when I look upon it, is more vivid, than when I only think of it. Our Idea of the sweet Relish of a delicious Fruit is usually stronger when we taste it, than when we only imagine it. And sometimes, the Ideas we have of Things by Contemplation, are much stronger & clearer, than at other Times. Thus, a Man at one Time has a much stronger Idea of the Pleasure which is to be enjoyed in eating some Sort of Food that he loves, than at another. Now the Degree, or Strength of the Idea or Sense that Men have of future Good or Evil, is one Thing that has great Influence on their Minds to excite Choice or Volition. When of two Kinds of future Pleasure, which the Mind considers of, and are presented for Choice, both are supposed exactly equal by the Judgment, and both equally certain, and all other Things are equal, but only one of them is what the Mind has a far more lively Sense of, than of the other ; this has the greatest Advantage by far to affect and attract the Mind, and move the Will. 'Tis now more agreable to the Mind, to take the Pleasure it has a strong and lively Sense of, than that which it has only a faint Idea of. The View of the former is attended with the strongest Appetite, and the greatest Uneasiness attends the Want of it ; and 'tis agreable to the Mind, to have Uneasiness removed, and it's Appetite gratified. And if several future Enjoyments are presented together, as Competitors for the Choice of the Mind, some of them judged to be greater, and others less ; the Mind also having a greater Sense and more lively Idea of the Good of some of them, and of others a less ; and some are view'd as of greater Certainty or Probability than others ; and those Enjoyments that appear most agreable in one of these Respects, appears least so in others : In this Case, all other Things being equal, the Agreableness of a proposed Object of Choice will be in a Degree some Way compounded of the Degree of Good supposed by the Judgment, the Degree of apparent Probability or Certainty of that Good, and the Degree of the View or Sense, or Liveliness of the Idea the Mind has, of that Good ; because all together concur to constitute the Degree in which the Object appears at present agreable ; and accordingly Volition will be determined.

I might further observe, the State of the Mind that views a proposed Object of Choice, is another Thing that contributes to the Agreableness or Disagreableness of that Object ; the particular Temper which the Mind has by Nature, or that has been introduced and established by Education, Example, Custom, or some other Means ; or the Frame

or

Figure 6.1 Occom's annotations in his copy of Edwards's *Freedom of the Will.* Long Island Collection, East Hampton (New York) Library. Photograph by the author.

even had these words from Edwards in mind when he wrote in his Montauk sermon, cited earlier, that "sinceless" people had no "*Rellish* for Divine Things." By 1760, Occom was well on his way toward becoming a sensationalist philosopher in his own right.

Over the course of his career, as Occom's ideas about perception got more and more nuanced, they also got more tightly integrated into his writings on historical and political topics, as well as religious ones. "People in general have been Slumbering and Sleeping together a long while," he observed in the 1780 letter to Solomon Welles mentioned at the end of the previous chapter; but "it is high Time to awake for the Night is far Spent and the Day at Hand."[6] This imminent awakening would give true believers the insight they needed to overthrow their earthly adversaries: "in the Time of Darkness the Enemy has been Very busy to Sow the Seeds of Discord and all manner of Strange and Damnable Doctrines, and it is time to See which is the right way."[7] Some people, at least, would finally be able to perceive the world for what it really was.

In the historical literature, Occom's attraction to the language of sleep and wakefulness has often been ascribed to his religion, specifically, his involvement in the "Great Awakening," a regional revival of Christian spirituality that swept across Coastal Algonquian homelands in the 1730s and 1740s.[8] In this chapter I want to suggest a more obvious reason for Occom's preoccupation with sleepiness and wakefulness: he wrote and preached about these topics because he was concerned about *perception*. To be asleep was to be "sinceless," and to be awakened was to move from this state of senselessness into a state of perceptual attunement to the world one belongs to.

Recontextualizing Occom's writings on sleep and wakefulness as part of a broader inquiry into perception is not incompatible with understanding him as a participant in the Great Awakening, as Occom's engagement with Jonathan Edwards, a key figure in the New England revivals, attests. But on its own, that familiar religious-historical narrative is both too broad and too narrow to capture why Occom was so intent on teaching people "to *See* which is the right way." It is too broad because, in most scholarly accounts of Native involvement in the Great Awakening, the specific theme of perception tends to get overlooked (as it were) in favor of other concerns, such as cultural difference and "adaption," the difficulty of measuring Native adherence, the historiography of assimilation, the difference between Native and non-Native understandings of conversion, and so on.[9]

The Great Awakening frame is too narrow, on the other hand, because it obscures how Occom's conceptualization of human history in terms of perception drew on a broad range of cultural resources, only some of which had any connection to the Great Awakening or, indeed, Christianity more generally.

Contextualizing Occom's writings on religious "awakenings" and "Sleepy people" alongside his nonreligious reflections on perception reminds us how often he invited others to *feel* the texture of the world as perceived through everyday bodily experience, and to reflect on the power of altered states of consciousness and sensation. In his journals, Occom puzzles over the meaning of his own "dreams or night visions," whose import (religious or otherwise) is not always clear. In one diary entry from 1786, Occom recounts a dream about George Whitefield in which the long-deceased English minister

> came to me, and took hold of my wright Hand and he put his face to my face, and rub'd his face to mine and Said,—I am glad that you preach the Excellency of Jesus Christ . . . and then he Stretchd himself upon the ground flat on his face and reachd his hands forward, and mad a mark with his Hand, and Said I will out doe and over reach all Sinners, and I thought he Barked like a Dog, with a Thundering Voice.[10]

What did the dream mean? Occom doesn't say, although he notes that it "put me much upon thinking of the End of my Journey."

In another manuscript from 1776, Occom records the fevered visions of a young Mohegan woman on her deathbed: "I saw a table, such a table as never was seen in this world, and my father and Uncle Sam sat near it, and this company was travelling together, and I saw Christ going before them, and his track was all bloody, and the company followed his footsteps, and I was bid to follow them."[11] Here, too, Occom declines to offer much by way of interpretation, although he does note in closing how, "a little while before she died," the woman declared: "No drunkards and frolickers shall ever enter into heaven." This sounds, at first, like a pious avowal of the evils of alcohol, a consciousness-altering substance that according to many people in the eighteenth century (as today) takes people farther away from God. But the story Occom tells is more complicated than that; he continues, "as the mother thought she was a' dying, she got some drink and put to her mouth, and she turned her head and said, 'I shan't drink till I get home.'" And so the manuscript ends, with a young Mohegan refusing earthly alcohol from her mother on the expectation that she will be able to get a proper quaff in heaven.

This conclusion does not seem to alarm Occom or affect his assessment that the young woman's visions "appear to be like the Gospel experience." But why would it? Occom's own relationship to alcohol was complex and seemingly ambivalent. He publicly deplored the "beastly and accursed sin of drunkenness" on more than one occasion and warned Native people in his sermon for Moses Paul how drinking negatively affected Indigenous communities' public image: "for this sin," he said, "we are despised in the world."[12] Nowhere, however, does Occom say that Native people were more guilty of drunkenness than non-Native people; nor does he even condemn alcohol *per se*. True, on one occasion Occom was compelled (unjustly, he thought) to issue a public apology for being "overtaken with strong drink" at a dinner.[13] On the other hand, his surviving account books indicate that he took a few gallons of wine or rum into his home from time to time; and during the fall of 1773 he complained to the Moor's Charity School trustees that "we Scarcely Drink anything else but Clear Water, I Cant afford my Family any thing else, except a little Beer some my family makes." Alcohol was part of Occom's life, just as it was for the vast majority of people in eighteenth-century New England. And it's plausible that he (or those in his household) valued it for its powerful effects on perception, or for the peculiar forms of experience to which it gave access.[14]

In any case, it is unlikely that anything Occom ingested ever had a perceptual effect as powerful as the substances the Montaukett powwaws took into their bodies. In his "Account of the Montauk Indians" (1761) Occom claims that the powwaws "get their art . . . part[l]y by dreams or night visions, and partly by the devil's immediate appearance to them by various shapes; sometimes in the shape of one creatures, sometimes in another, sometimes by a voice." The Montaukett powwaws accessed extraordinary sensory states through the application and removal of what Occom calls "poison":

> Poisoning one another, and taking out poison . . . puts them into great pain, and when a powaw takes out the poison they have found immediate relief; at other times they feel no manner of pain, but feel

strangely by degrees, till they are senseless, and then they will run mad. Sometimes they would run into the water; sometimes into the fire; and at other times run up to the top of high trees and tumble down headlong to the ground, yet receive no hurt by all these.

There is no evidence that Occom participated in these rituals, but he may have experimented with other perception-altering substances as a young person who grew up surrounded by traditional plant-based medicine. In the compendium of Montaukett herbal wisdom that he composed during his stay there in the 1750s, Occom noted at least four plants that could be used to assuage "Sore Eyes": "Wautouwox and Grape Vine Sap," "Sassarfax heart and Speccle beans," plus "another herb" whose name seems to have escaped him.[15] Out of all the plant-based remedies listed by Occom in his herbarium, he may have been especially drawn to these because of his own failing vision. Indeed, according to one of Occom's tutors in Connecticut, the whole impetus for his sojourn as a schoolteacher at Montauk was that he had been "taken off from his studies by a pain in his eyes."[16]

One wonders if it was around this time that Occom came upon (or was introduced to) the works of John Milton, perhaps the most famous poet in the American colonies, who in seventeenth-century England had breathed new poetic life into the classical literary persona of the blind seer.[17] Occom would have found much to relate to in Milton's poetic accounts of his blindness, and of how God, in his mysterious way, gave him tremendous powers of literacy—"that one talent, which is death to hide, / Lodged with me useless"—only to make it physically impossible for him to read or write.[18] This may explain the profusion of Miltonic motifs in Occom's writings after the 1750s, for instance his description of America as a "boundless continent," a turn of phrase that also appears in Book III of *Paradise Lost*.[19] Milton likely inspired Occom not merely owing to the courage with which he confronted his loss of eyesight, but also because of his extraordinary experimentations with language as a means of training other people to perceive the world in a certain way.[20] For Occom, as for Milton, language was a sensually "thick" medium, something that never disappeared from view so as to transparently disclose the meanings that lay behind it. Getting stuck in the muddle of linguistic communication was characteristic of the situatedness (Milton and Occom would both have called it fallenness) of human perception. Even the phrase "boundless continent," so familiar to readers of Occom, is a full-blown Miltonic paradox. Continents are, after all, continent: they contain things, and are therefore necessarily bounded. Occom, mindful of this, always used the phrase with the pronoun *this*, emphasizing that the continent he was referring to was one among others. America, "*this* boundless continent" really was discrete, but it had no boundaries that anyone living there could *perceive*. Here and elsewhere in his writings, Occom's language communicates the impossibility of human faculties ever completely comprehending a continent's worth of experience.

Although Occom, as a person of strong opinions, could be somewhat doctrinaire at times, his writings on altered perceptual states almost always have a tone of acceptance. He had a genuine curiosity about other ways of seeing the world, and in particular about whether he and the people he cared about were "see[ing] . . . the right way." He was interested in perception, in other words, not merely as a way of passively absorbing sense-data, but also as a normative practice through which people oriented themselves toward what matters most in the world.

Of course, Occom was neither the first nor the last Indigenous thinker to commit himself to exploring the variability (and normativity) of human perception—a fact that is easy to lose sight of if we attach him too strongly to the Great Awakening of the 1740s. Stepping back from eighteenth-century New England, we can see him as part of a longer history of Indigenous reflection upon the ethics and politics of perception. This history has been shaped by Native cultural and religious traditions, as well as transformations of political economy, the rise of mass media, and other historical developments unfolding on a global scale: a set of concerns that scholars today sometimes analyze using the Marxian (or really Hegelian) notion of *alienation*.

In Occom's homelands and other Native territories in eastern North America, the eighteenth century was a period of increasing alienation, and of prophesying against it. To the west and south of New England, leaders like Tenskwatawa and Tecumseh sought to bring about what historian Gregory Dowd calls—in a careful choice of words—an "Indian great awakening" *against* both colonialism and Christianity.[21] The authority of these prophets, according to Dowd, came from "visionary" encounters with a "remote" Great Spirit or "Master of Life" who empowered the prophets to see Indigenous futures that settler colonialism had obscured or foreclosed.[22] Their words inspired "a widespread, often divisive, yet intertribal movement" for cultural and religious revitalization that stretched from the Seminole nation in the south to Lake Winnebago in the west to the Six Nations in the north. It was in among the latter peoples—specifically, in Oneida territory, where he began working as a missionary in 1761—that Occom may have begun using some of the rhetorical moves characteristic of the "prophets of the Great Spirit" discussed by Dowd. He put these moves to use in texts like the letter "to all the Indians in this Boundless Continent" discussed at the end of chapter 2, where he demands that listeners "awake your Understanding" (as if it were asleep) and listen to the message he had to deliver on behalf of the "Great good Supream and Indepentant Spirit above." Indeed, it can be instructive to think of some of Occom's visionary writings as expressions of what Walter Breuggemann famously described as the "prophetic imagination," which seeks "to nurture, nourish, and evoke a consciousness and perception alternative to the consciousness and perception of the dominant culture."[23]

Yet one would not want to push this prophetic reading too far. Occom was, in a way, too busy to be a prophet: as a community leader and working minister who earned a living by teaching, reading, writing, and preaching, he wrote his fair share of workaday prose, and he saw that as an important part of his vocation. Nor did renouncing Christianity, as leaders like Tenskwatawa proposed, ever make it onto Occom's agenda for Indigenous liberation. He certainly shared other Native prophets' concern with seeing things from a perspective that had somehow been blocked by colonialism. Like them, he was committed to diagnosing and reversing the perceptual catastrophe that settler colonialism had brought about. But from Occom's vantage—and here he was a forerunner to many later liberation theologians—it was unnecessary to reject Christianity just because it was so strongly associated with the colonists. To the contrary: much as Occom was drawn to various nonreligious texts and practices that opened up altered states of consciousness, so too was he fascinated by Christianity—as it found expression in the distinctively eighteenth-century discourse of "awakening"—because he thought it had the potential to change the way he and his people perceived the world. The trick was to practice Christianity the right way, which definitely wasn't being done by the colonists.

In his highly critical attitude toward actually existing Christianity, but simultaneous open-mindedness about how it might serve as an aid to perception, Occom shared more than has previously been realized with the eminent twentieth-century religious thinker Vine Deloria Jr. Drawing inspiration from Christian theologians like Paul Tillich, Deloria emphasized the phenomenological and existential dimensions of religious experience much more than the institutional or cultural forms that a given religion took. In *God Is Red* (1973), *Metaphysics of Modern Existence* (1979), and "Perceptions and Maturity" (1991), Deloria offered an interpretation of "tribal" religious traditions that focused on human beings' *participation* in a living world, in contrast to the "alienation between the various life forms that Christian peoples read into the story in Genesis."[24] Deloria chose these words carefully: his point was that "alienation" is an outcome of what Christian people "*read into*" Genesis, not something inherent in the Bible itself. How one reads, Deloria argues, is connected to how one perceives: Christians read Genesis the way they do because they have a perspective on the world that tends "to reduce natural events to a sequence containing some form of predictability, to introduce the conception of law and regularity into the natural world," in contrast with the perspective of tribal peoples who "maintain a sense of mystery through their bond with nature."[25]

Interestingly, Deloria notes that this broad distinction between religious perspectives might oversimplify the complex historical relationship between tribal and Christian (also referred to as "world") religions.[26] Occom, as we shall see, would definitely have thought so, and so do I—although I am neither Christian nor tribal, so my opinion should be taken with a grain of salt. After all, mapping incommensurable "perspectives" onto different groups of people can itself be a way of imposing "predictability," "law," and "regularity" on the world, as in the famous "clash of civilizations" model of modern history made famous by Samuel Huntington and others.[27] As such, Deloria's totalizing and avowedly tendentious dichotomy between tribal and nontribal religions might be said to work at cross purposes to his more historically nuanced argument about the relationship between settler colonialism and "alienation": his argument, namely, that colonialism encourages Native and non-Native people alike to perceive the world in a way that privileges "law and regularity" as opposed to "mystery" and human beings' "bond with nature."

I put forward this admittedly revisionist interpretation of Deloria partly to align his analysis more closely with the structural analyses of settler colonialism that I mentioned in chapter 1, but also to bring him into dialogue with recent conversations about alienation and its historical relationship to colonialism. Here I am particularly interested in certain parallels between Deloria's account of colonial alienation and philosopher Akeel Bilgrami's notion of an "unalienated life." In a 2012 essay on Gandhi and Marx, Bilgrami argues that for all the differences between these two thinkers, they were in agreement on two crucial points: first, that an unalienated life should be the goal of emancipatory politics, and second, that living an unalienated life meant overcoming the numbing detachment brought about through the intertwined historical processes of capitalism and imperialism, which teach people to see one another and the natural world *instrumentally*, as "resources to be exploited."[28] Alienation, on this account, is a kind of perceptual blindness in which the world is seen as devoid of value except *the value that human beings project upon it*. An unalienated life, in contrast, is one in which the world is seen as "enchanted," in the sense of containing value-laden objects that call people into action because of their "normative directiveness."[29]

As I read them, there is a strong parallel between Bilgrami's account of unalienated "enchantment" and Deloria's discussion of Indigenous peoples' "sense of mystery through their bond with nature." The parallel exists because Deloria and Bilgrami agree on one fundamental point: being unalienated means getting out of one's own head and perceiving the world for what it is—which is to say, both value-laden and mysterious. It means attuning oneself to "the presence of value properties in the world (including nature) that we inhabit," instead of seeing the world as a disenchanted array of inert objects that value is "read into" (per Deloria) according to preexisting conceptual schemes characterized by "predictability," "law," and "regularity": "here it is," writes Deloria, "that Western science prematurely derives its scientific 'laws' and assumes that the products of its own mind are inherent in the structure of the universe."[30]

Following Deloria and Bilgrami, this chapter explores Occom's writings on altered states of perception with the following questions in mind: How did Northeast Native communities perceive the world before colonialism? What new forms of alienated perception did colonialism engender? And how could Native people get their old way of seeing back again? The next two sections of this chapter explore these questions, detailing how Occom thought colonialism changed the way Native people perceived, first, the land and, second, other human beings. The final section shows how Occom came to understand Bible-reading as a way of retraining Indigenous perception. Occom thought the Bible could be helpful to Native Americans as a way of recovering an unalienated life, but he also thought it was dangerous and not strictly necessary. In order to see how he came to that conclusion, however, we need to reembed Occom's writings about "awakening" in the context of both ancestral Indigenous and post-Edwardsean understandings of religious perception.

"All help we use to have"

Sometime in the late 1780s, Occom wrote a petition to the U.S. Congress on behalf of the Brothertown Tribe. In the petition, the tribe asks Congress to compensate them for economic losses they had suffered during the Revolutionary War. But Occom frames this request as the culmination of a long history of alienation, injustice, and environmental degradation. In doing so, he explains how colonization changed the way Native people perceived the world around them.

The Brothertown petition begins with an account of the world's creation:

> The Most Great, The Good and The Supream Spirit above Saw fit to Creat This World, and all Creatures and all things therein; and ... Saw fit in his good pleasure, to Divide this World by the Great Waters, and he fenced this great Continent by the Mighty Waters, all around, and it pleased him, to Plant our fore Fathers here first, and he gave them this Boundless Continent, and it was well furnishd ... [31]

This was not the sort of creation story the members of Congress would have been accustomed to hearing. The claim that "our Forefathers" were "planted" here first would have especially roused their attention, since it corresponds to no account of human origins that eighteenth-century Christians would have been familiar with.[32]

Even more important for the present purposes, however, is the petition's description of what it was like to *live* on this "boundless continent." As Occom writes,

> This World was full of all manner of four footed Wild Creatures great & small both on the Land and in the Waters, and Fowls Without Number on the dry & in the Waters ... and the Waters and our

Lakes, Ponds, Rivers, Brooks, and the Seas, were all alive, and fom'd with Fish of every Sort and Bigness, even our Sand and Mud were well Stord with Shell Fish, besids with Variety of Creeping Shell Fish great and Small.[33]

This language is intended to convey a sense not merely of how God "furnishd" North America but also of what it was like to *be there* before the colonists came. Note, for instance, how "four footed" animals (followed by "Fowls") are the animals Occom first describes as living in the water, well before he gets to the "Fish" and "Shell Fish." From the detached, third personal perspective of natural science, this may seem out of order, since fish are the animals science more strongly associates with aqueous habitats. But by introducing his audience to North American waters via "four footed Wild Creatures" and birds instead of fish, Occom captures something of what it is actually like to experience these habitats as a human being; after all, if you approach the water from the land, as people usually do, birds and wading quadrupeds are likely to be the first aquatic creatures you see.

Figure 6.2 The Thames River estuary between Mohegan and Long Island Sound. Photograph by the author.

Together with these amphibious quadrupeds, the Brothertown ancestors inhabited a landscape where "our Lakes, Ponds, Rivers, Brooks, and the Seas, were all alive." These waters were alive, for one thing, because so many creatures lived in them—they "foam'd with Fish"—but also because the waters themselves were constantly changing through their interaction with other elements. Not just the fish with which the waters "foam'd," but also the foam itself matters to Occom's depiction, since foam is a mixture of liquid, solid, and gas, just as the "sand and mud" where the "Creeping Shell Fish" live are mixtures containing elements of liquid and solid, animate and inanimate matter. Language itself seems scarcely capable of giving durable expression to all this change; all it can really do is channel it, as in Occom's impassioned discussion of fish: "Fish of every Sort and Bigness, even our Sand and Mud were well Stord with Shell Fish, besids with Variety of Creeping Shell Fish great and Small."

It is not an accident that Occom devotes so much effort here to putting fish, especially "Shell Fish," or "Creeping Shell Fish great and Small," into words—or, rather, letting them swim through his words. Shellfish, in particular, have a very specific significance to Native life in the Northeast because they are where wampum comes from. Wampum had by Occom's time been central for centuries to tribal ceremonial life over a geographical area stretching from the Eastern Seaboard to the Great Lakes and beyond. Wampum meant (and continues to mean) many things in Native communities.[34] Among the Coastal Algonquian peoples from whom Occom descended, writes Lisa Brooks, wampum bore a strong connection to *manit*, or "the power of transformation": "the purple and white beads, hand crafted from quahog shell, held the potential for transforming relationships in Native space."[35] Wampum also played a role in the creation (or severing) of relations of "political kinship" between different families and tribes, as Occom himself attested at various times.[36] In 1761, Wheelock wrote to George Whitefield that Occom had been entrusted with a wampum belt from the Oneida chief Connoquies, in recognition of a provisional agreement between the Oneidas and Occom (then working on behalf on the Scottish Society for the Propagation of Christian Knowledge) for Occom and David Fowler to live at Oneida as missionaries.[37] And in 1772, Occom wrote to Wheelock from Boston that, in advance of a congress of tribal nations to be held that March in Stockbridge, Massachusetts, "A Wampum of Friendship Flew from Massipi thro Various Tribes of Indians, Came to our Hands about Six Weeks ago, and we Receiv'd it

Cordially."[38] These letters attest to Occom's longstanding participation in the ceremonial exchange of wampum as a way of establishing "cordial[ity]" among different Northeastern tribes (with "Massipi" in the latter letter probably referring to Mashpee, on present-day Cape Cod). But they also indicate how Occom associated the circulation of wampum with a specific way of *perceiving* that saw the social and natural world as mutually interpenetrating.

Note, for instance, how Occom describes "Receiv[ing] it Cordially," implying that the "Wampum of Friendship" was itself a guest. This was not just a fanciful locution. In Native Northeast communities, wampum really *was* an object of care and hospitality, a benevolent visitor at once human and nonhuman, natural and artificial, bearing with it a "power of transformation" that connected human affairs to the depths of water and mud. During his travels in the Six Nations (or even before) Occom may have become familiar with the Haudenosaunee oral tradition related by Penelope Kelsey, which describes how wampum was first given to Ha:yëwënta':

> Ha:yëwënta' had quickly lost his three daughters and his wife to illness and accident in a shocking series of events, and he no longer wanted to carry on living. As he lay on the beach in grief, a large body of birds that had been floating on the waters of the lake arose in flight, and the tremendous force of so many wings drove the water from the lake, revealing the wampum shells on the floor of the lake. Ha:yëwënta' picked up the shells and strung them onto cord, repeating to himself "This would I do if I found anyone burdened with grief even as I am. I would take these shell strings in my hand and console them. The strings would become words and lift away the darkness with which they are covered. Holding these in my hand, my words would be true."[39]

This Haudenosaunee story recounts a moment of creation that is also an awakening. The "revealing" of wampum rouses Ha:yëwënta' from numbing grief and gives him, in turn, a power of enlightenment, of "lift[ing] away darkness" and guiding others toward truth. Occom, for his part, never explicitly linked wampum to the power of truth-telling or to the perceptual phenomenon of awakening. Yet the petition he sent from Brothertown, as it guides the reader through "our" semi-aqueous landscapes, shares with the Haudenosaunee narrative a profound sense of being looked after by the land, and in particular of relying on the natural world to summon human beings into a perceptual state attuned to what Brooks calls the "power of transformation," or (per Deloria) "a sense of mystery through their bond with nature."

As the Brothertown petition proceeds, however, it quickly becomes apparent how colonization, with its unending cycles of war and exploitation, came to obstruct Native peoples' ability to see the world as a place to live in and with. In contrast to precolonial times, when "our Forefathers lived upon the Spontaneous Product of this Country," now "we find that this late war [the American Revolution] has stript us of all help we use to have—All the Fountains abroad that use to water and refresh our Wilderness are Dryed up, and the Springs that use to rise near are all Ceased."[40] When Occom speaks here of the "drying up" of our waters, he may well be alluding to the desiccation of specific landscapes: to drained swamps, depleted aquifers, dammed streams, and depleted stocks of fish, game, and other sustenance. On the other hand, Brothertown was not itself near those ancestral homelands, but rather far inland, in upstate New York, near some significant rivers but not the kinds of "lakes" or "seas" that one would describe as "well Stord with Shell Fish." So it seems a little strange to contrast the richness of precontact *coastal* landscapes with the "dry[ness]" of post-Revolutionary Brothertown. This peculiar feature of the petition may reflect the views of Brothertown community members who were suffering from a sense of dislocation from their former homelands (and waterways) and the creatures residing therein. Such dislocation was something that many would-be migrants worried about during the early years of Brothertown's existence. In 1789, for instance, a group of Montauketts rebuffed Occom's invitation to relocate because of their concern that "they would suffer and come to poverty if they should move as a body into this part of the world, where there were no oysters and Clams."[41] Occom did not deny that moving to Brothertown meant dislocation; nor, however, did he think that relocating to Brothertown *in and of itself* had to be seen as a source of alienation. People's relationship to the land (and creatures living there) would have to change, but not necessarily in a bad way. In 1785, as mentioned in chapter 3, Occom called Brothertown "the best land I ever did see in all my Travils" owing to its incredible yields of potatoes, cabbage, beans, parsnips, beets, cucumbers, and watermelons.[42] Occom likely celebrated the prodigious harvests at Brothertown partly in order to assuage the concerns of kindred who had demurred from migrating owing to their attachment to coastal economies. As he told the Montauketts, it was time for Coastal Algonquian communities to join together as "one people": a sovereign nation with a renewed commitment to sharing the land.[43] From his point of view, that clearly required moving, but it did not entail becoming alienated from the land.

As we saw in chapter 3, historians of the Brothertown movement sometimes make it sound as if Occom wanted Brothertown families to model their domestic and economic lives on white farmers and thus to renounce traditional modes of subsistence (on oysters and clams, for instance) inherited from their ancestors.[44] The assumption often seems to be that Occom, unlike the Coastal Algonquians who stayed behind, was committed to a Euro-American (basically Lockean) conception of private property grounded in a labor theory of value. Occom was certainly familiar with that idea, which was loudly propounded by eighteenth-century Anglo colonists. But the truth about the early Brothertown migrants' understanding of the land, and the way they related to it, is much more complicated. Recall, for instance, how in the 1785 diary entry cited earlier, Occom describes the soil at Brothertown as yielding an abundance of crops without plowing or hoeing: "only leaves and Small Bushes were burnt on it and great many Logs ly on it now."[45] This certainly does not conform to the familiar Lockean view that the value of farmland derives from "the plough-man's pains, the reaper's and thresher's toil, and the baker's sweat."[46] On the contrary, Occom's description of charred fields on the margins of woodlands, with logs left lying on the ground, indicates that the people of Brothertown were cultivating their land much as their ancestors had been for centuries. They burned fuels made available by the land and thus invited the latter to regenerate itself from within, rather than plowing long furrows across its surface in order to maximize its per-acre yield in the short term. So there is good reason to be suspicious of the notion that Occom thought the Brothertown movement entailed Native people alienating themselves from the land and their ancestral ways of relating to it. If all went well, the founding families could still maintain a traditional relationship to the land, one based on collaboration rather than exploitation. That, at least, was Occom's vision in Brothertown's early years. Brothertown was a refuge from the labor theory of value, not an implementation of it.

But, to return to the petition and its account of a "dryed up" land: the fact remains that Occom wrote this text in his own hand as a Brothertown spokesperson, as he often did; and this indicates that he himself experienced some kind of alienation from the land. It just wasn't the sense of *geographical* dislocation (from coastal landscapes and the modes of subsistence attached to them) that his Montaukett correspondents worried about. The key phrase here is "all help": we are "stript," the petition says, "of all help we used to have—All the Fountains . . . are Dryed up." This loss of "all help" may refer to a loss of agricultural (or horticultural) yield due to a drought affecting the shoreline, the inland region around Brothertown, or both. But the phrase also describes a shift in perception, the loss of Native peoples' ability to *see* the land as a collaborator with whom communities lived in a relationship of mutual support, as when the Brothertown founders helped the land regenerate itself through burning. Instead of seeing the land in this way, as a place for a community to live in but also *with*, Native people had begun to see it more like the colonists did: as a passive resource available for exploitation by individual profit-seekers.

This shift in perspective, which Occom saw afflicting Native communities on the coast and around Brothertown, had brought about an alienated way of looking at the world that manifested itself most egregiously in the practice of leasing tribal land to white people. Occom first registered his unease about such leasing at Mohegan in the 1770s; and he complained about the practice more and more vociferously following his emigration to Brothertown, where he had hoped that Native communities would be able to live in a mutually supportive relationship with the land. In 1791, a letter penned by Occom from Brothertown deplores the "mad doings of our Crazy People," specifically a faction of "Stupid Creatures" who had "least out" a "Mill Spot [that] was reservd for the Benefit of the Whole Town" as well as "Lands where Pine Grew, intended for the Benefit of the Whole, and the Best spots of Land."[47] From Occom's point of view, the "mad," "Crazy," Stupid" individuals who had signed such leases had literally lost their senses. The only thing that could possibly explain such agreements was Native peoples' loss of their accustomed capacity to perceive the land in an unalienated way. As Occom wrote in a letter the same year representing Brothertown's leasing crisis to the New York State Assembly: "Your People are Flatering, treating, and urging our distracted Indians, to lease Lands to them, and our Crazy Indians have gone on, leasing Lands, without any regard . . . to Rule or order."[48] Occom saw what the New Yorkers were up to: if they could keep just a few Native individuals "distracted" from "regard" of their communities with the prospect of monetary reward, that could be enough to undermine the tribe's land base—and thus, by extension, Brothertown sovereignty.[49] Yet despite the pervasive political injustices wrought by the colonists, it was up to Native people, and only Native people, to reach back into their collective memory and recover the sense of connectedness they used to have to the land and to one another.

Occom never gave up on his mission of reawakening his "distracted" kin and neighbors from their compromised perceptual state: the last thing he wanted was for Brothertown to degenerate into a "Careless People, a Sleepy People, a Stuped People."[50] Yet he knew that the erosion of tribal solidarity around the issue of rents meant that he himself was often seen as the leader of a "Party" rather than a guardian of a "body politick." He struggled to keep himself from getting sucked into intra-Brothertown factionalism. New migrants kept arriving at Brothertown throughout the 1780s and 1790s, and he wanted them to share the founders' original vision of one people living on the land collaboratively, "for the Benefit of the Whole."[51] It was hard to stay true to this vision when these newcomers threw themselves in with the leasing party. As Occom wrote to Governor George Clinton in 1792, "these Strangers were taken in by Benevolence & Favour, and now they are picking out our Eyes."[52]

These may be the bitterest words Occom ever wrote, and it is no coincidence that they express his bitterness through the perceptual metaphor of blinding. Nor is it a coincidence that the "strangers" in question included "Three Families [who] are Mixtures or Molattoes" and who "did not come from the Tribes, to whom this Land was given."[53] In his very attempt to recover his ancestors' unalienated social ethic, Occom had taken on board a racial taxonomy with colonial origins. Perhaps this wasn't entirely by choice. Brothertown's supporters in the colonial administration had made it clear that their support of the tribe's autonomy would be contingent on its exclusion of people of African descent.[54] On the other hand, Occom sounds sincerely committed to the idea that people of "mixed" blood did not belong at Brothertown, even though that idea was without grounding in precolonial tradition. The bottom line is that Occom longed to see the way his ancestors had *because he could not*. The corrosive, exploitative way of looking at the world that colonialism had introduced into Indigenous communities was spreading. And it was affecting Native peoples' relationship not only with the land but also with one another and with strangers.

"Pure Religion"

I have been exploring Occom's writings on perception as a way of unpacking his diagnosis of colonialism as a process of alienation: a shift in Native peoples' perception of the world whose outcome was a lost sense of "help" from the land. According to Occom, this changed perception of the natural world coincided in the Brothertown rent crisis with a new desire among a "party" of migrants to exploit common lands and undermine "the Benefit of the Whole" for purposes of private gain. I have also indicated how Occom waged his own personal struggle against alienation at Brothertown, particularly against the blinding bitterness he experienced when newcomers failed to properly reciprocate the "benevolence" traditionally shown by Native communities toward "strangers."

The convergence, in Occom's letter to Clinton, of the themes of hospitality, strangerhood, and blindness ("These Strangers . . . are picking out our eyes") is highly revealing. Occom's longstanding interest in unalienated states of perception informed his choice of the "eyes" metaphor to describe having been betrayed by the Brothertown newcomers. But that same interest in perception also helps explain why he wrote about "strangers" with such passion, not only in this letter to Clinton but throughout his surviving writings. Talking about strangers—who are, after all, *strange*, in some sense that needs to be further unpacked—gave Occom a way of delineating the perceptual contours of his social world, much as talking about water gave him a way of describing how his ancestors experienced nature. This makes Occom's writings on strangers, and on how Native communities *perceived* them, a key point of reference for reconstructing his understanding of what it would take for Native people to reawaken to an unalienated life.

One of the most amazing things Occom wrote about strangers (or anything else) comes near the beginning of the Brothertown petition I have been considering over the past several pages. After recounting the creation of the world, the petition proceeds as follows:

> our Forefathers lived upon the Spontaneous Product of this Country,—and in Process of Time, The great Sovereign of the Universe, Saw fit to permit the Brethren of your fore Fathers to rise up against them for their maintaining the pure Religion of Jesus Christ,

and they killd many of them, and a few of them fled from the Face of their Cruel Bre[thr]en and the good Spirit above Directed their Course to the West, [an]d he brought them over into this Country, and here the Good Spirit made Room for them.[55]

What Occom seems to be saying here—is, in fact, saying—is that Indigenous people ("our Forefathers") practiced "the pure Religion of Jesus Christ" before colonization and thus before they had access to the Bible, or any other way of knowing who "Jesus Christ" was.

This is a surprising proposal on multiple levels. For one thing, it implies a highly unorthodox *historical* approach to Christianity. When eighteenth-century theologians spoke about "pure" Christianity or the "pure" Church, what they typically had in mind was the "primitive" or Apostolic church—in other words, Christianity before it was "the Church," back in the days when Jesus's own ministry was still a living memory. But Occom's idea of a "pure Religion of Jesus Christ" cannot have been the same thing as this more familiar "pure" or "primitive" church, because the Great Spirit had presumably "plant[ed]" Occom's ancestors in North America without any knowledge of the events recounted in the New Testament. In a letter from the 1750s, Occom describes his own youth as one of "Grosses[t] Paganism, where I was perishing without the least Glimpse of Gospel Light." Here, and in everything else he wrote, Occom's commonsensical view seems to have been that Native people knew nothing about the Bible or the historical religion known as "Christianity" prior to the European colonization of the Americas.[56]

If Occom meant what he said when he wrote about his "Forefathers" practicing the "pure Religion of Jesus Christ" before colonization, then, he can *only* have meant that this religion was independently discovered in two separate locations. The first of these was the ancient Near East in the days of "the holy prophets and apostles" as Occom put it in one sermon, who "are gone home to heaven, in chariots of fire."[57] And the second was North America in the days of Occom's precolonial ancestors. The remarkable historical question raised by the petition can thus be posed as follows: How did Native Americans arrive at the same "pure Religion" as Jesus's first followers without actually *being* followers of Jesus in the first place?

Before proceeding, I would like to acknowledge that it may seem strange to some readers that I am making so much of Occom's mention of a "pure Religion of Jesus Christ"; indeed, it may seem bizarre that Occom's petition even mentions such a religion in the first place. Perhaps especially for people who, like me, are neither Christian nor Native, it can be difficult to think of the "religion of Jesus Christ" as anything other than a foreign imposition on Native communities; certainly, it is very rarely described as something Native communities invented independently. Occom, however, thought about things in his own surprising way. From his point of view, the "pure Religion of Jesus Christ" wasn't something imported. Rather, it was just another name for an unalienated life. And Occom was convinced that his ancestors had lived this kind of life—that they inadvertently practiced the "pure Religion of Jesus Christ" without knowing the first thing about historical Christianity—in large part because of the way they interacted with strangers.

This point is not made *totally* explicit in the Brothertown petition, although it is strongly implied in the text's description of the first encounter between Native people and settlers. This encounter is related as an interaction between strangers, with one party responding to the other in ways that were horribly asymmetrical. When they met the colonists, the petition reads, the Brothertown ancestors "maintaine[d] the pure Religion of Jesus Christ"; and it was "for" this that the colonists "[rose] up against them." This account presupposes that Native people greeted the European newcomers with a kindness that the latter were unable to reciprocate. But that presupposition remains in the background: the petition does not connect "pure Religion" to Indigenous practices of hospitality explicitly.

If we look at Occom's sermon on the Good Samaritan, however, which was probably written around the same time as the Brothertown petition, we find that same connection celebrated, right out in the open. The character of the Samaritan, according to Occom, personifies the words of Christ ("thou shalt love thy neighbor as thyself") because he took care of people he didn't already know. And what is "very Remarkable among the Indian Heathen in this great Continent" is that they display this same exact virtue: they are "very Compassionate one to another, very Liberal among themselves, and also to Strangers."[58] Here, then, we find the teachings of Christ and the conduct of non-Christian Indigenous people ("the Indian Heathen") mirroring one another quite explicitly.

In order to see how Occom's observations about loving strangers support his assertion that Native people had a "pure Religion," it may be helpful to revisit Deloria's comments on the topic of prediction. In the passage quoted earlier, Deloria characterized Christianity in terms of an aspiration "to reduce natural events to *a sequence containing some form of predictability*, to introduce the conception of law and regularity into the natural world," in contrast to the perspective of tribal communities who "maintain a sense of mystery through their bond with nature."[59] As I suggested earlier, reading Deloria through the lens of Bilgrami, this passage implies that looking at the world *predictively* (according to "law and regularity") involves projecting one's own expectations onto it, since when people predict they imagine a future that is shaped by what they already know and value. As Deloria and Bilgrami emphasize, this can make it harder to see the world as a place where beings exist that have value independent of the expectations that are being projected upon them based on the predictor's prior experience. That's why people who only look at the world predictively are deprived of what Deloria calls "a sense of mystery through [a] bond with nature." If one is always trying to predict what the world will do, one will likely fail to notice when it reveals itself as value-laden in ways one doesn't expect. In order to have a "bond with nature," one has to let nature be its own thing. If one can do that, one can recover a sense of "mystery" or "enchantment."

In Occom's Good Samaritan sermon, there is something deeply predictive in the way the colonists go about their lives. Occom has many harsh things to say about people who fail to love their neighbors, but he devotes special attention to "Monopolizers" who "will Buy up evry Necessary of Life in the Town or State, even of the Whole World" today, with the expectation that doing so will help them profit from other peoples' misfortunes in the future:

> They will sell you their goods today, Yea this Morning . . . for So much, and if another Comes at Noon or before, he must give a Little more for the Same Commodity, and if another Comes towards Night, he must give more Still, and so they go on . . . And if the Times like to grow harder and Distresses increase in the Land, these People will Shut up their Stores, and will tell you a thousand Genteel Lies . . . they are only waiting for Worse Times,—I was going to Say . . . Praying for Worst Times, for Such Times Suits them.[60]

Profiting from others' misfortune during lean times proves monopolizers' blindness toward what other people *need*; they literally cannot see other people as free-standing sources of value that exist independent of their calculations of private risk and reward. In this respect, Occom goes on to show, monopolizers are the polar opposite of "Indian Heathen[s]," who "are very Compassionate one to another, very Liberal among themselves, and also to Strangers, When there is Scarsity of Food amongst them, they will yet Divide what little they have if there is but a mouth full a Piece. . . . This I take to be a Human Love or Being Neighbourly, according to our Text."[61]

Two points about this description of "Heathen" stranger-love bear emphasizing: first, it implies that Indigenous people act in response to others' need without projecting what kind of benefit will accrue to them in the future; and second, they extend generosity equally to "themselves" and to "Strangers." Both points support the claim that when Native people were "Being Neighborly," on Occom's account, they were not (like the monopolizers) looking at the world predictively. It was remarkable enough that they gave away their scarce food without calculating the costs or benefits that would accrue to them. But the point Occom really wants to drive home is that the "Indian Heathen" didn't even care *where the people they were caring for came from*, or how they were likely to respond in the future. "There [are] many who pretend to Love their Neighbours," Occom argues, "but their Neighbours are either of their own nation or party, either in their Spiritual or Temporal Concerns."[62] Such people mistake neighborly love for loving the people they already know; but, Occom shows, if you have to ask yourself "do I know this person?" before interacting with them, then you're not going to be able to show that person neighborly love at all, since you will be dealing with them from a *predictive* point of view in which your preexisting priorities determine your apportionment of future care.

The reason the Good Samaritan (as Occom represents him) so nearly approximates the "pure Religion" of the "Indian Heathen" is that he acts toward the wounded man as if he knew nothing about how the other person was likely to respond: "he . . . was a Stranger he was a Samaritan, one that had no manner of Connection with the Jews, Yea one that was Dispised and Set at Nought by the Jews yet this was a Neighbour." Note how Occom edits himself here, amending "one that had no manner of Connection" to "one that was Dispised and Set at Nought," in order to capture what he really thought was at stake in strangerly love. Acting kindly toward someone you have no "connection with" is nice enough; it might be seen as a sign that you are a moral universalist, albeit perhaps a naive one. But the Samaritan, who *knew* his people were at odds with the individual he was helping, did something even more remarkable than the universalist: he acted toward the wounded man *as if* he knew nothing at all about how the latter "Dispised and Set at Nought" strangers like him. He saw someone in need, and he responded, just as Native people did when strangers came to them in times of need. That is interacting with others from a nonpredictive point of view, or the unalienated life.

Seeing Like the Ancestors

I have no way of proving this definitively, but it has often occurred to me that when Occom ascribed to his "Forefathers" a "pure Religion" defined by unalienated relations with strangers and the natural world, he may have been trying to repair the reputation of his famous ancestor Uncas.

When Uncas allied with the English in their wars against the Pequots and Narragansetts, he put Northeast Native communities through tremendous hardships in order to help a foreign people. In return, Uncas was reviled by the chroniclers of early New England for his alleged duplicity and self-dealing. In 1677, the Massachusetts minister William Hubbard published his *Narrative of the Troubles with the Indians in New England*, a semi-official colonial history of Anglo-Indigenous relations up to that time. Hubbard's *Narrative* included several stories about Uncas, including the following one told to him by the Norwich minister James Fitch. During a prolonged period of drought, Fitch reported,

> Uncas with many *Indians* came to my house, Uncas lamented there was such Want of Rain; I asked, whether if God should send us Rain, he would not attribute it to their *Pawawes*? He answered No, for they had done their Uttermost, and all in vain . . . Then Uncas made a great Speech to the *Indians* . . . confessing, that if God should send Rain, it could not be ascribed to their Powawing, but must be acknowledged to be an Answer of our Prayers. . . . The next Day there was such a Plenty of Rain, that our River rose more than two Foot in Height.[63]

For Hubbard, this anecdote showed that Uncas lacked what he called a religion of the "heart": "In Uncas's heart, he is no better affected to the English; or their Religion, then the rest of his Country-men; and . . . it hath been his own advantage, that hath led him to be thus true to them who have upheld him." This was not entirely Uncas's fault, Hubbard argued, since "the hearts of all are in the hand of God, so he turns them as he pleases, either to favour his people, or to hate and deal subtilly with his Servants, as seems good to him."[64] Yet Hubbard thought history clearly showed that God, through what he called a "special providence," had "turned the hearts" of "his people"—that is, New Englanders—toward him. Thus Hubbard sought to demonstrate that Uncas's much celebrated kindness toward the colonists, his "faithfulness to the interest of the English," had nothing to do with "faith" in any meaningful sense, being totally devoid of affection to God, to God's chosen people, or indeed to anyone other than Uncas himself.

It was, I suspect, partly in opposition to this familiar sort of colonial narrative about his ancestors' allegedly counterfeit hospitality that Occom advanced his counternarrative about his "Forefathers" "maintaining the pure Religion of Jesus Christ," in defiance of the hard-hearted colonists "ris[ing] up against them." As I have been arguing, this counternarrative was highly unorthodox and resolutely anticolonial. Yet it had deep roots in both Northeast Native tradition and in Protestant theological inquiries into the nature of religious perception. One of the reasons Occom concerned himself with the theology of perception was that was that doing so gave him a way of refuting people like Hubbard, who insisted that his ancestors' "hearts" had been numb to true religion. The Anglo ministers whose theological guidance Occom came to trust—people like Jonathan Edwards, Samuel Hopkins, and Samuel Buell—acquainted him with intellectual tools that helped him undermine this decades-old stereotype.

A long-standing theological preoccupation of Edwards and those influenced by him (including Hopkins, Buell, and Occom) was the question of what, exactly, it means to have one's heart turned toward God. Edwards's answer to this question borrowed a page from British "moralists" such as Francis Hutcheson: he argued that God empowers human beings with a natural ability to sense the excellence of creation and thus participate in what Edwards called the "general good will" or "consent of being to being."[65] Sin, on the other hand, could be understood as a failure to perceive the world in this way; it flowed from human beings' willing refusal to "see" the "excellency" of God and his Creation. Occom's mentor (and Edwards's mentee) Samuel Hopkins put the point this way in 1773: human beings, he wrote, shut their own eyes, through an indisposition and perverse refusal to exert the powers they have in seeing and relishing divine things. The Spirit of God alone can cure this evil disease of the heart by removing this indisposition and perverse refusal to see, and so opening the eyes of the blind.[66]

New Divinity writings like this one provided Occom with an intellectual framework for describing precisely how, with the advent of colonialism, his people had lost their ability to "see" the sacredness of creation.[67] They also informed his evolving conception of Bible-reading, which he gradually came to see as a way Native people could train themselves to recover the unalienated point of view on the world that had allowed them to practice the "pure Religion of Jesus Christ" prior to colonial contact.

In 1774, just as Native Northeast families were preparing to migrate to Brothertown, Occom published a collection of hymns that he hoped would be of some use in their new home. Occom's book include many favorites of Anglophone hymnody, but he had also been writing some new ones of his own: "new Tunes for new singers," as he put it in the hymnal's preface. One of them, "Wak'd by the gospel's joyful sound," provides one of the clearest illustrations of what Bible-reading meant from a New Divinity perspective:

> Wak'd by the gospel's joyful sound
> My soul in guilt and thrall I found,
> Expos'd to endless woe. . . . [68]

These lines describe what typically happens when someone first reads the Bible seriously, according to Occom and other ministers in his milieu. There is an awakening to the Gospel, followed by an immediate realization of one's sinfulness (presumably the person who is "wak'd by the gospel's joyful sound" also dabbles a bit in Paul's letters). The hymn continues:

> I read my bible; it was plain
> The sinner must be born again,
> Or feel the wrath of God.
>
> I heard some tell how Christ did give
> His life, to let the sinner live;
> But him I could not see. . . .

These verses describe life during the problematic period when one has been exposed to the "means of grace" through the "bible" and its ministers ("I heard some tell") but has not yet "see[n]" God.[69] It is a period when one is fully conscious of one's sinfulness, but nevertheless spiritually "blind" due to what Hopkins had called a "perverse refusal to exert the powers [people] have in seeing and relishing divine things." At last, this refusal to see comes to an end, and Jesus appears:

> But as my soul, with dying breath,
> Was gasping in eternal death,
> Christ Jesus I did spy:
>
> Free grace and pardon he proclaim'd;
> The sinner then was born again,
> With raptures I did cry.[70]

Occom's hymn illustrates the importance of Bible-reading, but also its dangers. Reading the Bible makes the plight of the sinner "plain," and points a way out of that plight through the *perception* of a savior. But reading the Bible can cause only death and despair, absent the "free grace" that empowers the believer to "spy" Christ. Bible-reading, then, is not an intellectual process, but rather a preparation to see *again*. Why "again"? Because of the hymn's first line. In order to even begin the journey of rebirth Occom lays out, you have to be able to use your natural ability to be "waked," not by the Bible in general but by the Gospel promises specifically: that is, by God's love to creation as embodied in Christ. "Christ himself is the gift, and he is the christian's life," Occom wrote in his sermon for Moses Paul; "For [according to the Gospel of John] God so loved the world that he gave his only begotten Son, that whosoever believed in him should not perish but have everlasting life."[71] The point of Occom's hymn is that if you are incapable of using this natural, prebiblical capacity to be "waked" by God's love as manifest in the Gospel, then the Bible's warnings about "endless woe" will only cause you anguish.

For Occom, the approach to Bible-reading sketched in this hymn mattered greatly to Northeast Native communities. Before colonization, I have argued, Occom thought that Native people practiced the "pure Religion of Jesus Christ," which simply meant that they knew how to perceive—to "see" and "relish"—the world as a manifestation of divine love. This precolonial experience of "pure Religion" could be recaptured by Native people if they used Bible-reading to re-teach themselves to perceive the world in the right way.

Occom provided a concrete example of how this might work in a sermon he preached on September 7, 1766, at the Pithay Meeting in Bristol, England. Taking as his text John 10:27 ("My Sheep hear my Voice, and I know them, and they follow me"), he shared the following anecdote: "This makes me remember a poor Indian Woman, that some Years ago was converted. As soon as she knew this Book to be the Book of God, she said, that it was as Thunder and Lightning unto her Soul, and every Word that she read was against her; but a little while after she said, it was all sweet, it was pleasant to her Taste, and all for her Good."[72]

Here Occom recounts one Indigenous person's progress in the work of becoming unalienated. Having taken an interest in the Bible, thanks to her natural capacity to be "waked," she almost immediately sees the "Book of God" as "against" her: something opposed to herself and her interests, as she understood them. But to see the Bible as a threat to one's own self-interest is already to look at the world in an alienated, instrumentalizing way that is bound to bring about a predictive despair over the fate of one's soul. Fortunately, the distracting displays of psychic "Thunder and Lighting" soon subside, and the gates of religious perception are unlocked: "she said, it was all sweet, it was pleasant to her Taste, and all for her Good." Reading turns out to be a preparation to perceive the world's "sweet[ness]" again, as if for the first time.

Colonialism had been a source of alienation for Indigenous communities; but from Occom's perspective the Bible had the power to meet them where they were and get them back to a better way of seeing. Whether or not the Bible was strictly *necessary* for Indigenous communities to recover an unalienated life is a more complicated question. After all, they had practiced the "pure Religion of Jesus Christ" without the Bible before, so couldn't they do so again?

That Occom in his late writings brought himself to the threshold of this question—the mention of which would have seemed scandalous to his younger self—testifies to his courage and his restlessness as a religious thinker. After decades of reflection about whether and how the Bible mattered to Northeast Native communities, he had come to see Bible-reading as neither an end in itself nor as a *sine qua non* of "pure Religion," but rather as an aid to unalienated perception. This position reflected Occom's respect for his ancestors ("Forefathers") and his refusal of old colonial tales about how Native peoples' troubles began when Satan made it impossible for them to read scripture.[73] In refusing such colonial narratives, Occom made himself into an enemy of dogmatism. Teaching religion was about helping people see, not forcing them to adhere to some prescribed text or proposition.

What, then, were the underlying sources of biblical authority and textual authority more generally? This question, I think, was very much on Occom's mind in his later years. And, considering that this is a book about reading Occom's writings, it seems like a fitting one with which to conclude.

Conclusion

"Good Enthusiasm"

> At the Sellers Shops there's enough of the Word of God to be bought for Money, if the meer Letter were it, and a number of new Bibles for all Comers: Is it for want of hearing them read? No, they are read too much, and heard too often, unless they were more spiritually understood, and more carefully & practically observed.
> —SAMUEL FISHER, *RUSTICUS AD ACADEMICOS* (1660)

> The world is already full of books; and the people of God are abundantly furnished with excellent books upon divine subjects; and it seems that every subject has been written upon over and over again: And the people in very deed have had precept upon precept, line upon line, here a little and there a little; so in the whole, they have much, yea very much, they have enough and more than enough.
> —SAMSON OCCOM, PREFACE TO *A SERMON, PREACHED AT THE EXECUTION OF MOSES PAUL, AN INDIAN* (1772)

For most people reading this book, I would guess that it's hard to imagine what it's like to learn to read at age seventeen. By this age, most people have already gotten used to seeing the world in a certain way. Many have probably wondered if the way they see the world is, in fact, the only way. This must have been true of Occom, who would have been told from a young age how different the landscape his ancestors saw was from the one he grew up looking at in the first half of the eighteenth century. As I argued in the last chapter, Occom also understood that the *way* his ancestors looked at the world was different from his own. Colonialism had changed the landscape. It had also brought about a shift in perception that he wanted badly to undo.

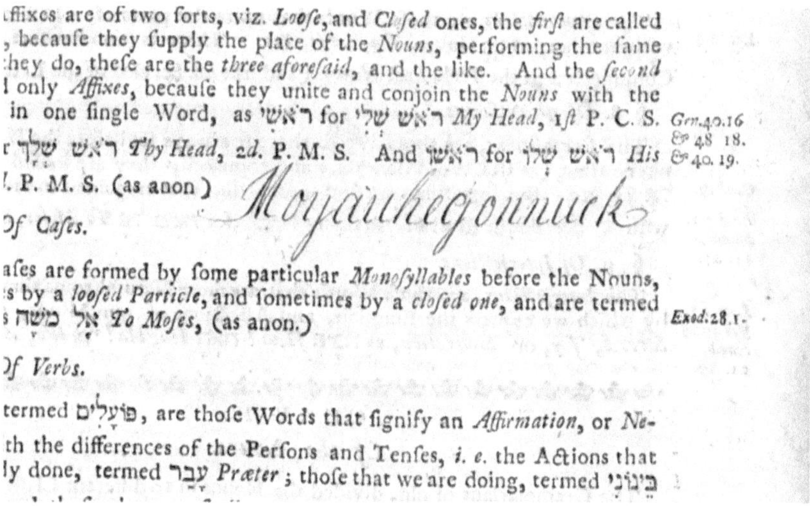

ıffixes are of two ſorts, viz. *Looſe*, and *Cloſed* ones, the *firſt* are called
, becauſe they ſupply the place of the *Nouns*, performing the ſame
hey do, theſe are the *three aforeſaid*, and the like. And the *ſecond*
l only *Affixes*, becauſe they unite and conjoin the *Nouns* with the
in one ſingle Word, as ראשי for ראש שלי *My Head*, *1ſt* P. C. S. *Gen.40.16*
r ראשך for ראש שלך *Thy Head*, *2d.* P. M. S. And ראשו for ראש שלו *His* *& 48 18. & 40. 19.*
l. P. M. S. (as anon)

Of Caſes.

aſes are formed by ſome particular *Monoſyllables* before the Nouns,
s by a *looſed Particle*, and ſometimes by a *cloſed one*, and are termed
s אל משה *To Moſes*, (as anon.) *Exod.28.1.*

Of Verbs.

termed פועלים, are thoſe Words that ſignify an *Affirmation*, or *Ne-*
th the differences of the Perſons and Tenſes, *i. e.* the Actions that
ly done, termed עבר *Præter*; thoſe that we are doing, termed בינוני

Figure C.1 Occom's "flip-book" in the margins of his copy of *Grammar of the Hebrew Tongue* by Judah Monis.
Photograph courtesy of Dartmouth College Library.

Once Occom started looking at books he had a very hard time stopping, so much so that he wrecked his eyesight. In his 1765 autobiography, Occom said he learned to read after "I began to think about Religion."[1] But as it turned out, he also simply *liked* reading, much more than Wheelock, Pomeroy, or any of his other teachers could have foreseen. Occom's surviving school books and exercises are an astonishing record of exuberant literacy in action. During the brief period when he was studying ancient languages more or less full time (this was before he was forced to give up his chance to go to Yale) Occom made incredible progress, as is documented nowhere better than in his copy of Judah Monis's *Grammar of the Hebrew Tongue* (1735). In the endpapers of this volume, Occom wrote exercises in five languages: Mohegan, English, Latin, Hebrew, and Greek. He also dabbled in apocalyptic numerology and transcribed a "Grammar in Verse" copied from a manual by John Brighton ("Grammar does all the Art and Knowledge Teach / According to the use of Every Speech," etc.). The volume also contains an intriguing flip-book of sorts that Occom penned for himself on pages 18 through 26, in the margins of a discussion by Monis "Concerning the Raupha and Dauguesh, forte and lene."[2]

Broken up over successive pages, in three languages, Occom repeats the ubiquitous slogan of eighteenth-century schoolchildren:

Samson
Occom An
Indian
of
Moyauhegonnuck
Jure Hunc
Librum Tenet

Or, I am Mohegan and this book is rightfully mine.

Occom devoured popular literature as well as this more recondite fare. At the bookshop nearest his house, run by Nathaniel Patten in Norwich, one could buy in the early 1770s "Large and small bibles," "Milton's Paradise Lost," "Pilgrim's Progress," "Watts' Lyric Poems," "Scripture Songs," "Account Books, bound in leather, cheaper than any imported," "surprising excellent Tooth-Drops," "the imperial Lip-Salve," and a "most excellent Worm-Powder."[3] These books by Watts, Bunyan, and Milton were among the most popular works of Anglophone literature in eighteenth-century North America, and Occom could have come across them anywhere. But given how often he alluded to them, cited them, copied from them, and even named his children after characters in them, he clearly came across them somewhere. Patten's seems as good a guess as any, since it was less than five miles from his house. And how can one resist wondering if he ever tried the lip salve or worm-powder?

In the zeal of his young faith, there is no doubt, Occom could be something of a Bible-thumper. In his twenties and thirties, he fashioned himself an enemy of "enthusiasts," those who proposed that the Spirit could be severed from the Word. Countering the "Inthusiastical Exhorters" who had corrupted the people of Montauk, Occom remembered, "I woud come to them with all Authority, Saying, thus Saith the Lord, and by this means, the Lord was pleased to Bless my poor Endeavours."[4] But this youthful zeal for biblically sanctioned "Authority" was what might fairly be termed, in modern parlance, a "phase." As Occom got older and began to think more critically about how religion actually worked in colonial society, he increasingly saw the tenuousness of the connection between the words of the Bible and the "True Religion of Jesus Christ, which Consists in the Power,

Figure C.2 Merchandise advertised by Nathaniel Patten of New London. *Norwich Packet*, November 4, 1774. Photograph courtesy of the American Antiquarian Society.

as well as in form."[5] And how could he not? He was confronted every day by the arrogance of the English, who misread the Bible as a mandate for greed and imperial conquest: "they have enjoyd the Gospel Priviledges for a long Time, and they are now greatly Degenerated from the Purity and Simplicity of the Gospel."[6] The crucial word here is "and." The English, from Occom's point of view, had immiserated themselves and Indigenous peoples alike precisely *because* they had had access to the Bible for so long, just like the ancient Jews who (according to the uncharitable account of Paul, which Occom followed closely) had come to suffer under the very law that should have made them free.

For all his love of reading, Occom was enough of an iconoclast to see that books—including the Bible itself—could be turned into false idols. By the time he published his Moses Paul sermon, he was writing that "the world is already full of books. . . . and the people in very deed have had precept upon precept, line upon line, here a little and there a little; so in the whole, they have much, yea very much, they have enough and more than enough."[7] Too many words, in other words, and not enough Spirit. Occom's late-career views on this topic were remarkably similar to those of the Quakers, with whom he became increasingly close over the course of his life. After a weeklong fundraising visit he and David Fowler made to Philadelphia in 1788, Occom wrote in his diary that "the Quakers in particular were exceeding kind to us and Freely Communicated their Substance to help our People in the Wilderness."[8] Presumably this "Substance" consisted mainly of money. But Occom was in Philadelphia for a week, and the Friends there may also have "Communicated" some of the doctrines passed down to them by early Quakers such as Margaret Fell, Samuel Fisher, and George Fox. These famous Friends were biblioclasts who held that "there's enough of the Word of God to be bought for Money," that eschatology concerned an inward "realizing" rather than a covenantal melodrama, and that "God was at work . . . restoring all creation, including political, social, economic, and ecclesiastical structures, to their pre-Edenic state."[9] In his thank-you letter "to the Friends of Philadelphia," Occom wrote, "The Lord God of Heaven and Earth your God and our God reward and Bless you all, with all the Blessing of Heaven and Earth."[10] The letter doesn't go into detail with regard to the Quakers' theology. But Occom was clearly convinced that they worshipped the same God.

Be that as it may, by the time he got to know the Philadelphia Quakers, Occom had already been worrying about Bible fetishization for a long time.

He saw it around him everywhere in New England, where God's "chosen" people had gotten themselves "caught in a bibliolatry of their own making," and Occom was dead set against the same thing happening in the communities among which he worked.[11] The Bible was indispensable for his work in helping Indigenous peoples recover an unalienated relationship with the world, but its imbrication with colonial history made his people understandably suspicious. In his work as a minister, Occom used scripture in ways designed to defamiliarize what reading even meant. Using his famous "Christian Cards," Occom broke scripture into little pieces, a literal act of biblioclasm.[12] Writing Bible verses onto loose leaves of paper, he passed them out to individuals who gathered around him in living rooms and public houses; he then shocked his listeners into attention by explaining how *this* one piece of scripture applied to *them*. His goal in this—and, for that matter, in most of his preaching—was not so much to teach people "the Bible" as it was to put them in a position of "answerability" to God.[13]

Occom was careful not to push his biblioclasm too far. In his own lifetime he had seen various pretenders to godliness lay claim to a false freedom by destroying books they deemed heretical. There was, for instance, James Davenport, who burned a whole "catalogue" of books on the New London town wharf in 1743, including the works of Occom's favorite Bible commentator, Matthew Henry.[14] He was also probably aware of the book-burning rituals conducted by the "Shaking Quakers," whom he learned about during a "long discourse" with the ex-Shaker Valentin Rathbun in 1785 in a tavern in New London.[15] In his diary entry on this meeting, Occom sized Rathbun up carefully, reaching a conclusion that is interestingly ambivalent with respect to the relationship between Word and Spirit: "He is a young man of good Sense, but in my Opinion he is altogether Caried away with very Strong Enthusiasm and I am afraid a bad one there is good Enthusiasm and there is a bad one, he Says they go by immediate opperation of the Spirit of God."[16] At this advanced stage of his career, Occom remained suspicious of anyone claiming to "go by the immediate opperation of the Spirit." But what exactly is "*good* Enthusiasm"? This can't have been a phrase Occom ever heard uttered by any of the New Divinity ministers who taught him theology in the 1740s and 1750s. Nor is it easy to imagine Occom himself uttering it during his earlier, anti-"Inthusiastical" phase.

Possibly Occom had hymnody in mind. Hymns (including Occom's own) typically alluded to Scripture without citing it directly. In a way, that was the whole point of them, at least according to Isaac Watts, whose path-breaking *Hymns and Spiritual Songs* (1709) furnished many of the hymns included in Occom's 1774 collection. In the preface to his unapologetically (and indeed polemically) modern verse translation of the *Psalms of David*, Watts had argued that

> the royal author is most honoured when he is made most intelligible; and when his admirable composures are copied in such language, as gives light and joy to the saints that live two thousand years after him. . . . How can we assume to ourselves all [David's] words . . . when our condition of life, our time, place, and religion, are so vastly different from those of *David*?[17]

This argument opened Watts up to "charges of antinomianism and enthusiasm," since it justified forms of text-based devotion that were unprecedently remote from the actual Bible.[18] Interestingly, Occom followed a parallel line of reasoning in the preface his own *Choice Collection of Hymns and Spiritual Songs*, insisting that "the People ought not to be contented with the outward Form of Singing, but should seek after the inward Part." Whether the "outward Forms" of songs were Scriptural or not, "when they are sung with the Spirit of the Gospel, [they] are very comforting, refreshing, and edifying to the Children of God."[19] The "Spirit of the Gospel," then, *could* be separated from the Gospel itself. This was presumably an example of what Occom would come to call "good Enthusiasm."

Hymn-singing mattered to Occom because it was something his people loved to do.[20] In 1791, Occom wrote to an unknown correspondent (possibly, per Joanna Brooks, the Philadelphia minister James Sprout) asking for books to be sent to Brothertown. The list of books he asked for included songbooks but not Bibles: "We are poorly of it for School books, and we are Scant of it for Psalm Books for the older People—They are good Singers as any People; it woud do you good to hear them once, and they are most all Singers old and Young."[21]

This passage testifies to Occom's pride in the Northeast Native practice of song, a custom that was being passed down the generations, from "the older People" to the "Young." It also reflects his belief that reading, whatever its problems, had to be at the center of Northeast Native education: "Psalm Books for the older People" and "School books" for the children. Clearly Occom saw literacy as central to his people's future, but it is important not to draw the wrong conclusions from this. As I argued in the last chapter, Occom grew increasingly averse over time to the dogmatic idea that Indigenous people should be compelled to read the Bible, or indeed any text. But neither was he particularly nostalgic for some precolonial condition of Indigenous "orality." As each of the preceding chapters shows in a different way, Occom refused to believe that the political or spiritual progress of Native communities ("our reformation") hinged on them adopting particular "outward Forms" in matters of devotion, agriculture, personal style, or anything else. The problem they confronted was one of perception: of alienation and numbness. Their task was to "stand fast" and *wake up* to the sacredness their ancestors saw immanent everywhere in creation.

Reading, writing, hearing, singing, talking, dwelling, living. It mattered to Occom what these modes of human existence achieved, but the best way of judging their rightness was to ask whether or not they were conducted in a spirit of "Gratitude" to God for having made the world in the first place:

> This Seems to be inate in the very Dumb Beasts of the Field, they Manifest a kind of Gratitude . . . by a Certain Noise, or the Motion of their Bodies,—the Fowls of the Air Mount up towards heaven and Sing forth their Artless to God,—Toads and Frogs and all the Venomous Kind, have their way of giving thanks to their Ma[ster], Yea the very Insects of the Earth Sing their Various Notes of Praise to god.[22]

Could human beings live up to this standard set by the "Toads" and "Frogs" and "Insects"? Occom hoped so, but people tended to get in their own way. They convinced themselves and one another that the way they saw the world was good enough, even when they were totally oblivious to God. That's one of the reasons why Occom placed so much emphasis on the "strange": on the "Strange State Situation and Appearance of the Indian Tribes in this Great Continent," "the Strange Call of Providence," "Strange Countries," "Strange things," and strangers.[23] Seeing the world aright required putting oneself in touch with the unfamiliar.

Occom thought his ancestors grasped this, as did the "Indian heathen" who blurred the line separating neighbor from stranger, inviting the unknown and unpredictable into the space of their homes. In this, they resembled the Good Samaritan of Jesus's parable, but unlike the Samaritan they avowed this hospitality as "our custom."[24] Perhaps assuming that this custom was universal, Occom as a young person had thrown himself upon the hospitality of the world beyond the Native Northeast, an act of courage and, probably, naivete that forever changed his life. Wheelock, to his credit, "received me with kindness and Compassion and in Stead of Staying a Fortnight or 3 Weeks, I Spent 4 Years with him."[25] Others were less welcoming, but by learning to read and to attune himself to God's "Strange Providence," Occom got from the wider world vital resources for helping his people see the world anew.[26] Looking back on his journeys in 1771, he wrote to Susanna Wheatley that "when I Come to recollect what I have Seen in my Travels, and what I have Read also, I am Struck with amazement and Stand Speechless."[27] Occom had trusted that a world of strangers, speaking strange words, would take care of him. In many ways he had been disappointed and betrayed. In others, his trust had been rewarded.

Occom never expected his kin to follow in his steps—as travelers or even as readers. On his tour of the British Isles, he had taken advantage of an unprecedented opportunity to witness the internal diversity and sheer vastness of English society, the good parts and the bad. But he never expressed even a shred of disapproval for Native peoples' "very [great] Prejudice against the English ministers and all English": "they have too much good reason for it—they have been imposed upon, too much."[28] The work of "Reformation" he and his people needed had to happen without English interference, inside their own communities.[29] Tending to their own affairs, they would be in a better position to answer his call to "Let there be Room for my words & keep them there Choice and loose them not . . . and Call home all your Roving Thoughts, and attend Diligently, and I Will Speak."[30]

Until the end of his days, Occom remained a self-styled "Strange Creature," broadcasting "amazement" to all who would listen, but especially to his "kindred according to the flesh," who knew the value of strangers in their bones.[31] A radical in the truest sense, what he wanted most was for his kindred not to be a "sleepy people." Calling forth all their powers of perception, they would rediscover what they always were.

APPENDIX

Two Letters from Susanna Wheatley to John Thornton Concerning Samson Occom

These letters from Susanna Wheatley to John Thornton are housed in the "Leslie Family Papers, Earls of Leven and Melville" (reference GD26/13/663) at the National Records of Scotland. I have not been able to ascertain how exactly the letters came to be included in this collection, which also includes several letters by Phillis Wheatley, which were found by Kenneth Silverman and published in the winter 1974 issue of *American Literature*. However, the eighteenth-century earls of Melville had connections with several of Occom's evangelical friends, including Thornton and Selina, Countess of Huntingdon (See Sir William Fraser, *The Melvilles, Earls of Melville, and the Leslies, earls of Leven* [Edinburgh, 1890], I:349–50, 360–63). More research into the Leven and Melvilles' circle could help further clarify these manuscripts' history and, more generally, the precise contours of Occom's evangelical network. I am grateful to the Earl of Leven and Melville for his encouragement to reprint the letters here.

Boston Ocr. 26 1771

Hon'd Sir,

I rec'd your Agreeable and instructive favour of 7th August for which I thank you. It's a duty incumbent On us to help each other in our

Christian course. The earnest of the Spirit and foretaste of the glory which Shall be reveal'd, has been long the Object of my pursuit. O that we might so successfully seek, as at length to Obtain that refreshing cordial, to animate us in the way To heaven! May we be more ready to draw from this Inexhaustible fountain, and Seek its life giving influences. We know that it never diminishes, yet we come more slowly to partake Of its benefits than the important man at the pool of Bethesda. Will it never raise emulation in us To See so many taking the Kingdom of heaven with a Sacred violence? Let us complain like him to Jesus, that He would make his Strength manifest in our weakness: to give us that water of life which others are drinking in full draughts of. What a glorious privilege is this to be the Children of the Living God! I contemplate with astonishment the honour that an Infinite God Confers upon us in calling us his Children. And taking upon himself in unspeakable love the affectionate title Of "Heavenly Father." How Sweet and at the Same time how mysterious is this love of God to man who is in Perpetual rebellion Against him in thought word and Action. Who then, can call him unmerciful. Let us Strive earnestly then to lay aside the weapons with which we have been daring him ever Since the fall, for the whole armour of God, to fight against his, and our enemies. O that I might be like the importunate Widow, who never left pleading till she had Obtain'd her request. I beg you to carry me to God as a Sinner, who Am made Sensible that I have no Righteousness of my Own: that I might be invested with the perfect Righteousness of Christ. I beg the continuance of your prayers for my Husband and Son, and my whole Family. I am under great weakness of Body and very low in Spirit. I thank you heartily for your repeated favors to Mr. Occom which is come very seasonably to him, for I am afraid he must have suffer'd both hunger and cold this winter.

As to the report which is Spread about him, I have made it my business to inquire into it, and by What I can learn, it was a design'd thing by a wicked Sett of men who were with him. I am intimately acquainted with a young Gentleman who went from this Town to settle Near to Mr. Occom; he has a great opinion of him & gives him the Character of an honest and worth man. He has Promis'd me that he would make it his endeavor to get a Number of good sort of people to write home in Mr Occom's behalf to clear up his Character. I am of your Opinion that he has had very hard treatment, I love him for his humility. They hear that somebody has wrote against him. My Son rec'd a letter from Dr. Wheelock, in which he told him that Mr. Occom had behav'd in Christian Character. Ask'd Dr. Whitaker whether he thought it was a thing that Mr. Occom was fond of? To which he reply'd he never had such a thought, and believ'd it to be a mere Accident. For he was sure, when he was in England there was liquor enough to swim in, But he never perceiv'd that he was in the least fond of it. He came passenger With Capt Calef, who said, that he behav'd extremely well. You best know what Dr. Wheelock & Dr. Whitaker have wrote you: but this I affirm for truth. I wrote to Mr. Occom to know how he came to be so poor When He was paid so much a year for preaching, & he return'd the following answer.

> A few days after I got home, I went to see Dr. Wheelock, and he was very urgent, to have me go up into the wilderness immediately; but I did not think it duty to leave my family again so soon, as I had been Gone from home two years and half, and was but Just got home, and I told him that I thought it was rather my duty to stay at home till another Spring as I had a large family of Children and had neglected them, whilst I have been preaching and Teaching others and so I stay'd at home, but contrary to his mind. The Spring following, I was ready to go, and went up to the Dr.'s But he said he had no money to assist me with to go, and so did not go that Spring again, Since that time I have been so infirm, I have not been able to undertake Such arduous Journies: Riding hurts me as much as Any thing, I had several invitations early this Spring from Naraganset both by the Indians and English, and I went but that Journey hurt me much I have not got over it yet. And I never expect to be able to go such Journies as I have done

   I am Sir with great respect your Sincere
   friend and humble Ser't Susanna Wheatly
PS I am much oblig'd to you for the soul refreshing tract which you inclos'd me, and that you bear me so much upon your mind.

I forwarded your letter by the first post after Capt. Calef arrived But I have had no answer. I believe he was gone from home

Susanna Wheatley
Boston 26 Oct 1771
Rec'd 18 Dec.
Ans 24 Jan'y 1772

To
John Thornton Esq
Merchant
London

Boston Feb'y 9 1773

Hon'd Sir

I should not have wrote before I had heard from you; but having a good opportunity to inform you that the rev'd Mr. Occom has been to Boston & resided at my house almost a fortnight, we had the satisfaction of having his heavenly conversation and his earnest Prayers not only for my Family, but for his dear friends in England we set apart one evening to be by our Selves, in which you and your Family were particularly remember'd & I wish you had been here to have Joined us.—He has preach'd here 2 sabbaths, on the first he preach'd twice and on the 2nd 3 times and so great was the number of People to hear him that it was as tho 300 were about the door. People of the first rank in Town went to hear him and he was much admired. The numerous Auditories of the rev'd Mr. Whitfield came to my mind upon Sight of the Concourse that followed the rev'd Mr. Occom His preaching seems to be attended with great success, and has put some young People under great concern for their Souls, and they came to converse with him.

I am sorry he went away so soon, for he had the offer of 2 collections being made for him, at 2 meeting Houses, but he said he could not tarry a day longer, but must make haste home, expecting that the Indians were already come from a distant part upon some Public business that requir'd him to be present. I wish he could have staid a few days longer for I am sure he has need enough of those collections, for tho' he has a Salary of 50£sterl. It seems he has but little benefit of it: for his house is almost always fill of Indians, 30 of whom come and reside with him several days together. I told him I did not think it was his duty and that the Salary was given for the Support of his family which is very Large— But he said he thot he was doing his duty to let as many come as would for then he had an Opportunity of Preaching and conversing with them, and they are very attentive to his instructions. He has nothing from the English or Indians for preaching, only his Salary from England.

He says he does not preach for gain for if he had nothing he would still go on preaching, his view is the good of Souls. ——

I hope by this time you are convinced that my Son has been Falsely accus'd; but if he Suffers, he is not the first who has suffer'd wrongfully. It is my earnest desire that this trouble may be sanctified to us both— I must repeat that it is a great grief to me. ——

When I consider that a man's ways are not at his own disposal but his heart is in the hands of God— there, I leave it begging the Continuance of your prayer for me and my Family, I remain your sincere friend & well wisher

Susanna Wheatley

To
John Thornton Esq
Merchant
Capt. Hatch
London
Susanna Wheatley

Boston 9 Feb'y 1773
Rec'd 7 April
Ans. 2nd Jany

Notes

Introduction

1. Samson Occom, *The Collected Writings of Samson Occom, Mohegan: Leadership and Literature in Eighteenth-Century Native America*, ed. Joanna Brooks (New York: Oxford University Press, 2006), 52–53. Following recent scholarly practice, I use the term "Native Northeast" to refer to all of the Native nations of which Occom likely had some firsthand knowledge. (See, for instance, the Native Northeast Research Collaborative: https://www.thenativenortheast .org/about.html.) As a descriptor of Occom's home communities and the communities that neighbored them, "Native Northeast" has the advantage of being broader than the familiar "Coastal Algonquian," which refers more narrowly to eastern Algonquian languages and the peoples who speak them; this term can be confusing as a descriptor of the Brothertown Nation, which was located in Occom's lifetime at a considerable distance from the coast. I will still sometimes use "Coastal Algonquian" when referring to the tribes whose families participated in the formation of Brothertown: Narragansett, Niantic, Groton Pequot, Stonington Pequot, Tunxis, Montauk, and Mohegan. Another advantage of "the Native Northeast" (which I use as a noun) and "Northeast Native" (which I use as an adjective) is that these terms are more specific than "Indigenous peoples" or "Native Americans." When I use the latter terms, it is almost always when I am trying to draw a sharp distinction (typically cultural or political) between Native peoples and colonizers—not in order to generalize about what Native people "are like." In chapter 3,

the term "Turtle Island" refers more generally to North America and all the originally precolonial peoples living there. It is worth emphasizing that Occom himself used none of these terms. He referred to his Northeast Native communities by their tribal names, a practice I follow whenever appropriate. He spoke of Indigenous people more generally as "kindred," "Indians," and occasionally—when he wanted to make a point—"heathens." I sometimes use the first of these terms but avoid the latter two because of their colonial connotations. I capitalize "Indigenous," "Native," and "Black," but not "white," extending to Indigenous people Kimberlé Crenshaw's reasoning that "Blacks . . . Asians, Latinos, and other 'minorities' constitute a specific cultural group and, as such, require denotation as a proper noun." Kimberle Crenshaw, "Mapping the Margins: Intersectionality, Identity Politics, and Violence Against Women of Color," *Stanford Law Review* 43, no. 6 (1991): 1244n6.

2. For details of Occom's biography, see William DeLoss Love, *Samson Occom and the Christian Indians of New England* (Boston: Pilgrim Press, 1899); Harold William Blodgett, *Samson Occom* (Hanover, NH: Dartmouth College Publications, 1935); and Joanna Brooks, "Chronology," in *The Collected Writings of Samson Occom.*

3. Bruce Hindmarsh, *The Spirit of Early Evangelicalism: True Religion in a Modern World* (New York: Oxford University Press, 2018), 30; Thomas S. Kidd, *George Whitefield: America's Spiritual Founding Father* (New Haven, CT: Yale University Press, 2014); Frank Lambert, *Pedlar in Divinity: George Whitefield and the Transatlantic Revivals, 1737–1770* (Princeton, NJ: Princeton University Press, 1994).

4. Colin G. Calloway, *The Indian History of an American Institution: Native Americans and Dartmouth* (Hanover, NH: University Press of New England, 2010), 26.

5. Paul Joseph Grant-Costa, "The Last Indian War in New England: The Mohegan Indians v. The Governour and Company of the Colony of Connecticut, 1703–1774" (PhD dissertation, Yale University, 2008), 308.

6. Audra Simpson, *Mohawk Interruptus: Political Life Across the Borders of Settler States* (Durham, NC: Duke University Press, 2014), citing Robert Allen Warrior, *Tribal Secrets: Recovering American Indian Intellectual Traditions* (Minneapolis: University of Minnesota Press, 1995). It is worth noting that Warrior does not actually use the term "literary sovereignty" in this text but rather "intellectual sovereignty," although both terms capture aspects of his argument in *Tribal Secrets*. (I am grateful to Robert Warrior for pointing this out to me.) Regardless of who first coined it, I am happy to borrow this term here.

7. This construal of Occom's literary sovereignty is inspired by Hilary Wyss's claim that Northeast Native people "who *did* write, no matter what they wrote, fundamentally altered the relationship between missionary culture and Native people through the simple act of self-expression." Hilary E. Wyss, *English Letters and Indian Literacies: Reading, Writing, and New England Missionary Schools, 1750–1830* (Philadelphia: University of Pennsylvania Press, 2012), 7, emphasis in original. However, I am somewhat more optimistic than Wyss sometimes appears to be about the possibility of recovering an Indigenous cultural perspective from the content of Occom's writings. See chapter 2.
8. Occom, *Collected Writings*, 203–4.
9. Timothy D. Hall, *Contested Boundaries: Itinerancy and the Reshaping of the Colonial American Religious World* (Durham, NC: Duke University Press, 1994), 2.
10. Occom, *Collected Writings*, 52, emphasis added; Sandra M. Gustafson, *Eloquence Is Power: Oratory and Performance in Early America* (Chapel Hill: University of North Carolina Press, 2000), 94.
11. Occom, *Collected Writings*, 52. A more modern scholarly term for this "wandering life" lived by Coastal Algonquian peoples is "conditional sedentism." See Jean M. O'Brien, *Dispossession by Degrees: Indian Land and Identity in Natick, Massachusetts, 1650–1790* (New York: Cambridge University Press, 1997), 17n23, citing Kathleen Bragdon, *Native People of Southern New England, 1500–1650* (Norman: University of Oklahoma Press, 1996), 36–39.
12. "Alas!," exclaimed Connecticut minister William Worthington in 1774 about the recent upsurge in revivalism and itinerancy: "We have taught them to love Strangers, and now after them they will go"; cited in Hall, *Contested Boundaries*, 70.
13. Occom, *Collected Writings*, 53.
14. Lisa Brooks, *The Common Pot: The Recovery of Native Space in the Northeast* (Minneapolis: University of Minnesota Press, 2008).
15. See, for instance, Yael Ben-zvi, *Native Land Talk: Indigenous and Arrivant Rights Theories* (Hanover, NH: Dartmouth College Press, 2018), 60–90; Kathleen Brown-Pérez, "A Right Delayed: The Brothertown Indian Nation's Story of Surviving the Federal Acknowledgment Process," in *Recognition, Sovereignty Struggles, & Indigenous Rights in the United States: A Sourcebook*, ed. Amy E. Den Ouden and Jean M. O'Brien (Chapel Hill: University of North Carolina Press, 2013); Craig N. Cipolla, James Quinn, and Jay Levy, "Theory in Collaborative Indigenous Archaeology: Insights from Mohegan," *American Antiquity* 84, no. 1 (January 2019); Courtney Cottrell, "NAGPRA's Politics of Recognition: Repatriation Struggles of a Terminated Tribe," *American Indian Quarterly* 44, no. 1 (2020); Amy E. Den Ouden, *Beyond Conquest: Native Peoples and the Struggle for History in New England* (Lincoln: University of

Nebraska Press, 2005); Craig Yirush, "Claiming the New World: Empire, Law, and Indigenous Rights in the Mohegan Case, 1704," *Law and History Review* 29, no. 2 (2011).

16. Glen Sean Coulthard, *Red Skin, White Masks: Rejecting the Colonial Politics of Recognition* (Minneapolis: University of Minnesota Press, 2014); Cottrell, "NAGPRA's Politics of Recognition"; Simpson, *Mohawk Interruptus*; Patchen Markell, *Bound by Recognition* (Princeton, NJ: Princeton University Press, 2003). I revisit the idea of recognition in chapter 2.
17. Brown-Pérez, "A Right Delayed"; Cottrell, "NAGPRA's Politics of Recognition."
18. I examine the relationship between Indigenous studies and settler colonial studies in chapter 1.
19. Linda Tuhiwai Smith, *Decolonizing Methodologies: Research and Indigenous Peoples* (New York: St. Martin's Press, 1999); Alyssa Mt. Pleasant, Caroline Wigginton, and Kelly Wisecup, "Materials and Methods in Native American and Indigenous Studies: Completing the Turn," *Early American Literature* 53, no. 2 (2018): 409.
20. Robert Innes, "Introduction: Native Studies and Native Cultural Preservation, Revitalization, and Persistence," *American Indian Culture and Research Journal* 34, no. 2 (October 2010): 6; see also Chris Andersen and Jean M. O'Brien, "Introduction: Indigenous Studies: An Appeal for Methodological Promiscuity," in *Sources and Methods in Indigenous Studies*, ed. Chris Andersen and Jean M. O'Brien (New York: Routledge, 2017).
21. From this point of view, "modernity" itself can be described as an "epistemic condition that Europeans created to distinguish the nation as civilized and thereby justify aggrandizing the nation at the expense of the uncivilized." Mahmood Mamdani, *Neither Settler nor Native: The Making and Unmaking of Permanent Minorities* (Cambridge, MA: Belknap Press of Harvard University Press, 2020), 3, 37–101; cited in Timothy Bowers Vasko, "Nature and the Native," *Critical Research on Religion* 10, no. 1 (April 2022): 19n2. Arguing along similar lines, the late Patrick Wolfe drew on postcolonial theory, particularly the work of Gayatri Spivak, in voicing skepticism about "any attempt on my part to recuperate a pristine Indigenous trace from behind the surface of the anthropological text." Patrick Wolfe, *Settler Colonialism and the Transformation of Anthropology: The Politics and Poetics of an Ethnographic Event* (New York: Cassell, 1999), 4.
22. Moreover, and more basically, Innes argues that the term "Indigenous knowledge" is notoriously difficult to define. Innes, "Native Studies," 6. I return to these questions of subject-positionality and disciplinary knowledge in chapter 2.
23. Occom, *Collected Writings*, 177.
24. Andersen and O'Brien, "Indigenous Studies."

25. Occom, *Collected Writings*.
26. Joanna Brooks, "'This Indian World': An Introduction to the Writings of Samson Occom," in *The Collected Writings of Samson Occom*, 36.
27. Matt Cohen, *The Networked Wilderness: Communicating in Early New England* (Minneapolis: University of Minnesota Press, 2010); Phillip H. Round, *Removable Type: Histories of the Book in Indian Country, 1663–1880* (Chapel Hill: University of North Carolina Press, 2010); Wyss, *English Letters and Indian Literacies*; Kelly Wisecup, *Assembled for Use: Indigenous Compilation and the Archives of Early Native American Literatures* (New Haven, CT: Yale University Press, 2021).
28. Angela Calcaterra, *Literary Indians: Aesthetics and Encounter in American Literature to 1920* (Chapel Hill: University of North Carolina Press, 2018), 47–82; Wisecup, *Assembled for Use*, 23–59.
29. Brooks, *The Common Pot*; Roman Jakobson, "Metalanguage as a Linguistic Problem," in *Contributions to Comparative Mythology* (Berlin: De Gruyter Mouton, 1985); Michael Silverstein, "Metapragmatic Discourse and Metapragmatic Function," in *Reflexive Language: Reported Speech and Metapragmatics*, ed. John Arthur Lucy (New York: Cambridge University Press, 1993). I describe my approach to Occom's metalanguage at much greater length in chapters 2 and 4.
30. On evangelicalism as an interactional form, see Michael Warner, "The Preacher's Footing," in *This Is Enlightenment* (Chicago: University of Chicago Press, 2010).
31. On the periodization of Puritanism see, for instance, Thomas S. Kidd, *The Protestant Interest: New England After Puritanism* (New Haven, CT: Yale University Press, 2004), 1–19; David Hall, *The Puritans: A Transatlantic History* (Princeton, NJ: Princeton University Press, 2019), 252–354; and Richard L. Bushman, *From Puritan to Yankee: Character and the Social Order in Connecticut, 1690–1765* (Cambridge, MA: Harvard University Press, 1998).
32. Douglas L. Winiarski, *Darkness Falls on the Land of Light: Experiencing Religious Awakenings in Eighteenth-Century New England* (Chapel Hill: University of North Carolina Press, 2017), 14; Linford D. Fisher, *The Indian Great Awakening: Religion and the Shaping of Native Cultures in Early America* (New York: Oxford University Press, 2012), 10.
33. Julius H. Rubin, *Tears of Repentance: Christian Indian Identity and Community in Colonial Southern New England* (Lincoln: University of Nebraska Press, 2013), 126–28; Brooks, "This Indian World," 3–4; Gustafson, *Eloquence Is Power*, 77.
34. Alan Heimert, *Religion and the American Mind, from the Great Awakening to the Revolution* (Cambridge, MA: Harvard University Press, 1966). Like other Americanist scholarship of this period, Heimert's concern with democracy as a supposedly intrinsic feature of the American way of life reflected Cold

War cultural priorities. Other midcentury work in this vein includes Reinhold Niebuhr and Alan Heimert, *A Nation So Conceived: Reflections on the History of America from Its Early Visions to Its Present Power* (New York: Scribner, 1963); and F. O. Matthiessen, *From the Heart of Europe* (New York: Oxford University Press, 1948).

35. Jay Fliegelman, *Declaring Independence: Jefferson, Natural Language and the Culture of Performance* (Stanford, CA: Stanford University Press, 1993), 38, 109, 398n21; Nancy Ruttenburg, *Democratic Personality: Popular Voice and the Trial of American Authorship* (Stanford, CA: Stanford University Press, 1998), 17, 24; Nancy Ruttenburg, "George Whitefield, Spectacular Conversion, and the Rise of Democratic Personality," *American Literary History* 5, no. 3 (1993): 452n7; Gustafson, *Eloquence Is Power*, xixn11; Philip F. Gura, "Eloquence Is Power: Oratory and Performance in Early America," *Journal of American History* 88, no. 2 (September 2001): 638. For a critical perspective on Fliegelman's appropriation of Heimert's "democratic" vision, and on the relation of that vision to Native-settler relations in the eighteenth century, see Robert Allen Warrior, "'The Finest Men We Have Ever Seen': Reading Jefferson's Osage Encounters Through *Orientalism*," *Ariel: A Review of International English Literature* 51, no. 1 (2020): 74.

36. Jace Weaver, *The Red Atlantic: American Indigenes and the Making of the Modern World, 1000–1927* (Chapel Hill: University of North Carolina Press, 2014); Nick Estes, *Our History Is the Future: Standing Rock Versus the Dakota Access Pipeline, and the Long Tradition of Indigenous Resistance* (London: Verso, 2019); Kidd, *The Protestant Interest*; Susan O'Brien, "A Transatlantic Community of Saints: The Great Awakening and the First Evangelical Network, 1735," *American Historical Review* 91, no. 4 (October 1986); Douglas L. Winiarski, "Native American Popular Religion in New England's Old Colony, 1670–1770," *Religion and American Culture: A Journal of Interpretation* 15, no. 2 (2005): 152; Annette G. Aubert and Zachary Purvis, eds., *Transatlantic Religion: Europe, America, and the Making of Modern Christianity* (Leiden: Brill, 2021); D. Bruce Hindmarsh, *The Spirit of Early Evangelicalism: True Religion in a Modern World* (New York: Oxford University Press, 2018).

37. See chapters 3 and 6.

38. See, for instance, Margaret Bruchac, "Broken Chains of Custody: Possessing, Dispossessing, and Repossessing Lost Wampum Belts," *Proceedings of the American Philosophical Society* 162, no. 1 (March 2018); Erin Debenport, *Fixing the Books: Secrecy, Literacy, and Perfectibility in Indigenous New Mexico* (Santa Fe, NM: School for Advanced Research Press, 2015); Simpson, *Mohawk Interruptus*. I return to this paradox in chapter 2.

39. Occom, *Collected Writings*, 176.

1. "Asylum for Strangers"

1. Samson Occom, *The Collected Writings of Samson Occom, Mohegan: Leadership and Literature in Eighteenth-Century Native America*, ed. Joanna Brooks (New York: Oxford University Press, 2006), 96.
2. Colin G. Calloway, *The Indian History of an American Institution: Native Americans and Dartmouth* (Hanover, NH: University Press of New England, 2010), 26.
3. Standish Meacham, *Henry Thornton of Clapham, 1760–1815* (Cambridge, MA: Harvard University Press, 1964). Thornton had signed on as one of Dartmouth's founding trustees but remained loyal to Occom even after Wheelock's betrayal. William DeLoss Love, *Samson Occom and the Christian Indians of New England* (Boston: Pilgrim Press, 1899), 156.
4. Susanna Wheatley to John Thornton, October 26, 1771, Papers of the Leslie family, Earls of Leven and Melville, National Records of Scotland, GD26/13/663/1. See also the appendix.
5. Occom, *Collected Writings*, 204.
6. Occom, *Collected Writings*, 203, 201.
7. Occom, *Collected Writings*, 206.
8. Occom, *Collected Writings*, 55.
9. Wheatley to Thornton, October 26, 1771.
10. Susanna Wheatley to John Thornton, February 9, 1773, Papers of the Leslie family, Earls of Leven and Melville, National Records of Scotland, GD26/13/663/3. See the appendix.
11. John Thornton to Samson Occom. February 19, 1773, Samson Occom Papers, Connecticut Historical Society, http://hdl.handle.net/11134/40002:395.
12. On Paul's background and the circumstances of his arrest see Ava Chamberlain, "The Execution of Moses Paul: A Story of Crime and Contact in Eighteenth-Century Connecticut," *New England Quarterly* 77, no. 3 (2004): 416–19.
13. Occom, *Collected Writings*, 178, citing Romans 5:23. Unless otherwise noted, I follow Occom in using the King James Version when referring to scripture.
14. Occom, *Collected Writings*, 177.
15. G. S. Rousseau and Roy Porter, eds., *Exoticism in the Enlightenment* (New York: St. Martin's Press, 1989); Christa Knellwolf and Iain McCalman, "Introduction: Exoticism and the Culture of Exploration," *Eighteenth-Century Life* 26, no. 3 (September 2002); Susan Scott Parrish, *American Curiosity: Cultures of Natural History in the Colonial British Atlantic World* (Chapel Hill: University of North Carolina Press, 2012).

16. Occom, *Collected Writings*, 206.
17. Mandy Suhr-Sytsma, "The View from Crow Hill: An Interview with Melissa Tantaquidgeon Zobel," *Studies in American Indian Literatures* 27, no. 2 (2015): 83.
18. Jean M. O'Brien, *Dispossession by Degrees: Indian Land and Identity in Natick, Massachusetts, 1650–1790* (New York: Cambridge University Press, 1997), 17n23, citing Kathleen Bragdon, *Native People of Southern New England, 1500–1650* (Norman: University of Oklahoma Press, 1996), 36–9.
19. Jeffrey C. Bendremer et al., "Mohegan Oral Tradition, Archaeology and the Legacy of Uncas," *Bulletin of the Archaeological Society of Connecticut* 70 (2008): 79.
20. Occom, *Collected Writings*, 52, 248.
21. O'Brien, *Dispossession by Degrees*, 24.
22. O'Brien, *Dispossession by Degrees*, 207–13.
23. While Northeast Native peoples had been practicing horticulture for half a millennium or more, the fact that *men* were growing crops was new, and it created a further set of economic, social, and psychological challenges for Native women due to their "separation from agricultural tasks." Jean M. O'Brien, "'Divorced from the Land': Resistance and Survival of Indian Women in Eighteenth-Century New England," in *After King Philip's War: Presence and Persistence in Indian New England*, ed. Colin G. Calloway (Hanover, NH: University Press of New England, 1997), 148.
24. Strother E. Roberts, *Colonial Ecology, Atlantic Economy: Transforming Nature in Early New England* (Philadelphia: University of Pennsylvania Press, 2019), 71.
25. Joseph Johnson, *To Do Good to My Indian Brethren: The Writings of Joseph Johnson, 1751–1776*, ed. Laura J. Murray (Amherst: University of Massachusetts Press, 1998), 123.
26. Paul Joseph Grant-Costa, "The Last Indian War in New England: The Mohegan Indians v. The Governour and Company of the Colony of Connecticut, 1703–1774" (PhD dissertation, Yale University, 2008), 242. See also chapter 3.
27. See, for instance, O'Brien, *Dispossession by Degrees*; Amy E. Den Ouden, *Beyond Conquest: Native Peoples and the Struggle for History in New England* (Lincoln: University of Nebraska Press, 2005); Calloway, *After King Philip's War*.
28. On the Mason guardianship see Wendy B. St. Jean, "Inventing Guardianship: The Mohegan Indians and Their 'Protectors,'" *New England Quarterly* 72, no. 3 (September 1999): 362. The most thorough study of the Mason land case or "Mohegan Affair" is Grant-Costa, "The Last Indian War in New England."
29. Grant-Costa, "The Last Indian War in New England," 147.
30. Grant-Costa, "The Last Indian War in New England," 303, 242.

31. Bragdon, *Native People of Southern New England, 1500–1650*, 150. Occom may have been alluding to these customary attitudes toward the sachemship in a 1764 letter to William Johnson: "we have a Law and a Custom to make a Sachem over us Without the help of any People or Nation in the World, and When he makes himself unworthy of his Station we put him down—ourselves." Occom, *Collected Writings*, 145. In the scholarly literature Native communities choosing sachems in this way are sometimes described as "voting with their feet." See, for instance, Jenny Hale Pulsipher, *Subjects Unto the Same King: Indians, English, and the Contest for Authority in Colonial New England* (Philadelphia: University of Pennsylvania Press, 2005), 11; Alan Taylor, *The Divided Ground: Indians, Settlers and the Northern Borderland of the American Revolution* (New York: Knopf, 2006), 20.
32. Grant-Costa, "The Last Indian War in New England," 242.
33. Connecticut Archives: Indians, First Series, volume 2: 310, 319, https://findit.library.yale.edu/bookreader/BookReaderDemo/index.html?oid=10682281, https://findit.library.yale.edu/bookreader/BookReaderDemo/index.html?oid=10682290.
34. "Samson Occom, Autobiography," 1768, Samson Occom Papers, Mohegan Tribe (reproduction by the Occom Circle Project, Dartmouth College), https://collections.dartmouth.edu/occom/html/diplomatic/768517-diplomatic.html.
35. In this respect Occom's act reflects what many scholars see as a broader pattern in the history of settler colonialism, which is that the lines between "Native" and "Settler" tend to become sharper over time; see Nancy Shoemaker, *A Strange Likeness: Becoming Red and White in Eighteenth-Century North America* (New York: Oxford University Press, 2004), and Patrick Wolfe, ed., *The Settler Complex: Recuperating Binarism in Colonial Studies* (Los Angeles: UCLA American Indian Studies Center, 2016).
36. Occom, *Collected Writings*, 294, 201.
37. Occom, *Collected Writings*, 204.
38. Occom, *Collected Writings*, 203.
39. Occom, *Collected Writings*, 205.
40. Occom, *Collected Writings*, 55, 138, 308; see also chapter 3.
41. Occom, *Collected Writings*, 277.
42. While some Coastal Algonquians rejected the ideas behind the movement, others probably couldn't afford to move, even if they had wanted to. Still others stayed back or returned midway through their migration because of the violence of the American Revolution. Brad Jarvis, *The Brothertown Nation of Indians: Land Ownership and Nationalism in Early America, 1740–1840* (Lincoln: University of Nebraska Press, 2010), 13–57; Roberts, *Colonial Ecology, Atlantic Economy*, 71; Anthony Wonderley, "Brothertown, New York, 1785," *New York*

History 81, no. 4 (2000): 465; Colin Calloway, *The American Revolution in Indian Country: Crisis and Diversity in Native American Communities* (New York: Cambridge University Press, 1995), 91–92.

43. Occom, *Collected Writings*, 233.
44. This event is described in a speech by Gladys Tantaquidgeon transcribed in "Mohegan Church Observes 100th Anniversary Corner Stone Laying," *Norwich Bulletin*, August 1 1931: 9. I am indebted to archivist David Freeburg at the Mohegan Tribe for sharing this source with me.
45. Melissa Tantaquidgeon Zobel, *Medicine Trail: The Life and Lessons of Gladys Tantaquidgeon* (Tucson: University of Arizona Press, 2000); Melissa Tantaquidgeon Zobel, *The Lasting of the Mohegans: Part I, the Story of the Wolf People* (Uncasville, CT: Mohegan Tribe, 1995), 23–29.
46. Joanna Brooks, "'This Indian World': An Introduction to the Writings of Samson Occom," in *The Collected Writings of Samson Occom*, 39.
47. See, for instance, Julius H. Rubin, *Tears of Repentance: Christian Indian Identity and Community in Colonial Southern New England* (Lincoln: University of Nebraska Press, 2013), 141; Linford D. Fisher, *The Indian Great Awakening: Religion and the Shaping of Native Cultures in Early America* (New York: Oxford University Press, 2012), 18–19; and Brooks's editorial remarks in Occom, *Collected Writings*, 251, 252n11.
48. For a useful discussion of this assumption and its history, particularly among non–Native Americans, see Philip Jenkins, *Dream Catchers: How Mainstream America Discovered Native Spirituality* (New York: Oxford University Press, 2004), esp. 3–28.
49. Kimberly TallBear, *Native American DNA: Tribal Belonging and the False Promise of Genetic Science* (Minneapolis: University of Minnesota Press, 2013).
50. Phillis Wheatley, *Complete Writings* (New York: Penguin Books, 2001), 153.
51. Occom, *Collected Writings*, 206.
52. Jonathan Edwards, for example, developed an elaborate historical narrative to explain how "Native Americans . . . had become Satan's peculiar people, and their religion nothing more than devil worship." Gerald R. McDermott, *Jonathan Edwards Confronts the Gods: Christian Theology, Enlightenment Religion, and Non-Christian Faiths* (New York: Oxford University Press, 2000), 194
53. Occom, *Collected Writings*, 97; Rebecca Larson, *Daughters of Light: Quaker Women Preaching and Prophesying in the Colonies and Abroad, 1700–1775* (Chapel Hill: University of North Carolina Press, 2000).
54. Occom, *Collected Writings*, 206. Occom's views on abolition may also have been influenced by fellow evangelicals such as Phillis Wheatley and Samuel Hopkins, who, like Occom, connected slavery to capitalism's "monopolizing" tendencies and to its valorization of rational self-interest. See Michael Monescalchi, "Phillis Wheatley, Samuel Hopkins, and the Rise of

Disinterested Benevolence," *Early American Literature* 54, no. 2 (2019); Catherine A. Brekus, *Sarah Osborn's World: The Rise of Evangelical Christianity in Early America* (New Haven, CT: Yale University Press, 2013), 284–87.

55. Eva Marie Garroutte, *Real Indians: Identity and the Survival of Native America* (Berkeley: University of California Press, 2003); Scott Richard Lyons, "Actually Existing Indian Nations: Modernity, Diversity, and the Future of Native American Studies," *American Indian Quarterly* 35, no. 3 (2011); Patrick Wolfe, *Settler Colonialism and the Transformation of Anthropology: The Politics and Poetics of an Ethnographic Event* (New York: Cassell, 1999), 163–64.

56. O'Brien, *Dispossession by Degrees*, 3–8.

57. Patrick Wolfe, "Settler Colonialism and the Elimination of the Native," *Journal of Genocide Research* 8, no. 4 (December 2006).

58. J. Kēhaulani Kauanui, "'A Structure, Not an Event': Settler Colonialism and Enduring Indigeneity," *Lateral* 5, no. 1 (June 2016).

59. Occom, *Collected Writings*, 200, emphasis added; Wolfe, "Introduction," in Wolfe, *Settler Complex*.

60. James Axtell, *The Invasion Within: The Contest of Cultures in Colonial North America* (New York: Oxford University Press, 1986), 284.

61. On the structure-agency problem generally see, for instance, Anthony Giddens, *The Constitution of Society: Outline of the Theory of Structuration* (Berkeley: University of California Press, 1984); and the essays in Craig J. Calhoun et al., eds., *Contemporary Sociological Theory*, 4th ed. (Hoboken, NJ: John Wiley & Sons, 2022), 77–128. For an overview of this problem as it pertains to the analysis of settler colonialism, see Alexander Page and Theresa Petray, "Agency and Structural Constraints: Indigenous Peoples and the Australian Settler-State in North Queensland," *Settler Colonial Studies* 6, no. 1 (January 2016).

62. Lorenzo Veracini, "Is Settler Colonial Studies Even Useful?" *Postcolonial Studies* 24, no. 2 (April 2021): 270.

63. Chris Andersen and Jean M. O'Brien, "Introduction: Indigenous Studies: An Appeal for Methodological Promiscuity," in *Sources and Methods in Indigenous Studies*, ed. Chris Andersen and Jean M. O'Brien (New York: Routledge, 2017).

64. See, for instance, Jean M. O'Brien, "Tracing Settler Colonialism's Eliminatory Logic in *Traces of History*," *American Quarterly* 69, no. 2 (2017): 252.

65. See, for instance, Occom's comments on the Mohegan "custom" of selecting and deposing sachems; Occom, *Collected Writings*, 145.

66. Suhr-Sytsma, "The View from Crow Hill," 83.

67. Occom, *Collected Writings*, 202–3.

68. I revisit this distinction, with reference to Occom's writings on perception, in chapter 6.

69. This way of talking about love was becoming increasingly common in Occom's lifetime. His contemporary Adam Smith wrote in *Theory of Moral Sentiments* that "the passion [of love] appears to every body, but the man who feels it, entirely disproportioned to the value of the object; and love, though it is pardoned in a certain age because we know it is natural, is always laughed at, because we cannot enter into it. All serious and strong expressions of it appear ridiculous to a third person; and though a lover may be good company to his mistress, he is so to nobody else." Adam Smith, *The Theory of Moral Sentiments*, ed. Knud Haakonssen (New York: Cambridge University Press, 2002), 23. For a historical and sociological treatment of love covering this period, see Niklas Luhmann, *Love as Passion: The Codification of Intimacy*, trans. Jeremy Gaines and Doris L. Jones (Stanford, CA: Stanford University Press, 1998).
70. Occom, *Collected Writings*, 308.
71. Occom, *Collected Writings*, 50, 53, 174, 180.
72. Occom, *Collected Writings*, 49.
73. Webb Keane, *Christian Moderns: Freedom and Fetish in the Mission Encounter* (Berkeley: University of California Press, 2007), 60.
74. Occom, *Collected Writings*, 218.
75. Occom lived during a period in which this term was beginning to shed the negative connotation it had had since early modernity. See, for instance, M. H. Abrams, *The Mirror and the Lamp: Romantic Theory and the Critical Tradition* (New York: Oxford University Press, 1971), 161–63.
76. Occom, *Collected Writings*, 49.
77. Occom, *Collected Writings*, 185.
78. Occom, *Collected Writings*, 170.
79. Occom, *Collected Writings*, 196.
80. Occom, *Collected Writings*, 49.
81. Occom, *Collected Writings*, 201.
82. Occom, *Collected Writings*, citing Luke 10:34–35.
83. Occom, *Collected Writings*, 218.
84. Matthew Engelke, "Reading and Time: Two Approaches to the Materiality of Scripture," *Ethnos* 74, no. 2 (June 2009). On iconoclasm beyond Protestantism see, for instance, Naomi Janowitz, *Acts of Interpretation: Ancient Religious Semiotic Ideologies and Their Modern Echoes* (Boston: Walter de Gruyter, 2022) and W. J. T. Mitchell, *Iconology: Image, Text, Ideology* (Chicago: University of Chicago Press, 1986), 160–208.
85. Occom, *Collected Writings*, 216.
86. James Clifford, *The Predicament of Culture* (Cambridge, MA: Harvard University Press, 1988), 303; Fisher, *The Indian Great Awakening*, 8.

87. Fisher, *The Indian Great Awakening*, 66.
88. Fisher, *The Indian Great Awakening*, 8, 64; Michael McNally, *Ojibwe Singers: Hymns, Grief, and a Native Culture in Motion* (New York: Oxford University Press, 2000), 34-38; Tisa Wenger, *Religious Freedom: The Contested History of an American Ideal* (Chapel Hill: University of North Carolina Press, 2017), 2-6; Axtell, *The Invasion Within*, 132-36; Neal Salisbury, "Red Puritans: The 'Praying Indians' of Massachusetts Bay and John Eliot," *William and Mary Quarterly* 31, no. 1 (1974): 28–29; Hilary E. Wyss, *English Letters and Indian Literacies: Reading, Writing, and New England Missionary Schools, 1750–1830* (Philadelphia: University of Pennsylvania Press, 2012), 8–9.
89. Christopher Hill, *The World Turned Upside Down: Radical Ideas During the English Revolution* (New York: Viking, 1972), 15.
90. Yehezkel Kaufmann, *The Religion of Israel: From Its Beginnings to the Babylonian Exile* (Chicago: University of Chicago Press, 1960), 23.
91. Kaufmann, *Religion of Israel*, 80.
92. Kaufmann, *Religion of Israel*, 347; Naomi Janowitz, "Do Jews Make Good Protestants?: The Cross-Cultural Study of Ritual," in *Beyond Primitivism: Indigenous Religious Traditions and Modernity*, ed. Jacob Olupona (New York: Routledge, 2004), 32.
93. Janowitz, "Do Jews Make Good Protestants?" 28.
94. Kaufmann, *Religion of Israel*, 2.
95. I am grateful to Martha Himmelfarb for pointing this out to me.
96. This was Occom's message as reported by a group of Montauketts in 1789 to Samuel Kirkland; Samuel Kirkland, *The Journals of Samuel Kirkland: 18th Century Missionary to the Iroquois, Government Agent, Father of Hamilton College*, ed. Walter Pilkington (Clinton, NY: Hamilton College, 1980), 162, emphasis added.
97. Fisher, *The Indian Great Awakening*.
98. Rubin, *Tears of Repentance*, 119–20.
99. Merrell, *The Indians' New World*, 44.
100. Tisa Wenger, "'A New Form of Government': Religious-Secular Distinctions in Pueblo Indian History," in *Religion as a Category of Governance and Sovereignty*, ed. Trevor Stack and Naomi R. Goldenberg (Leiden: Brill, 2015), 69.

2. Occom Obviously

1. Samson Occom, *The Collected Writings of Samson Occom, Mohegan: Leadership and Literature in Eighteenth-Century Native America*, ed. Joanna Brooks (New York: Oxford University Press, 2006), 178, 102, 134, 127.

2. Occom, *Collected Writings*, 255; William DeLoss Love, *Samson Occom and the Christian Indians of New England* (Boston: Pilgrim Press, 1899), 94; "Samson Occom's Hebrew Textbook," Samson Occom Papers, Mohegan Tribe (online reproduction by the Occom Circle Project, Dartmouth College), https://collections.dartmouth.edu/occom/html/diplomatic/pj4566-m7-1735-diplomatic.html. See also the conclusion to this book.
3. A noteworthy possible exception is Ely Parker, the first Indigenous U.S. Secretary of Indian Affairs, who penned countless official documents through his government work; these included the terms of Confederate surrender agreed to by Ulysses Grant and Robert E. Lee at Appomattox Courthouse, which Parker put down on paper during his time as Grant's personal secretary.
4. Drew Lopenzina makes a similar point about the writings of Charles Alexander Eastman in "'Good Indian': Charles Eastman and the Warrior as Civil Servant," *American Indian Quarterly* 27, nos. 3–4 (2003): 728–29.
5. This bedrock principle is taught to undergraduates everywhere by professors who insist that if you want to get an "A" on an English paper, it is not enough to summarize what a literary text is "about." Some sort of formal analysis is typically required.
6. Occom, *Collected Writings*, 92.
7. Angela Calcaterra, *Literary Indians: Aesthetics and Encounter in American Literature to 1920* (Chapel Hill: University of North Carolina Press, 2018), 75.
8. Calcaterra, *Literary Indians*, 49.
9. Robert Innes, "Introduction: Native Studies and Native Cultural Preservation, Revitalization, and Persistence," *American Indian Culture and Research Journal* 34, no. 2 (October 2010): 2.
10. Chris Andersen and Jean M. O'Brien, "Introduction: Indigenous Studies: An Appeal for Methodological Promiscuity," in *Sources and Methods in Indigenous Studies*, ed. Chris Andersen and Jean M. O'Brien (New York: Routledge, 2017).
11. Joanna Brooks, " 'This Indian World': An Introduction to the Writings of Samson Occom," in *The Collected Writings of Samson Occom*, 38; Kelly Wisecup, *Assembled for Use: Indigenous Compilation and the Archives of Early Native American Literatures* (New Haven, CT: Yale University Press, 2021), 3; Drew Lopenzina, *Red Ink: Native Americans Picking Up the Pen in the Colonial Period* (Albany: SUNY Press, 2012), 16; see also Hilary E. Wyss, *Writing Indians: Literacy, Christianity, and Native Community in Early America* (Amherst: University of Massachusetts Press, 2000), 10. For a helpful discussion of how this critique of "the archive" migrated out postcolonial studies into Indigenous studies, see Melissa Adams-Campbell, Ashley Glassburn Falzetti, and Courtney Rivard, "Introduction: Indigeneity and the Work of Settler Archives," *Settler Colonial Studies* 5, no. 2 (April 2015).

12. Wisecup, *Medical Encounters: Knowledge and Identity in Early American Literatures* (Amherst: University of Massachusetts Press, 2013), 8, citing Ed White, "Invisible Tagkanysough," *PMLA* 120, no. 3 (2005); Lopenzina, *Red Ink*, 17.
13. Kelly Wisecup, *Assembled for Use*, 17; Lopenzina, *Red Ink*, 8.
14. Wisecup, *Assembled for Use*, 26; Lopenzina, *Red Ink*, 209.
15. I take this to be one of the central claims of Scott Richard Lyons's *X-Marks: Native Signatures of Assent* (Minneapolis: University of Minnesota Press, 2010).
16. Innes, "Introduction," 4; Andersen and O'Brien, "Indigenous Studies," 1–4.
17. Lyons, *X-Marks*, 53, 104; Robert Allen Warrior, *Tribal Secrets: Recovering American Indian Intellectual Traditions* (Minneapolis: University of Minnesota Press, 1995), 106, 85, 124.
18. Lyons, *X-Marks*, 60.
19. Linda Alcoff, "The Problem of Speaking for Others," *Cultural Critique* 20 (1991).
20. My claim here, which calls into question the recovery of Indigenous knowledge as a literary-historical methodology is informed by feminist standpoint theories advocated by Alcoff, Miranda Fricker, and others. While it is beyond my scope to engage fully with that literature here, I follow standpoint theorists in supposing that where knowledge comes from matters, as does who is doing the knowing. I am less sure about the stronger, properly epistemological claim that "knowledge reflects the perspectives of the knower." For a useful discussion of standpoint epistemology see Elizabeth Anderson, "Feminist Epistemology and Philosophy of Science," *The Stanford Encyclopedia of Philosophy* (Spring 2020 Edition), ed. Edward N. Zalta, https://plato.stanford.edu/archives/spr2020/entries/feminism-epistemology. My own understanding of the "authority" that knowers have over their own knowledge is informed by Akeel Bilgrami, *Self-Knowledge and Resentment* (Cambridge, MA: Harvard University Press, 2006), and "Notes Toward the Definition of 'Identity,'" *Daedalus* 135, no. 4 (2006).
21. Innes, "Native Studies," 6; Chris Andersen and Jean M. O'Brien, "Indigenous Studies," 3–4, emphasis in original.
22. Andersen and O'Brien, "Indigenous Studies," 2.
23. Andersen and O'Brien, "Indigenous Studies," 1–2.
24. Innes argues that this applies to Native and non-Native scholars alike: "being Native does not automatically mean a person understands [a] Native cultural perspective." Innes, "Native Studies," 3–4.
25. Innes, "Native Studies," 4; Andersen and O'Brien, "Indigenous Studies," 4.
26. Andersen and O'Brien, "Indigenous Studies," 4.

27. Audra Simpson, *Mohawk Interruptus: Political Life Across the Borders of Settler States* (Durham, NC: Duke University Press, 2014), 11.
28. Simpson, *Mohawk Interruptus*, 95.
29. Patchen Markell, *Bound by Recognition* (Princeton, NJ: Princeton University Press, 2003), 34.
30. Markell, *Bound by Recognition*, 35.
31. Simpson, *Mohawk Interruptus*, 105.
32. Simpson, *Mohawk Interruptus*, 105. Robert Warrior, whom Simpson credits with fleshing out the meaning of "literary sovereignty," has used the term "hermeneutic" to talk about the sort of reading that would be capable of acknowledging Indigenous writers' creative agency. I am happy to take that term on board here too, at least as Warrior propounds it; see Warrior, "Afterword," in *Crossing Waters, Crossing Worlds: The African Diaspora in Indian Country*, ed. Tiya Miles and Sharon Patricia Holland (Durham, NC: Duke University Press, 2006), 324.
33. Courtney Cottrell, "NAGPRA's Politics of Recognition: Repatriation Struggles of a Terminated Tribe," *American Indian Quarterly* 44, no. 1 (2020): 78.
34. Cottrell, "NAGPRA's Politics of Recognition," 81n9, 64, emphasis added.
35. Cottrell, "NAGPRA's Politics of Recognition," 62.
36. From this point of view, "tradition indeed brings the past into the future, not by being rigid but by providing a bundle of constraints within which a spectrum of practices and possible innovations can take place," as Stephen A. Mrozowski, D. Rae Gould, and Heather Law Pezzarossi argue; "the 'deepest' traditions," then, may well be "those that lend themselves best to negotiation in practice." See their "Rethinking Colonialism: Indigenous Innovation and Colonial Inevitability," in *Rethinking Colonialism: Comparative Archaeological Approaches* (Gainesville: University Press of Florida, 2015), 130.
37. Occom, *Collected Writings*, 177.
38. Occom, *Collected Writings*, 177, 203.
39. Stephen Best and Sharon Marcus, "Surface Reading: An Introduction," *Representations* 108, no. 1 (2009): 3.
40. Best and Marcus, "Surface Reading," 9, 10; Erving Goffman, *The Presentation of Self in Everyday Life* (Garden City, NY: Doubleday, 1959), 8.
41. Best and Marcus, "Surface Reading," 10, 12.
42. Bernd Peyer, *The Tutor'd Mind: Indian Missionary-Writers in Antebellum America* (Amherst: University of Massachusetts Press, 1997), 95; see also Lopenzina, *Red Ink*, 199; and Laura Murray, "'Pray Sir, Consider a Little': Rituals of Subordination and Strategies of Resistance in the Letters of Hezekiah Calvin and David Fowler to Eleazar Wheelock," *Studies in American Indian Literatures* 4, nos. 2–3 (1992): 53.

43. James C. Scott, *Domination and the Arts of Resistance: Hidden Transcripts* (New Haven, CT: Yale University Press, 1990), x.
44. Simpson, *Mohawk Interruptus*, 95.
45. Scott, *Domination and the Arts of Resistance*, ix–x.
46. Leo Strauss, *Persecution and the Art of Writing* (Chicago: University of Chicago Press, 1952), 25.
47. Strauss, *Persecution and the Art of Writing*, 25.
48. Scott, *Domination and the Arts of Resistance*, 183n1.
49. Scott, *Domination and the Arts of Resistance*, xii.
50. Occom, *Collected Writings*, 52.
51. Joanna Brooks, "Prose Writings," in *The Collected Writings of Samson Occom*, 43.
52. Dana Nelson, "'(I Speak Like a Fool but I Am Constrained)': Samson Occom's Short Narrative and Economies of the Racial Self," in *Early Native American Writing: New Critical Essays*, ed. Helen Jaskoski (New York: Cambridge University Press, 1996), 52.
53. Occom, *Collected Writings*, 51.
54. See chapter 5.
55. Occom, *Collected Writings*, 183.
56. Michael Silverstein, "Metapragmatic Discourse and Metapragmatic Function," in *Reflexive Language: Reported Speech and Metapragmatics*, ed. John Arthur Lucy (New York: Cambridge University Press, 1993); G. Urban, "Metasemiosis and Metapragmatics," in *Encyclopedia of Language & Linguistics* (The Hague: Elsevier, 2006). See also the special issue of *Representations* (137, no. 1 [Winter 2017]) devoted to linguistic-anthropological approaches to literature.
57. I have been especially inspired by Erin Debenport, *Fixing the Books: Secrecy, Literacy, and Perfectibility in Indigenous New Mexico* (Santa Fe, NM: School for Advanced Research Press, 2015); see also Leighton Peterson, "Reflections on Navajo Publics, 'New' Media, and Documentary Futures," in *Engaging Native American Publics: Linguistic Anthropology in a Collaborative Key*, ed. Paul V. Kroskrity and Barbra A. Meek (London: Routledge, 2017), 175; and Justin B. Richland, "Pragmatic Paradoxes and Ironies of Indigeneity at the 'Edge' of Hopi Sovereignty," *American Ethnologist* 34, no. 3 (August 2007).
58. Occom, *Collected Writings*, 177, 233, 172, 228, 201, 116.
59. My understanding of this term follows Michael Warner, *Publics and Counterpublics* (New York: Zone Books, 2005), 65–123.
60. Phillip H. Round, *Removable Type: Histories of the Book in Indian Country, 1663–1880* (Chapel Hill: University of North Carolina Press, 2010), 67; Heather Bouwman, "Samson Occom and the Sermonic Tradition," in *Early Native*

Literacies in New England: A Documentary and Critical Anthology, ed. Kristina Bross and Hilary E. Wyss (Amherst: University of Massachusetts Press, 2008), 66.
61. Matt Cohen suggests an alternative approach in The Networked Wilderness: Communicating in Early New England (Minneapolis: University of Minnesota Press), 6-7.
62. Round, Removable Type, 67.
63. Occom, Collected Writings, 197.
64. Michael Silverstein, "Metapragmatic Discourse and Metapragmatic Function," 36–38.
65. Michael Silverstein and Greg Urban, "The Natural History of Discourse," in Natural Histories of Discourse, ed. Michael Silverstein and Greg Urban (Chicago: University of Chicago Press, 1996), 10.
66. Asif Agha, Language and Social Relations (New York: Cambridge University Press, 2007), 84–103.
67. Michael Silverstein, "Discourse and the No-thing-ness of Culture," Signs and Society 1, no. 2 (September 2013): 333; Occom, Collected Writings, 196.
68. Occom, Collected Writings, 55.
69. Occom, Collected Writings, 201.
70. Occom, Collected Writings, 176.
71. Samson Occom and Nathaniel Whitaker, Extracts of Several Sermons, Preached Extempore at Different Places of Divine Worship, in the City of Bristol, by the Rev. Mr. Nathaniel Whitaker, Minister of the Gospel at Norwich, in New-England, and the Rev. Mr. Samson Occom, an Indian Minister (Bristol, 1766), 3–4.
72. Lisa Brooks, The Common Pot: The Recovery of Native Space in the Northeast (Minneapolis: University of Minnesota Press, 2008).
73. For instance: "I thought it my Duty to give a Short Plain and Honest Account of myself, that those *who may hereafter see it*, may know the Truth Concerning me." Occom, Collected Writings, 52. See also chapter 5.
74. In disaggregating technological change from "forms of address" in the history of broadcast media, I follow the lead of Michael Warner, Letters of the Republic: Publication and the Public Sphere in Eighteenth-Century America (Cambridge, MA: Harvard University Press, 1990). On forms of address in broadcast media more generally, see, for example, Ian Hutchby, Media Talk: Conversation Analysis and the Study of Broadcasting (New York: Open University Press, 2006).
75. Elias Boudinot, Cherokee Editor: The Writings of Elias Boudinot, ed. Theda Perdue (Athens: University of Georgia Press, 1996), 75–76.
76. Arthur Parker (?), "The New Quarterly Journal," "Think Upon These Things," Quarterly Journal of the Society of Americans 1, no. 1 (April 1913): 2–8.

77. Concerning this paradox, Deloria writes in an essay on Paul Feyerabend, "I could rephrase these same [metaphysical] ideas, pass them off in the format of ancient teachings of American Indians, and have Harper's publicity department declare that they were being revealed for the first time. . . . But in adopting that format, I would then be attracting hundreds of hippies, disgruntled ex-Christians, and the usual scattering of affluent white youths whose most philosophical moments occurred while backpacking the continental divide." Vine Deloria Jr., "Perceptions and Maturity: Reflections on Feyerabend's Point of View," in *Beyond Reason: Essays on the Philosophy of Paul Feyerabend*, ed. Paul Feyerabend and Gonzalo Munévar (Boston: Kluwer Academic Publishers, 1991), 391. See also *Custer Died for Your Sins* (Norman: University of Oklahoma Press, 1988), 78–100; and Philip Jenkins, *Dream Catchers: How Mainstream America Discovered Native Spirituality* (New York: Oxford University Press, 2004).
78. Simpson, *Mohawk Interruptus*, 102; Vine Deloria, *We Talk, You Listen: New Tribes, New Turf* (New York: Macmillan, 1970), 172.
79. Innes, "Native Studies," 2.
80. W. K. Wimsatt and M. C. Beardsley, "The Intentional Fallacy," *Sewanee Review* 54, no. 3 (1946): 471.
81. Steven Knapp and Walter Benn Michaels, "Against Theory," *Critical Inquiry* 8, no. 4 (July 1982).
82. Jace Weaver, *That the People Might Live: Native American Literatures and Native American Community* (New York: Oxford University Press), ix; cited in Daniel Heath Justice, *Why Indigenous Literatures Matter* (Waterloo, ON: Wilfrid Laurier University Press, 2018), 21.
83. Lyons, *X-Marks*, 129–31, 160.
84. Mikhail Bakhtin, "The Problem of Speech Genres," in *Speech Genres and Other Late Essays*, ed. Michael Holquist and Caryl Emerson (Austin: University of Texas Press, 1986), 99, 95.
85. In his discussion of addressivity, Bakhtin devotes much attention to the historical variability of the speech genres' imagined "addressees," but comparatively little to the way people imaginatively construct *addressors*. In observing that these two imagined subject positions often fail to match up in the case of Indigenous literature and its sites of (often non-Indigenous) reception, I am questioning Bakhtin's claim that literary texts typically belong to "secondary" or complex speech-genres rather than "primary" or "everyday" ones. Bakhtin, "Problem of Speech Genres," 98. Bakhtin might reply that if the mismatch between imagined addressee and imagined addressor is sufficiently serious and systematic, then one may not be dealing with a "speech genre" at all.
86. Simpson, *Mohawk Interruptus*, 107.

87. Wimsatt and Beardsley, "The Intentional Fallacy," 476.
88. Occom, *Collected Writings*, 200–201.
89. Occom, *Collected Writings*, 204.
90. Thus Simpson describes how "*refusal worked in everyday encounters to enunciate repeatedly to* [Kahnawà:ke people] themselves and to outsiders: "This is who we are; this is who you are; these are my rights." Simpson, *Mohawk Interruptus*, 106, emphasis added.
91. Stanley Cavell, "Knowing and Acknowledging," in *Must We Mean What We Say?* (New York: Cambridge University Press, 1976), 257.
92. Stanley Cavell, *The Claim of Reason: Wittgenstein, Skepticism, Morality, and Tragedy* (New York: Oxford University Press, 1999), 23.
93. When Occom talks about "owning" God he means something different from what Cavell means when he speaks of taking ownership of his country ("recogniz[ing] the society and government . . . as mine"). Having a national identity, for Cavell, means that you have to *answer for* your nation to others, when they ask you why certain things happen in "your" country. But "owning God" does not put you in that position, because God exists on a metaphysical plane that transcends human relations of ownership. Occom is using "own" in a slightly archaic way here, much as Herman Melville does in *Moby-Dick* when Ishmael encourages the reader to "own the whale." Making something one's own, in this archaic sense, means "taking something on board," as we might say today—that is, "owning up" to it in the sense of avowing one's accountability *to* some third party.
94. Edward W. Said, *Orientalism* (New York: Vintage Books, 1979), 282.

3. A Theology of Land and Peoplehood

1. Samson Occom, *The Collected Writings of Samson Occom, Mohegan: Leadership and Literature in Eighteenth-Century Native America*, ed. Joanna Brooks (New York: Oxford University Press, 2006), 149, 187.
2. Reiner Smolinski, "Israel Redivivus: The Eschatological Limits of Puritan Typology in New England," *New England Quarterly* 63, no. 3 (1990); John F. Berens, *Providence & Patriotism in Early America, 1640–1815* (Charlottesville: University Press of Virginia, 1978), 14–31.
3. Robert Allen Warrior, "Canaanites, Cowboys, and Indians: Deliverance, Conquest, and Liberation Theology Today," *Christianity and Crisis* 49, no. 12 (September 1989): 263.
4. Occom, *Collected Writings*, 215.

5. See, for instance, Occom, *Collected Writings*, 149.
6. David J. Silverman, *Red Brethren: The Brothertown and Stockbridge Indians and the Problem of Race in Early America* (Ithaca, NY: Cornell University Press, 2010), 105; Julius H. Rubin, *Tears of Repentance: Christian Indian Identity and Community in Colonial Southern New England* (Lincoln: University of Nebraska Press, 2013), 114.
7. Margaret Connell Szasz, "Samson Occom: Mohegan as Spiritual Intermediary," in *Between Indian and White Worlds: The Cultural Broker*, ed. Margaret Connell Szasz (Norman: University of Oklahoma Press, 1994), 76.
8. William DeLoss Love, *Samson Occom and the Christian Indians of New England* (Boston: Pilgrim Press, 1899), 137, 41.
9. Love, *Samson Occom and the Christian Indians of New England*, 277.
10. Love, *Samson Occom and the Christian Indians of New England*, 2.
11. Love, *Samson Occom and the Christian Indians of New England*, 209, 14.
12. Love, *Samson Occom and the Christian Indians of New England*, 284.
13. Love, *Samson Occom and the Christian Indians of New England*, 152, 1.
14. Silverman, *Red Brethren*, 7.
15. Silverman, *Red Brethren*, 143.
16. Silverman, *Red Brethren*, 91, 105; Jarvis, *The Brothertown Nation of Indians*, 5.
17. Silverman, *Red Brethren*, 101, 105.
18. Jarvis, *The Brothertown Nation of Indians*, 89.
19. Silverman, *Red Brethren*, 143; see also Rubin, *Tears of Repentance*, 243.
20. Paul Joseph Grant-Costa, "The Last Indian War in New England: The Mohegan Indians v. The Governour and Company of the Colony of Connecticut, 1703–1774" (PhD dissertation, Yale University, 2008), 308.
21. Melissa Tantaquidgeon Zobel, *The Lasting of the Mohegans: Part I, the Story of the Wolf People* (Uncasville, CT: Mohegan Tribe, 1995), 17–18, 40; cited in Amy E. Den Ouden, *Beyond Conquest: Native Peoples and the Struggle for History in New England* (Lincoln: University of Nebraska Press, 2005), 255n21.
22. Connecticut Archives: Indians, First Series (hereafter "Indian Papers"), Volume 2, no. 310, https://findit.library.yale.edu/bookreader/BookReaderDemo/index.html?oid=10682281.
23. Indian Papers 2:315a, https://findit.library.yale.edu/bookreader/BookReaderDemo/index.html?oid=10682286. Earlier Johnson had provided a "List of Mohegan Indians Agreeable to the Mind of Zachary, Simon & Noah [Uncas] & Samuel Dantaquegin"; Indian Papers 2:316.
24. Silverman, *Red Brethren*, 105–14; Jarvis, *Brothertown Nation*, 38, 256n39. In their accounts of the Occom/Johnson controversy, both Silverman and Jarvis refer to the nineteenth-century historian William De Forest, whose misreading of the Connecticut Indian Papers may be the original source of

this misunderstanding. De Forest bought into the crude dichotomy between the followers of the "enlightened" Occom and the traditional Mohegans who followed the "old councilor" Johnson in resisting Occom's supposed innovations; John William De Forest, *History of the Indians of Connecticut from the Earliest Known Period to 1850* (Hartford, CT: W. J. Hamersley, 1852), 471–76.

25. Indian Papers 2:312a, https://findit.library.yale.edu/bookreader/BookReader Demo/index.html?oid=10682283.
26. Den Ouden, *Beyond Conquest*, 190–96; Silverman, *Red Brethren*, 104–5.
27. Occom, *Collected Writings*, 138.
28. Den Ouden, *Beyond Conquest*, 196.
29. Den Ouden, *Beyond Conquest*, 195–96.
30. Silverman, *Red Brethren*, 133.
31. Cited in Joseph Johnson, *To Do Good to My Indian Brethren: The Writings of Joseph Johnson, 1751–1776*, ed. Laura J. Murray (Amherst: University of Massachusetts Press, 1998), 242; see also Love, *Samson Occom and the Christian Indians of New England*, 222
32. Occom, *Collected Writings*, 138.
33. Silverman, *Red Brethren*, 105, 143, 52.
34. Occom, *Collected Writings*, 147.
35. Occom, *Collected Writings*, 106, 104.
36. Joseph Johnson identified March 13, 1773 as the date of a decisive planning meeting at Brothertown; "Joseph Johnson's Speech to the Oneidas," in Johnson, *To Do Good to My Indian Brethren*, 207.
37. Occom, *Collected Writings*, 203–4.
38. Occom, *Collected Writings*, 107.
39. Indian Papers, 2:321a, https://findit.library.yale.edu/bookreader/BookReader Demo/index.html?oid=10682292.
40. Indian Papers 2:312a, https://findit.library.yale.edu/bookreader/BookReader Demo/index.html?oid=10682283.
41. Indian Papers 2:319, https://findit.library.yale.edu/bookreader/BookReader Demo/index.html?oid=10682290.
42. Indian Papers 2:322a-b, https://findit.library.yale.edu/bookreader/BookReaderDemo/index.html?oid=10682293.
43. Indian Papers 2:313a, https://findit.library.yale.edu/bookreader/BookReader Demo/index.html?oid=10682284.
44. Occom, *Collected Writings*, 147.
45. Grant-Costa, "The Last Indian War in New England," 308.
46. Zobel, *The Lasting of the Mohegans*, 41.
47. Occom, *Collected Writings*, 147; see also 145, 132.
48. Occom, *Collected Writings*, 104.

49. Occom, *Collected Writings*, 137.
50. Jarvis, *The Brothertown Nation of Indians*, 11, 89.
51. Occom, *Collected Writings*, 221.
52. Jarvis, *The Brothertown Nation of Indians*, 89; Silverman, *Red Brethren*, 7.
53. Love, *Samson Occom and the Christian Indians of New England*, 284, emphasis added.
54. Love, *Samson Occom and the Christian Indians of New England*, 108.
55. Margaret Connell Szasz, *Indian Education in the American Colonies, 1607–1783* (Lincoln: University of Nebraska Press, 2007), 239–41.
56. Cited in Love, *Samson Occom and the Christian Indians of New England*, 111–12.
57. Cited in Szasz, *Indian Education in the American Colonies*, 242.
58. Lucianne Lavin, *Connecticut's Indigenous Peoples: What Archaeology, History, and Oral Traditions Teach Us About Their Communities and Cultures* (New Haven, CT: Yale University Press, 2013), 209.
59. Jean M. O'Brien, *Dispossession by Degrees: Indian Land and Identity in Natick, Massachusetts, 1650–1790* (New York: Cambridge University Press, 1997), 7; Den Ouden, *Beyond Conquest*, 28.
60. Occom, *Collected Writings*, 273; see also 266.
61. Occom, *Collected Writings*, 273.
62. Occom, *Collected Writings*, 102.
63. Occom, *Collected Writings*, 309n120.
64. Occom, *Collected Writings*, 102–3.
65. Samuel Kirkland wrote of Brothertown in 1795 that "these Indians have none of the spirit, industry, and perseverance, necessary in those who subdue a wilderness. A small number only have brought their farms into tolerable order. The principal part clear one field for corn, beans, and potatoes, and give themselves no further trouble; but either suffer their remaining tracts to be wild, or lease them for a small rent to the neighbouring whites." "Answer to the Foregoing Queries, Respecting Indians," *Collections of the Massachusetts Historical Society*, First Series, 4 (1795): 68. In the 1810s, the Connecticut minister Timothy Dwight reported that "forty families" had "fixed themselves in the business of agriculture" at Brothertown; Dwight, *Travels in New-England and New-York* (London: W. Baynes and Son, 1823), 4: 168–69.
66. Many from the original Stockbridge community in the Berkshires had earned a living by plowing and brought that skill with them when they migrated west; the plowing Occom saw at New Stockbridge may have been a continuation of that practice. William A. Starna, *From Homeland to New Land: A History of the Mahican Indians, 1600–1830* (Lincoln: University of Nebraska Press, 2013), 182, 189–90.
67. Occom, *Collected Writings*, 57.
68. Occom, *Collected Writings*, 58.

69. Eleazar Wheelock, *Continuation of the Narrative of the Indian Charity-School in Lebanon, in Connecticut* (Hartford, CT: Ebenezer Watson, 1771), 5.
70. On Native Americans as "Canaanites" see Alfred A. Cave, "Canaanites in a Promised Land: The American Indian and the Providential Theory of Empire," *American Indian Quarterly* 12, no. 4 (1988); Steven T. Newcomb, *Pagans in the Promised Land: Decoding the Doctrine of Christian Discovery* (Golden, CO: Fulcrum, 2008), 38–54; and Warrior, "Canaanites, Cowboys, and Indians."
71. Various factors conspired to make this view relatively unpopular in seventeenth- and eighteenth-century America. Sacvan Bercovitch argues persuasively that the Israelite interpretation of Indigenous nationhood "violated the Puritans' concept of themselves, their fundamental distinction between Christ's Army and its Satanic enemies. In any case, by the time King Philip's War broke out the Indians were unequivocally identified with the doomed 'dark brothers' of Scripture—Cain, Ishmael, Esau, and above all the heathen natives of the promised land, who were to be dispossessed by divine decree of what really belonged to God's chosen." See Sacvan Bercovitch, *The American Jeremiad* (Madison: University of Wisconsin Press, 2012), 75n; cited in Richard W. Cogley, "John Eliot and the Origins of the American Indians," *Early American Literature* 21, no. 3 (1986): 223–24n12.
72. Gerald R. McDermott, *Jonathan Edwards Confronts the Gods: Christian Theology, Enlightenment Religion, and Non-Christian Faiths* (New York: Oxford University Press, 2000), 194, 94.
73. McDermott, *Jonathan Edwards Confronts the Gods*, 8; E. Brooks Holifield, *Theology in America: Christian Thought from the Age of the Puritans to the Civil War* (New Haven, CT: Yale University Press, 2003), 106.
74. Romans 2:15.
75. Roger Williams, *A Key into the Language of America* (London: Gregory Dexter, 1643), 7–8.
76. George Fox, *The Heathens Divinity Set Upon the Heads of All Called Christians That Say They Had Not Known That There Had Been a God or a Christ Unless the Scripture Had Declared It to Them* ([London?], 1671), 28; see also Kristen Block, "Quaker Evangelization in Early Barbados: Forging a Path Toward the Unknowable," in *Quakers and Abolition*, ed. Brycchan Carey and Geoffrey Plank (Urbana: University of Illinois Press, 2014), 91.
77. Occom, *Collected Writings*, 206.
78. Samuel Buell, *The Excellence and Importance of the Saving Knowledge of the Lord Jesus Christ in the Gospel-Preacher, Plainly and Seriously Represented and Enforced: And Christ Preached to the Gentiles in Obedience to the Call of God* (New York: J. Parker and Company, 1761), 16.
79. Buell, *Excellence and Importance*, v.

80. Buell, *Excellence and Importance*, 15–16.
81. Occom, *Collected Writings*, 52. It seems significant that Occom dates his interest in Christianity to the year or two immediately preceding the arrival of the Great Awakening in his homeland. While Occom clearly wanted to affiliate himself with the revivalists to a certain extent, he may have wanted to communicate that the awakening of his own faith was a relatively private event that predated the more spectacular (and hence more easily criticized) displays of religiosity that started happening in 1741.
82. Harry S. Stout and Peter Onuf, "James Davenport and the Great Awakening in New London," *Journal of American History* 70, no. 3 (1983): 560, 556–57.
83. A. LaVonne Brown Ruoff, "Introduction," *Studies in American Indian Literatures* 4, nos. 2–3 (1992); Michael Elliott, "'This Indian Bait': Samson Occom and the Voice of Liminality," *Early American Literature* 29, no. 3 (1994): 235; Sandra M. Gustafson, *Eloquence Is Power: Oratory and Performance in Early America* (Chapel Hill: University of North Carolina Press, 2000), 95; Joanna Brooks, "Introduction," in Occom, *Collected Writings*, 3.
84. Stout and Onuf, "James Davenport and the Great Awakening in New London," 557.
85. Occom, *Collected Writings*, 56.
86. Occom, *Collected Writings*, 56.
87. Holifield, *Theology in America*, 136.
88. George Marsden, *Jonathan Edwards: A Life* (New Haven, CT: Yale University Press, 2003), 103.
89. On the Edwardsean sources of New Divinity theology, see especially Holifield, *Theology in America*, 102–56. For treatments of Hopkins and Bellamy specifically see Joseph A. Conforti, *Samuel Hopkins and the New Divinity Movement: Calvinism, the Congregational Ministry, and Reform in New England Between the Great Awakenings* (Grand Rapids, MI: Christian University Press, 1981); and Mark Valeri, *Law and Providence in Joseph Bellamy's New England: The Origins of the New Divinity in Revolutionary America* (New York: Oxford University Press, 1994). On the afterlives of Edwardsean theology in the New Divinity and other movements, see Oliver D. Crisp and Douglas A. Sweeney, *After Jonathan Edwards: The Courses of the New England Theology* (New York: Oxford University Press, 2012). On the relationship between the New Divinity and "Old" Calvinism, see, for instance, Mark A. Noll, "Moses Mather (Old Calvinist) and the Evolution of Edwardseanism," *Church History* 49, no. 3 (1980).
90. On Wheelock's connection to Edwards and Davenport, see Marsden, *Jonathan Edwards*, 232; John Fea, "Wheelock's World: Letters and the Communication of Revival in Great Awakening New England," *Proceedings of the American Antiquarian Society* 109, no. 1 (April 1999): 120–21; and Stout and

Onuf, "James Davenport and the Great Awakening in New London." According to Onuf and Stout (573n41), Wheelock was the "next most successful itinerant" associated with the 1740s revivals after Davenport.

91. Wheelock maintained one of eighteenth-century Connecticut's most extensive networks of correspondence, as John Fea has shown; the letters he sent and received "extended Wheelock's parish, in an imagined sense, throughout the region" of southern New England. Fea, "Wheelock's World," 129.

92. Wheelock also stayed in touch with Edwards himself, who wrote to Lebanon about Occom on at least one occasion; Jonathan Edwards, "To the Reverend Eleazar Wheelock," in *Letters and Personal Writings* (New Haven, CT: Yale University Press, 1998), 146.

93. Occom, *Collected Writings*, 98, 103, 127, 280; Bobby Wright, "'For the Children of the Infidels?': American Indian Education in the Colonial Colleges," *American Indian Culture and Research Journal* 12, no. 3 (January 1988); Colin G. Calloway, *The Indian History of an American Institution: Native Americans and Dartmouth* (Hanover, NH: University Press of New England, 2010), ch. 2.

94. Ava Chamberlain, "The Execution of Moses Paul: A Story of Crime and Contact in Eighteenth-Century Connecticut," *New England Quarterly* 77, no. 3 (2004): 447; Bernd Peyer, *The Tutor'd Mind: Indian Missionary-Writers in Antebellum America* (Amherst: University of Massachusetts Press, 1997), 91–95.

95. Hopkins did not rule out the possibility of God conveying knowledge via an immediate revelation, but this did not play a major role in his arguments about salvation; see, for instance Samuel Hopkins, *The Works of Samuel Hopkins, D.D.*, ed. Edwards Amasa Park (Boston: Doctrinal Tract and Book Society, 1854), 3:356.

96. Hopkins, *Works*, 3:344.

97. Holifield, *Theology in America*, 141.

98. Jedediah Mills, *An Inquiry Concerning the State of the Unregenerate Under the Gospel* (New Haven, CT: B. Mecom, 1767), 18–19.

99. Mills, *Inquiry*, 10–11.

100. Hopkins, *Works*, 3:307.

101. Hopkins, *Works*, 3:306.

102. Occom, *Collected Writings*, 188–89.

103. Hopkins, *Works*, 3:308.

104. According to Occom's ledger book from 1761, "Esqr. Hopkins of Waterbury Gave me a Dollar," and we know from Occom's journal that he stayed with Hopkins at least once during his periods of itinerancy in the 1770s: "was at Esqr Hopkins all Day," he wrote on Saturday, January 7, 1775; and then, on Sunday, "Preached here all Day." Samson Occom, "Samson Occom, Receipts

and Expenses, 1761," Samson Occom Papers, Mohegan Tribe (online reproduction by the Occom Circle Project, Dartmouth College), https://collections.dartmouth.edu/occom/html/diplomatic/761290-diplomatic.html; Occom, *Collected Writings*, 280. Hopkins had been aware of Occom's missionary work among the Oneidas as early as 1751; see Edwards Amasa Park, *Memoir of the Life and Character of Samuel Hopkins, D.D.* (Boston: Doctrinal Tract and Book Society, 1854), 45.

105. A. LaVonne Brown Ruoff, *American Indian Literatures: An Introduction, Bibliographic Review, and Selected Bibliography* (New York: Modern Language Association of America, 1990), 62.

106. As Holifield writes, "the New Divinity allowed no middle ground between sinners and saints. One either loved God above self or one loved self above God." Holifield, *Theology in America*, 140.

107. Occom, *Collected Writings*, 167; Samson Occom, Sermon on John 8:31-32, Samson Occom Papers, Connecticut Historical Society, http://hdl.handle.net/11134/40002:389. See also Occom's sermon on John 3:4: "It is impossible for unregenerate man to serve & enjoy God. . . . Consider, Can the Dead Serve the Living, Can a Dead Sinner serve and Injoy the Living God? Don't your Bibles tell you?" Samson Occom Papers, Connecticut Historical Society, http://hdl.handle.net/11134/40002:389.

108. Holifield, *Theology in America*, 140. On disinterested benevolence more generally, see Conforti, *Samuel Hopkins*, ch. 7.

109. Covenant theology also concerned itself with the formation and government of local churches, a topic I pass by here; see, for instance, William Kenneth Bristow Stoever, *A Faire and Easie Way to Heaven: Covenant Theology and Antinomianism in Early Massachusetts* (Middletown, CT: Wesleyan University Press, 1978). On federal theology in early New England, see, for instance, Smolinski, "Israel Redivivus." On the specific relationship of the New Divinity to covenant theology, see Valeri, *Joseph Bellamy's New England*, 29–31; and Harry S. Stout, *The New England Soul: Preaching and Religious Culture in Colonial New England* (New York: Oxford University Press, 1986), 10.

110. Valeri, *Joseph Bellamy's New England*, 148–49; Conforti, *Samuel Hopkins*, 59–61.

111. Holifield, *Theology in America*, 125.

112. Gilbert Tennent, *The Happiness of Rewarding the Enemies of Our Religion and Liberty: Represented in a Sermon Preached in Philadelphia, Feb. 17, 1756. To Captain Vanderspiegel's Independent Company of Volunteers, at the Request of Their Officers* (Philadelphia: James Chattin, 1756), 4.

113. Berens, *Providence & Patriotism in Early America, 1640–1815*, 32–50.

114. Such a national self-understanding, it might be argued, was implicit in the slightly later idea of a "benevolent empire." On continuities between the New

Divinity and the benevolent empire ideal see Conforti, *Samuel Hopkins*, ch. 11; Holifield, *Theology in America*, 149; and George Marsden, *The Evangelical Mind and the New School Presbyterian Experience: A Case Study of Thought and Theology in Nineteenth-Century America* (Eugene, OR: Wipf and Stock, 2003), 35.

115. Bercovitch, *The American Jeremiad*, ch. 4. For a discussion of how the jeremiad tradition was revitalized at midcentury during the French and Indian War, see Berens, *Providence & Patriotism in Early America, 1640–1815*, ch. 2.

116. Occom, *Collected Writings*, 191.

117. Ruoff, "Introduction," 28.

118. Occom, *Collected Writings*, 191–92.

119. Ephesians 2:11. I set aside here the modern debate about whether Paul actually wrote the letter to the Ephesians, since Occom knew nothing of it. See, for instance, Carl R. Holladay, *Introduction to the New Testament: Reference Edition* (Waco, TX: Baylor University Press, 2017), 628–30; C. Leslie Mitton, *The Epistle to the Ephesians: Its Authorship, Origin, and Purpose* (Oxford: Clarendon Press, 1951).

120. Laura K. Arnold, "Crossing Cultures: Algonquian Indians and the Invention of New England" (PhD diss., University of California, Los Angeles, 1995), 138. This dissertation was perhaps the first study to acknowledge Occom's interest in Paul, and especially in the Gentiles as discussed by Paul, as a model of Indigenous identity.

121. Occom, *Collected Writings*, 191, 177.

122. Occom, *Collected Writings*, 189.

123. The end of the sermon includes a discussion of the American trade in African slaves, a topic that elsewhere appears in texts composed by Occom only after 1783. Occom, *Collected Writings*, 58, 124.

124. Occom, *Collected Writings*, 215.

125. Jason Byassee, "Typology," in Ian A. McFarland, ed., *The Cambridge Dictionary of Christian Theology* (New York: Cambridge University Press, 2011), 523.

126. Eleazar Wheelock, *A Plain and Faithful Narrative of the Original Design, Rise, Progress and Present State of the Indian Charity-School at Lebanon, in Connecticut* (Boston: Richard and Samuel Draper, 1763), 10.

127. Occom, *Collected Writings*, 215.

128. Occom, *Collected Writings*, 215.

129. In his anti-Catholicism, Occom was an avid partisan of what Thomas Kidd describes as a post-Puritan "Protestant interest." See Thomas S. Kidd, *The Protestant Interest: New England After Puritanism* (New Haven, CT: Yale University Press, 2004).

130. Occom, *Collected Writings*, 217.

131. Occom, *Collected Writings*, 217.

132. 1 Corinthians 5:1.
133. Romans 2:14–15.
134. Romans 2:29.
135. Occom, *Collected Writings*, 224. For early American examples of the broader literary tradition inspired by typology, see Sacvan Bercovitch, *Typology and Early American Literature* (Amherst: University of Massachusetts Press, 1972).
136. Eleazar Wheelock, *A Sermon Preached Before the Second Society in Lebanon, June 30. 1763: At the Ordination of the Rev. Mr Charles-Jeffry Smith, with a View to His Going as a Missionary to the Remote Tribes of the Indians in This Land* (London: E. and C. Dilly, 1767), 3–4.
137. Wheelock, *Plain and Faithful Narrative*, 12.
138. Wheelock, *Plain and Faithful Narrative*, 11; Eleazar Wheelock, *A Continuation of the Narrative of the State, &c. Of the Indian Charity-School, at Lebanon, in Connecticut* (Boston: Richard and Samuel Draper, 1765), 20.
139. Wheelock, *Plain and Faithful Narrative*, 10.
140. It should be noted that Edwards's own views on federal theology were less univocal, and possibly more subtle, than those of his students; see, for instance, Harry S. Stout, "The Puritans and Edwards," in Nathan O. Hatch and Harry S. Stout, eds., *Jonathan Edwards and the American Experience* (New York: Oxford University Press, 1988).
141. Occom, *Collected Writings*, 203.
142. Occom, *Collected Writings*, 201.
143. Occom, *Collected Writings*, 183.
144. Matthew Henry, *An Exposition of the Old and New Testament* (Philadelphia: Barrington & Haswell, 1828 [1721–1725]), 5:535.
145. Occom, *Collected Writings*, 201.
146. Occom, *Collected Writings*, 119, citing Matthew 8:20.
147. Warrior, "Canaanites, Cowboys, and Indians," 264, 263. For an excellent discussion of Warrior's essay in the broader context of liberation theology, see Joel S. Baden, *The Book of Exodus: A Biography* (Princeton, NJ: Princeton University Press, 2019), 187–215.
148. Warrior, "Canaanites, Cowboys, and Indians," 264.
149. Warrior, "Canaanites, Cowboys, and Indians," 261.
150. David J. Silverman, "To Become a Chosen People: The Missionary Work and Missionary Spirit of the Brothertown and Stockbridge Indians, 1775–1835," in *Native Americans, Christianity, and the Reshaping of the American Religious Landscape*, ed. Joel W. Martin and Mark A. Nicholas (Chapel Hill: University of North Carolina Press, 2010).
151. Rubin, *Tears of Repentance*, 282; Zuck, "William Apess, the 'Lost Tribes,' and Indigenous Survivance," 7; both citing Arnold, "Crossing Cultures," ch. 4.

152. More generally, even though Occom's diaries often reveal what scripture passages he preached from, relatively few of his sermon notes from this period survive.
153. Warrior, "Canaanites, Cowboys, and Indians," 261.
154. Romans 2:28–29.
155. See, for instance, Paula Fredriksen, *Paul: The Pagan's Apostle* (New Haven, CT: Yale University Press, 2017).
156. Jarvis, *The Brothertown Nation of Indians*, 86; see also Rubin, *Tears of Repentance*, 147.
157. Warrior, "Canaanites, Cowboys, and Indians," 264.
158. Fredriksen, *Paul*, 167.
159. Fredriksen, *Paul*, 167, 145.
160. "Samson Occom's Hebrew Textbook," 64v, Samson Occom Papers, Mohegan Tribe (online reproduction by the Occom Circle Project, Dartmouth College), https://collections.dartmouth.edu/occom/html/diplomatic/pj4566-m7-1735-diplomatic.html.
161. Occom, *Collected Writings*, 207.
162. Jonathan Edwards, *The Works of President Edwards* (New York: S. Converse, 1829), 3:366.
163. William Apess, *The Increase of the Kingdom of Christ: A Sermon* (New York: G. F. Bunce, 1831), 22.
164. Genesis 1:27, 2:6; Occom, *Collected Writings*, 294, 320, 340, 344, 367.
165. Occom, *Collected Writings*, 149. I return to this passage in greater detail in chapter 6.
166. Exodus 25:8.
167. Occom, *Collected Writings*, 149.
168. Occom, *Collected Writings*, 197.
169. Occom, *Collected Writings*, 224.
170. Occom, *Collected Writings*, 224.
171. Jean M. O'Brien, "'Divorced from the Land': Resistance and Survival of Indian Women in Eighteenth-Century New England," in *After King Philip's War: Presence and Persistence in Indian New England*, ed. Colin G. Calloway (Hanover, NH: University Press of New England, 1997), 153, 156.
172. Jason Byassee, "Typology," in *The Cambridge Dictionary of Christian Theology*, ed. Ian A. McFarland (New York: Cambridge University Press, 2011).
173. Occom, *Collected Writings*, 223.
174. Occom, *Collected Writings*, 225.
175. Matthew 4:7, Luke 4:12.
176. Occom's engagements with these authors are further discussed in chapters 4 and 6.

177. John Milton, *Paradise Regain'd*, Poetry Foundation, https://www.poetryfoundation.org/poems/45752/paradise-regaind-book-4-1671-version; emphasis added.
178. John Bunyan, *Pilgrim's Progress* (London: Scott, Webster and Geary, 1845), 404.
179. Bunyan, *Pilgrim's Progress*, 404.
180. Occom, *Collected Writings*, 145.
181. Occom, *Collected Writings*, 224.
182. Henry, *Exposition*, I.25, emphasis in original.
183. Occom, *Collected Writings*, 310.
184. Occom, *Collected Writings*, 380.
185. Occom, *Collected Writings*, 186.
186. John Bunyan, *The Works of That Eminent Servant of Christ, Mr. John Bunyan* (London: W. Johnston, 1768), 2:344.
187. Occom, *Collected Writings*, 306.
188. "Protology," OED; Stephen Ward Angell, Pink Dandelion, and Douglas Gwyn, eds., "Quakers, Eschatology, and Time," in *The Oxford Handbook of Quaker Studies* (New York: Oxford University Press, 2013), 202.

4. Piety and Placemaking

1. This episode and all quotations drawn from it appear in Samson Occom, *The Collected Writings of Samson Occom, Mohegan: Leadership and Literature in Eighteenth-Century Native America*, ed. Joanna Brooks (New York: Oxford University Press, 2006), 302–3; the capitalization in my retelling has been selectively modernized. On Occom's gold-headed cane—reportedly a gift from King George III of England—see, for instance, Henry C. Rogers, *History of the Town of Paris* (Utica, NY: White & Floyd, 1881), 390; and *Our Country and Its People: A Descriptive Work on Oneida County, New York* (Boston: Boston History Company, 1896), 116. This cane was part of the nineteenth-century lore about Occom and should be taken with a grain of salt.
2. Occom, *Collected Writings*, 303.
3. David Freeman Hawke, *Everyday Life in Early America* (New York: Harper & Row, 1988), 149.
4. Adam Jaworski, "Silence and Small Talk," in *Small Talk*, ed. Justine Coupland (New York: Longman, 2000), 117.
5. Occom, *Collected Writings*, 326, 349, 362.
6. For such a conception of piety as applied to Occom specifically, see Julius H. Rubin, *Tears of Repentance: Christian Indian Identity and Community in Colonial Southern New England* (Lincoln: University of Nebraska Press, 2013), 114; and

Eileen Razzari Elrod, *Piety and Dissent: Race, Gender, and Biblical Rhetoric in Early American Autobiography* (Amherst: University of Massachusetts Press, 2008), 2, 22.

7. Saba Mahmood, *Politics of Piety: The Islamic Revival and the Feminist Subject* (Princeton, NJ: Princeton University Press, 2005), 73.
8. Mahmood, *Politics of Piety*, 4, 152, 193, emphasis in the original.
9. Mahmood, *Politics of Piety*, 106.
10. Christine M. DeLucia, *Memory Lands: King Philips War and the Place of Violence in the Northeast* (New Haven, CT: Yale University Press, 2018); Heather L. Pezzarossi, "Native Basketry and the Dynamics of Social Landscapes in Southern New England," in *Things in Motion: Object Itineraries in Anthropological Practice*, ed. Rosemary A. Joyce and Susan D. Gillespie (Santa Fe, NM: School for Advanced Research Press, 2015), 179; Patricia E. Rubertone, ed., *Archaeologies of Placemaking: Monuments, Memories, and Engagement in Native North America* (Walnut Creek, CA: Left Coast Press, 2008).
11. Rubertone, *Archaeologies of Placemaking*, 13.
12. Rubin, *Tears of Repentance*, 114; Mahmood, *Politics of Piety*, 106.
13. Occom, *Collected Writings*, 233.
14. Erving Goffman, "The Nature of Deference and Demeanor," *American Anthropologist* 58, no. 3 (1956).
15. Erving Goffman, *Behavior in Public Places* (New York: Simon & Schuster, 2008), 137, citing Cornelia Skinner, "Where to Look," in *Bottoms Up!* (New York: Dodd, Mead, 1955), 29–30.
16. Here I am loosely paraphrasing an argument from Georg Simmel, *The Sociology of Georg Simmel*, ed. Kurt H. Wolff (Glencoe, IL: Free Press, 1950), 329.
17. Samson Occom and Nathaniel Whitaker, *Extracts of Several Sermons, Preached Extempore at Different Places of Divine Worship, in the City of Bristol, by the Rev. Mr. Nathaniel Whitaker, Minister of the Gospel at Norwich, in New-England, and the Rev. Mr. Samson Occom, an Indian Minister* (Bristol, 1766), 4.
18. "Why do I, why do we, have to answer these questions from strangers and strangers with attitudes!?" Audra Simpson, *Mohawk Interruptus: Political Life Across the Borders of Settler States* (Durham, NC: Duke University Press, 2014), 118; see also chapter 2.
19. Philip Joseph Deloria, *Indians in Unexpected Places* (Lawrence: University Press of Kansas, 2004), 4, 11.
20. Deloria, *Indians in Unexpected Places*, 4, 20.
21. Alden T. Vaughan and Daniel K. Richter, "Crossing the Cultural Divide: Indians and New Englanders, 1605–1763," *Proceedings of the American Antiquarian Society* 90, no. 1 (January 1980): 25; James Axtell, *The Invasion Within: The*

Contest of Cultures in Colonial North America (New York: Oxford University Press, 1986), 19.

22. See, for instance, Laura J. Murray, "Vocabularies of Native American Languages: A Literary and Historical Approach to an Elusive Genre," *American Quarterly* 53, no. 4 (2001): 613; Lisa Brooks, "Turning the Looking Glass on King Philip's War: Locating American Literature in Native Space," *American Literary History* 25, no. 4 (2013): 739.

23. Elizabeth A. Povinelli, *The Empire of Love: Toward a Theory of Intimacy, Genealogy, and Carnality* (Durham, NC: Duke University Press, 2006), 86; Mark Rifkin, *When Did Indians Become Straight? Kinship, the History of Sexuality, and Native Sovereignty* (New York: Oxford University Press, 2011), 268; Mark Rifkin, *Beyond Settler Time: Temporal Sovereignty and Indigenous Self-Determination* (Durham, NC: Duke University Press, 2017), 165. See also Nayan Shah, *Stranger Intimacy: Contesting Race, Sexuality, and the Law in the North American West* (Berkeley: University of California Press, 2011) and Rita Keresztesi, *Strangers at Home: American Ethnic Modernism Between the World Wars* (Lincoln: University of Nebraska Press, 2005), 112–60.

24. Jean M. O'Brien, "'Divorced from the Land': Resistance and Survival of Indian Women in Eighteenth-Century New England," in *After King Philip's War: Presence and Persistence in Indian New England*, ed. Colin G. Calloway (Hanover, NH: University Press of New England, 1997), 149.

25. It is important to note that the Occom-Fowler marriage had important political implications that went well beyond their forms of interpersonal interaction. In the early eighteenth century, the New York colonial assembly "reached an agreement with the [Montaukett] tribe that prohibited non-Montaukett men from marrying Montaukett women, effectively creating through legislation a means of ensuring a decline in the Montaukett population." Brad Jarvis, *The Brothertown Nation of Indians: Land Ownership and Nationalism in Early America, 1740–1840* (Lincoln: University of Nebraska Press, 2010), 54; see also R. Todd Romero, *Making War and Minting Christians: Masculinity, Religion, and Colonialism in Early New England* (Amherst: University of Massachusetts Press, 2011), 165.

26. David McClure, *Diary of David McClure: Doctor of Divinity, 1748–1820*, ed. Franklin Bowditch Dexter (New York: Knickerbocker Press, 1899), 192, spelling modernized.

27. Jeffrey Andrew Dolven, *Senses of Style: Poetry Before Interpretation* (Chicago: University of Chicago Press, 2017), 153, 183.

28. Occom, *Collected Writings*, 78.

29. Nathaniel Hawthorne, *Twice-Told Tales* (Boston: American Stationery Co., John B. Russell, 1837), 65, emphasis added.

30. Dolven, *Senses of Style*, 183.

31. Sermons and fragments of sermons by Samson Occom, undated, Samson Occom Papers, Connecticut Historical Society, http://hdl.handle.net/11134/40002:389. It should be noted that at least one (unknown) person has questioned whether this manuscript was really written by Occom. At the top of the manuscript, a modern reader has written "Not in S. O.'s hand." Library records do not indicate who wrote this or what their qualifications were, and it may be simply the private judgment of a patron. It is true that the handwriting does not look identical to manuscripts written later in Occom's career; then again, a certain amount of change in an individual's handwriting is to be expected over the course of a lifetime. In trying to ascertain the authorship of the piece, I consulted archivists and scholars at the Connecticut Historical Society, Dartmouth College, Yale University, and the Native Northeast Research Collaborative. All of them agree with me that the handwriting on the manuscript, while different from some of Occom's later writings, has enough in common with those later writings to raise doubts about the aforementioned assertion that it is not in Occom's hand. This is a question for further research that could potentially be settled by an expert in paleography. Meanwhile, I have opted to quote from the manuscript here because it his filed among Occom's other papers; because the identity, qualifications, and motivations of the person who deemed it not to be in Occom's hand are unknown; and because it is not clear who else would have written it.
32. Sermons and fragments of sermons by Samson Occom, undated, Samson Occom Papers, Connecticut Historical Society, http://hdl.handle.net/11134/40002:389.
33. Samuel Buell, *The Excellence and Importance of the Saving Knowledge of the Lord Jesus Christ in the Gospel-Preacher, Plainly and Seriously Represented and Enforced: And Christ Preached to the Gentiles in Obedience to the Call of God* (New York: J. Parker and Company, 1761), 12–13.
34. Buell, *Excellence and Importance*, iii. There exists a rich historical literature on ancient and modern parrhesia. See, for instance, Dana Farah Fields, *The Rhetoric of Parrhesia in Roman Greece* (Princeton, NJ: Princeton University Press, 2009); Stanley Marrow, "Parrhēsia and the New Testament," *Catholic Biblical Quarterly* 44, no. 3 (1982); and David Colclough, "Parrhesia: The Rhetoric of Free Speech in Early Modern England," *Rhetorica: A Journal of the History of Rhetoric* 17, no. 2 (1999). I borrow the formulation of parrhesia as a form of "truth-telling" from Michel Foucault, *The Government of Self and Others: Lectures at the Collège de France 1982–1983* (New York: Palgrave Macmillan, 2010), 42–43.
35. Buell, *Excellence and Importance*, 11.
36. Geoffrey F. Nuttall, *The Holy Spirit in Puritan Faith and Experience* (Oxford: Blackwell, 1946), 26.

37. Cited in Norman Penney, ed., *The First Publishers of Truth: Being Early Records (Now First Printed) of the Introduction of Quakerism into the Counties of England and Wales* (London: Headley, 1907), 367.
38. Acts 14:3.
39. Whether early modern Quakers explicitly described their acts of piety as *parrhesia* seems doubtful. For an argument that they nevertheless belonged to the same broad rhetorical and intellectual tradition, see Martin L. Warren, "The Quakers as Parrhesiasts: Frank Speech and Plain Speaking as the Fruits of Silence," *Quaker History* 98, no. 2 (2009): 1–25.
40. See chapter 3.
41. Charles Chauncy, *Enthusiasm Described and Caution'd Against: A Sermon Preach'd at the Old Brick Meeting-House in Boston, the Lord's Day After the Commencement, 1742* (Boston: J. Draper, 1742), 12.
42. Chauncy, *Enthusiasm Described and Caution'd Against*, 7–8.
43. Occom, *Collected Writings*, 56; see also chapter 3.
44. Occom, *Collected Writings*, 97, 128–29, 156n15.
45. Occom, *Collected Writings*, 177.
46. Occom, *Collected Writings*, 183.
47. Occom, *Collected Writings*, 183.
48. Occom, *Collected Writings*, 99; Michael Elliott, "'This Indian Bait': Samson Occom and the Voice of Liminality," *Early American Literature* 29, no. 3 (1994): 245–46; Rochelle Raineri Zuck, "Staging the Empire: Samson Occom and the Eighteenth-Century London Theater," *Eighteenth-Century Studies* 54, no. 3 (2021): 565.
49. Thomas Heath to Samson Occom, September 3, 1776, Samson Occom Papers, Connecticut Historical Society, http://hdl.handle.net/11134/40002:391.
50. Unsigned letter to Samson Occom, 1776–1777, Samson Occom Papers, Connecticut Historical Society, http://hdl.handle.net/11134/40002:391.
51. Jos(eph?) Green to Samson Occom, April 15, 1767, Samson Occom Papers, Connecticut Historical Society, http://hdl.handle.net/11134/40002:392.
52. John Thornton to Samson Occom, February 19, 1773 and June 3, 1772, Samson Occom Papers, Connecticut Historical Society, http://hdl.handle.net/11134/40002:394.
53. Occom, *Collected Writings*, 185.
54. Occom, *Collected Writings*, 187, emphasis added.
55. Susan O'Brien, "A Transatlantic Community of Saints: The Great Awakening and the First Evangelical Network, 1735," *American Historical Review* 91, no. 4 (October 1986); Shelby M. Balik, "'Scattered as Christians Are in This Part of Our Country': Layfolk's Reading, Writing, and Religious Community in New England's Northern Frontier, 1780," *New England Quarterly* 83, no. 4 (December 2010): 609.

56. John Thornton to Samson Occom, February 19, 1773, Samson Occom Papers, Connecticut Historical Society, http://hdl.handle.net/11134/40002:395; see also Galatians 6:14.
57. Occom, *Collected Writings*, 97.
58. Susanna Wheatley to John Thornton, October 26, 1771, Papers of the Leslie family, Earls of Leven and Melville, National Records of Scotland, GD26/13/663/1. See also the appendix.
59. Occom, *Collected Writings*, 183.
60. Occom, *Collected Writings*, 291, 315.
61. Occom, *Collected Writings*, 293, 329.
62. See chapter 3.
63. Occom, *Collected Writings*, 178.
64. Occom, *Collected Writings*, 73, 97n67.
65. Occom, *Collected Writings*, 365, 267; Ernest Marshall Howse, *Saints in Politics: The "Clapham Sect" and the Growth of Freedom* (London: Allen & Unwin, 1952), 15.
66. Occom, *Collected Writings*, 59, 224.
67. Occom, *Collected Writings*, 178.
68. Joseph Johnson, *To Do Good to My Indian Brethren: The Writings of Joseph Johnson, 1751–1776*, ed. Laura J. Murray (Amherst: University of Massachusetts Press, 1998), 160–61.
69. Rubertone, *Archaeologies of Placemaking*, 14; DeLucia, *Memory Lands*, 2.
70. Lisa Brooks, *The Common Pot: The Recovery of Native Space in the Northeast* (Minneapolis: University of Minnesota Press, 2008), 88.
71. Occom, *Collected Writings*, 149; see also chapters 3 and 6.
72. Occom and Whitaker, *Extracts of Several Sermons*, 3–4.
73. Occom and Whitaker, *Extracts of Several Sermons*, 7, 5, emphasis in original.
74. Augustine, *The City of God Against the Pagans*, ed. R. W. Dyson (New York: Cambridge University Press, 1998), 48, 26.
75. Charles E. Hambrick-Stowe, *The Practice of Piety: Puritan Devotional Disciplines in Seventeenth-Century New England* (Chapel Hill: University of North Carolina Press, 1982), 36.
76. Hambrick-Stowe, *The Practice of Piety*, 71
77. Stephen Foster, *Their Solitary Way: The Puritan Social Ethic in the First Century of Settlement in New England* (New Haven, CT: Yale University Press, 1971), 63. On disinterested benevolence, see chapter 3.
78. Occom, *Collected Writings*, 103.
79. Vincent Carretta, *Phillis Wheatley: Biography of a Genius in Bondage* (Athens: University of Georgia Press, 2011), 148. Occom may also have met the Black painter Scipio Moorhead, who was enslaved to Moorhead until being sold at auction after the minister's death in 1775.

80. William Sprague, *Annals of the American Pulpit* (New York: Robert Carter & Brothers, 1858), 3:44–45.
81. Andrew Pettegree, "The Spread of Calvin's Thought," in *The Cambridge Companion to John Calvin*, ed. Donald K. McKim (New York: Cambridge University Press, 2004), 207; on stranger churches more generally, see Silke Muylaert, *Shaping the Stranger Churches: Migrants in England and the Troubles in the Netherlands, 1547–1585* (Leiden: Brill, 2021).
82. Occom, *Collected Writings*, 215. See also chapter 3.
83. See, for instance, Hannah Arendt, *The Human Condition* (Chicago: University of Chicago Press, 1998), 53–54.
84. Rubin, *Tears of Repentance*, x.
85. David J. Silverman, *Red Brethren: The Brothertown and Stockbridge Indians and the Problem of Race in Early America* (Ithaca, NY: Cornell University Press, 2010), 112.
86. I explore the issue of Occom's secularity in greater detail in "Indigenous Secularism and the Secular-Colonial," *Critical Research on Religion* 10, no. 1 (April 2022).
87. Occom, *Collected Writings*, 380.
88. Silverman, *Red Brethren*, 112; see also chapter 3.
89. Occom, *Collected Writings*, 23.
90. Occom, *Collected Writings*, 232.
91. See chapter 5.
92. Norman Fiering, *Jonathan Edwards's Moral Thought and Its British Context* (Chapel Hill: University of North Carolina Press, 1981), 196.
93. Johnson, *To Do Good to My Indian Brethren*, 113.
94. Isaac Watts, *Hymns and Spiritual Songs* (London: W. Strahan et al., 1772), 240.
95. Johnson, *To Do Good to My Indian Brethren*, 160.
96. Johnson, *To Do Good to My Indian Brethren*, 183.
97. Johnson, *To Do Good to My Indian Brethren*, 207.
98. Occom, *Collected Writings*, 25n28; Megan Fulopp, "What's in a Name?," Life of the Brothertown Indians, November 7, 2017, https://brothertowncitizen.wordpress.com/2017/11/07/whats-in-a-name-part-iv-happy-eeyawquittoo wauconnuck-day/.

5. Seft at Last

1. Lisa Peet, "Dartmouth Returns Occom Papers to Mohegan Tribe," *Library Journal* 147, no. 7 (June 2022): 11.

2. "Samson Occom, Autobiography," 1768, Samson Occom Papers, Mohegan Tribe (online reproduction by the Occom Circle Project, Dartmouth College), https://collections.dartmouth.edu/occom/html/diplomatic/768517-diplomatic.html. All future citations of the autobiography in this chapter refer to this version.
3. See, for instance, Samson Occom, *The Collected Writings of Samson Occom, Mohegan: Leadership and Literature in Eighteenth-Century Native America*, ed. Joanna Brooks (New York: Oxford University Press, 2006), 58; Robert S. Levine, ed., *The Norton Anthology of American Literature*, 9th ed. (New York: Norton, 2017), A:595; Derrick R. Spires et al., eds., *The Broadview Anthology of American Literature: Beginnings to Reconstruction* (Peterborough, ON: Broadview Press, 2022), A:462.
4. "Samson Occom, Autobiography."
5. Joan H. Hall and Frederic Gomes Cassidy, eds., *Dictionary of American Regional English* (Cambridge, MA: Harvard University Press, 1985), 4:756.
6. *Oxford English Dictionary*, s.v. "saught, n.," https://doi.org/10.1093/OED/9298581264 "Saught, n.," OED Online; "seft" is listed here as an alternate spelling.
7. Occom, *Collected Writings*, 84; Colin G. Calloway, *The Indian History of an American Institution: Native Americans and Dartmouth* (Hanover, NH: University Press of New England, 2010), 18; National Archives Currency Converter, https://www.nationalarchives.gov.uk/currency-converter/.
8. "Samson Occom, Autobiography."
9. Drew Lopenzina, *Red Ink: Native Americans Picking Up the Pen in the Colonial Period* (Albany: SUNY Press, 2012), 245; Bernd Peyer, ed., *The Elders Wrote: An Anthology of Early Prose by North American Indians, 1768–1931* (Berlin: Reimer, 1982), 12–18.
10. Lopenzina, *Red Ink*, 240.
11. Joanna Brooks, "Prose Writings," in *The Collected Writings of Samson Occom*, 43.
12. Arjun Appadurai, "Introduction: Commodities and the Politics of Value," in *The Social Life of Things: Commodities in Cultural Perspective*, ed. Arjun Appadurai (New York: Cambridge University Press, 1986), 56.
13. Webb Keane, *Christian Moderns: Freedom and Fetish in the Mission Encounter* (Berkeley: University of California Press, 2007), 59–82.
14. Lopenzina, *Red Ink*, 237.
15. Occom, *Collected Writings*, 96.
16. Penelope Myrtle Kelsey, *Reading the Wampum: Essays on Hodinöshö:ni' Visual Code and Epistemological Recovery* (Syracuse, NY: Syracuse University Press, 2014).
17. Heather L. Pezzarossi, "Native Basketry and the Dynamics of Social Landscapes in Southern New England," in *Things in Motion: Object Itineraries in*

Anthropological Practice, ed. Rosemary A. Joyce and Susan D. Gillespie (Santa Fe, NM: School for Advanced Research Press, 2015), 194.

18. Akeel Bilgrami, "The Visibility of Value," *Social Research: An International Quarterly* 83, no. 4 (2016): 920.
19. Eileen Razzari Elrod, "'I Did Not Make Myself so . . .': Samson Occom and American Religious Autobiography," in *Piety and Dissent: Race, Gender, and Biblical Rhetoric in Early American Autobiography* (Amherst: University of Massachusetts Press, 2008).
20. "Samson Occom, Autobiography."
21. Personal email; see also William Leete Stone Jr., "Letter, to the President of Dartmouth College, 1866 December 12," Occom Circle Project, Dartmouth College Library, https://collections.dartmouth.edu/occom/html/diplomatic/866662-diplomatic.html.
22. For a remarkable account of this episode see Wayne Franklin, *James Fenimore Cooper: The Later Years* (New Haven, CT: Yale University Press, 2017), 213–50.
23. *Appleton's Cyclopedia of American Biography* (New York: Appleton, 1888), 5:705.
24. William Leete Stone, *The Family of John Stone: One of the First Settlers of Guilford, Conn* (Albany, NY: J. Munsell's Sons, 1888), 66–67.
25. Stone, *Family of John Stone*, 46.
26. "Samson Occom, Autobiography."
27. "Miscellany. For the Norwich Courier. The Mohegan Indians," *Norwich Courier*, December 8, 1830: 1.
28. David McClure, *Memoirs of the Rev. Eleazar Wheelock, D.D: Founder and President of Dartmouth College and Moor's Charity School* (Newburyport, MA: Edward Little & Co., 1811), 175–76, 176n. Neither is the autobiography mentioned in any of the letters by Wheelock published via the Occom Circle Project.
29. "[Notice]," *Norwich Courier*, December 8, 1830: 3.
30. Michael Leroy Oberg, *Uncas: First of the Mohegans* (Ithaca, NY: Cornell University Press, 2003), 1–5.
31. *The Uncas Monument* (Norwich, CT: J. G. Cooley, 1842), 1–8; cited in Oberg, *Uncas*, 4.
32. Cited in Oberg, *Uncas*, 4.
33. Jean M. O'Brien, *Firsting and Lasting: Writing Indians Out of Existence in New England* (Minneapolis: University of Minnesota Press, 2010), 169–71.
34. William L. Stone, *Uncas and Miantonomoh: A Historical Discourse, Delivered at Norwich, (Conn.,) On the Fourth Day of July, 1842, on the Occasion of the Erection of a Monument to the Memory of Uncas, the White Man's Friend, and First Chief of the Mohegans* (New York: Dayton & Newman, 1842), i.
35. Stone, *Uncas and Miantonomoh*, 153.

36. Cited in Emma Sternlof, "History, Language, and Power: James Hammond Trumbull's Native American Scholarship," 41, April 2013, Trinity College Digital Repository, https://digitalrepository.trincoll.edu/theses/303; see also Emma Sternlof, "Of Pequots and Postscripts," October 2011, Trinity College Library, https://commons.trincoll.edu/rring/2011/10/19/of-pequots-and-postscripts/.
37. Sternlof, "History, Language, and Power," 41.
38. Stone, *Uncas and Miantonomoh*, 183–94.
39. Stone, *Uncas and Miantonomoh*, 186–87, 191; see also William Allen, *An American Biographical and Historical Dictionary* (Boston: William Hyde & Co, 1832), 619–20.
40. Stone, *Uncas and Miantonomoh*, 188–89.
41. Stone, *Uncas and Miantonomoh*, 193–94.
42. Stone, *The Family of John Stone*, 66, emphasis added.
43. Having said this, there is in my view no *a priori* political or methodological reason to celebrate the thingness of Occom's manuscript over and above its textuality. I agree with Holly Herbster that it is problematic to assume that "'factual' Euroamerican history was written down while an 'authentic' Native American history was not." As Herbster writes, "there is a danger in assuming that colonial-era documents did not record the individual and collective actions and reactions of Native people." Holly Herbster, "The Documentary Archaeology of Magunkaquog," in *Historical Archaeology and Indigenous Collaboration: Discovering Histories That Have Futures* (Gainesville: University Press of Florida, 2020), 98.
44. "Review of The Life and Times of Sir William Johnson," *North American Review* 101, no. 208 (1865): 249.
45. There is no mention of any Occom-related manuscript or archive anywhere in the Dartmouth College Library's twelve volumes of accession records or in the minutes of the meetings of the Library Board.
46. 1 Corinthians 14:13–14.
47. Occom, *Collected Writings*, 233.
48. Occom, *Collected Writings*, 74.
49. "Andrew Oliver," Personography, Occom Circle Project, https://collections.dartmouth.edu/occom/html/ctx/personography/personography.html.
50. Andrew Oliver, "Company for Propagation of the Gospel in New England and the Parts Adjacent in America, Letter, to Eleazar Wheelock, 1767 September 3," Occom Circle Project, Dartmouth College Library, https://collections.dartmouth.edu/occom/html/diplomatic/767503-3-diplomatic.html.
51. Eileen Razzari Elrod, *Piety and Dissent: Race, Gender, and Biblical Rhetoric in Early American Autobiography* (Amherst: University of Massachusetts Press, 2008), 32.

52. Keely McCarthy, "Conversion, Identity, and the Indian Missionary," *Early American Literature* 36, no. 3 (2001): 366.
53. Dana Nelson, "'(I Speak Like a Fool but I Am Constrained)': Samson Occom's Short Narrative and Economies of the Racial Self," in *Early Native American Writing: New Critical Essays*, ed. Helen Jaskoski (New York: Cambridge University Press, 1996), 47.
54. Michael Omi and Howard Winant, *Racial Formation in the United States* (New York: Routledge, 2014), 7.
55. Occom, *Collected Writings*, 145.
56. Occom, *Collected Writings*, 99.
57. Rey Chow, *The Protestant Ethnic and the Spirit of Capitalism* (New York: Columbia University Press, 2002), 95–127; similar pressures are described in the Haudenosaunee context in Audra Simpson, *Mohawk Interruptus: Political Life Across the Borders of Settler States* (Durham, NC: Duke University Press, 2014), 81.
58. "Samson Occom, Autobiography."
59. "Samson Occom, Autobiography."
60. "Samson Occom, Autobiography."
61. Matthew Henry, *An Exposition of the Old and New Testament* (Philadelphia: Barrington & Haswell, 1828 [1721–1725]), 5:64.
62. "Samson Occom, Autobiography."
63. 1 Corinthians 1:27.
64. Simpson, *Mohawk Interruptus*, 67–94.
65. Eve Kosofsky Sedgwick, "Paranoid Reading and Reparative Reading, or, You're So Paranoid, You Probably Think This Essay Is About You," in *Touching Feeling: Affect, Pedagogy, Performativity* (Durham, NC: Duke University Press, 2003).
66. H. J. Jackson, *Those Who Write for Immortality: Romantic Reputations and the Dream of Lasting Fame* (New Haven, CT: Yale University Press, 2015); Sheldon I. Pollock, *The Language of the Gods in the World of Men: Sanskrit, Culture, and Power in Premodern India* (Berkeley: University of California Press, 2006), 142–43; Ryan Carr, "Lyric X-Marks: Genre and Self-Determination in the Harp Poems of John Rollin Ridge," *MELUS* 43, no. 3 (August 2018).
67. Rosabeth Moss Kanter, *Men and Women of the Corporation* (New York: Basic Books, 1993), 236.
68. "Samson Occom, Autobiography."
69. Occom, *Collected Writings*, 183.
70. Jean-Jacques Rousseau, *The Confessions: And, Correspondence, Including the Letters to Malesherbes* (Hanover, NH: University Press of New England, 1995), 5:5, emphasis in original.

71. Occom, *Collected Writings*, 211–12.
72. Occom, *Collected Writings*, 213.
73. See chapter 4.
74. "Samson Occom, Autobiography."
75. "Samson Occom, Autobiography," emphasis added. The manuscript is difficult to read at this point, having been overwritten by the nineteenth-century editor.
76. 2 Corinthians 11:12.
77. Matthew Henry, *Exposition*, VI:501.
78. Ryan S. Schellenberg, "Paul, Samson Occom, and the Constraints of Boasting: A Comparative Rereading of 2 Corinthians 10," *Harvard Theological Review* 109, no. 4 (October 2016).
79. 2 Corinthians 11:23–27.
80. Occom, *Collected Writings*, 186, 58.
81. Henry, *Exposition*, VI:502.
82. Occom, *Collected Writings*, 79; "Samson Occom, Autobiography."
83. Occom, *Collected Writings*, 74.
84. Jos(eph?) Green, "Jos. Green to Samson Occom," April 1767.
85. Jonathan Edwards, *A Divine and Supernatural Light, Immediately Imparted to the Soul by the Spirit of God, Shown to Be Both a Scriptural, and Rational Doctrine; in a Sermon Preach'd at Northampton, and Published at the Desire of Some of the Hearers* (Boston: S. Kneeland and T. Green, 1734), 12.
86. My understanding of "acknowledgment" here is informed by Patchen Markell, *Bound by Recognition* (Princeton, NJ: Princeton University Press, 2003), 9–38.
87. Michael J. McClymond, "Spiritual Perception in Jonathan Edwards," *Journal of Religion* 77, no. 2 (1997): 211–12.
88. Occom, *Collected Writings*, 168–69.
89. Occom, *Collected Writings*, 126.
90. Occom, *Collected Writings*, xxiv.
91. Occom, *Collected Writings*, 203.
92. Occom, *Collected Writings*, 102; D. Rae Gould and Stephen A. Mrozowski, "Introduction: Histories That Have Futures," in *Historical Archaeology and Indigenous Collaboration: Discovering Histories That Have Futures* (Gainesville: University Press of Florida, 2020), 11; Courtney Cottrell, "NAGPRA's Politics of Recognition: Repatriation Struggles of a Terminated Tribe," *American Indian Quarterly* 44, no. 1 (2020): 62.
93. Brad Jarvis, *The Brothertown Nation of Indians: Land Ownership and Nationalism in Early America, 1740–1840* (Lincoln: University of Nebraska Press, 2010), 21–56; Cottrell, "NAGPRA's Politics of Recognition," 62.

94. Occom, *Collected Writings*, 55.
95. Lisa Brooks, *Our Beloved Kin: A New History of King Philip's War* (New Haven, CT: Yale University Press, 2018), 4.

6. "Time to Awake"

1. Samson Occom, *The Collected Writings of Samson Occom, Mohegan: Leadership and Literature in Eighteenth-Century Native America*, ed. Joanna Brooks (New York: Oxford University Press, 2006), 168.
2. Occom, *Collected Writings*, 49; Michael McNally, "Native American Visionary Experience and Christian Missions," in *Religions of the United States in Practice*, ed. Colleen McDannell (Princeton, NJ: Princeton University Press, 2001).
3. Edwards responded to Wheelock's request in a letter from July 13, 1744: "As to the Indian which you are instructing, such are the present circumstances of our people, that I have not courage to set forward any collection for him among them. They have been moved to many contributions of late, and they have now one in consideration for the promotion of a free boarding school for the Indians at Housatonic. . . . And it is a time of the greatest scarcity of money among them." Jonathan Edwards, "To the Reverend Eleazar Wheelock," in *Letters and Personal Writings* (New Haven, CT: Yale University Press, 1998), 146.
4. On moral sense philosophy and *Freedom of the Will*, see Paul Helm, "John Locke and Jonathan Edwards: A Reconsideration," *Journal of the History of Philosophy* 7, no. 1 (1969). On Edwards and the British "moralists" more generally, see Norman Fiering, *Jonathan Edwards's Moral Thought and Its British Context* (Chapel Hill: University of North Carolina Press, 1981).
5. Jonathan Edwards, *A Careful and Strict Enquiry into the Modern Prevailing Notions of That Freedom of Will Which Is Supposed to Be Essential to Moral Agency, Vertue and Vice, Reward and Punishment, Praise and Blame* (Boston: S. Kneeland, 1754), 10.
6. Occom, *Collected Writings*, 126.
7. Occom, *Collected Writings*, 126.
8. See, for instance, Linford D. Fisher, *The Indian Great Awakening: Religion and the Shaping of Native Cultures in Early America* (New York: Oxford University Press, 2012); Thomas S. Kidd, *The Great Awakening: The Roots of Evangelical Christianity in Colonial America* (New Haven, CT: Yale University Press, 2007), 189–212.
9. Fisher, *The Indian Great Awakening*, 8.

10. Occom, *Collected Writings*, 334.
11. Samson Occom, "Samson Occom's Account of the Death of a Christian Mohegan Indian," May 10, 1776, Native Northeast Portal, https://nativenortheastportal.com/digital-heritage/samson-occoms-account-death-christian-mohegan-indian.
12. Occom, *Collected Writings*, 192.
13. Occom, *Collected Writings*, 88, 89.
14. "Samson Occom, Receipts and Expenses, 1761," Samson Occom Papers, Mohegan Tribe (online reproduction by the Occom Circle Project, Dartmouth College), https://collections.dartmouth.edu/occom/html/normalized/761290-normalized.html, 1761; Nathaniel Shaw, "Nathaniel Shaw Jr., Account, 1765 to 1767," Occom Circle Project, Dartmouth College, https://collections.dartmouth.edu/occom/html/diplomatic/767900-10-diplomatic.html, 1767; Occom, *Collected Writings*, 107. Megan Fulopp (personal communication) also suggests that alcohol may have been a component of medicines made in Occom's home.
15. Occom, *Collected Writings*, 46.
16. William DeLoss Love, *Samson Occom and the Christian Indians of New England* (Boston: Pilgrim Press, 1899), 44.
17. George Frank Sensebaugh, *Milton in Early America* (Princeton, NJ: Princeton University Press, 2015), viii.
18. John Milton, *Poems, &c. Upon Several Occasions* (London: Tho. Dring, 1673), 59.
19. Occom, *Collected Writings*, 149.
20. Stanley Fish, *Surprised by Sin: The Reader in Paradise Lost* (Cambridge, MA: Harvard University Press, 1998).
21. Gregory Evans Dowd, *A Spirited Resistance: The North American Indian Struggle for Unity, 1745–1815* (Baltimore: Johns Hopkins University Press, 1992), 23–46; on the specificity of this type of prophecy to the eighteenth century, see Alfred A. Cave, *Prophets of the Great Spirit: Native American Revitalization Movements in Eastern North America* (Lincoln: University of Nebraska Press, 2006), 3.
22. Dowd, *A Spirited Resistance*, 27.
23. Walter Brueggemann, *The Prophetic Imagination* (Minneapolis: Fortress Press, 2018), 3.
24. Vine Deloria Jr., *God Is Red: A Native View of Religion* (Golden, CO: Fulcrum, 2003), 88.
25. Vine Deloria Jr., *The Metaphysics of Modern Existence* (Golden, CO: Fulcrum, 2012), 204, 207.
26. Deloria, *The Metaphysics of Modern Existence*, 206.

27. Samuel P. Huntington, *The Clash of Civilizations and the Remaking of World Order* (New York: Simon & Schuster, 2011).
28. Akeel Bilgrami, *Secularism, Identity, and Enchantment* (Cambridge, MA: Harvard University Press, 2014), 154.
29. Akeel Bilgrami, "The Philosophical Significance of the Commons," *Social Research: An International Quarterly* 88, no. 1 (2021): 214.
30. Vine Deloria Jr., "Perceptions and Maturity: Reflections on Feyerabend's Point of View," in *Beyond Reason: Essays on the Philosophy of Paul Feyerabend*, ed. Paul Feyerabend and Gonzalo Munévar (Boston: Kluwer Academic, 1991), 399.
31. Occom, *Collected Writings*, 149.
32. See chapter 3.
33. Occom, *Collected Writings*, 149.
34. Lynn Ceci, "The Value of Wampum Among the New York Iroquois: A Case Study in Artifact Analysis," *Journal of Anthropological Research* 38, no. 1 (1982); Penelope Myrtle Kelsey, *Reading the Wampum: Essays on Hodinöshö:ni' Visual Code and Epistemological Recovery* (Syracuse, NY: Syracuse University Press, 2014); Evan Haefeli, "On First Contact and Apotheosis: Manitou and Men in North America," *Ethnohistory* 54, no. 3 (July 2007): 431. It is also worth keeping in mind Paul Otto's warning that "Wampum, shorn of the complex history in which it first appeared, has become little more than a hackneyed term that can mean just about anything related to Native Americans or money"; Paul Otto, "'This Is That Which . . . They Call Wampum:' Europeans Coming to Terms with Native Shell Beads," *Early American Studies* 15, no. 1 (2017): 36.
35. Lisa Brooks, *The Common Pot: The Recovery of Native Space in the Northeast* (Minneapolis: University of Minnesota Press, 2008), 8, 54.
36. Brooks, *The Common Pot*, 93.
37. Eleazar Wheelock, Letter to George Whitefield, 1761 November 25, Samson Occom Papers, Mohegan Tribe, https://collections.dartmouth.edu/occom/html/diplomatic/761404-diplomatic.html.
38. Occom, *Collected Writings*, 102.
39. Kelsey, *Reading the Wampum*, xiii–xiv.
40. Occom, *Collected Writings*, 150.
41. Samuel Kirkland, *The Journals of Samuel Kirkland: 18th Century Missionary to the Iroquois, Government Agent, Father of Hamilton College*, ed. Walter Pilkington (Clinton, NY: Hamilton College, 1980), 162; cited in Anthony Wonderley, "Brothertown, New York, 1785," *New York History* 81, no. 4 (2000): 472.
42. Occom, *Collected Writings*, 309.
43. Kirkland, *The Journals of Samuel Kirkland*, 162.

44. See the first section of chapter 3.
45. Occom, *Collected Writings*, 309.
46. John Locke, *Two Treatises of Government*, ed. Peter Laslett (New York: Cambridge University Press, 1988), 298.
47. Occom, *Collected Writings*, 132.
48. Occom, *Collected Writings*, 157.
49. A similar insight would later be voiced by Patrick Wolfe, who observed that "though assimilation operates at the level of the individual—incrementally absorbing individuals and families into settler society—its target is not individuals but Indian collectivity." Patrick Wolfe, ed., *The Settler Complex: Recuperating Binarism in Colonial Studies* (Los Angeles: UCLA American Indian Studies Center, 2016), 8.
50. Occom, *Collected Writings*, 211.
51. Occom, *Collected Writings*, 132.
52. Occom, *Collected Writings*, 138.
53. Occom, *Collected Writings*, 138.
54. Joseph Johnson, *To Do Good to My Indian Brethren: The Writings of Joseph Johnson, 1751–1776*, ed. Laura J. Murray (Amherst: University of Massachusetts Press, 1998), 242. See also chapter 3.
55. Occom, *Collected Writings*, 149.
56. Occom, *Collected Writings*, 65. See also chapter 2.
57. Occom, *Collected Writings*, 187.
58. Occom, *Collected Writings*, 203.
59. Deloria, *The Metaphysics of Modern Existence*, 204, 207.
60. Occom, *Collected Writings*, 202–3.
61. Occom, *Collected Writings*, 203–4.
62. Occom, *Collected Writings*, 202.
63. William Hubbard, *A Narrative of the Indian Wars in New-England, from the First Planting Thereof in the Year 1607, to the Year 1677. Containing a Relation of the Occasion, Rise and Progress of the War with the Indians, in the Southern, Western, Eastern and Northern Parts of Said Country* (Boston: John Boyle, 1775), 193.
64. Hubbard, *Indian Wars*, 113, 106.
65. E. Brooks Holifield, *Theology in America: Christian Thought from the Age of the Puritans to the Civil War* (New Haven, CT: Yale University Press, 2003), 120, 105.
66. Samuel Hopkins, *The Works of Samuel Hopkins, D.D.*, ed. Edwards Amasa Park (Boston: Doctrinal Tract and Book Society, 1854), 3:88.
67. On Occom and the New Divinity, see chapter 3.
68. Occom, *Collected Writings*, 237.
69. On the "means of grace," see chapter 3.
70. Occom, *Collected Writings*, 237.
71. Occom, *Collected Writings*, 187.

72. Samson Occom and Nathaniel Whitaker, *Extracts of Several Sermons, Preached Extempore at Different Places of Divine Worship, in the City of Bristol, by the Rev. Mr. Nathaniel Whitaker, Minister of the Gospel at Norwich, in New-England, and the Rev. Mr. Samson Occom, an Indian Minister* (Bristol, 1766), 27–28.
73. Gerald R. McDermott, *Jonathan Edwards Confronts the Gods: Christian Theology, Enlightenment Religion, and Non-Christian Faiths* (New York: Oxford University Press, 2000), 194.

Conclusion

1. Samson Occom, *The Collected Writings of Samson Occom, Mohegan: Leadership and Literature in Eighteenth-Century Native America*, ed. Joanna Brooks (New York: Oxford University Press, 2006), 52.
2. "Samson Occom's Hebrew Textbook," Samson Occom Papers, Mohegan Tribe (online reproduction by the Occom Circle Project, Dartmouth College), https://collections.dartmouth.edu/occom/html/diplomatic/pj4566-m7-1735-diplomatic.html.
3. "Advertisement," *Norwich Packet*, November 4, 1774: 1.
4. Occom, *Collected Writings*, 56. See also chapter 3.
5. Occom, *Collected Writings*, 277.
6. Occom, *Collected Writings*, 215; see also chapter 3.
7. Occom, *Collected Writings*, 177.
8. Occom, *Collected Writings*, 392.
9. Samuel Fisher, *Rusticus Ad Academicos in Exercitationibus Expostulatoriis, Apologeticis Quatuor [or] The Rustick's Alarm to the Rabbies* (London: R. Wilson, 1660), 191; Stephen Ward Angell and Pink Dandelion, eds., *The Oxford Handbook of Quaker Studies* (New York: Oxford University Press, 2013), 205, 233.
10. Occom, *Collected Writings*, 129.
11. I borrow this phrase from Matthew Engelke's study of biblical authority in postcolonial Zimbabwe, *A Problem of Presence: Beyond Scripture in an African Church* (Berkeley: University of California Press, 2007), 245.
12. Occom, *Collected Writings*, 222, 291, 292, 293, 296, 299, 301, 304, 313, 314, 315, 329, 330, 331, 340, 341.
13. See chapter 2.
14. Harry S. Stout and Peter Onuf, "James Davenport and the Great Awakening in New London," *Journal of American History* 70, no. 3 (1983): 556.
15. Occom, *Collected Writings*, 290; Valentine Rathbun, "A Brief Account of a Religious Scheme," in *Writings of Shaker Apostates and Anti-Shakers, 1782–1850*, ed. Christian Goodwillie (London: Pickering & Chatto, 2013), 16.

16. Occom, *Collected Writings*, 290.
17. Isaac Watts, *Works, Published by Himself* (London, T. & T. Longman, 1753), xiii–xiv; see also Rochelle Stackhouse, "Hymnody and Politics," in *Wonderful Words of Life: Hymns in American Protestant History and Theology*, ed. Richard J. Mouw and Mark A. Noll (Grand Rapids, MI: W. B. Eerdmans, 2004), 45–46.
18. Stephen A. Marini, "Isaac Watts and the Theological Aesthetics of Evangelical Sacred Song," in *Protestant Aesthetics and the Arts*, ed Sarah Covington and Kathryn Reklis (New York: Routledge, 2020), 141.
19. Occom, *Collected Writings*, 233.
20. Occom, *Collected Writings*, 56, 94; Joanna Brooks, *American Lazarus: Religion and the Rise of African American and Native American Literatures* (New York: Oxford University Press, 2003), 51–86.
21. Occom, *Collected Writings*, 133.
22. Occom, *Collected Writings*, 222.
23. Occom, *Collected Writings*, 59, 265, 99, 135, 96.
24. Occom, *Collected Writings*, 55.
25. Occom, *Collected Writings*, 54.
26. Occom, *Collected Writings*, 74.
27. Occom, *Collected Writings*, 96.
28. Occom, *Collected Writings*, 108, 133.
29. Courtney Cottrell, "NAGPRA's Politics of Recognition: Repatriation Struggles of a Terminated Tribe," *American Indian Quarterly* 44, no. 1 (2020): 81n8.
30. Occom, *Collected Writings*, 196.
31. Occom, *Collected Writings*, 192.

Bibliography

Manuscript Sources

Connecticut Archives: Indians. First Series, 1647–1789. Connecticut State Library, Hartford, CT. Reproduced online by the Yale Indian Papers Project. https://web.library.yale.edu/collection/new-england-indian-papers-series.

Edwards, Jonathan. *A careful and strict enquiry into the modern prevailing notions of that freedom of the will, which is supposed to be essential to moral agency, vertue and vice, reward and punishment, praise and blame.* Boston: S. Kneeland, 1754. Bound and annotated by Samson Occom. Long Island Collection. East Hampton Library, East Hampton, NY.

Occom, Samson. "Samson Occom's Account of the Death of a Christian Mohegan Indian." May 10, 1776. Thomas Leffingwell House Museum, Norwich, CT. Reproduced online by the Northeast Native Portal. https://nativenortheastportal.com/digital-heritage/samson-occoms-account-death-christian-mohegan-indian.

Samson Occom Papers. Connecticut Historical Society, Hartford, CT. http://hdl.handle.net/11134/40002:Occom.

Samson Occom Papers. Mohegan Tribe, Uncasville, CT. Reproduced online by the Occom Circle Project, Dartmouth College. https://www.library.dartmouth.edu/digital/digital-collections/occom-circle.

Papers of the Leslie family, Earls of Leven and Melville. GD26/13/663/1. National Records of Scotland, Edinburgh, Scotland.

Published Sources

Abrams, M. H. *The Mirror and the Lamp: Romantic Theory and the Critical Tradition.* New York: Oxford University Press, 1971.

Adams-Campbell, Melissa, Ashley Glassburn Falzetti, and Courtney Rivard. "Introduction: Indigeneity and the Work of Settler Archives." *Settler Colonial Studies* 5, no. 2 (April 2015): 109–16.

"Advertisement." *Norwich Packet*, November 4, 1774: 1.

Agha, Asif. *Language and Social Relations.* New York: Cambridge University Press, 2007.

Alcoff, Linda. "The Problem of Speaking for Others." *Cultural Critique* 20 (1991): 5–32.

Allen, William. *An American Biographical and Historical Dictionary.* Boston: William Hyde & Co, 1832.

Andersen, Chris, and Jean M. O'Brien. "Introduction: Indigenous Studies—An Appeal for Methodological Promiscuity." In *Sources and Methods in Indigenous Studies*, ed. Chris Andersen and Jean M. O'Brien, 1–11. New York: Routledge, 2017.

Anderson, Elizabeth. "Feminist Epistemology and the Philosophy of Science." *Stanford Encyclopedia of Philosophy.* https://plato.stanford.edu/archives/spr2020/entries/feminism-epistemology/.

Angell, Stephen Ward, and Pink Dandelion, eds. *The Oxford Handbook of Quaker Studies.* New York: Oxford University Press, 2013.

Apess, William. *The Increase of the Kingdom of Christ: A Sermon.* New York: G. F. Bunce, 1831.

Appadurai, Arjun. "Introduction: Commodities and the Politics of Value." In *The Social Life of Things: Commodities in Cultural Perspective*, ed. Arjun Appadurai, 3–63. New York: Cambridge University Press, 1986.

Appleton's Cyclopedia of American Biography, Vol. 5. New York: Appleton, 1888.

Arendt, Hannah. *The Human Condition.* Chicago: University of Chicago Press, 1998.

Arnold, Laura K. "Crossing Cultures: Algonquian Indians and the Invention of New England." PhD diss., University of California, Los Angeles, 1995.

Aubert, Annette G., and Zachary Purvis, eds. *Transatlantic Religion: Europe, America, and the Making of Modern Christianity.* Boston: Brill, 2021.

Augustine. *The City of God Against the Pagans.* Ed. R. W. Dyson. New York: Cambridge University Press, 1998.

Axtell, James. *The Invasion Within: The Contest of Cultures in Colonial North America.* New York: Oxford University Press, 1986.

Baden, Joel S. *The Book of Exodus: A Biography.* Princeton, NJ: Princeton University Press, 2019.

Bakhtin, Mikhail. "The Problem of Speech Genres." In *Speech Genres and Other Late Essays*, ed. Michael Holquist and Caryl Emerson, 60–102. Austin: University of Texas Press, 1986.

Balik, Shelby M. "'Scattered as Christians Are in This Part of Our Country': Layfolk's Reading, Writing, and Religious Community in New England's Northern Frontier, 1780." *New England Quarterly* 83, no. 4 (December 2010): 607–40.

Bendremer, Jeffrey C., Elaine L. Thomas, Faith Damon Davison, and Mohegan Tribe Cultural and Community Programs. "Mohegan Oral Tradition, Archaeology and the Legacy of Uncas." *Bulletin of the Archaeological Society of Connecticut* 70 (2008): 75–86.

Ben-zvi, Yael. *Native Land Talk: Indigenous and Arrivant Rights Theories.* Hanover, NH: Dartmouth College Press, 2018.

Bercovitch, Sacvan. *The American Jeremiad.* Madison: University of Wisconsin Press, 2012.

———. *Typology and Early American Literature.* Amherst: University of Massachusetts Press, 1972.

Berens, John F. *Providence & Patriotism in Early America, 1640–1815.* Charlottesville: University Press of Virginia, 1978.

Best, Stephen, and Sharon Marcus. "Surface Reading: An Introduction." *Representations* 108, no. 1 (2009): 1–21.

Bilgrami, Akeel. "Notes Toward the Definition of 'Identity.'" *Daedalus* 135, no. 4 (2006): 5–14.

———."The Philosophical Significance of the Commons." *Social Research: An International Quarterly* 88, no. 1 (2021): 203–39.

———. *Secularism, Identity, and Enchantment.* Cambridge, MA: Harvard University Press, 2014.

———. "The Visibility of Value." *Social Research: An International Quarterly* 83, no. 4 (2016): 917–43.

Block, Kristen. "Quaker Evangelization in Early Barbados: Forging a Path Toward the Unknowable." In *Quakers and Abolition*, ed. Brycchan Carey and Geoffrey Plank, 89–105. Urbana: University of Illinois Press, 2014.

Blodgett, Harold William. *Samson Occom.* Hanover, NH: Dartmouth College Publications, 1935.

Boudinot, Elias. *Cherokee Editor: The Writings of Elias Boudinot.* Ed. Theda Perdue. Athens: University of Georgia Press, 1996.

Bragdon, Kathleen. *Native People of Southern New England, 1500–1650.* Norman: University of Oklahoma Press, 1996.

Brekus, Catherine A. *Sarah Osborn's World: The Rise of Evangelical Christianity in Early America.* New Haven, CT: Yale University Press, 2013.

Brooks, Joanna. *American Lazarus: Religion and the Rise of African American and Native American Literatures.* New York: Oxford University Press, 2003.

Brooks, Lisa. *The Common Pot: The Recovery of Native Space in the Northeast.* Minneapolis: University of Minnesota Press, 2008.

———. *Our Beloved Kin: A New History of King Philip's War.* New Haven, CT: Yale University Press, 2018.

———. "Turning the Looking Glass on King Philip's War: Locating American Literature in Native Space." *American Literary History* 25, no. 4 (2013): 718–50.

Bross, Kristina, and Hilary E. Wyss, eds. *Early Native Literacies in New England: A Documentary and Critical Anthology.* Amherst: University of Massachusetts Press, 2008.

Brown-Pérez, Kathleen. "A Right Delayed: The Brothertown Indian Nation's Story of Surviving the Federal Acknowledgment Process." In *Recognition, Sovereignty Struggles, & Indigenous Rights in the United States: A Sourcebook,* ed. Amy E. Den Ouden and Jean M. O'Brien, 237–61. Chapel Hill: University of North Carolina Press, 2013.

Bruchac, Margaret. "Broken Chains of Custody: Possessing, Dispossessing, and Repossessing Lost Wampum Belts." *Proceedings of the American Philosophical Society* 162, no. 1 (March 2018): 56–105.

Brueggemann, Walter. *The Prophetic Imagination.* Minneapolis: Fortress Press, 2018.

Buell, Samuel. *The Excellence and Importance of the Saving Knowledge of the Lord Jesus Christ in the Gospel-Preacher, Plainly and Seriously Represented and Enforced: And Christ Preached to the Gentiles in Obedience to the Call of God.* New York: J. Parker and Company, 1761.

Bunyan, John. *Pilgrim's Progress.* London: Scott, Webster and Geary, 1845.

———. *The Works of That Eminent Servant of Christ, Mr. John Bunyan.* London: W. Johnston, 1768.

Bushman, Richard L. *From Puritan to Yankee: Character and the Social Order in Connecticut, 1690–1765.* Cambridge, MA: Harvard University Press, 1998.

Byassee, Jason. "Typology." In *The Cambridge Dictionary of Christian Theology,* ed. Ian A. McFarland. New York: Cambridge University Press, 2011.

Calcaterra, Angela. *Literary Indians: Aesthetics and Encounter in American Literature to 1920.* Chapel Hill: University of North Carolina Press, 2018.

Calhoun, Craig J., Joseph Gerteis, James W. Moody, Steven Pfaff, and Indermohan Virk, eds. *Contemporary Sociological Theory.* 4th ed. Hoboken, NJ: John Wiley & Sons, 2022.

Calloway, Colin G., ed. *After King Philip's War: Presence and Persistence in Indian New England*. Hanover, NH: University Press of New England, 1997.

———. *The American Revolution in Indian Country: Crisis and Diversity in Native American Communities*. New York: Cambridge University Press, 1995.

———. *The Indian History of an American Institution: Native Americans and Dartmouth*. Hanover, NH: University Press of New England, 2010.

Carr, Ryan. "Indigenous Secularism and the Secular-Colonial." *Critical Research on Religion* 10, no. 1 (April 2022): 24–40.

———. "Lyric X-Marks: Genre and Self-Determination in the Harp Poems of John Rollin Ridge." *MELUS* 43, no. 3 (August 2018): 42–63.

Carretta, Vincent. *Phillis Wheatley: Biography of a Genius in Bondage*. Athens: University of Georgia Press, 2011.

Cave, Alfred A. "Canaanites in a Promised Land: The American Indian and the Providential Theory of Empire." *American Indian Quarterly* 12, no. 4 (1988): 277–97.

———. *Prophets of the Great Spirit: Native American Revitalization Movements in Eastern North America*. Lincoln: University of Nebraska Press, 2006.

Cavell, Stanley. *The Claim of Reason: Wittgenstein, Skepticism, Morality, and Tragedy*. New York: Oxford University Press, 1999.

———. *Must We Mean What We Say? A Book of Essays*. New York: Cambridge University Press, 2015.

Ceci, Lynn. "The Value of Wampum Among the New York Iroquois: A Case Study in Artifact Analysis." *Journal of Anthropological Research* 38, no. 1 (1982): 97–107.

Chamberlain, Ava. "The Execution of Moses Paul: A Story of Crime and Contact in Eighteenth-Century Connecticut." *New England Quarterly* 77, no. 3 (2004): 414–50.

Charles, Mark, and Soong-Chan Rah. *Unsettling Truths: The Ongoing, Dehumanizing Legacy of the Doctrine of Discovery*. Downers Grove, IL: InterVarsity Press, 2019.

Chauncy, Charles. *Enthusiasm Described and Caution'd Against: A Sermon Preach'd at the Old Brick Meeting-House in Boston, the Lord's Day After the Commencement, 1742*. Boston: J. Draper, 1742.

Chow, Rey. *The Protestant Ethnic and the Spirit of Capitalism*. New York: Columbia University Press, 2002.

Cipolla, Craig N., James Quinn, and Jay Levy. "Theory in Collaborative Indigenous Archaeology: Insights from Mohegan." *American Antiquity* 84, no. 1 (January 2019): 127–42.

Clifford, James. *The Predicament of Culture*. Cambridge, MA: Harvard University Press, 1988.

Cogley, Richard W. "John Eliot and the Origins of the American Indians." *Early American Literature* 21, no. 3 (1986): 210–25.

Cohen, Matt. *The Networked Wilderness: Communicating in Early New England.* Minneapolis: University of Minnesota Press, 2010.

Colclough, David. "Parrhesia: The Rhetoric of Free Speech in Early Modern England." *Rhetorica: A Journal of the History of Rhetoric* 17, no. 2 (1999): 177–21.

Conforti, Joseph A. *Samuel Hopkins and the New Divinity Movement: Calvinism, the Congregational Ministry, and Reform in New England Between the Great Awakenings.* Grand Rapids, MI: Christian University Press, 1981.

Corbett, Mary Jean. *Representing Femininity: Middle-Class Subjectivity in Victorian and Edwardean Womens' Autobiographies.* New York: Oxford University Press, 1992.

Cottrell, Courtney. "NAGPRA's Politics of Recognition: Repatriation Struggles of a Terminated Tribe." *American Indian Quarterly* 44, no. 1 (2020): 59–85.

Coulthard, Glen Sean. *Red Skin, White Masks: Rejecting the Colonial Politics of Recognition.* Minneapolis: University of Minnesota Press, 2014.

Crenshaw, Kimberle. "Mapping the Margins: Intersectionality, Identity Politics, and Violence against Women of Color." *Stanford Law Review* 43, no. 6 (1991): 1241–99.

Crisp, Oliver D., and Douglas A. Sweeney. *After Jonathan Edwards: The Courses of the New England Theology.* New York: Oxford University Press, 2012.

Debenport, Erin. *Fixing the Books: Secrecy, Literacy, and Perfectibility in Indigenous New Mexico.* Santa Fe, NM: School for Advanced Research Press, 2015.

De Forest, John William. *History of the Indians of Connecticut from the Earliest Known Period to 1850.* Hartford: W. J. Hamersley, 1852.

Deloria, Philip Joseph. *Indians in Unexpected Places.* Lawrence: University Press of Kansas, 2004.

Deloria, Vine, Jr. *Custer Died for Your Sins.* 1969. Norman: University of Oklahoma Press, 1988.

———. *God Is Red: A Native View of Religion.* Golden, CO: Fulcrum, 2003.

———. *The Metaphysics of Modern Existence.* Golden, CO: Fulcrum, 2012.

———. "Perceptions and Maturity: Reflections on Feyerabend's Point of View." In *Beyond Reason: Essays on the Philosophy of Paul Feyerabend,* ed. Paul Feyerabend and Gonzalo Munévar, 389–401. Boston: Kluwer Academic Publishers, 1991.

———. *We Talk, You Listen: New Tribes, New Turf.* New York: Macmillan, 1970.

DeLucia, Christine M. *Memory Lands: King Philips War and the Place of Violence in the Northeast.* New Haven, CT: Yale University Press, 2018.

Den Ouden, Amy E. *Beyond Conquest: Native Peoples and the Struggle for History in New England.* Lincoln: University of Nebraska Press, 2005.

Dolven, Jeffrey Andrew. *Senses of Style: Poetry Before Interpretation.* Chicago: University of Chicago Press, 2017.

Dowd, Gregory Evans. *A Spirited Resistance: The North American Indian Struggle for Unity, 1745–1815*. Baltimore: Johns Hopkins University Press, 1992.

Dwight, Timothy. *Travels in New-England and New-York*. London: W. Baynes and Son, 1823.

Edwards, Jonathan. *A Careful and Strict Enquiry into the Modern Prevailing Notions of That Freedom of Will Which Is Supposed to Be Essential to Moral Agency, Vertue and Vice, Reward and Punishment, Praise and Blame*. Boston: S. Kneeland, 1754.

———. *A Divine and Supernatural Light, Immediately Imparted to the Soul by the Spirit of God, Shown to Be Both a Scriptural, and Rational Doctrine; in a Sermon Preach'd at Northampton, and Published at the Desire of Some of the Hearers*. Boston: S. Kneeland and T. Green, 1734.

———. *Letters and Personal Writings*. Ed. George S. Claghorn. The Works of Jonathan Edwards, vol. 16. New Haven, CT: Yale University Press, 1998.

———. *The Works of President Edwards*. New York: S. Converse, 1829.

Elliott, Michael. "'This Indian Bait': Samson Occom and the Voice of Liminality." *Early American Literature* 29, no. 3 (1994): 233–53.

Elrod, Eileen Razzari. *Piety and Dissent: Race, Gender, and Biblical Rhetoric in Early American Autobiography*. Amherst: University of Massachusetts Press, 2008.

Engelke, Matthew. *A Problem of Presence: Beyond Scripture in an African Church*. Berkeley: University of California Press, 2007.

———. "Reading and Time: Two Approaches to the Materiality of Scripture." *Ethnos* 74, no. 2 (June 2009): 151–74.

Estes, Nick. *Our History Is the Future: Standing Rock Versus the Dakota Access Pipeline, and the Long Tradition of Indigenous Resistance*. London: Verso, 2019.

Fea, John. "Wheelock's World: Letters and the Communication of Revival in Great Awakening New England." *Proceedings of the American Antiquarian Society* 109, no. 1 (April 1999): 99–144.

Fields, Dana Farah. *The Rhetoric of Parrhesia in Roman Greece*. Princeton, NJ: Princeton University Press, 2009.

Fiering, Norman. *Jonathan Edwards's Moral Thought and Its British Context*. Chapel Hill: University of North Carolina Press, 1981.

Fish, Stanley. *Surprised by Sin: The Reader in Paradise Lost*. Cambridge, MA: Harvard University Press, 1998.

Fisher, Linford D. *The Indian Great Awakening: Religion and the Shaping of Native Cultures in Early America*. New York: Oxford University Press, 2012.

Fisher, Samuel. *Rusticus Ad Academicos in Exercitationibus Expostulatoriis, Apologeticis Quatuor [or] The Rustick's Alarm to the Rabbies*. London: R. Wilson, 1660.

Fliegelman, Jay. *Declaring Independence: Jefferson, Natural Language and the Culture of Performance*. Stanford, CA: Stanford University Press, 1993.

Foster, Stephen. *Their Solitary Way: The Puritan Social Ethic in the First Century of Settlement in New England*. New Haven, CT: Yale University Press, 1971.

Foucault, Michel. *The Government of Self and Others: Lectures at the Collège de France 1982-1983*. New York: Palgrave Macmillan, 2010.

Fox, George. *The Heathens Divinity Set Upon the Heads of All Called Christians That Say They Had Not Known That There Had Been a God or a Christ Unless the Scripture Had Declared It to Them.* [London?], 1671.

Franklin, Wayne. *James Fenimore Cooper: The Later Years*. New Haven, CT: Yale University Press, 2017.

Fredriksen, Paula. *Paul: The Pagan's Apostle*. New Haven, CT: Yale University Press, 2017.

Fulopp, Megan. Life of the Brothertown Indians. https://brothertowncitizen.wordpress.com/.

Garroutte, Eva Marie. *Real Indians: Identity and the Survival of Native America*. Berkeley: University of California Press, 2003.

Giddens, Anthony. *The Constitution of Society: Outline of the Theory of Structuration*. Berkeley: University of California Press, 1984.

Goffman, Erving. *Behavior in Public Places*. New York: Simon & Schuster, 2008.

———. "The Nature of Deference and Demeanor." *American Anthropologist* 58, no. 3 (1956): 473–502.

———. *The Presentation of Self in Everyday Life*. Garden City, NY: Doubleday, 1959.

Gould, D. Rae, and Stephen A. Mrozowski. "Introduction: Histories That Have Futures." In *Historical Archaeology and Indigenous Collaboration: Discovering Histories That Have Futures*, ed. D. Rae Gould, Holly Herbster, Heather Law Pezzarossi, and Stephen A. Mrozowski, 1–26. Gainesville: University Press of Florida, 2020.

Gould, D. Rae, Stephen A. Mrozowski, and Heather L. Pezzarossi. "Rethinking Colonialism: Indigenous Innovation and Colonial Inevitability." In *Rethinking Colonialism: Comparative Archaeological Approaches*, ed. Craig N. Cipolla and Katherine Howlett Hayes, 121–42. Gainesville: University Press of Florida, 2015.

Grant-Costa, Paul Joseph. "The Last Indian War in New England: The Mohegan Indians v. The Governour and Company of the Colony of Connecticut, 1703–1774." PhD dissertation, Yale University, 2008.

Gura, Philip F. "Eloquence Is Power: Oratory and Performance in Early America." *Journal of American History* 88, no. 2 (September 2001): 638.

Gustafson, Sandra M. *Eloquence Is Power: Oratory and Performance in Early America*. Chapel Hill: University of North Carolina Press, 2000.

Gwyn, Douglas. "Quakers, Eschatology, and Time." In Ward and Dandelion, *The Oxford Handbook of Quaker Studies*, 202–7.

Haefeli, Evan. "On First Contact and Apotheosis: Manitou and Men in North America." *Ethnohistory* 54, no. 3 (July 2007): 407–43.

Hall, David. *The Puritans: A Transatlantic History*. Princeton, NJ: Princeton University Press, 2019.

Hall, Joan H., and Frederic Gomes Cassidy, eds. *Dictionary of American Regional English*. Cambridge, MA: Harvard University Press, 1985.

Hall, Timothy D. *Contested Boundaries: Itinerancy and the Reshaping of the Colonial American Religious World*. Durham, NC: Duke University Press, 1994.

Hambrick-Stowe, Charles E. *The Practice of Piety: Puritan Devotional Disciplines in Seventeenth-Century New England*. Chapel Hill: University of North Carolina Press, 1982.

Hatch, Nathan O., and Harry S. Stout, eds. *Jonathan Edwards and the American Experience*. New York: Oxford University Press, 1988.

Hawke, David Freeman. *Everyday Life in Early America*. New York: Harper & Row, 1988.

Hawthorne, Nathaniel. *Twice-Told Tales*. Boston: American Stationery Co., John B. Russell, 1837.

Heimert, Alan. *Religion and the American Mind, from the Great Awakening to the Revolution*. Cambridge, MA: Harvard University Press, 1966.

Helm, Paul. "John Locke and Jonathan Edwards: A Reconsideration." *Journal of the History of Philosophy* 7, no. 1 (1969): 51–61.

Henry, Matthew. *Exposition of the Old and New Testament*. Philadelphia: Barrington & Haswell, 1828.

Herbster, Holly. "The Documentary Archaeology of Magunkaquog." In *Historical Archaeology and Indigenous Collaboration: Discovering Histories That Have Futures*, ed. D. Rae Gould, Holly Herbster, Heather Law Pezzarossi, and Stephen A. Mrozowski, 74–100. Gainesville: University Press of Florida, 2020.

Hill, Christopher. *The World Turned Upside Down: Radical Ideas During the English Revolution*. New York: Viking, 1972.

Hindmarsh, D. Bruce. *The Spirit of Early Evangelicalism: True Religion in a Modern World*. New York: Oxford University Press, 2018.

Holifield, E. Brooks. *Theology in America: Christian Thought from the Age of the Puritans to the Civil War*. New Haven, CT: Yale University Press, 2003.

Holladay, Carl R. *Introduction to the New Testament: Reference Edition*. Waco, TX: Baylor University Press, 2017.

Hopkins, Samuel. *The Works of Samuel Hopkins, D.D.* Ed. Edwards Amasa Park. Boston: Doctrinal Tract and Book Society, 1854.

Howse, Ernest Marshall. *Saints in Politics: The "Clapham Sect" and the Growth of Freedom*. London: Allen & Unwin, 1952.

Hubbard, William. *A Narrative of the Indian Wars in New-England, from the First Planting Thereof in the Year 1607, to the Year 1677. Containing a Relation of the Occasion, Rise and Progress of the War with the Indians, in the Southern, Western, Eastern and Northern Parts of Said Country*. Boston: John Boyle, 1775.

Huntington, Samuel P. *The Clash of Civilizations and the Remaking of World Order*. New York: Simon & Schuster, 2011.

Hutchby, Ian. *Media Talk: Conversation Analysis and the Study of Broadcasting.* New York: Open University Press, 2006.

Innes, Robert. "Introduction: Native Studies and Native Cultural Preservation, Revitalization, and Persistence." *American Indian Culture and Research Journal* 34, no. 2 (October 2010): 1–9.

Jackson, H. J. *Those Who Write for Immortality: Romantic Reputations and the Dream of Lasting Fame.* New Haven, CT: Yale University Press, 2015.

Jakobson, Roman. "Metalanguage as a Linguistic Problem." In *Contributions to Comparative Mythology*, 113–21. Berlin: De Gruyter Mouton, 1985.

Janowitz, Naomi. *Acts of Interpretation: Ancient Religious Semiotic Ideologies and Their Modern Echoes.* Boston: Walter de Gruyter, 2022.

———. "Do Jews Make Good Protestants? The Cross-Cultural Study of Ritual." In *Beyond Primitivism: Indigenous Religious Traditions and Modernity*, ed. Jacob Olupona, 23–36. New York: Routledge, 2004.

Jarvis, Brad. *The Brothertown Nation of Indians: Land Ownership and Nationalism in Early America, 1740–1840.* Lincoln: University of Nebraska Press, 2010.

Jaworski, Adam. "Silence and Small Talk." In *Small Talk*, ed. Justine Coupland, 110–32. New York: Longman, 2000.

Jenkins, Philip. *Dream Catchers: How Mainstream America Discovered Native Spirituality.* New York: Oxford University Press, 2004.

Johnson, Joseph. *To Do Good to My Indian Brethren: The Writings of Joseph Johnson, 1751–1776.* Ed. Laura J. Murray. Amherst: University of Massachusetts Press, 1998.

Justice, Daniel Heath. *Why Indigenous Literatures Matter.* Waterloo, ON: Wilfrid Laurier University Press, 2018.

Kanter, Rosabeth Moss. *Men and Women of the Corporation.* New York: Basic Books, 1993.

Kauanui, J. Kēhaulani. "'A Structure, Not an Event': Settler Colonialism and Enduring Indigeneity." *Lateral* 5, no. 1 (June 2016). https://csalateral.org/issue/5-1/forum-alt-humanities-settler-colonialism-enduring-indigeneity-kauanui/.

Kaufmann, Yehezkel. *The Religion of Israel: From Its Beginnings to the Babylonian Exile.* Chicago: University of Chicago Press, 1960.

Keane, Webb. *Christian Moderns: Freedom and Fetish in the Mission Encounter.* Berkeley: University of California Press, 2007.

Kelsey, Penelope Myrtle. *Reading the Wampum: Essays on Hodinöshö:ni' Visual Code and Epistemological Recovery.* Syracuse, NY: Syracuse University Press, 2014.

Kidd, Thomas S. *George Whitefield: America's Spiritual Founding Father.* New Haven, CT: Yale University Press, 2014.

———. *The Great Awakening: The Roots of Evangelical Christianity in Colonial America.* New Haven, CT: Yale University Press, 2007.

———. *The Protestant Interest: New England After Puritanism.* New Haven, CT: Yale University Press, 2004.

Kirkland, Samuel. "Answer to the Foregoing Queries, Respecting Indians." *Collections of the Massachusetts Historical Society*, First Series, 4 (1795): 67–74.

———. *The Journals of Samuel Kirkland: 18th Century Missionary to the Iroquois, Government Agent, Father of Hamilton College.* Ed. Walter Pilkington. Clinton, NY: Hamilton College, 1980.

Knapp, Steven, and Walter Benn Michaels. "Against Theory." *Critical Inquiry* 8, no. 4 (July 1982): 723–42.

Knellwolf, Christa, and Iain McCalman. "Introduction: Exoticism and the Culture of Exploration." *Eighteenth-Century Life* 26, no. 3 (September 2002): 1–9.

Lambert, Frank. *Pedlar in Divinity: George Whitefield and the Transatlantic Revivals, 1737–1770.* Princeton, NJ: Princeton University Press, 1994.

Larson, Rebecca. *Daughters of Light: Quaker Women Preaching and Prophesying in the Colonies and Abroad, 1700–1775.* Chapel Hill: University of North Carolina Press, 2000.

Lavin, Lucianne. *Connecticut's Indigenous Peoples: What Archaeology, History, and Oral Traditions Teach Us About Their Communities and Cultures.* New Haven, CT: Yale University Press, 2013.

Levine, Robert S., ed. *The Norton Anthology of American Literature.* 9th ed. New York: Norton, 2017.

Locke, John. *Two Treatises of Government.* Ed. Peter Laslett. New York: Cambridge University Press, 1988.

Lopenzina, Drew. "'Good Indian': Charles Eastman and the Warrior as Civil Servant." *American Indian Quarterly* 27, nos. 3–4 (2003): 727–57.

———. *Red Ink: Native Americans Picking Up the Pen in the Colonial Period.* Albany: SUNY Press, 2012.

Love, William DeLoss. *Samson Occom and the Christian Indians of New England.* Boston: Pilgrim Press, 1899.

Luhmann, Niklas. *Love as Passion: The Codification of Intimacy.* Trans. Jeremy Gaines and Doris L. Jones. Stanford, CA: Stanford University Press, 1998.

Lyons, Scott Richard. "Actually Existing Indian Nations: Modernity, Diversity, and the Future of Native American Studies." *American Indian Quarterly* 35, no. 3 (2011): 294–312.

———. *X-Marks: Native Signatures of Assent.* Minneapolis: University of Minnesota Press, 2010.

Mahmood, Saba. *Politics of Piety: The Islamic Revival and the Feminist Subject.* Princeton, NJ: Princeton University Press, 2005.

Mamdani, Mahmood. *Neither Settler nor Native: The Making and Unmaking of Permanent Minorities.* Cambridge, MA: Belknap Press of Harvard University Press, 2020.

Marini, Stephen A. "Isaac Watts and the Theological Aesthetics of Evangelical Sacred Song." In *Protestant Aesthetics and the Arts*, ed. Heather Covington and Kathryn Reklis, 130–45. New York: Routledge, 2020.

Marrow, Stanley. "Parrhēsia and the New Testament." *The Catholic Biblical Quarterly* 44, no. 3 (1982): 431–46.

Markell, Patchen. *Bound by Recognition*. Princeton, NJ: Princeton University Press, 2003.

Marsden, George. *The Evangelical Mind and the New School Presbyterian Experience: A Case Study of Thought and Theology in Nineteenth-Century America*. Eugene, OR: Wipf and Stock, 2003.

———. *Jonathan Edwards: A Life*. New Haven, CT: Yale University Press, 2003.

Matthiessen, F. O. *From the Heart of Europe*. New York: Oxford University Press, 1948.

McCarthy, Keely. "Conversion, Identity, and the Indian Missionary." *Early American Literature* 36, no. 3 (2001): 353–69.

McClure, David. *Diary of David McClure: Doctor of Divinity, 1748–1820*. Ed. Franklin Bowditch Dexter. New York: Knickerbocker Press, 1899.

———. *Memoirs of the Rev. Eleazar Wheelock, D.D: Founder and President of Dartmouth College and Moor's Charity School*. Newburyport, MA: Edward Little & Co., 1811.

McClymond, Michael J. "Spiritual Perception in Jonathan Edwards." *Journal of Religion* 77, no. 2 (1997): 195–216.

McDermott, Gerald R. *Jonathan Edwards Confronts the Gods: Christian Theology, Enlightenment Religion, and Non-Christian Faiths*. New York: Oxford University Press, 2000.

McFarland, Ian A., ed. *The Cambridge Dictionary of Christian Theology*. New York: Cambridge University Press, 2011.

McNally, Michael. "Native American Visionary Experience and Christian Missions." In *Religions of the United States in Practice*, ed. Colleen McDannell, 445–51. Princeton, NJ: Princeton University Press, 2001.

———. *Ojibwe Singers: Hymns, Grief, and a Native Culture in Motion*. New York: Oxford University Press, 2000.

Meacham, Standish. *Henry Thornton of Clapham, 1760–1815*. Cambridge, MA: Harvard University Press, 1964.

Merrell, James H. *The Indians' New World: Catawbas and Their Neighbors from European Contact Through the Era of Removal*. Chapel Hill: University of North Carolina Press, 2012.

Mills, Jedediah. *An Inquiry Concerning the State of the Unregenerate Under the Gospel*. New Haven, CT: B. Mecom, 1767.

Milton, John. *Paradise Regain'd*. Poetry Foundation. December 2022. https://www.poetryfoundation.org/poems/45752/paradise-regaind-book-4-1671-version.

———. *Poems, &c. Upon Several Occasions*. London: Tho. Dring, 1673.

"Miscellany. For the Norwich Courier. The Mohegan Indians." *Norwich Courier*, December 8, 1830: 1.

Mitchell, W. J. T. *Iconology: Image, Text, Ideology*. Chicago: University of Chicago Press, 1986.

Mitton, C. Leslie. *The Epistle to the Ephesians: Its Authorship, Origin, and Purpose*. Oxford: Clarendon Press, 1951.

"Mohegan Church Observes 100th Anniversary Corner Stone Laying." *Norwich Bulletin*, August 1 1931: 5–9.

Monescalchi, Michael. "Phillis Wheatley, Samuel Hopkins, and the Rise of Disinterested Benevolence." *Early American Literature* 54, no. 2 (2019): 413–44.

Mt. Pleasant, Alyssa, Caroline Wigginton, and Kelly Wisecup. "Materials and Methods in Native American and Indigenous Studies: Completing the Turn." *Early American Literature* 53, no. 2 (2018): 407–44.

Murray, Laura. "'Pray Sir, Consider a Little': Rituals of Subordination and Strategies of Resistance in the Letters of Hezekiah Calvin and David Fowler to Eleazar Wheelock." *Studies in American Indian Literatures* 4, nos. 2–3 (1992): 48–74.

———. "Vocabularies of Native American Languages: A Literary and Historical Approach to an Elusive Genre." *American Quarterly* 53, no. 4 (2001): 590–623.

Muylaert, Silke. *Shaping the Stranger Churches: Migrants in England and the Troubles in the Netherlands, 1547–1585*. Leiden: Brill, 2021.

Nelson, Dana. "'(I Speak Like a Fool but I Am Constrained)': Samson Occom's Short Narrative and Economies of the Racial Self." In *Early Native American Writing: New Critical Essays*, ed. Helen Jaskoski, 42–65. New York: Cambridge University Press, 1996.

Newcomb, Steven T. *Pagans in the Promised Land: Decoding the Doctrine of Christian Discovery*. Golden, CO: Fulcrum, 2008.

Niebuhr, Reinhold, and Alan Heimert. *A Nation So Conceived: Reflections on the History of America from Its Early Visions to Its Present Power*. New York: Scribner, 1963.

Noll, Mark A. "Moses Mather (Old Calvinist) and the Evolution of Edwardseanism." *Church History* 49, no. 3 (1980): 273–85.

"[Notice]." *Norwich Courier*, December 10, 1830: 3.

Nuttall, Geoffrey F. *The Holy Spirit in Puritan Faith and Experience*. Oxford: Blackwell, 1946.

O'Brien, Jean M. *Dispossession by Degrees: Indian Land and Identity in Natick, Massachusetts, 1650–1790*. New York: Cambridge University Press, 1997.

———. "'Divorced from the Land': Resistance and Survival of Indian Women in Eighteenth-Century New England." In *After King Philip's War: Presence and Persistence in Indian New England*, ed. Colin G. Calloway, 144–61. Hanover, NH: University Press of New England, 1997.

———. *Firsting and Lasting: Writing Indians Out of Existence in New England*. Minneapolis: University of Minnesota Press, 2010.

——. "Tracing Settler Colonialism's Eliminatory Logic in *Traces of History*." *American Quarterly* 69, no. 2 (2017): 249–55.

Oberg, Michael Leroy. *Uncas: First of the Mohegans*. Ithaca, NY: Cornell University Press, 2003.

O'Brien, Susan. "A Transatlantic Community of Saints: The Great Awakening and the First Evangelical Network, 1735." *American Historical Review* 91, no. 4 (October 1986): 811–32.

Occom, Samson. *The Collected Writings of Samson Occom, Mohegan: Leadership and Literature in Eighteenth-Century Native America*. Ed. Joanna Brooks. Oxford and New York: Oxford University Press, 2006.

Occom, Samson, and Nathaniel Whitaker. *Extracts of Several Sermons, Preached Extempore at Different Places of Divine Worship, in the City of Bristol, by the Rev. Mr. Nathaniel Whitaker, Minister of the Gospel at Norwich, in New-England, and the Rev. Mr. Samson Occom, an Indian Minister*. Bristol, 1766.

Oliver, Andrew. "Company for Propagation of the Gospel in New England and the Parts Adjacent in America, Letter, to Eleazar Wheelock, 1767 September 3." Occum Circle Project. Dartmouth College Library. https://collections.dart mouth.edu/occom/html/normalized/767503-3-normalized.html, 1767.

Omi, Michael, and Howard Winant. *Racial Formation in the United States*. New York: Routledge, 2014.

Otto, Paul. "'This Is That Which ... They Call Wampum': Europeans Coming to Terms with Native Shell Beads." *Early American Studies* 15, no. 1 (2017): 1–36.

Page, Alexander, and Theresa Petray. "Agency and Structural Constraints: Indigenous Peoples and the Australian Settler-State in North Queensland." *Settler Colonial Studies* 6, no. 1 (January 2016): 88–98.

Park, Edwards Amasa. *Memoir of the Life and Character of Samuel Hopkins, D.D.* Boston: Doctrinal Tract and Book Society, 1854.

Parrish, Susan Scott. *American Curiosity: Cultures of Natural History in the Colonial British Atlantic World*. Chapel Hill: University of North Carolina Press, 2012.

Penney, Norman, ed. *The First Publishers of Truth: Being Early Records (Now First Printed) of the Introduction of Quakerism into the Counties of England and Wales*. London: Headley, 1907.

Peterson, Leighton. "Reflections on Navajo Publics, 'New' Media, and Documentary Futures." In *Engaging Native American Publics: Linguistic Anthropology in a Collaborative Key*, ed. Paul V. Kroskrity and Barbra A. Meek, 169–83. London: Routledge, 2017.

Pettegree, Andrew. "The Spread of Calvin's Thought." In *The Cambridge Companion to John Calvin*, ed. Donald K. McKim, 207–24. New York: Cambridge University Press, 2004.

Peyer, Bernd, ed. *The Elders Wrote: An Anthology of Early Prose by North American Indians, 1768–1931*. Berlin: Reimer, 1982.

——. *The Tutor'd Mind: Indian Missionary-Writers in Antebellum America*. Amherst: University of Massachusetts Press, 1997.

Pezzarossi, Heather L. "Native Basketry and the Dynamics of Social Landscapes in Southern New England." In *Things in Motion: Object Itineraries in Anthropological Practice*, ed. Rosemary A. Joyce and Susan D. Gillespie, 179–99. Santa Fe, NM: School for Advanced Research Press, 2015.

Pollock, Sheldon I. *The Language of the Gods in the World of Men: Sanskrit, Culture, and Power in Premodern India*. Berkeley: University of California Press, 2006.

Povinelli, Elizabeth A. *The Empire of Love: Toward a Theory of Intimacy, Genealogy, and Carnality*. Durham, NC: Duke University Press, 2006.

Pulsipher, Jenny Hale. *Subjects Unto the Same King: Indians, English, and the Contest for Authority in Colonial New England*. Philadelphia: University of Pennsylvania Press, 2005.

Rathbun, Valentine. "A Brief Account of a Religious Scheme." In *Writings of Shaker Apostates and Anti-Shakers, 1782–1850*, ed. Christian Goodwillie, 1-28. London: Pickering & Chatto, 2013.

"Review of The Life and Times of Sir William Johnson." *North American Review* 101, no. 208 (1865): 249–56.

Richland, Justin B. "Pragmatic Paradoxes and Ironies of Indigeneity at the 'Edge' of Hopi Sovereignty." *American Ethnologist* 34, no. 3 (August 2007): 540–57.

Rifkin, Mark. *Beyond Settler Time: Temporal Sovereignty and Indigenous Self-Determination*. Durham, NC: Duke University Press, 2017.

——. *When Did Indians Become Straight? Kinship, the History of Sexuality, and Native Sovereignty*. New York: Oxford University Press, 2011.

Roberts, Strother E. *Colonial Ecology, Atlantic Economy: Transforming Nature in Early New England*. Philadelphia: University of Pennsylvania Press, 2019.

Rogers, Henry C. *History of the Town of Paris*. Utica, NY: White & Floyd, 1881.

Romero, R. Todd. *Making War and Minting Christians: Masculinity, Religion, and Colonialism in Early New England*. Amherst: University of Massachusetts Press, 2011.

Round, Phillip H. *Removable Type: Histories of the Book in Indian Country, 1663–1880*. Chapel Hill: University of North Carolina Press, 2010.

Rousseau, G. S., and Roy Porter, eds. *Exoticism in the Enlightenment*. New York: St. Martin's Press, 1989.

Rousseau, Jean-Jacques. *The Confessions: And, Correspondence, Including the Letters to Malesherbes*. Hanover, NH: University Press of New England, 1995.

Rubertone, Patricia E., ed. *Archaeologies of Placemaking: Monuments, Memories, and Engagement in Native North America*. Walnut Creek, CA: Left Coast Press, 2008.

Rubin, Julius H. *Tears of Repentance: Christian Indian Identity and Community in Colonial Southern New England.* Lincoln: University of Nebraska Press, 2013.

Ruoff, A. LaVonne Brown. *American Indian Literatures: An Introduction, Bibliographic Review, and Selected Bibliography.* New York: Modern Language Association of America, 1990.

———. "Introduction." *Studies in American Indian Literatures* 4, nos. 2–3 (1992): 75–81.

Ruttenburg, Nancy. *Democratic Personality: Popular Voice and the Trial of American Authorship.* Stanford, CA: Stanford University Press, 1998.

———. "George Whitefield, Spectacular Conversion, and the Rise of Democratic Personality." *American Literary History* 5, no. 3 (1993): 429–58.

Said, Edward W. *Orientalism.* New York: Vintage Books, 1979.

Salisbury, Neal. "Red Puritans: The "Praying Indians" of Massachusetts Bay and John Eliot." *William and Mary Quarterly* 31, no. 1 (1974): 27–54.

Schellenberg, Ryan S. "Paul, Samson Occom, and the Constraints of Boasting: A Comparative Rereading of 2 Corinthians 10." *Harvard Theological Review* 109, no. 4 (October 2016): 512–35.

Scott, James C. *Domination and the Arts of Resistance: Hidden Transcripts.* New Haven, CT: Yale University Press, 1990.

Sedgwick, Eve Kosofsky. "Paranoid Reading and Reparative Reading, or, You're So Paranoid, You Probably Think This Essay Is About You." In *Touching Feeling: Affect, Pedagogy, Performativity,* 123–51. Durham, NC: Duke University Press, 2003.

Sensebaugh, George Frank. *Milton in Early America.* Princeton, NJ: Princeton University Press, 2015.

Shah, Nayan. *Stranger Intimacy: Contesting Race, Sexuality, and the Law in the North American West.* Berkeley: University of California Press, 2011.

Shaw, Nathaniel. "Nathaniel Shaw Jr., Account, 1765 to 1767." Occom Circle Project. Dartmouth College Library. https://collections.dartmouth.edu/occom/html/diplomatic/767900-10-diplomatic.html, 1767.

Shoemaker, Nancy. *A Strange Likeness: Becoming Red and White in Eighteenth-Century North America.* New York: Oxford University Press, 2004.

Silverman, David J. *Red Brethren: The Brothertown and Stockbridge Indians and the Problem of Race in Early America.* Ithaca, NY: Cornell University Press, 2010.

———. "To Become a Chosen People: The Missionary Work and Missionary Spirit of the Brothertown and Stockbridge Indians, 1775–1835." In *Native Americans, Christianity, and the Reshaping of the American Religious Landscape,* ed. Joel W. Martin and Mark A. Nicholas, 250–75. Chapel Hill: University of North Carolina Press, 2010.

Silverstein, Michael. "Discourse and the No-thing-ness of Culture." *Signs and Society* 1, no. 2 (September 2013): 327–66.

———. "Metapragmatic Discourse and Metapragmatic Function." In *Reflexive Language: Reported Speech and Metapragmatics*, ed. John Arthur Lucy, 33–58. New York: Cambridge University Press, 1993.

Silverstein, Michael, and Greg Urban, eds. *Natural Histories of Discourse*. Chicago: University of Chicago Press, 1996.

Simmel, Georg. *The Sociology of Georg Simmel*. Ed. Kurt H. Wolff. Glencoe, IL: Free Press, 1950.

Simpson, Audra. *Mohawk Interruptus: Political Life Across the Borders of Settler States*. Durham, NC: Duke University Press, 2014.

Smith, Adam. *The Theory of Moral Sentiments*. Ed. Knud Haakonssen. New York: Cambridge University Press, 2002.

Smith, Linda Tuhiwai. *Decolonizing Methodologies: Research and Indigenous Peoples*. New York: St. Martin's Press, 1999.

Smolinski, Reiner. "Israel Redivivus: The Eschatological Limits of Puritan Typology in New England." *New England Quarterly* 63, no. 3 (1990): 357–95.

Spires, Derrick R., Christina Roberts, Joseph Rezek, Justine S. Murison, Laura L. Mielke, Christopher Looby, Rodrigo Lazo, et al., eds. *The Broadview Anthology of American Literature: Beginnings to Reconstruction*. Peterborough, ON: Broadview Press, 2022.

Sprague, William Buell. *Annals of the American Pulpit*. 9 vols. New York: Robert Carter and Brothers, 1858.

St. Jean, Wendy B. "Inventing Guardianship: The Mohegan Indians and Their 'Protectors.'" *New England Quarterly* 72, no. 3 (September 1999): 362.

Stackhouse, Rochelle. "Hymnody and Politics." In *Wonderful Words of Life: Hymns in American Protestant History and Theology*, ed. Richard J. Mouw and Mark A. Noll, 42–65. Grand Rapids, MI: W. B. Eerdmans, 2004.

Starna, William A. *From Homeland to New Land: A History of the Mahican Indians, 1600–1830*. Lincoln: University of Nebraska Press, 2013.

Sternlof, Emma. "History, Language, and Power: James Hammond Trumbull's Native American Scholarship." Trinity College Digital Repository. https://digitalrepository.trincoll.edu/theses/303, April 2013.

———. "Of Pequots and Postscripts." Trinity College Library. https://commons.trincoll.edu/rring/2011/10/19/of-pequots-and-postscripts/, October 2011.

Stoever, William Kenneth Bristow. *A Faire and Easie Way to Heaven: Covenant Theology and Antinomianism in Early Massachusetts*. Middletown, CT: Wesleyan University Press, 1978.

Stone, William L. *Uncas and Miantonomoh: A Historical Discourse, Delivered at Norwich, (Conn.,) On the Fourth Day of July, 1842, on the Occasion of the Erection of a*

Monument to the Memory of Uncas, the White Man's Friend, and First Chief of the Mohegans. New York: Dayton & Newman, 1842.

Stone, William Leete. *The Family of John Stone: One of the First Settlers of Guilford, Conn*. Albany, NY: J. Munsell's Sons, 1888.

Stone, William Leete, Jr. "Letter, to the President of Dartmouth College, 1866 December 12." Occom Circle Project. Dartmouth College Library. https://collections.dartmouth.edu/occom/html/validation/866662-validation.html, 1866.

Stout, Harry S. *The New England Soul: Preaching and Religious Culture in Colonial New England*. New York: Oxford University Press, 1986.

Stout, Harry S., and Peter Onuf. "James Davenport and the Great Awakening in New London." *Journal of American History* 70, no. 3 (1983): 556–78.

Strauss, Leo. *Persecution and the Art of Writing*. Chicago: University of Chicago Press, 1952.

Suhr-Sytsma, Mandy. "The View from Crow Hill: An Interview with Melissa Tantaquidgeon Zobel." *Studies in American Indian Literatures* 27, no. 2 (2015): 80.

Szasz, Margaret Connell. *Indian Education in the American Colonies, 1607–1783*. Lincoln: University of Nebraska Press, 2007.

———. "Samson Occom: Mohegan as Spiritual Intermediary." In *Between Indian and White Worlds: The Cultural Broker*, ed. Margaret Connell Szasz, 61–78. Norman: University of Oklahoma Press, 1994.

TallBear, Kimberly. *Native American DNA: Tribal Belonging and the False Promise of Genetic Science*. Minneapolis: University of Minnesota Press, 2013.

Taylor, Alan. *The Divided Ground: Indians, Settlers and the Northern Borderland of the American Revolution*. New York: Knopf, 2006.

Tennent, Gilbert. *The Happiness of Rewarding the Enemies of Our Religion and Liberty: Represented in a Sermon Preached in Philadelphia, Feb. 17, 1756. To Captain Vanderspiegel's Independent Company of Volunteers, at the Request of Their Officers*. Philadelphia: James Chattin, 1756.

The Uncas Monument. Norwich, CT: J. G. Cooley, 1842.

Urban, G. "Metasemiosis and Metapragmatics." In *Encyclopedia of Language & Linguistics*, 88–91. The Hague: Elsevier, 2006.

Valeri, Mark. *Law and Providence in Joseph Bellamy's New England: The Origins of the New Divinity in Revolutionary America*. New York: Oxford University Press, 1994.

Vasko, Timothy Bowers. "Nature and the Native." *Critical Research on Religion* 10, no. 1 (April 2022): 7–23.

Vaughan, Alden T., and Daniel K. Richter. "Crossing the Cultural Divide: Indians and New Englanders, 1605–1763." *Proceedings of the American Antiquarian Society* 90, no. 1 (January 1980): 23–99.

Veracini, Lorenzo. "Is Settler Colonial Studies Even Useful?" *Postcolonial Studies* 24, no. 2 (April 2021): 270–77.

Warner, Michael. *The Letters of the Republic: Publication and the Public Sphere in Eighteenth-Century America*. Cambridge, MA: Harvard University Press, 1990.

———. "The Preacher's Footing." In *This Is Enlightenment*, 368–83. Chicago: University of Chicago Press, 2010.

———. *Publics and Counterpublics*. New York: Zone Books, 2005.

Warren, Martin L. "The Quakers as Parrhesiasts: Frank Speech and Plain Speaking as the Fruits of Silence." *Quaker History* 98, no. 2 (2009): 1–25.

Warrior, Robert Allen. "Afterword." In *Crossing Waters, Crossing Worlds: The African Diaspora in Indian Country*, ed. Tiya Miles and Sharon Patricia Holland, 321–26. Durham, NC: Duke University Press, 2006.

———. "Canaanites, Cowboys, and Indians: Deliverance, Conquest, and Liberation Theology Today." *Christianity and Crisis* 49, no. 12 (September 1989): 261–65.

———. "'The Finest Men We Have Ever Seen': Reading Jefferson's Osage Encounters Through *Orientalism*." *Ariel: A Review of International English Literature* 51, no. 1 (2020): 57–80.

———. *Tribal Secrets: Recovering American Indian Intellectual Traditions*. Minneapolis: University of Minnesota Press, 1995.

Watts, Isaac. *Hymns and Spiritual Songs*. London: W. Strahan et al., 1772.

———. *Works, Published by Himself.* London: T. & T. Longman, 1753.

Weaver, Jace. *The Red Atlantic: American Indigenes and the Making of the Modern World, 1000–1927*. Chapel Hill: University of North Carolina Press, 2014.

———. *That the People Might Live: Native American Literatures and Native American Community*. New York: Oxford University Press, 1997.

Wenger, Tisa. "'A New Form of Government': Religious-Secular Distinctions in Pueblo Indian History." In *Religion as a Category of Governance and Sovereignty*, ed. Trevor Stack and Naomi R. Goldenberg, 68–89. Leiden: Brill, 2015.

———. *Religious Freedom: The Contested History of an American Ideal*. Chapel Hill: University of North Carolina Press, 2017.

Wheatley, Phillis. *Complete Writings*. New York: Penguin Books, 2001.

Wheeler, Rachel. *To Live Upon Hope: Mohicans and Missionaries in the Eighteenth-Century Northeast*. Ithaca, NY: Cornell University Press, 2013.

Wheelock, Eleazar. *A Continuation of the Narrative of the State, &c. Of the Indian Charity-School, at Lebanon, in Connecticut*. Boston: Richard and Samuel Draper, 1765.

———. *A Continuation of the Narrative of the Indian Charity-School, Begun in Lebanon, in Connecticut: From the Year 1768, to the Incorporation of It with Dartmouth-College, and Removal and Settlement of It in Hanover, in the Province of New-Hampshire, 1771*. Hartford, CT: Ebenezer Watson, 1771.

———. *A Plain and Faithful Narrative of the Original Design, Rise, Progress and Present State of the Indian Charity-School at Lebanon, in Connecticut*. Boston: Richard and Samuel Draper, 1763.

———. *A Sermon Preached Before the Second Society in Lebanon, June 30. 1763: At the Ordination of the Rev. Mr Charles-Jeffry Smith, with a View to His Going as a Missionary to the Remote Tribes of the Indians in This Land*. London: E. and C. Dilly, 1767.

Williams, Roger. *A Key into the Language of America*. London: Gregory Dexter, 1643.

Wimsatt, W. K., and M. C. Beardsley. "The Intentional Fallacy." *Sewanee Review* 54, no. 3 (1946): 468–88.

Winiarski, Douglas L. *Darkness Falls on the Land of Light: Experiencing Religious Awakenings in Eighteenth-Century New England*. Chapel Hill: University of North Carolina Press, 2017.

———. "Native American Popular Religion in New England's Old Colony, 1670–1770." *Religion and American Culture: A Journal of Interpretation* 15, no. 2 (2005): 147–86.

Wisecup, Kelly. *Assembled for Use: Indigenous Compilation and the Archives of Early Native American Literatures*. New Haven, CT: Yale University Press, 2021.

———. *Medical Encounters: Knowledge and Identity in Early American Literatures*. Amherst: University of Massachusetts Press, 2013.

Wolfe, Patrick, ed. "Introduction." In *The Settler Complex: Recuperating Binarism in Colonial Studies*, 1–24. Los Angeles: UCLA American Indian Studies Center, 2016.

———. "Settler Colonialism and the Elimination of the Native." *Journal of Genocide Research* 8, no. 4 (December 2006): 387–409.

———. *Settler Colonialism and the Transformation of Anthropology: The Politics and Poetics of an Ethnographic Event*. New York: Cassell, 1999.

———, ed. *The Settler Complex: Recuperating Binarism in Colonial Studies*. Los Angeles: UCLA American Indian Studies Center, 2016.

Wonderley, Anthony. "Brothertown, New York, 1785." *New York History* 81, no. 4 (2000): 457–92.

Wright, Bobby. "'For the Children of the Infidels?': American Indian Education in the Colonial Colleges." *American Indian Culture and Research Journal* 12, no. 3 (January 1988): 1–14.

Wyss, Hilary E. *English Letters and Indian Literacies: Reading, Writing, and New England Missionary Schools, 1750–1830*. Philadelphia: University of Pennsylvania Press, 2012.

———. *Writing Indians: Literacy, Christianity, and Native Community in Early America*. Amherst: University of Massachusetts Press, 2000.

Yirush, Craig. "Claiming the New World: Empire, Law, and Indigenous Rights in the Mohegan Case, 1704." *Law and History Review* 29, no. 2 (2011): 333–73.

Zobel, Melissa Tantaquidgeon. *The Lasting of the Mohegans: Part I, the Story of the Wolf People*. Uncasville, CT: Mohegan Tribe, 1995.

——. *Medicine Trail: The Life and Lessons of Gladys Tantaquidgeon*. Tucson: University of Arizona Press, 2000.

Zuck, Rochelle Raineri. "Staging the Empire: Samson Occom and the Eighteenth-Century London Theater." *Eighteenth-Century Studies* 54, no. 3 (2021): 555–75.

——. "William Apess, the 'Lost Tribes,' and Indigenous Survivance." *Studies in American Indian Literatures* 25, no. 1 (2013): 1–26.

Index

abolitionism, 36, 158, 254n54
"aboutness" of writing by S. Occom, 57, 72
accountability, 192–94, 264n93
"Account of the Montauk Indians" (Occom, S.), 51
acknowledgment, 58–59, 66, 79, 286n86
Adair, James, 103
Adam (biblical figure), 131–32, 160
"addressivity," 17, 76–80, 263n85; broadcast-oriented forms of, 16, 72–74, 262n74
adultery, 119, 121
agency, 7, 34, 139; collective, 77; Indigenous, 39–40; settler colonialism and, 38–39
agriculture/agricultural, 91, 96, 122, 252n23, 267n65; at Brothertown, 100–101, 132–33; D. Fowler on, 99–100; harvests, 100–101, 157, 215–16; S. Occom on, 98–101, 132–33
Alcoff, Linda, 56
alcohol, 204–5

alienation, 155, 192, 207, 209–11, 215–17, 228; colonialism as a process of, 219
alphabetic literacy, 68
altered states of consciousness, 200, 204–8, 210
American Indian Movement, 73
American Indian Quarterly (journal), 59
American Literature (journal), 239
American Revolution, 4, 15, 171, 198, 215, 253n42
ancient religions, 46, 114
Andersen, Chris, 12, 53, 56–57
"answerability," 77–81
anti-Catholicism, 272n129
anticolonialism, 88, 112, 225
anti-Indigenous prejudice, 8, 185–90
Apess, William, 129
apocalypticism, 128–29
Appadurai, Arjun, 173
"the archive," 54–55, 62, 175
archives, colonialism, 53–55, 70, 172
Arnold, Laura K., 115–16

[315]

assimilation, 12, 68, 90, 121–22, 290n49; historiography of, 203–4; S. Occom opposing, 127–28
"Asylum for Strangers." *See* hospitality
audiences, 24, 72–74, 116–19, 172–73, 212; co-participation of, 70; Paul's epistles, 127
Augustine and Augustinian piety, 26, 160–62, 164–65
authenticity, 186; assimilation and, 37; cultural, 10, 187
authority, 7, 10, 58, 74–75, 85, 141; biblical, 229, 291n11; deference and, 158; of Indigenous prophets, 207–8; personal, 56, 138, 145–46; political, 93–94, 187; power and, 138–39
autobiography, S. Occom (1765), 8, 65, 186, 231
autobiography, S. Occom (1768), 1, 51, 101, 191–99, 231; academia on, 173–74; language in, 169–71, *170*, 175–77, 187–88; manuscript, 17–18, 28–29, *29*, 169–80, *171*, 183–84; repatriated to Mohegan, 176, 184; "social life" of, 18, 174–75, 183, 198; on theology, 106–7; on traditional hospitality, 22, 28–29, *29*; on traditional mobility, 26
autonomy, 218; S. Occom on, 12; political, 15, 27, 29
Avery, David, 52
Axtell, James, 38, 142–43

Bakhtin, Mikhail, 76, 78–79, 263n85
Bellamy, Joseph, 107–8, 112–13
belonging, 13, 75, 79, 160, 164, 177; Indigenous, 26–28, 31, 91; political, 89, 94
"Benefit of the Whole," 97–98, 132, 217–19
benevolent empire, 114, 271n114

Ben's Town, 4, 27–28
Bercovitch, Sacvan, 268n71, 273n135
betrayal, 4, 219
Bible/biblical, 3, 146, 149, 251n12; Adam/Eve in, 131–32, 160; authority, 229, 291n11; bibliolatry, 44, 234–35; book of Exodus, 35, 86, 89, 125–26, 129; book of Genesis, 88, 129–33, 209; commentary, 123, 235; Gentiles in, 16, 103–5, 115, 119–23, 127–28; hymns and, 235–37; on Native Americans, 102–3; S. Occom on, 68–69, 85–86, 129–31, 210–11, 226–28; Old Testament, 103, 118, 120–21, 125–26, 130; Promised Land in, 86, 89, 102, 114, 125, 268n71; Satan in, 103, 131. *See also* "chosen people"/"chosenness"; Jesus Christ (biblical figure); New Testament, Bible; Paul (apostle); scriptural interpretation, by S. Occom
biblioclasm, 235
bibliolatry, 44, 234–35
Bilgrami, Akeel, 209–10, 222
Black Skin, White Masks (Fanon), 35
Blake, William, 184, 198
blindness, 150, 206, 218, 226–27
boarding schools, 287n3. *See also* education
books. *See* literature/books
Boudinot, Elias, 73
Bound by Recognition (Markell), 58–59
Brighton, John, 231
British Isles, 151, 171, 238
broadcast-oriented forms of address, Indigenous, 16, 72–74, 262n74
Brooks, Joanna, 12, 33, 51, 53–54, 101, 275n1; on S. Occom autobiography, 172
Brooks, Lisa, 9, 72, 199, 213, 215
Brothertown Indian Nation/movement, 32–33, 127–28, 198–99, 245n1,

267n65; agriculture at, 100–101, 132–33; Christianity and, 90–91; diary entries about, 162; factionalism, 218; migration and, 97, 126, 216–18; Mohegan and, 59–60; S. Occom in, 4, 6, 13, 31–33, 129, 159, 162–66, 172–73, 216–18; S. Occom manuscripts and, 17–18, 172, 174; S. Occom petitioning on behalf of, 211–12, 214–15, 219–20; racial exclusion and, 87–88; settler colonialism impacting, 9–10
Buell, Samuel, 9, 98, 108, 148–50, 201, 225; peaching at S. Occom ordination, 105, 122, 146–47
Bunyan, John, 131–32, 153
burning, book, 106, 235

Calcaterra, Angela, 14, 52–53
Canaanite interpretation of Indigenous nationhood, 102–3, 114, 125, 268n71
cane, gold-headed, belonging to S. Occom, 135, 275n1
capitalism, 210, 254n54
Carini, Peter, 177, 183
Catholic Church/Catholicism, 118–19, 161, 272n129
causality, traditionalism and, 35–36, 38–41
Cavell, Stanley, 59–61, 78–80, 264n93
Chauncy, Charles, 149–50
Cherokee Nation, 73
childhood of Occom, S., 1, 27, 230–31
children, Native, 4, 21, 150–51, 171, 179, 236, 241
Choice Collection of Hymns and Spiritual Songs (Occom, S.), 31, 141, 162–64, 226–27, 236
"chosen people"/"chosenness," biblical, 17, 47, 102, 120, 123–26, 129, 134, 225, 234–35; Gentiles as, 104, 115–16; S. Occom on, 86–89, 118

Chow, Rey, 189
Christiana (character in *Pilgrim's Progress*), 131–32
Christian cards, 235
Christianity and Crisis (journal), 125
Christianity/Christians, 3, 128, 207–8, 220, 269n81; Brothertown and, 90–91; Deloria on, 221–22; fellowship, 115, 162; mobility in, 31–32; Mohegan, 34, 44; Native, 16, 44–46, 125; New Light, 13–15, 106; of S. Occom, 17, 34–37, 44, 106; S. Occom on, 67, 85–86; Old Light, 14–15, 107; social ethic of, 34, 36. *See also* evangelicalism/evangelicals
circular letters, 68–69
circumcision, 120–21
Claim of Reason, The (Cavell), 79–80
Clinton, George, 218–19
Coastal Algonquian tribes, 1, 4, 13, 28, 31, 41, 47, 54, 88, 100–101, 159, 166, 245n1. *See also* Northeast Native
Cold War, 33, 249n34
Collected Writings of Samson Occom, Mohegan, The (Brooks, J.), 51, 275n1
collective: agency, 77; identity, 114; life, 13, 90, 198
colonialism/settler colonialism, 7, 9–11, 30–31, 81, 198–99, 230, 252n35; alienation and, 209–10, 228; archives, 53–55, 70, 172; Indigenous mobility and, 26–27; Indigenous survival during, 25–26; Northeast Native diaspora and, 131; S. Occom on, 18, 33, 210, 219; religion and, 220–21, 232–32, 234–35; sachemship and, 27–28; "spiritual life" under, 155; strangerhood, 143. *See also* precolonial Indigenous peoples/traditions
colonial knowledge, 10, 54–55

commentary, Bible, 123, 235
Commercial Advertiser (newspaper), 178
Common Pot, The (Brooks, L.), 12, 72
"common pot" ethos, 9, 132
communicative methods, of S. Occom, 50; broadcast-oriented, 16, 72–74, 262n74; publishing as, 24–25, 66, 73; transatlantic, 72–73. *See also* letters, from S. Occom
"conditional sedentarism," 26
conformity/conformism, 13–14, 139
Conforti, Joseph, 112
Congress, U.S., 129–30, 211
Connecticut Colony, 4, 27; General Assembly, 28, 92–93, 95–97; New London, 106–8, 149, 155, 235
Connecticut Historical Society, 146
Connecticut Indian Papers, 265n24
Connell Szasz, Margaret, 88, 99
consciousness, altered states of, 200, 204–8, 210
Constitution, U.S., 35
conversion, religious, 68, 121–22, 269n81; Great Awakening and, 203–4
Cooper, James Fenimore, 177–78
co-participatory, writings by S. Occom as, 69–70
correspondences. *See* letters
Cottrell, Courtney, 59–60
Coulthard, Glen, 9–10
courage, of S. Occom, 30–31, 172, 206
Courier (newspaper), 179–82
covenant theology, 36–37, 89, 112–14, 117, 119, 271n109, 273n140; chosenness and, 87; Indigenous sovereignty and, 16; Wheelock and, 118, 121–22
creation, divine, 42–43, 134, 160, 214; perception of, 15–16, 211–13, 219–20, 226
Crenshaw, Kimberlé, 245n1

crime, 110, 121, 126
culturalism, 64, 141
culture/cultural: authenticity, 10, 187; dominant, 30, 35, 187, 208; English, 8, 29, 88, 144; Native, 48, 53, 57, 74, 121, 207; textual, 140. *See also* missionaries/missionary culture
customs, tribal. *See* traditions/traditionalism

Dartmouth College, 4, 22, 171–72, 176–80, 183
Davenport, James, 106–8, 149–50, 155, 235
Dayton & Newman (publisher), 181
death/s, 3, 96, 204; of Moses Paul, 51–52, 117; by murder, 23–24, 110–11, 120; of S. Occom, 5, 32, 172, 178; of Uncas III, 27–28
deference, 17, 140–42, 144, 158
De Forest, William, 265n24
Deloria, Philip, 142
Deloria, Vine, Jr., 16, 73–74, 208–10, 221–22
DeLucia, Christine, 139–40, 159
democracy, 15, 249n34
denotational text, 69
"devil worship," 254n52
diaries, of S. Occom, 50–51, 135–37, 141–42, 204, 234, 274n152; on agriculture, 100–101; on Brothertown, 162; on "Christian Cards," 155; piety in, 138–39; on Valentin Rathburn, 235
diplomacy, 25–26, 43, 61, 224–25
"disinterested benevolence," 112–14
dispossession, 26, 98, 126, 131
Divine and Supernatural Light, A (Edwards), 196
divine transcendence, 45–49
Dolven, Jeff, 144, 146

[318] INDEX

dominant culture, 30, 35, 187, 208
Douglass, Frederick, 35
Dowd, Gregory, 207
dual identity, 124
Dumpert, Hazel-Dawn, 177
Dwight, Timothy, 267n65

Eastman, Charles Alexander, 51, 73
education, 21–22, 122; Moor's Indian Charity School and, 3–4, 95–96, 150–51, 205; of Northeast Natives, 236–37; of S. Occom, 3, 105–6, 185–86. *See also* literacy
Edwards, Jonathan, 15–16, 103, 225, 254n52, 287n3; New Divinity and, 107–9, 113; S. Occom influenced by, 164, 201, *202*, 203
election, national, 112, 114, 117–18, 119, 123, 126
Elrod, Eileen, 176, 185
"enduring Indigeneity," 37–38
England, 3–4, 21–22, 100, 152, 158, 186; fundraising in, 71–72, 150–51, 171; S. Occom sermon in, 160, 228
English: culture, 88; language, 50, 90, 143, 171, 179; literature, 7, 131, 169, 206, 233; morals, 15–16, 119–20
enthusiasm (religious), 107–8, 149–50, 235–36
epistemology, 11, 56–57, 259n20
eschatology, 121–22, 128, 134, 234
esotericism, 59, 63–66
Estes, Nick, 15
ethnographic refusal, 59, 77, 142–45
ethnohistory, 142
ethnonational identity, 87
evangelicalism/evangelicals, 14; hospitality and, 72; Indigenous, 73–74, 103–4; mobility and, 8–9, 31; of S. Occom, 16, 71, 200; piety, 62, 151–52, 154, 159; pilgrimage and, 8, 31, 67, 141, 158, 160–64; of Thornton, 22; transatlantic, 3, 15, 26
Eve (biblical figure), 131–32
exceptionalism, Anglo-American, 87
Exodus, book of, 35, 86, 89, 125–26, 129
exploitation, 210, 216, 218
Exposition of the Old and New Testaments (Henry), 123, 132, 187
eyesight, loss of, 3, 206, 231

factionalism: Brothertown, 218; Mohegan, 27–29
family, of S. Occom, 21–22, 143–44, 150–51; parents in, 1, 3, 25, 33, 186
Fanon, Frantz, 35
farming. *See* agriculture
federal theology, 112–14, 273n140. *See also* covenant theology
Fell, Margaret, 234
fellowship, Christian, 115, 162
Fielding, Fidelia, 32, 34
Fielding, Stephanie, 165
finances/financial support, 4, 171, 201; land and, 96–98; of S. Occom, 21–23, 150–51, 185, 190–91, 193–94, 242; tribal revenue as, 27, 97–98. *See also* fundraising, by S. Occom
fires/burning of books, 106, 236
fish, 212–13
Fisher, Samuel, 47, 230, 234
Fitch, James, 224
"fool"/foolish, 184–85, 187–88, 190, 194–97
forms of address: broadcast-oriented, 16, 72–74, 262n74; evangelical, 8–9, 14, 16, 38, 71, 155
Fowler, David, 99, 132–33, 213, 234
Fowler, Mary. *See* Occom, Mary Fowler
Fox, George, 104, 234
Fredriksen, Paula, 128
Freeburg, David, 176

freedom of speech. *See parrhesia*
Freedom of the Will (Edwards), 15, 201, 202, 203
fundraising, by S. Occom, 3–4, 21–22, 108; in England, 71–72, 150–51, 171

Gandhi, 35
gardens/gardening. *See* horticulture
gender/gender norms, 26, 143–44, 148–50, 252n23
General Assembly of Connecticut, 28, 92–93, 95–97
Genesis, book of, 88, 129–33, 209
genres, literary, 6, 50, 54–55, 61, 175, 186, 191. *See also* speech genres
Gentiles (biblical), 16, 103–5, 115, 119–23, 127–28
Goffman, Erving, 62, 141–42
Good Samaritan (biblical figure), 237–38; S. Occom sermon on, 8, 25, 29–30, 38, 43, 77, 123–24, 198–99, 222–23
Gospel, 8, 71, 75, 86, 105, 109–11, 147, 150, 200, 206–7, 236
Grammar of the Hebrew Tongue (Monis), 231–32, 232
Grant-Costa, Paul, 28, 97
"Gratitude," 136–37, 237
Great Awakening, 15, 106, 148, 204, 207; religious revivalism and, 203, 269n81
Great Britain, 122
Green, Jos., 151–52
Green Corn ceremony (Mohegan), 32
"gross mistakes" about Native Americans, 171, 174, 185

handwriting, 169–71, *170*, 177, *231*, 277n31
harvests, agricultural, 100–101, 157, 215–16

Haudenosaunee Confederacy (Six Nations), 3, 52–53, 207–8, 214–15
Hawthorne, Nathaniel, 145
Ha:yëwënta:', 214
Haynes, Lemuel, 158
health, of S. Occom, 4, 101; loss of eyesight and, 3, 206, 231
"Heathenism"/heathens, Indigenous people as, 1, 16, 104–6, 187–88, 223
Heathens Divinity, The (Fox), 104
Hebrew (language), *231*, 231–32
hegemony, 54, 64
Heimert, Alan, 15, 115, 249nn34–35
Henry, Matthew, 123–24, 132, 187, 195–96, 235
"Herbs and Roots" (Occom, S.), 51
Herbster, Holly, 284n43
hereditary sachemship, 27–28, 92, 97–98
heretical/heretics, 36, 106, 235
hierarchies, 15, 171
Hill, Christopher, 45
Hind Swaraj (Gandhi), 35
historiography, 15, 17, 45–46, 119; of assimilation, 203–4
History of the Work of Redemption (Edwards), 129
Holifield, E. Brooks, 107
Holmes, Abiel, 182
"holy conversation," 50, 154, 157
Hopkins, Samuel, 107–13, 254n54, 270n95, 270n104
horticulture, 26, 100–101, 143, 252n23
hospitality, 1, *29*, 31, 33, 61–62, 135–38; of Christians, 34–35; evangelicalism and, 72; of S. Occom, 21–26, 28–30, 43, 95–96; S. Occom on, 70–71, 123–25; "stranger-love" as, 8, 32, 37–38, 40, 223; of Uncas I, 25–26, 29
Hubbard, William, 224–25
humor, 137, 145
Huntington, Samuel, 209

Hutcheson, Frances, 225
Hymns and Spiritual Songs (Watts), 236
hymns/hymnals, 235–37; by S. Occom, 31, 50–51, 141, 162–64, 226–27
hypocrisy, 149–50, 157

iconoclasm, 41–47
identity, 15, 79, 128; collective, 114; dual, 124; ethnonational, 87; as "fool"/foolish, 184–85, 187–88, 190, 194–97; Indigenous, 36–37, 56, 272n120; national, 87, 264n93; as unchosen people, 16, 114, 120–21, 123–25
idolatry, 41–44, 46–47
ignorance, 150, 154, 194
"images," idolatry and, 41–44
imagination, 42, 44, 208
imperialism, 121–22, 210
income/salary, of S. Occom, 22, 190–91, 193–94, 242
Increase of the Kingdom of Christ (Apess), 129
Indian law, U.S., 32
"Indian Moses," misperception of S. Occom as, 13, 47, 87, 89–90, 95, 102, 134
"Indianness," 10, 172, 185, 194
Indians in Unexpected Places (Deloria, P.), 142
Indigeneity, 11, 38, 55–56; acknowledgment and, 60; broadcast conception of, 16, 72–74, 262n74; of S. Occom, 24–25, 61–62, 112; settler colonialism and, 37
Indigenous knowledge, 10–11, 54–59, 66, 70, 248n22, 259n20
Indigenous people. *See* Northeast Native; *specific topics*
Indigenous studies, 11, 15–17, 53, 74–75, 143; Indigenous knowledge and,

56–58; metapragmatics, 66; politics of recognition and, 79; settler colonial studies and, 9–10, 37–39, 45, 248n18
"industriousness," 91, 98–99
inequality, 185–87, 189
Innes, Robert, 11, 53, 55–57, 248n22, 259n24
intentionality/intentionalism, 61–62, 75, 78
interactional text, 69
"interlopers," tribal, 28, 92–96
intertextuality, 141
Invasion Within, The (Axtell), 142–43
Ireland, 3–4, 21–22, 150
Israelite interpretation of Indigenous nationhood, 102–3, 115–16, 268n71
Israelites/Israelite religion, 47, 102–3, 115–16, 123–25, 127–28, 268n71; ancient, 46, 114
itinerancy, 14, 149–50, 247n12, 270n104; of S. Occom, 111, 136–37; Wheelock and, 108

Jackson, Andrew, 180
Janowitz, Naomi, 46, 49
Jarvis, Brad, 91–93, 99, 128
jeremiad tradition, 114
Jesus Christ (biblical figure), 78, 110–11, 127, 131, 152; S. Occom, on, 71, 124–25, 219–20, 226–28
Johnson, Guy, 94
Johnson, Joseph, 4, 159, 164–66
Johnson, William, 253n31
Johnson, Zachary, 28, 92–97
John's Town, 4, 27–28, 96–97
Judaism/Jews, 115–21, 127, 234; Hebrew language and, 231, 231–32

Kahnawà:ke Mohawk people, 57–58
Kanter, Rosabeth, 189–90

Kauanui, J. Kēhaulani, 37–39
Kaufmann, Yehezkel, 46–47
Keane, Webb, 173–74
Keen, Robert, 180
Kelsey, Penelope, 214
Kidd, Thomas, 272n129
King Philip's War, 199, 268n71
kinship, political, 213
Kirkland, Samuel, 267n65
knowledge, 74–75, 141, 146, 158; academic, 10–11; colonial, 10, 54–55; Indigenous, 10–12, 16, 54–59, 66, 70, 248n22, 259n20; production, 10–11, 54–55, 57–58

labor, 216; of the enslaved, 157–58; wage, 100–101, 193–94
land/land use, 13, 87–88, 92–93, 132–33, 212; alienation from, 216; colonialism impacting, 143; Haudenosaunee traditions respecting, 214–15; Mason land case, 27, 92–94 150–151, 96–98, 252n28; ownership, 264n93; placemaking and, 159–60, 162; as private property, 98, 216; Promised, 86, 89, 102, 114, 125, 268n71; rents/leasing of, 96–98, 101, 217–19; tribal/Indigenous, 27, 92, 98, 129–30, 216–18. *See also* agriculture/agricultural; horticulture; migration; mobility
language/s, 53–54, 66, 184, 213, *231*; ancient, 3, 147, 231; Coastal Algonquian, 166, 245n1; English, 50, 90, 143, 171, 179; Hebrew, *231*, 231–32; metaphoric, 70, 160–61, 188, 218–19; Milton on, 206–7; Mohegan, 32, 50; in S. Occom autobiography, 169–71, *170*, 175–77, 187–88; understandability of, 52–53, 61–64, 66–68, 72; of

wakefulness/awakening, 203, 208, 214, 228
Lasco, John à, 161
Latin (language), 50
LaVigne, Jason, 176
Lavin, Lucianne, 100
"law of righteousness," 120, 126
leasing/rents, land, 96–98, 101, 217–19
letters, 18, 153–56, 165–66, 270n91; from English admirers, 151–52; from Thornton, 23; from S. Wheatley, 22–23, 35, 153–54, 239–43
letters, from S. Occom, 21, 23, 50–51, 144–45, 153–56, *156*; circular, 68–69; to Clinton, 218–19; from English admirers, 151–52; to Keen, 180; to Poquiantup, 52; to S. Wheatley, 28, 95, 157–58; to Wheelock, 151, 185, 213–14
liberation, Indigenous, 35, 72, 125–26, 208
liberation theology, 208
linguistic anthropology, 66
literacy, 17–18, 90, 230–31; alphabetic, 68; "literary sovereignty" and, 7, 59, 66, 77, 246nn6–7, 260n32; of Northeast Native peoples, 236–37; of S. Occom, 3, 6, 28, 238; powers of, 206
Literary Indians (Calcaterra), 52
"literary sovereignty," 7, 59, 61–63, 66, 77, 246nn6–7, 260n32
literary studies, 14, 17, 53–54, 56–57, 61–62, 75
literature/books, 8, *231*, 231–32, *233*, 234–35; Anglophone, 7, 169, 232; heretical, 106; Indigenous, 53–54, 75–77, 81, 189, 263n85; published, 24–25, 50, 73, 181; religious, 3, 14–15
Lopenzina, Drew, 53–54, 172, 174, 179–80

love, 41, 43, 164, 256n69; national, 38, 40, 124–26; self, 65, 191–92, 196; "stranger-love" as, 8, 32, 37–38, 40, 223
Love, William DeLoss, 13, 89–90, 99, 102
Lyons, Scott, 55–56, 75

Mahmood, Saba, 139, 145–46, 150, 154, 162
manuscripts, of S. Occom, 5, 277n31, 284n43, 284n45, 286n75; autobiography as, 17–18, 28–29, 29, 169–80, *171*, 183–84; unpublished, 8, 12; unsigned, 146. *See also* writings, by S. Occom
marginalia, 50, 201, *202*, *203*, *231*, 231–32
Markell, Patchen, 58–61
marriage, 3, 143, 277n25
Mason, John, 27, 92
Mason land case, 27, 92–94 150–151, 96–98, 252n28
mass media, 73, 207
material world/materialism, 41–42; "thingness" and, 173–74, 284n43
Mather, Cotton, 160
Mather, Moses, 107–8, 113
Mayhew, Jonathan, 107–8
McCarthy, Keely, 185
McClure, David, 143–44, 179–80
McClymond, Michael, 197
McNickle, D'Arcy, 73
media, mass, 73, 207
medicine, plant-based, 206
Melville, Herman, 264n93
Memoirs of the Rev. Eleazar Wheelock (McClure), 179–80
Merrell, James, 47–48
metalanguage, 14, 70, 73
metaphoric language, 70, 160–61, 188, 218–19

"metapragmatic regimentation," 66, 73–74
"methodological promiscuity," 12, 39, 53, 57
"micropractices," political, 139–40, 145–46, 159, 162
migration, 4, 31, 41, 134, 172; Brothertown, 97, 126, 216–18; "wandering life" and, 1, 8, 12, 25, 32, 247n11. *See also* mobility
Mills, Jedediah, 109–11, 117
Milton, John, 131, 206
missionaries/missionary culture, 38, 171, 194–95, 247n7; S. Occom as, 3–4, 52, 148, 213; women as, 36
mobility, 27, 41, 61, 143; evangelicals and, 8–9, 31; hospitality and, 25–26; S. Occom on, 31, 95; "wandering life" and, 1, 8, 12, 25, 32, 247n11
Moby-Dick (Melville), 51, 264n93
"modernity," 248n21
Mohawk Interruptus (Simpson), 57–58
Mohegan Church, 31, 32, 54, 254n44
Mohegan Tribe, 1, 4, 31–32, 127–28, 158–59, *212*, 265n24; Brothertown and, 59–60; Christianity and, 34, 44; factionalism in, 27–29; *Norwich Courier* on, 180–81; S. Occom in, 22, 33, 85, 169; S. Occom papers repatriated to, 176, 184; religious revivalism and, 8, 106; settler colonialism impacting, 9–10; sovereignty of, 4, 85; traditionalism of, 17; tribal councils, 3, 27, 32
"Molattoes," 94, 218
Monis, Judah, *231*, 231–32
monopolizers/monopoly, 222–23
monotheism, 46–47, 68
Montauk, 101, 108; sermons by S. Occom in, 200–201, 203

INDEX [323]

Montaukett tribe, 41–42, 107, 205–6, 216–17; marriage and, 277n25; S. Occom teaching among, 3, 179
Montezuma, Carlos, 51
Moorhead, John, 95, 161
Moorhead, Scipio, 280n79
Moor's Indian Charity School, 3–4, 95–96, 108, 150–51, 205
morality/moralism, 88, 160, 192–93, 225; Anglo-American, 15–16; Gentile, 120–21
moral universalism, 29-30, 116, 123
Moses Paul sermon, 51–52, 85, 152, 195–96, 227; on alcohol, 205; New Divinity theology and, 108, 114–18; publishing of, 24, 234; self-love in, 191; on sin, 111; understandability of, 61
Mr. Stand-fast (*Pilgrim's Progress*), 131–32
murder, 23–24, 110–11, 120

NAGPRA. *See* Native American Graves Protection and Repatriation Act
Narragansett tribe, 100, 104, 199, 224
Narrative of the Troubles with the Indians in New England (Hubbard), 224
national: election, 112, 114, 117–18, 119, 123, 126; identity, 87, 264n93; love, 38, 40, 124–26
nationalism, 15, 73–75
"national love," 38, 40, 124–26
nationhood, Indigenous, 86–87, 128, 268n71; Canaanite interpretation of, 102–3, 114, 125, 268n71; Israelite interpretation of, 102–3, 115–16, 268n71
Native American Graves Protection and Repatriation Act (NAGPRA), U.S., 59–60
Native Americans. *See specific topics*

Native spaces, 71–77, 169, 172–73, 195–96, 213; "social life" in, 18, 174–75, 183, 198
neighborliness, 28–29, 36, 40, 77–78, 123–24, 223; biblical, 71; of unconverted Indigenous people, 30. *See also* hospitality
neighbors, non-Indigenous, 25–26, 39. *See also* white people/"English Neighbours"
Nelson, Dana, 185
New Divinity theology, 107–18, 127–28, 226, 235
"New Light" Christianity, 13–15, 106
New London, Connecticut, 106–8, 149, 155, 235
New Stockbridge community, 5–6, 101
New Testament, Bible, 103–5, 111, 118; Gentiles in, 16, 120–21; S. Occom on, 127
New York, 3, 94, 178, 215, 217; Montauk, 101, 108, 200–201, 203
Niantic tribe, 28, 148, 199
nonalphabetic literacy, 68
nonbelievers (unregenerate), 109, 112, 122, 155, 216–17
nonchosenness, Native, 16, 114, 120–21, 123–25
nonhereditary sachemship, 28
norms, 61, 162; gender, 26, 143–44, 148–50, 252n23; religious, 139; social, 70, 72
"Northeast Native"/"Native Northeast," 139–40, 245n1, 252n23; as a diasporic population, 131; gender norms, 26, 143, 252n23; literacy for, 236–37; missionaries and, 38; S. Occom as, 1, 3; precolonial, 200–201; settler colonialism impacting, 9–10; song practices of, 236; traditional hospitality of, 30; traditional

mobility of, 26. *See also* Coastal Algonquian; *specific tribal nations*
nudity, 148–49
numerology, 128, 231

O'Brien, Jean, 37, 53, 56–57, 131, 181; on methodological promiscuity, 12; on mobility, 26; on settler colonialism, 143
Occom, Christiana, 132, 153
Occom, Jonah, 138
Occom, Mary Fowler, 3–5, 143–44, 159
Occom, Samson, 2. *See also specific topics*
Occom Circle Project, 170, 176–77
"Old Light" Christianity, 14–15, 107
Old Testament, Bible, 103, 118, 120–21, 125–26, 130
Oliver, Andrew, 185–86
Oneida Nation, 3–4, 94–95, 207–8, 213
Onuf, Peter, 106
oppression, 11, 35, 87, 188
orality/oral tradition, 50, 68, 214, 237
ordination, of S. Occom, 3, 14, 23, 200; Buell at, 105, 122, 146–47; Presbyterian, 105, 115
Orientalism, 74, 80
"Other," 45–46, 80
Our Beloved Kin (Brooks, L.), 199
ownership, 264n93

"pagan"/paganism, 46, 48, 128, 220
Paradise Lost (Milton), 206
parents, of S. Occom, 1, 3, 25, 33, 186
Parker, Arthur, 73
Parker, Ely, 258n3
parrhesia (freedom of speech), 147–50, 157, 189, 279n39
patrimony, 16, 77
Patten, Nathaniel, 232, *233*

Paul (apostle), 104, 119, 194–96, 272n119, 272n120; S. Occom on, 16, 114–17, 120–21, 127–28, 131, 188–90
Paul, Moses, 24, 117, 251n12. *See also* Moses Paul sermon
Peabody Museum, 59
Pemberton, Ebenezer, 185
Penn, William, 104
Pennsylvania, 234
peoplehood, 12, 85, 87–88, 90–91, 102
perception, 9, 140, 196; of creation stories, 15–16, 211–13, 219–20, 226; S. Occom on, 17, 200, 203–4, 206–10, 214–15, 227; religious, 211, 225, 228; spiritual, 197
performativity, 141
Perkins, George, 180
personal authority, 56, 138, 145–46
personhood, 33, 74–75
Peyer, Bernd, 172
Pezzarossi, Heather Law, 139–40
Philadelphia, Pennsylvania, 234
piety, 87, 138, 161, 279n39; Augustinian, 26, 160–62, 165; evangelical, 62, 151–52, 154, 159; of S. Occom, 17, 139–40, 145–46, 149–51, 161–64; Quaker, 148–50; strangerhood and, 140–44
pilgrimages, 8, 31, 67, 141, 158, 160–64
Pilgrim's Progress (Bunyan), 131–32, 153
placemaking, 139–40, 158–66
Plain and Faithful Narrative (Wheelock), 122
plowing, symbolism of, 101–2
political: authority, 93–94, 187; autonomy, 15, 27, 29; belonging, 89, 94; kinship, 213; "micropractices," 139–40, 145–46, 159, 162
Politics of Piety (Mahmood), 139
polytheism, 42–43
Pomeroy, Benjamin, 3, 231

population, diasporic, 131
Poquiantup, Esther, 52
postcolonial studies, 53–54, 248n21
Postcolonial Studies (journal), 38–39
Povinelli, Elizabeth, 143
power, 35, 42–43, 141–42; authority and, 138–39; colonial, 31, 54–55, 186; of Indigenous literature, 75–76; of language, 78; of literacy, 206; political, 41, 88; of public discourse, 74; of sin, 164
powwaws, 41–42, 200, 205–6
preaching, by S. Occom, 23, 71, 135–37, 193, 243–44
precolonial Indigenous peoples/traditions, 7–8, 13, 200–201, 245n1; Christianity and, 31–32; S. Occom on, 33–34
prejudices, 101, 172, 193–94; anti-Indigenous, 8, 185–90
Presbyterian Church, 105, 115, 148, 161
pride, 73, 89, 191–92, 236
Promised Land, biblical, 86, 89, 102, 114, 125, 268n71
property, private, 98, 216
prophecy/prophets, 138; Indigenous, 207–8
Protestant Church/Protestants, 160–61, 173–74, 272n129; iconoclasm and, 43–47; international, 15; S. Occom as, 3, 47, 118–19; scholarly critique of, 45, 47; transatlantic, 26
protology, 36–37, 134
public/publicness, 16, 74; discourse, 68, 74; language as, 67–68; space, 71–77
published writings, by S. Occom, 24–25, 50, 73, 181; Moses Paul sermon as, 24, 234. *See also Choice Collection of Hymns and Spiritual Songs*; Moses Paul sermon

"pure religion," 219–28
Puritans, 14, 103, 142–43, 268n71

Quakers, 36, 104–5, 234–35, 279n39; piety of, 148–50
queer theory, 143

race, 73, 90, 91, 93, 102, 156–58, 185–86; anxieties regarding mixing, 94, 218; exclusivity, 87, 94–95
Rathbun, Valentin, 235
recognition, politics of, 9–10, 55, 57–58, 60; Indigenous studies and, 79
Red Ink (Lopenzina), 179
Reformed: Christians, 51, 191–92; Protestantism, 43–44
"reform," religious, 41–42, 60
refusal, 57–58, 79, 227, 264n90; ethnographic, 59, 77, 142–45
Religion of Israel, The (Kaufmann), 46
religion/religious, 45, 231–32; ancient, 46, 114; bibliolatry in, 44, 235; Edwards on, 254n52; "Enthusiasm," 107–8, 149–50, 235–36; Great Awakening, 15, 106, 148, 203–4, 207, 269n81; Indigenous, 41–49, 209; pure, 22–228. *See also* conversion, religious; revivalism, religious; *specific religions*
rents/leasing, land, 96–98, 101, 217–19
repatriation, 59, 176, 184
revenue, tribal, 27, 97–98
revivalism, religious, 3, 106–8, 247n12; the Great Awakening and, 203, 269n81; Mohegan nation and, 8, 106; S. Occom and, 14, 106
Revolutionary War. *See* American Revolution
Richter, Daniel, 142–43
Rifkin, Mark, 143
rights, 157–58, 164n90

rituals, Indigenous, 46–47; of powwaws, 41–42, 200, 205–6
"role entrapment," 189–90
Rousseau, Jean-Jacques, 191–92
Rubertone, Patricia, 139–40, 159
Rubin, Julius, 47, 161–62

sachemship, 3, 4, 180–81, 253n31; hereditary, 27–28, 92, 97–98
sacredness, 15–16, 129, 152, 184, 190, 196, 226–37
SAI. *See* Society of American Indians
Said, Edward, 80
salary/income, of S. Occom, 22, 190–91, 193–94, 242
salvation, 51, 62, 87, 109–10, 118, 121, 154, 158
Samson Occom and the Christian Indians of New England (Love), 13, 89–90
Satan (biblical figure), 103, 131
"savagism," 90
Schellenberg, Ryan, 195
schoolteacher, S. Occom as, 3, 179, 206
Scotland, 3–4, 21–22, 171
scriptural interpretation, by S. Occom, 51–52, 79–80, 88, 115–16, 126–27; of Genesis, 129–33; of Samaritan parable, 8, 25, 29–30, 38, 43, 77, 123–24, 198–99, 222–23
secularism, 129, 139, 145, 160
Sedgwick, Eve, 189
self-determination, 6–7, 32, 34; Indigenous, 48–49, 85, 112, 114, 128
self-love, 65, 191–93, 196
self-presentation, 17, 62, 138–39
self-sufficiency, Anglo-American ideal of, 87, 91, 98–100
separatism, Indigenous, 112, 126
sermons, by S. Occom, 8, 50, 71–72, 112, 125–26, 129, 277n31; Apostle Paul in, 114–17, 120–21; in England, 160, 228; Good Samaritan sermon, 29, 38, 43, 77, 123–24, 198–99, 222–23; at Montauk, 200–201, 203; against pride and self-sufficiency, 98–99, 192–93; on sin, 192. *See also* Moses Paul sermon
settler colonial studies, 9–10, 37–39, 45, 248n18
Seven Years' War, 113
Shakers, 150, 235
Silverman, David, 90–93, 99
Silverman, Kenneth, 239
Silverstein, Michael, 69, 173–74
Simpson, Audra, 9–10, 57–61, 74–76, 189, 264n90; on ethnographic refusal, 59, 77, 142–43
singing/song, 50, 164, 236–37
sin/sinners, 109–11, 116–20, 124, 131, 150, 192, 225–27; powerlessness of, 164
Six Nations (Haudenosaunee Confederacy), 3, 52–53, 207–8, 214–15
slavery, 26, 156–57, 254n54, 273n123, 280n79; abolitionism and, 36, 158, 254n54
sleep/slumber, language of, 200, 203–4
Smith, Adam, 192–93, 256n69
social distance, 141–45, 154
social ethics, 34, 36, 71, 218
Society of American Indians (SAI), 73
songs. *See* hymns/hymnals
soteriology, 124–25. *See also* salvation
sovereignty, Indigenous, 16, 30, 32, 59, 112; of Mohegan nation, 4, 85; S. Occom on, 6–7, 86–87, 127–28, 217–18; politics of recognition and, 9–10; refusal and, 58
speech genres, 61, 263n85
spiritual: deadness, 150, 154–55; life, 152, 155

"spiritual perception," 197
Spivak, Gayatri, 24n21
"standpoint epistemology," 259n20
stereotype, "Indian Moses," 89–91, 102, 126
Stiles, Ezra, 182
Stockbridge tribe, 267n66
Stone, William Leete, Jr., 178, 183–84
Stone, William Leete, Sr., 177–79, 181–84
Stout, Harry, 106
"stranger-love," 8, 32, 37–38, 40, 223. *See also* hospitality
stranger/strangerhood, 8–9, 25–29, 138, 140–45, 159–60, 165, 219
"Strange"/"Strange Creature," S. Occom on the, 135–39, 141–42, 169, 237–38
structural: causality, 35–36, 38–41; violence, 38
structuralism, 38–41
subaltern, 54
subject-positionality, 24, 56
subsistence practices, 1, 26, 99
survival, 25–26, 39–40, 52–53, 172, 183
syncretism, 47–48

Tantaquidgeon, Gladys, 32, 34, 254n44
Tantaquidgeon, Lucy, 183
temptation, 131–32
Tennent, Gilbert, 106, 113
Te Punga Somerville, Alice, 38–39
Thames (Pequot) River, 1, 106, *212*
That the People Might Live (Weaver), 75
theology, 208; federal, 112–14, 273n140; New Divinity, 107–18, 127–28, 225–26, 235. *See also* covenant theology
theology, of S. Occom, 15–16, 51–52, 87–89, 105–6, 123–28, 134; Edwards impacting, 201

"thingness," 173–74, 284n43
Thornton, John, 151–52, 158; letters from S. Wheatley to, 22–23, 35, 153–54, 239–43; letters to S. Occom from, 23
Tillich, Paul, 208–9
tokenization, 186–89
traditionalism, of S. Occom, 7–9, 13–14, 16–17, 30–35, 72; Christianity of S. Occom and, 36–37; hospitality in, 22–26, 28–29, 70–71; iconoclasm and, 43–45, 49; structuralist perspectives on, 35–36, 38–41
traditions/traditionalism, Indigenous, 1, 32–37, 45, 47, 159, 260n36; of M. Fowler Occom, 143–45; hospitality as, 22–26; mobility as, 25, 143; recognition and, 60; settler colonialism and, 37–38
Trail of Broken Treaties, 74
transatlantic, 72–73; evangelicalism, 3, 15, 26
transcendence, divine, 45–49
translation, 235–36
transnationality, 1, 3, 7–8, 52–53, 115
tribal councils, Mohegan, 3, 27, 32
True State and Character of the Unregenerate (Mills), 110
Trumbull, James Hammond, 181–82
truth-telling, 146, 150–51, 154, 159, 214, 262n73
Tuhy, John, 100–101
Tunxis people, 26, 199
"Turtle Island," 245n1
typology, 118, 120–21, 123, 126, 130–31

Uncas, Ben, II, 3–4, 27
Uncas, Ben, III, 27–28, 92
Uncas, John, 27
Uncas, Noah, 97–98
Uncas and Miantonomoh (Stone), 181–83

Uncas I, 25–27, 39, 180–81, 224–25
unchosen people/nonchosenness, Native, 16, 114, 120–21, 123–25
understandability, 52–53, 61–64, 66–68, 72
United States (U.S.), 180; American Revolution, 4, 15, 171, 198, 215, 253n42; Congress, 129–30, 211; Constitution, 35; NAGPRA, 59–60; Secretary of Indian Affairs, 258n3. *See also specific states*
universal benevolence, 112–14, 116, 122–23, 160
universalism, 29–30, 116
unpublished manuscripts, of S. Occom, 8, 12, 146, 176
unregenerate (nonbelievers), 109, 112, 122, 155, 216–17
U.S. *See* United States

"vagrancy"/vagrants, 26, 131
Valeri, Mark, 112
Vaughan, Alden, 142–43
Veracini, Lorenzo, 38–39
violence, 181, 253n42; of colonialism, 38

wage labor, 100–101, 193–94
wakefulness/awakening, language of, 203, 208, 214, 228. *See also* Great Awakening
Wampanoag people, 23
wampum, 50, 175, 213–15, 289n34
"wandering life," 1, 8, 12, 25, 32, 247n11
Warrior, Robert, 38–39, 55, 86, 125–26, 260n32
Wars: American Revolution, 4, 15, 171, 198, 215, 253n42; Cold War, 33, 249n34; King Philip's War, 199, 268n71; Seven Years' War, 113
Watts, Isaac, 164–65, 236
Weaver, Jace, 15, 75

Webster, Noah, 180
Welles, Solomon, 198, 203
Wenger, Tisa, 48
We Talk, You Listen (Deloria), 16, 74, 263
Wheatley, Phillis, 35, 150, 161, 239, 254n54
Wheatley, Susanna, 161; on hospitality of S. Occom, 21; letters from, 22–23, 35, 153–54, 238, 239–43; S. Occom letters to, 28, 153–57, *156*
Wheelock, Eleazar, 99, 201, 231, 238, 241, 270nn91–92, 287n3; as advocate of assimilation, 121–22; covenant theology and, 118, 121–22; missionary work by, 52; Moor's Indian Charity School operated by, 3–4, 95–96, 150–51, 205; New Divinity theology and, 108; S. Occom falling-out with, 172; S. Occom fundraising on behalf of, 21–22, 150–51, 171; S. Occom manuscripts in possession of, 171–72, 179; S. Occom taught by, 3, 28–29; Whitefield and, 213
Whitaker, Nathaniel, 187, 241
Whitefield, George, 3, 148, 153, 204, 213
white people/"English Neighbours," 4, 6, 21–23, 185, 194; as audience, 172; land rented to, 96–98, 101, 217–19; S. Occom on, 28–29, 116–17, 187–88
"wickedness," 44, 109–10, 115–17, 148, 192
Williams, Roger, 104
Wisecup, Kelly, 14, 53–54
Wolfe, Patrick, 37, 248n21, 290n49
women, 139; as missionaries, 36; Native, 143, 204–5, 228, 252n23, 277n25; Quaker, 148, 150
Worthington, William, 247n12

writings, by S. Occom, 3, 6–7, 13–15, 52, 95; "aboutness" of, 57, 72; addressivity of, 76–80; as co-participatory, 69–70; on hospitality, 61–62; hymns/hymnals, 31, 50–51, 226–27; on perception, 17, 200, 203–4, 206–10, 214–15, 227; published, 24–25, 50, 73, 181; traditionalism and, 33–34; understandability of, 24–25, 52–53, 61–64, 66–68, 72. *See also* "Account of the Montauk Indians"; autobiography, S. Occom (1768); diaries, of S. Occom; "Herbs and Roots"; letters, from S. Occom; sermons, by S. Occom

writing/writers, Indigenous, 6, 51, 61, 76, 163, 260n32; assimilation and, 68; broadcast forms of address and, 73; Indigenous knowledge and, 11–12

Wyss, Hilary, 12, 247n7

X-Marks (Lyons), 55–56

Yale College, 3, 59, 107–8

Zionism, 87, 102
Zitkala-Ša, 51, 73
Zobel, Melissa Tantaquidgeon, 25–26, 39–40, 97–98

GPSR Authorized Representative: Easy Access System Europe, Mustamäe tee 50, 10621 Tallinn, Estonia, gpsr.requests@easproject.com